MARK STEVENS has been riding motorcycles for almost forty years and in over fifty countries. A PADI Staff Instructor, his love for scuba diving and the underwater world is matched by his passion for exploring the lands above. A twenty-eight-year career, served in the Royal Air Force, has taken him from Alaska to Australia. He lives in rural Norfolk, England with his fiancée, Selly; two dogs; two motorcycles and several world maps!

IT WAS A GOOD PLAN!

...AND THEN THE WORLD SPUN UPSIDE DOWN...

Written by
MARK STEVENS

Cover design and illustrations by
SELEN CINUS

Matador
Unit E2 Airfield Business Park,
Harrison Road, Market Harborough,
Leicestershire. LE16 7UL
Tel: 0116 2792299
Email: books@troubador.co.uk
Web: www.troubador.co.uk/matador
Twitter: @matadorbooks

ISBN 978 1800465 503

British Library Cataloguing in Publication Data.
A catalogue record for this book is available from the British Library.

Printed and bound in the UK by TJ Books Limited, Padstow, Cornwall
Typeset in 12pt Minion Pro by Troubador Publishing Ltd, Leicester, UK

Matador is an imprint of Troubador Publishing Ltd

In memory of my dear departed brother. Ian, you may not be able to read this story, but your constant inspiration for me to live 'two lives' contributed vastly to making this happen.

Acknowledgements

Sincere thanks go first to my wonderfully versatile and resilient fiancée. Over many thousands of miles Selly has experienced the best and the worst of motorcycling, yet she considers herself no more than a 'passenger' sharing and enjoying my dreams. I wish I could convince her otherwise. She might not be sat at the front of the bike, but has endured equally all that I have and is 'a biker' in my books (excuse the pun!).

To all those who feature in these pages, thank you so much for contributing to our adventure and wonderful memories. In particular and with good fortune, we thank those of you that we found ourselves stranded with. As a pandemic locked down the world, you turned our 2020 around. We consider ourselves incredibly lucky to have landed where we did, and not just survived this turbulent year, but had it made so very special.

Many of my earliest and happiest childhood memories are of fun-filled holidays abroad. Coach trips to the south of France, living in tents, or flights to the sun-blessed Mediterranean. My brother and

I found these trips magically exciting. I believe a seed was planted and certainly geography became a favourite subject at school! I owe a heartfelt thank you to my parents for filling our young lives with so many adventures. My parents often juggled two or three jobs to make these affordable and I now realise how lucky we were, that they made these family holidays a priority for us all.

Final thanks go to you, the readers. Modern living doesn't leave much room for relaxation, for reading. I sincerely hope you enjoy this book and I sincerely hope it inspires even just one person to enjoy creating an adventure from one of your own cherished dreams!

Contents

Prologue

Those Early Days

A story would ordinarily start at the very beginning, I was once taught. Wanting to share a little background as to how I ended up riding on the Pan-American Highway with this Italian sweetheart, I offer you a condensed love story. For in truth, the beginning of this book was an innocent dalliance of hearts, between a seventeen and twenty-three-year-old, over thirty years prior. I really won't be offended if you skip straight to Chapter One, though!

In our youth, the light-headed excitement of seemingly being paid to hit the beach was infectious. At least those were our feelings on that scorching hot day back in July 1989. The crammed public bus had several stops along this eight-mile stretch of Mediterranean sand and it really didn't matter which one the four of us alighted at, for beach shacks, tanned bodies and warm water seemed to stretch out endlessly. It was a Saturday afternoon and Sardinia's nearby capital had practically emptied to help fill the entire length and width of available space. There must have been 80,000 tanned beach lovers, but I was about to meet just one that would, decades later, turn my life around.

Of course, we weren't literally being paid to swim, drink and throw frisbees at each other, but a weekend away from the nearby air base had to be exploited to the full. Life in the Royal Air Force had had its pros and cons, but deploying to Sardinia a couple of times a year felt epic, and falling in love with this island was effortless. Requiring much more effort was any conversation; armed with a well-thumbed phrase book, an eighties 'Boogie Box' and a cheeky grin, I hoped to break the ice with those unfortunate enough to endure close proximity to four deathly white foreigners.

I've often wondered how my life would be now if we hadn't squeezed our collection of four large towels, music, Panama hats and bags into that particular spot. It had looked much bigger from a distance, and picking our way through the maze of colourful beach paraphernalia revealed that most of the sand was already occupied by empty towels, the owners no doubt away enjoying the sparkling blue sea. Squeezing in and trying not to overly intrude, my eyes fell upon my new and nearest neighbour, a beautiful young girl either pretending to be asleep, behind her stylish sunglasses, or actually asleep under the sun's mid-afternoon rays. For me, in that lingering moment, she was simply as pretty as a girl could be, with long dark hair, deep Mediterranean tan and a clearly wonderful figure. I just knew this first image would be a lasting one. I actually felt my stomach flutter and my heart skip; really, can love at first sight actually exist?

I made a fuss of arranging my stuff and from the sanctuary of my own, though fake, sunglasses, tried to see if our arrival had elicited any small reaction. I just wanted the opportunity to smile and say hello. OK, maybe she was playing it cool, or truly was asleep, or was just wishing I would go away! The four of us hit the water, joking around, throwing balls and frisbees and striking up a game with two female Italians, who humoured our dismal language skills with unhidden giggles. Leaving the water revealed these were also our neighbours, owners of the remaining towels and clearly with Miss Beautiful, who was now definitely awake and in my imaginative mind, seemingly happy to acknowledge our (read, 'my'!) presence.

She introduced herself as Selly and her companions were one of her five older sisters and a college friend. In truth, Selly was a nickname. Her real name was Selen but it was rarely used by anybody. We laughed and joked into the early evening, played Guns N' Roses, enjoyed shared smiles and flipped endlessly through the phrase book ('translating' smartphones were still waiting to be invented!) to learn what we could of each other's lives. Selly loved and studied art, especially painting, could enjoy everything from rock to classical music, had read many of the great scholarly works and wanted desperately to travel, but then dropped a bombshell: she had a dislike of motorbikes. She hadn't actually sat on one, definitely didn't want to ride on one and didn't yet know I had ridden my very quick sports bike, quite quickly, down to Sardinia for this working holiday!

For now, this would remain untold, and with her parents' phone number scribbled on a scrap of paper we promised to meet again. This we did, frequently, for trips to ice-cream parlours, cafés, the cinema, walks around the city, the beaches, of course, and even her local disco, as long as she got home early enough not to cause any trouble. It was all good harmless fun, no kissing and just a little holding hands, for Selly was just seventeen and at twenty-three, I felt helplessly too old. We had our favourite go-to restaurant, our favourite spot on the beach and our collection of in-jokes, but despite what my heart felt, my head just couldn't push, or see, beyond the strong friendship we were nurturing. I went on to enjoy home-cooked meals at her parents', get to know her sisters and their boyfriends, or husbands, and felt thoroughly happy and in love with it all, except the age difference. Leaving the island was heart-wrenching and the only silver lining was that we were due to come back again, in just a few months' time. I just had to get chosen to return, and I also needed permission to get the extra time off to ride down and back again; my heart was demanding it! My boss relented to my persistence and in the months between, Selly and I sent postcards and letters to each other that never arrived in order and had to be translated as best they could.

I rode down with Chris. We were pretty inseparable as mates, and I was due to be best man for his and Caroline's upcoming wedding. He didn't hesitate in agreeing to a November ride down through Europe and the return ride back, in early December. North of the Alps was just numbingly cold, but crossing them was painfully fingertip-freezing! I don't know what had kept Chris going, but my head had never really left the warmth of Sardinia. Dropping out of the mountains, we felt milder winds thawing us and by the time we had the two bikes strapped into the depths of the overnight ferry, it was nearly a balmy twenty degrees. The following year was much the same, except Selly was now eighteen! We had become avid penfriends, exchanging letters way before the last reply had arrived, and I sent postcards from every corner of the world the RAF sent us to. For me, the trips to Sardinia felt like work-hard, play-hard romantic holidays and I shunned the flights in order to ride motorbikes down. I relished and cherished spending these happy, innocent, carefree times together.

Of course, it couldn't remain so sweet and dandy, could it! A growing complication, all of my own making, tempered the excitement of the next ride down. A cloud was hovering, one that couldn't any longer be pushed aside. A blind date, embarked upon years previously, had resulted in a fragile 'on-off' relationship of sorts. I say of sorts, as a once-strong friendship had petered down to a distant one, metaphorically and literally, after I found myself posted overseas to Germany. We'd tried taking a holiday together, just a week away in a friend's caravan, but the relationship had stalled and didn't seem to have the legs to be going anywhere fast. I had to face the fact that I had spent more time with Selly that year than I had back in England. So I did what my heart insisted was the right thing to do: I took Selly to our favourite restaurant and without so much as a kiss ever being exchanged between us, proposed to her! Showing maturity beyond mine, she quite rightly declined, stating she was too young and, additionally, had college the next day!

The truth smarted, but with Selly, I was learning. She was probably the most honest person I had met, seemingly incapable of telling even a white lie. From her, I would often hear the truth I needed to, but didn't necessarily want to. (To meet her approval, this book hasn't been allowed even the slightest of exaggerations, let alone anything remotely made up!) Yes, an age gap of nearly seven years was still too much. We carried on much as we were, even if I struggled to know exactly how I should be feeling about it all. To be honest, I was just relieved that I hadn't ruined our friendship and lost my gorgeous penfriend. We danced, laughed, swam and made heady imaginary plans to explore the world, but still she wouldn't get on a bike, not even for a single photograph!

Eventually, though, life inevitably moved on for both of us and within a few years we were both to be found married to other people. Our friendship had lasted seven wonderful years, but ultimately we even stopped writing, shortly after Selly's daughter, Giulia, was born. So sad, but it was just easier for me to think of my first love as happily surrounded by her many children and cared for by a loving husband. It was just painful to think in any other way, and I let the years slip on by, believing in this comforting scenario. It took the invention and emergence of Facebook to prove just how wrong I had been.

Fast forward sixteen years to October 2012. Everybody had the internet, hardly anyone wrote letters anymore, iPads and smartphones were now extensions of the body, and social media connected the world instantaneously. My embarrassingly second-hand and battered iPhone 2 pinged, informing me I had a new friend request. Although I had hung up my uniform some years earlier, I was at work, driving across a Saudi Arabian airport, avoiding taxiing aircraft and trying to make a meeting on time. I left the message unopened until later in the day, when coffee and some peace could be found. That morning, unbeknown to me, a mother of a now sixteen-year-old Giulia had woken with an overwhelming urge to try and find me one last time. Three years earlier, after her mum separated from a toxic marriage, it had been Giulia's idea for her to open a Facebook account and reconnect with past friends, maybe even try to find her long-lost Mark. There had been fruitless searches over these three years; why should this day be any more productive? In hindsight, I hadn't made it an easy task, with a rolling succession of diving profile pictures, complete with masks, regulators and hats, etc. No, I hadn't made it easy for Selly to find me, but find me she did!

Escaping the unrelenting desert heat and in the cool of the office, I opened the app and clicked on the friend request. I looked twice, three times maybe. It couldn't be, could it? My heart jumped and my head spun, absolutely it was Selly's picture and absolutely I accepted her request. We were connected again! The timing was unbelievably good and exactly the mood-lift I needed. Although I had been divorced for almost a decade, earlier that summer I'd left a soured relationship. My heart was free to do as it pleased, and in that moment, it chose to sing! Instant curiosity, on both sides, had us looking through each other's online photo albums and secretly hoping neither of us was committed to serious relationships. It was hard for either of us to stay grounded and open-minded; it was clear we both just wanted to physically see each other after all this time. Joyful video calls ensued, filled with reminiscing and endless questions as we completed the sixteen-year jigsaw puzzle of our lives spent apart.

The timing of our reconnection really did seem to be perfect. There were no skeletons hiding in the closets, no relationships complicating our growing feelings for each other. We took up writing again, physically writing to each other and regaining that anxious trepidation and excitement of waiting for the post to arrive. Selly was now an accomplished portrait painter and to brighten up the villa I shared, sent over beautiful sketches and illustrations. I didn't need to hesitate when she invited me over to Sardinia for the forthcoming New Year.

That first hug on arriving was magical. In those few seconds of holding each other tightly, I let those missing years melt away, away into unimportance. This felt so right, and I knew I was exactly where I was meant to be. Even more wonderful was sensing that she felt it too. Selly was dazzling, same infectious smile, and looking so smart in her heels and tailored winter coat. What a week we had. We were no longer seventeen and twenty-three; there wasn't any shyness, or innocence, to hold us back anymore. The whole world seemed to exist outside our bubble of kisses, love and excitement. Within a couple more months, we were in a solid and giddy relationship, travelling here, there and everywhere for weeks away, or romantic city-break weekends. The cheeky, innocent girl I had first met was now a wonderful, bright, talented and loving woman. She seemed to take my imperfections in her stride, and honest as ever, I was apparently far from perfect, but perfect for her. I knew I could learn a lot from her, I needed to; a lengthy career in the military had left me with some rough edges. I felt pride, knowing the woman at my side held a very strong sense of right and wrong, despised injustice, or unfairness, at any level and remains unwavering in her beliefs. Unless I had a spare couple of hours, I learnt to avoid engaging her in world politics or religion; both to her were just corrupted and in dire need of overhauling. It was pointless anyway; she kept herself far better informed than I did. I loved her selfless, passionate and positive personality, though, and marvelled that she loved me so unconditionally, so completely. I vowed to never take this for granted, just to cherish and try to return it twofold.

Within a couple of years, I had quit my job so that we could be together twenty-four seven and to whet our travelling appetites, celebrated with a three-month round-the-world backpacking trip. Within a few short years, we'd visited several more countries, some of which, as youngsters, we'd fantasised about seeing together. For my itchy feet, it was never enough, though. I had ambitions of bona fide adventures, trips that would take a year or more, and would test us both individually and as a couple. I would be asking a lot of her, though; she was busy painting, entering or organising exhibitions and even teaching. Just to compound the task of selling these dreams of mine, my thoughts most often gravitated to long-distance motorcycle adventures. I really was asking a lot of a woman who was still apprehensive about even getting onto a motorcycle.

I manned up and put my burning obsession to her, the trip I most wanted to do first. The one I considered sensible for novices, despite being seventeen countries, give or take, 30,000 miles give or take, and spanning several climates and seasons. To me, it seemed a logical start; it was well trodden, could be comfortably achieved in a year (or so I believed!), was 'mostly' on asphalt and between us we had the languages covered off. I wanted to ride the length of the Pan-American Highway, with my motorbike-wary woman as pillion. To my delight, she didn't hesitate to say 'yes' and the trip instantly gained a skilled photographer, excellent chef, competent navigator and for South and Central America, a much-needed translator! I could hardly believe she so readily agreed, and reiterated that it meant pushing through the winds and potentially freezing climate of southern Patagonia (this particular warm-blooded Sardinian's nemesis). I elaborated on the searing heat of the Atacama Desert, the potential altitude sickness of both crossing the Altiplano and multiple high passes of the Andes, the jungle humidity and the complications of border crossings, but still she gave an emphatic 'yes'. And so it was on!

February the sixth 2020, somewhere high in the Peruvian Andes, both of us soaked, numb with cold and nagged by hunger. I heard her scream above the roar of the water.

"More power, Mark, more power," rang in my ears.

Was this the same girl, now woman, that wouldn't pose for a bike photo shouting for more power, with pure fear and urgency in her voice? We were sliding off the road, being pushed sideways to tell the truth, and less than 2 metres separated us from an almost sheer drop of who knew what, maybe 200 metres. More power wouldn't work anymore, though; we had put paid to that an hour or so before.

Yes, this was turning into a really bad day.

Chapter One

The Dream Begins

The planning for the Pan-American trip kicked off in Hungary of all places, a full year prior to when we had hoped to be setting off. Ironic really, as we were currently away touring on a bike that I knew would have to be sold to finance a much lighter and more suitable machine. One that I was already convinced I'd have to pick up now and again from some remote Andean dirt road, or hot sandy desert floor. I wanted one last memorable blast on our big 'fat 'n' comfy' Kawasaki. In the country's capital, we took a break from the riding and camping, rented a cheap apartment for a week and just enjoyed the eclectic Danube-divided city.

Despite the sightseeing, I still found I had some spare time on my hands and whether trying to fall asleep or just taking a shower, thoughts often gravitated to the big trip, the PAH – Pan-American Highway. On a tiny travel laptop, in that Budapest apartment, I started a simple spreadsheet. It would go on to grow arms and legs, drawing me back at the oddest moments, after some new brainwave or afterthought needed to be recorded. It was the only way I knew how to consolidate the information flowing in from internet searches, books, or just something picked up in a TV documentary. As exciting as it all was, one answered question invariably led to three more, and it was getting harder to switch off from it, even midway through a motorcycle tour!

In its own way, this trip, through the Balkans and down to Montenegro, was proving very useful. I'd brought with us the majority of our camping, cooking and touring gear. Unfortunately, it had spent the last six years laid up in the garage loft and I needed to see what we could salvage and possibly make use of. It turned into a bit of a comedy; the twenty-five-year-old tent had way more repairs and peeling patches than I'd ever admitted to remembering. Selly remembered quite clearly, though; she had laboured on it with sewing machine, glues and repair kits prior to us setting off, but I was just too stubborn and reluctant to listen to her suggestions that we replace it, until now. The clever Khyam 'quick erect' poles now resembled a cheap, tangled umbrella in a whirlwind; they had become so twisted that it didn't seem to matter how long you spent, or how carefully you repacked them, they would only open in a jumbled mess. I was the taller by several inches, but even Selly's slight frame couldn't stand upright in any part of it. My back complained just attempting to get dressed and tie up shoelaces in the mornings. Maybe I was the one who'd aged. Anyway, it leaked as well, condemning it to post-trip retirement.

Its demise was only surpassed by the equally aging multi-stove. It had the audacity to shoot flames sideways the first time we pressurised and lit it, resulting in me having to kick the damn thing down into the River Rhine, before it blew up in our faces. Retrieving it, I joyfully introduced it to the campsite's metal recycling bin, never to be seen again. The theme continued with supposedly non-stick pots and pans now too pitted to save, along with an ad hoc selection of flimsy cutlery. Completing the failures were several items of waterproof biking gear that defied their description and most annoyingly, an airbed that resented retaining air for more than four hours. The hard ground would be digging into me around 3am, letting me know it was time to put my back out finding my clothes, dress and wander off to find the toilet. Oh well, only another five weeks of this! Hence I started the spreadsheet by overlooking the bigger concerns, like whether to start from the north, or south, what bike, or how long we should go for, etc. Instead, I made a shopping list of all the exhausted kit that we couldn't wait to replace. Of this, Selly and I were in complete agreement and I reminded myself (again) to listen to her more often.

As the research kicked in, one comforting fact became apparent: the PAH had been walked, cycled, hitchhiked, driven, probably skateboarded and, on almost every variety of two wheels from moped to street cruiser, ridden. It was uplifting to know that the vast majority of these adventurers seemed to have successfully crossed the expanse of countries and endured the harsh climates, high altitudes and differing seasons. There were those that clearly hadn't completed the journey and to the list of the obvious – breakdowns, injuries and robbery – my sleepless and furtive imagination added chloroform kidnappings, with a kidney each removed for the black market. I couldn't stop there, though; there was a lifetime in a filthy prison after secreted drugs were unknowingly stashed into our luggage and then discovered at a corrupt border, death by malaria, zika virus, or dengue fever, attacked by packs of rabid dogs and then eaten by grizzly bears. It was never-ending if you tried hard enough. I tried to stick to the simpler scenarios, like the bike getting nicked, or an emergency back home, or running out of cash from enjoying ourselves too much, or even a worldwide pandemic halting us in our tracks; you just never know!

Needless to say, we returned back across the Channel with less kit than we'd set off with, having dispersed various expired items in campsite bins across southern Europe. By now, Selly had moved full time to the UK, and her apartment in Sardinia became our holiday retreat from the all-too-often-disappointing British weather. As best she could, she was still painting portraits, in between my spontaneous purchases of last-minute flight deals that were just too good to pass up. With neither of us now working a traditional nine-to-five, we were dabbling in the rental market, with a couple of buy-to-lets. The income was needed to bolster the small RAF pension I was receiving and would hopefully cover the monthly budget of a longer trip. We still needed to save, though. The more we researched, the more the costs were mounting; vaccinations, travel insurance, new passports, shipping the bike both ways, our flights, plus all the new gear we needed, for us and for eventually prepping the bike. It wasn't hundreds of pounds, but mounting thousands, and I really needed to rein in the impulsive trips I continued to dream up along the way. In this respect, I was, and still am, hopelessly undisciplined and as if it were needed, about to prove it to myself yet again.

To this day, Chris and Caroline remain wonderful and close friends, despite them now living halfway around the world in Australia. Caroline's fiftieth was coming up and though I knew I shouldn't and knew the PAH trip could be delayed because of it, I hatched a plan for the four of us to get together. We couldn't justify the trip but went anyway, meeting them down in Indonesia and then heading over to theirs for a few more weeks. It was a thoroughly awesome and overdue catch-up. Chris and I rented a pair of off-road bikes and a guide, to explore around Bali's mountain tracks and beaches. For me, it was much-needed practice in tackling the softer surfaces. (Read: picking my bike up too often!) Enthused by the details of our trip, they pledged to take time out, rent a bike and join us somewhere in the USA for a few weeks.

Back home and at a more leisurely pace, Selly and I continued with the planning, finally settling one of the bigger decisions after catching an episode of the Alaskan-based *Ice Road Truckers* one evening. The northern end of the Pan-American is generally accepted as ending in the town of Deadhorse, Prudhoe Bay. This is reached via the Dalton Highway, a road we had just seen portrayed on TV as scarily daunting for vehicles usually benefitting from at least twenty more wheels than we had. It was also aptly 666km long; the last few hundred are unpaved and sprayed with calcium chloride, which turns into a slippery but sticky clay-like substance when wet. In a few miles, it could turn a shiny bike into one that looked fossilised and calcified. I both bricked it and made a profound decision. I turned to Selly and strongly suggested we went from south to north; I just didn't want us to fail before we'd even reached the starting point, before we had gained plenty of miles and experience on our loaded-up bike! If we had planned to start north to south, the weather window needed us to be in Alaska mid-July, so leaving the UK around May. To start the other way around, we needed to be in Tierra del Fuego, southern Argentina, around the middle of November to catch their summer, so leaving the UK in October. Our minds now agreed on the south-to-north route, but with no bike and not nearly enough money yet saved, it wouldn't be October this year. The best guess was a departure sometime in October 2019. Making it two long summers away.

Yes, two long summers; they had to be productive, and not in a gardening or decorating sense. The ZZR1400 we'd ridden down to the Balkans had been yet another of my impulse purchases, not a regretted purchase, just a misplaced one. It was just bought out of frustration, because my then twenty-six-year-old ZZR1100, that I'd proudly owned from new, was finally playing up. It had stood silent for too long whilst I had worked away in Saudi Arabia and now that it was being coaxed back into life, showed all the signs of worn and difficult-to-set-up carbs. I'd had them strip-cleaned to no avail, and so rode the rough-running bike to a specialist outside London, for a good old tinkering. In the meantime, rather than waiting patiently for an answer, I committed the crime of drinking and shopping on a well-known auction site. I won the bid on the 1400 the very night before the carb specialist rang to say he'd fixed my 1100. Swapping my worn carbs for a low mileage set, it was now running sweet and dandy.

I tried but just couldn't justify two ZZRs sat side by side in the garage (they were even the same colour, black). The 1400 was the logical one to sell, the one that would give us the most money towards an adventure bike. We'd enjoyed a good trip away the previous year, but it still pained us to let it go. Polished spotless and advertised at a fair price, the first viewer bought it without so much as a haggle. We took the money, splashing out on a new tent, airbed, cooking gear and a host of other bits and pieces we absolutely thought we needed.

I put the idea to Selly that we should go on a camping trip, to try out all this new gear. Here in Norfolk? she responded. The coast, or the Norfolk Broads maybe? I was thinking Morocco actually. Ferry to Spain, down through Portugal, another ferry from Spain to Morocco and back up through the Pyrenees, say, three months?

"Can we afford another big trip?" she rightly enquired.

"We'll be camping mostly, and it'll keep me away from shopping. Probably be cheaper than being at home?" I offered, not sure which one of us I was trying to convince.

I didn't have to waffle too much; Morocco seemed to have it clinched. It was a country she'd long wanted to explore and having our own wheels would give us all the freedom we fancied. The old ZZR was loaded up and pointed south, never missing a beat. Halfway back, the clocks wound past 100,000 miles, revealing a fresh row of zeros and the chance for me to reminisce about that far-off day when, still in my twenties, I had excitedly taken delivery. The new gear was a transformation; a watertight tent we could easily stand in, an airbed that was comfier than many a hostel we'd stayed in and brand-new cooking equipment. Overall, the trip was a prudent and successful experience, with some useful lessons learnt. The packing certainly improved along the way! Inadvertently, if usefully, I'd also notched up a little more practice in riding on softer sandy surfaces and coping with the strong, persistent winds of the Rif and Atlas Mountains. We were on a high and feeling much more confident, but not long after returning, our excitement was tempered by some disheartening news from home.

My father's knee had finally packed up, after a football injury incurred in his youth. He had struggled, on and off, for fifty-odd years, but now it had practically seized up and X-rays confirmed replacing it was the only option left. The issue wasn't just the operation, though; he was also the full-time carer for my mum, after she'd unfortunately suffered a stroke some years before. Caring was becoming physically impossible for him. Post-op, they would need to come and live with us for a while. I couldn't have my mum living off his banana sandwiches, however legendary they were! He was put on an NHS waiting list and warned it could be a six-to-twelve-month wait. Selly and I assured them we would delay our departure and be on hand to help. There was nothing for it; we pulled together and crossed fingers he would be operated on and out of pain as soon as possible.

With cash still remaining in the bank from the 1400 sale, my thoughts swung towards the next bike. Within reason and budget, all cards were on the table, with the exception of many overlanders' firm favourite, the larger BMWs. In Morocco, we had fortuitously crossed paths with a friendly Pernod-loving French couple, eventually staying at the same kasbah on the very edge of the Sahara dunes. Fabrice had insisted several times, until I relented, that I take his immaculate and expensive-looking R1250 GSA for a spin. Something I was definitely curious to do, but with it being both new and somebody else's, I was reluctant all the same. We happened to be on sand at the time, more by accident, as I had intended avoiding the desert on a sports-tourer. However, since the photos of our accommodation had been taken several years earlier, the Saharan sands had continued their relentless shifting, to engulf our kasbah by several hundred metres!

I hopped on and took off round what was remaining of the wide-open sandy car park and after a few laps, began tackling the smaller dunes close by, before bringing the bike safely back to its proud owner. Fabrice jumped on and headed to the same small dunes, eventually laying the bike down on its side to show me how easy it was to pick up. It wasn't and I dived in, grabbing one end as both of us struggled to keep our feet from sliding and disappearing into the scorching hot desert. Eventually, if reluctantly, the bike relinquished its horizontal friendship with gravity. We retired, hot and sweaty, to Pernod and cold beers. I was grateful for the fun and games, but I just knew that with two of us and all the gear, this was not going to be the bike for us. What I was searching for was a lighter bike, one that gave me a feeling of instantly being at ease, as if I'd owned it six months already. Selly had a say in all this, of course; it just needed to have a super comfy seat that was heated!

The months drifted into the winter of 2018. I read magazines and books, blogs and posts, until my shortlist came down to just a few bikes that I really fancied, none of which we would end up buying! Even in the chills of November and December, test riding was fun and exciting. For sure, there were some bikes that really were too expensive for us. We'd had a conversation whilst building the packing list that we had to be prepared to lose anything, or everything in the worst case. That included the bike, and so long as we were safe, the material stuff shouldn't be classed as too important. I said all these things, not ever believing it would come close to this, but I didn't have any hindsight back then, did I?

Some bikes were just too gimmicky for my liking, with umpteen power modes, hill starts and a host of sensors and microswitches that spelt trouble if they failed out in the sticks, or worse, up in the freezing mountains. There's a lot of choice, but none were jumping out as being 'the one' and I began to get a little frustrated. I went to yet another dealership and over a coffee was thrown a curve ball, a suggestion that for reasons unknown hadn't even crossed my radar.

"Have you taken out a V-Strom 650 yet?" I was asked.

"Er, no," I could only reply.

I rode home wondering why it hadn't occurred to me; probably too small and underpowered were my first thoughts. I hit the internet and the more I read, the more curious I became. It was getting rave reviews on rider and pillion comfort. With an intrigued but still open mind, I set up a test ride.

The December day was fresh but dry. A low winter sun did little to lift the temperature above five degrees. I parked up the aging ZZR and with a few formalities out of the way, swung my leg over the slim 650. Unsurprisingly, as I lifted the bike upright and thumbed the starter, it felt half the weight and size of the 1100. I'd never actually owned a twin before, and it just seemed to sit quietly purring, in an understated way. Nudging it down into first, I pulled out onto the near empty Sunday morning roads, hoping that reality would match the reviews. Tap dancing through the gear box soon had me grinning like a kid; it was just so light and flickable, a real joy compared to the succession of heavier bikes I had become so used to over the years. It was reminding me of being a teenager again, those early learning exploits on ER50s and GP100s. It was just so long since I'd been on a smaller machine.

I went via the house, to ask Selly if she wanted to come out and try it. The Sardinian in her felt and breathed in the crisp, cold air and promptly declined, taking my word for it that whatever bike we chose would be made as comfy as could be. The bike was a joy and after a couple of hours playing on the Norfolk country roads, I reluctantly took the little machine back to the dealers. Ten minutes later, I was being walked around a brand-new 650XT Adventure model that just happened to also be black. It was a back-to-basics machine, everything simple to get at and thus work on. A big bonus was the spoked wheels that took tubeless tyres. Yes, I liked it. Currently, this one was unregistered and unridden, but if unsold, was destined in the New Year to become the dealership's demonstrator. I had just a few remaining days to make up my mind and make an offer. As their display model, it had been draped in various Suzuki accessories, centre stand, crash guards, touring screen, hand guards and a few other 'bits 'n' pieces' that would, upon shaking hands, all be thrown in for free. Along with an end-of-the-year discount, it clinched the deal and a couple of weeks later I happily rode it home, now resplendent with a matching black aluminium luggage set. Finally, we had the PAH bike sorted!

With winter weather upon us, running-in was postponed and instead, the little machine was stripped down for prepping and to remedy some problems already emerging. The rear storage rack was clearly going to be too small and despite the luggage-set being Suzuki supplied, Selly couldn't get her feet on the rear foot pegs properly. I guess for centre of gravity reasons, the side panniers were positioned quite far forward and were digging into her calves. I mused over this as I continued pulling the bike apart, making a list of any tools I used that weren't already contained in the little 'under seat' tool kit. With the bike strewn around the garage floor, I could now easily wire up a satnav and mobile phone holder, USB chargers, fit a K&N air filter and put an extra 12V power socket under the seat. I had kindly been given a spare seat with the bike and sent this to Tony Archer, up in Yorkshire, for reshaping, recovering and the installation of heated seat pads, bought off the internet. Once returned, I wired these up and mounted a waterproof switch for each seat. As far as Selly was concerned, the prepping was complete; it was now a bum's dream!

I had a little more to do, though. The aesthetic but functionally useless plastic sump guard was swapped for a tough steel one, along with metal radiator and headlight protectors. Despite the finger-numbing cold, I was enjoying this time in the garage, kept company by the radio and our cat and Giulia's dog finding inappropriate places to lie down. Every so often, Selly would pop in with a cup of tea and a sandwich and ask if she could help. Even with the bike stripped down, her tinier hands could feed and route cables far easier than me. With the various power leads neatly cable-tied to existing looms, fused and labelled up, we finally wired all these accessories through a marine isolation switch. Tucked away under the seat, the key to this could be turned off and removed.

For the camping gear, I mocked up a larger full-scale rack in cardboard and took it to a sheet metal fabricator. His laser cutter beautifully replicated the design in 3-millimetre steel, complete with bungee points and attachment holes. I sourced a backrest for Selly, mainly to stop any luggage moving forward and digging into her back. After collecting the new rack, I set about making a steel bracket that could secure the backrest at the right angle, but also allow the rest to be easily removed for crating and shipping purposes. Once shaped, this was welded securely to the new rack. To sort out the panniers digging in, a second-hand set of rear pegs were cut up, repositioned and welded, to bring her feet further forward and a little higher. The finished rack and pegs were powder-coated and once fitted, looked virtually original.

It had taken a few weeks, but putting the bike back together felt like we were getting there, and the weather had improved enough to get out and finally enjoy running it in. Brimming the 20-litre tank and turning on the ignition displayed a respectable range of 304 miles. Fuel stations in the more remote parts of Patagonia could easily be over 200 miles apart, so we should be fine, except we had no experience of the notorious winds yet!

We planned away as my dad continued to wait on news from the NHS. A spare room was turned into our packing area and as we filled it with thermals, tent and sleeping gear, riding gear, waterproofs, clothing, cooking gear, medications, cameras, documents, tools and bike spares, I remember having a minor panic that it simply wasn't all going to fit. The doorbell seemed to shout out daily of more and more stuff arriving, all of it considered necessary in one way or another. We needed to get clever; we needed to practice pack! Everything got divided into piles of 'undeniably essential' and 'nice to have with us'. We condensed the clothing using vacuum bags and checked we weren't duplicating chargers, leads, or adapters. We shared what we could and still there didn't seem to be enough room. We purchased two waterproof roll bags, to be strapped on top of the side panniers, and Selly now found she had armrests to compliment the backrest! We repacked the tent bag, panniers, tank bag and the two new roll bags. Everything now seemed to fit, even our diving logbooks and my much-needed (if I wanted to dive) prescription mask.

That went a little easier than I had expected; there had to be a catch. We weighed it all, bag by bag and pannier by pannier, then the pair of us in our biking gear. We were just over the bike manual's recommended gross weight. Bugger, we were going to have to join the local gym! We had one summer left to try to lose as many kilos as we could and maybe a few more from another rinse-through of the gear. The leisure centre became an obsession, even addictive, as we counted steps, watched our calories and shed a few kilos each.

In the May, my father finally got the news we'd all been hoping for; a new knee was scheduled to be fitted the third week in June and it was agreed they would move in with us for the post-op weeks. In all honesty, the timing couldn't have been much more perfect if we'd chosen it ourselves. We desperately wanted, and needed, to fully load up the bike and take it on a mini-tour, a dry run so to speak. It would be tight, but there should be time to test out the bike in August, fly to Sardinia in September and then deliver a prepped bike to London sometime in October. This all hinged on my dad regaining his fitness enough to be able to care for my mum, though.

So, with this timeline to work to, we started looking at flights and shipping options for South America. Buenos Aries was our preferred option, allowing us to ride down the Atlantic east coast 2,500 miles into, and through, Patagonia to Ushuaia. This city, at the southern tip of Argentina, would be the true starting point of our PAH adventure. We would then be able to, without retracing our steps, head north through western Patagonia for a similar distance. Oh, how simple and easy it sounded from the warm comfort of our spare room, even if it did resemble a Sunday car boot sale cum flea market! Buenos Aires wasn't the cheapest option, though. Port and customs fees were hundreds of dollars higher than in neighbouring Chile, but besides the routing benefits, we really wanted to see and experience this immense capital. Scrutinising flights almost daily, we eventually dropped on a Norwegian Air sale, covering the route from Gatwick to Buenos Aires. We snapped up two seats for late October, immediately excited and then daunted by the reality that this was now actually happening, and then giddily excited again! With celebratory drinks in hand, we watched an awe-inspiring documentary, on Patagonia, of course.

The TV screen showed us whales, penguins, condors, llamas, mountains and glaciers in abundance. Would we really be there soon, amongst all that breathtaking wildlife and scenery? It was hard to comprehend this was soon to be our next destination, that we were really going. For the most part, our families and friends just seemed amazed and a little in awe of the length and mileage of the trip; we struggled to take it all in ourselves.

In various conversations, we answered many similar questions with information only gleaned through reading but never experienced. Country names rolled off our tongues as if we hid expert knowledge, Guatemala this and El Salvador that… no, we won't go to Venezuela, as it's almost in civil war… yes, we know about the Darién Gap and lack of any road through it. The Darién Gap, that little slice of jungle between Panama and Colombia that stopped the PAH, by just a few hundred miles, from being a continuous road. It was essentially a lawless swath of jungle, a conduit for criminal gangs to smuggle people and narcotics and to be avoided by happy-go-lucky tourists like us. A bit more research was necessary and, we guessed, another thousand pounds or so might be needed to transport us and the bike over or around it.

Unbeknown to Selly, I was also researching and planning behind her back. This had to happen when she was out of the house and I could safely plot away undetected. As a precaution, I had even set up a new and encrypted email address. It felt so alien; we had happily been in each other's company twenty-four seven for years and I wasn't used to having to be secretive. It had taken her six long years to finally win her divorce just four years earlier; it still isn't easy for an Italian woman to initiate and achieve this. I had wanted Selly to enjoy being single again, and it was a great comfort knowing she was with me because she wanted to be. Neither of us was in the slightest bit religious and hadn't discussed getting married, but I was just so proud of her. I really did want to see an engagement ring on her finger. I'd learned years before that she preferred emeralds over diamonds, and I wanted to make this trip even more memorable than she could imagine. So my research took me to Colombia, specifically Bogotá. In this capital could be found the Emerald Trading Centre, 120 dealers under one roof, and selling directly to the paying public.

Yes, she would be in gem heaven. I had no idea when, or where, I would propose, or even if our journey would be successful enough to take us all the way up to Bogotá. Assuming she would said 'yes' (this time around!), I took the planning further and wondered where we could marry. Italy wasn't fair to my parents, as following the stroke, my mum wasn't able to fly, and the UK wasn't fair to Selly's mum, who was turning ninety and also not well enough to fly. It made practicable sense to get married somewhere on our route, a cosy ceremony in a fun place. It needed to be somewhere I could convince Chris and Caroline to join us, and allow him to return the favour of being my best man. In my mind, Las Vegas was the obvious city for an easily arranged wedding, with plenty of fun and entertainment on tap. We had stayed there a few nights during our whirlwind 'round-the-world' trip, and as Selly had loved the place, I set about emailing various venues in secret. Though the age gap was far from any issue now, I really was getting ahead of myself and didn't dare harbour the thought she might actually say 'no'. Who knew, though? Maybe she was already as happy as she needed to be. What I did know for sure was I now needed to find another chunk of cash from somewhere; the trip was growing beyond our bank balance and savings!

After a short discussion, we decided where we wanted to test ride the loaded-up bike. It had been a no-brainer for me; if we wanted some Patagonian conditions then it needed to be Scotland, in the height of summer, when it would most likely rain and howl a gale! Having previously lived up there for a year, I had nurtured Selly's imagination with stories of its rugged beauty, deep fried pizza and unpredictable weather. As soon as I'd put the idea to her, she excitedly wanted to go (probably not for the pizza!), but we had the makings of a plan no less.

June arrived, the knee operation was a success and my dad strived to regain his fitness on a diet of Selly's cooking and my gin & tonics; he couldn't fail. With the flights booked, we started to iron out the finer details of the grand departure. To avoid any unforeseen shipping delays, we booked with a London freight company to crate up and fly the bike to Buenos Aires. It was more expensive upfront, but likely cheaper than the accommodation and living costs if the ship got delayed, or was diverted for unknown weeks. We had a range of NHS vaccinations each and stockpiled medications we either needed or packed as a precaution. Satnav and hardcopy maps were bought, and a request was sent to the US Environmental Protection Agency for a temporary import exemption for the bike. A few hours were spent researching travel insurance, visas and visa waivers. It was a nice surprise that for Italian and British passport holders, not a single visa was required throughout the seventeen countries we hoped to visit; only the USA and Canada required us to pay for visa waivers. Where it was obligatory, it seemed that bike insurance could be arranged either online or directly at the various borders themselves, along with the important 'Temporary Vehicle Import Permits' (TIPs). With no *Carnet de Passage* bond needed either, the Pan-American trip didn't seem to be any kind of bureaucratic nightmare at all? Oh, what naivety we planned away in!

For each country, we made a short list of places we most wanted to experience, followed by other sights to see, if time allowed. The framework for the trip was to generally follow the PAH up, timed between the southern and northern summers, but deviate for must-sees like Iguazu Falls, Uyuni Salt Flats and Machu Picchu, etc. These were exciting months, with no room for boredom; there was always something to do. I helped my dad with his daily rounds of strengthening exercises, before Selly and I hit the gym ourselves, or took lengthy dog walks to keep the Fitbit steps up. Giulia had moved in full time with us, secured a job and would kindly be looking after the house and animals whilst we were away. It felt like it was all falling into place, up until you watched the news anyway. The Amazon was sadly on fire, like never before. It was disheartening; we didn't have anything specific planned at this stage but had hoped at some point during the trip to fit in a little Amazonian detour.

By mid-July, my father was walking unaided and even back riding a pushbike again. It had been a painful six-week journey for him to get to this stage, but by the end of the month he was doing so well we could drop them back home. Within the following few days, we and the bike were all packed up and the weatherman kindly gave us a timely warning of gale force winds and flooding across west and central Scotland; it hadn't let me down!

Double-checking the waterproofs were easy to get at, we squeezed everything onto the little 650 for our first fully loaded ride. We had arranged to swing by and stay with friends in North Yorkshire and as the sun was shining in a cloudless Norfolk sky, a last-minute packed lunch was prepared for the journey up. With the remaining weeks to departure rapidly diminishing, this innocuous 'lunch' revealed the first potentially serious flaw of our chosen set-up. Fully loaded, the bike was certainly squatting lower, despite having already wound the rear shock's pre-load to its maximum setting. Later that afternoon, we hungrily pulled off the road, following signs to a panoramic picnic area that happened to be blessed with speed bumps (that I would come to hate across Latin America)! At just a moderate speed, the new steel belly pan collected its first scrapes. That's a pretty dismal start, I thought, accepting the reality that the rear shock would have to be replaced for something considerably beefier.

As the miles that first day progressed, yet another, and in my mind, much worse problem was unbelievably manifesting. The engine was worryingly developing a loud tick. It sounded like it was coming from the top-end and occasionally felt like it was missing. How could this be? With barely a thousand miles on the clock? Plodding up the road, I had too much time inside my helmet to ponder over the worst-case scenarios; blocked oil feeds, loose cam chain, or just an incorrectly assembled engine? The demons ran loose in my head and I just didn't know what to think. By the time we arrived at my mate's house, it had become quite loud and definitely not a figment of my imagination. John was not just a lifelong biker himself, but the first mate to let me ride a proper big bike, his beloved CB900 back in 1984. I spilled out my concerns and fired up the bike for a second opinion.

After a little head scratching, and clearly audible to him as well, he fetched a very large screwdriver and proceeded to place the blade against different parts of the engine's cases, whilst the plastic handle was wedged against his ear. With the blade acting like a stethoscope, he listened quite cleverly to the various interior moving parts. In less than a minute, a beaming smile spread across John's face, and above the rattle of the engine I heard his broad Scouse accent calling me a plonker, whilst pointing down at the right side. I followed his accusing finger, looked closer and sure enough a spark plug cap was floating loose and happily rattling away against the cylinder vanes. A simple firm push had it back to its proper place and the twin instantly returned to its quiet contented purring. The V-Strom actually has two plugs per cylinder, and losing the spark from one plug was virtually unnoticeable, unlike my embarrassment! I remembered removing that cap just days earlier to check that the long reach socket I intended packing comfortably fitted. I happily got the fish 'n' chips in that night!

With this panic behind me, I could press on with showing Selly as much of North Yorkshire and the Lake District as time allowed. We were taken on hikes up fells, given tips for riding some of the more scenic routes and enjoyed a top meal of 'bangers 'n' mash' in Britain's highest pub, the Tan Hill Inn. They truly are beautiful riding roads and suspension issues aside, the bike happily powered up the steeper hills without a stutter, or a plug cap rattle. As we continued further north, though, the winds picked up and the rain started to fall. It was the first week of August 2019, and the M74 greeted us with sign after sign warning of *Severe Winds – Heavy Rain*. How could I complain? It was, after all, what we needed to experience, if not what we actually wanted! The temperatures were also dropping, and crossing the Trossachs National Park in pounding hail, we got our first real chance to test both settings of the heated seats: one – comfortable, two – BBQ your backside!

If it wasn't hailing, then it was horizontal rain and my new waterproof boots filled up quickly and kept the water nicely inside, in some form of irritating reverse waterproofing. I had to admit that they were comfortable, though, so I added overboots and waterproof socks to my mental shopping list. As we arrived in Oban and alighted from the bike, the rain mockingly stopped. The clouds exited the wings to present us with a stunning sunset, reflecting off a flat, calm mirror of a sea. We were still fairly wet and cold, but absolutely happy and smiling. After a very sociable week crisscrossing Scotland, Selly still couldn't be convinced to try deep fried pizzas (or battered and fried Mars Bars)!

Once home, we ordered a replacement shock. Built to order, it would be at least a three-week wait but would come pre-set up to our all-up weight. We wouldn't see it until after our visit to Selly's family and would just have to hope this would leave enough time to fit, test and put the issue to bed.

Flying to Sardinia proved a relief, an enforced break from the four walls of our house and all the time spent either in the garage or in our makeshift packing and planning room. As we made final tweaks to exactly what would go and what could be left behind, I was still feeling nervous about the total amounts. For personal stuff, we had a pannier and roll bag each, mounted to the pannier's lids. Camping, sleeping and cooking gear was stashed behind Selly on the new larger steel rack, and a tank bag had cameras, phones, locks and other day-to-day stuff. Other than to make sure we weren't duplicating anything, we didn't question what each other was packing. We packed what was important to each of us, and my only input was that our panniers should end up roughly weighing the same.

What was frustrating for me, though, was that her clothes pile seemed to be a third the size of mine! I might be the one with thirty-five years of motorcycle touring experience, but I was also the one who was considerably taller and wider. It seemed that just two pairs of my boxer shorts annoyingly took up the same packing space as all of her underwear. I seriously needed to rethink my clothes before we flew to Argentina!

Sardinia wasn't helping matters; we were enjoying too many delicious pizzas and endless dinner invites. I could feel all our hard work in the gym coming apart. It was all just too irresistible, though, good old homely Italian hospitality that had lunches rolling seamlessly through into dinners and me considering ringing a certain shock manufacturer to add another 10 kilograms! I had work to do, though, and spent the best part of two days phoning and emailing my way through the list of potential travel insurance providers, and then getting denied cover for a variety of reasons. The trip was too long, you couldn't ride your own bike and definitely not off-road, etc, etc. Eventually, one ticked all the boxes and another chunk of our savings disappeared.

Over these fun and sun-filled three weeks, we got around all of Selly's family and friends, answering many of the same questions as we had back in the UK, the main difference being that they were aimed more at Selly than me this time around. Occasionally, she was asked if she wasn't scared to be on the back of a motorbike anymore. With ease, I could recall the exact pivotal moment that I finally stopped worrying about whether Selly was enjoying being a pillion. Several years earlier, we had gone to India and I was determined to rent a bike of some kind and get Selly to try out two wheels for the first time in her life. I'd wanted to jump straight in with an iconic Royal Enfield Bullet, but knew this was most likely a one-time chance to give her a positive and enjoyable experience. The rear seat on the Enfield resembled a small solid lunchbox, and as my future worldly touring aspirations hinged on these next few days, I walked past it and instead paid to rent a little scooter.

I remember just two things about this little Honda: the seat was more than half the size of the whole machine and it was bright yellow. Yes, it was a sofa on wheels, as comfy as you could find, and Selly quickly named it 'Girasole', Sunflower. I don't know who was more nervous as she first sat down behind me. I'm sure it must have been me, and as we pulled out into the Indian traffic of tuk-tuks, cows and bikes, I tried to detect any tensing, or overly holding on from behind me. For days we explored villages and beaches, country roads and markets, with me staying under the speed limits and eyes glued to the road ahead, trying to miss potholes, speed bumps and elephants. I'd never ridden so slowly in my life and it came to a head one afternoon as I eased back on the throttle to point out some water buffalo in a nearby field. A nun on a pushbike came flying past us, bell ringing furiously to get us out of her way and Selly burst out laughing.

"You can ride faster, you know. We don't have to go slowly everywhere. I am enjoying this!" she ribbed me.

In my defence, the road was slightly downhill, and it looked like a very fast pushbike, honestly! I sheepishly returned Girasole and rented the Enfield Bullet; the rest is history.

At the beginning of October, three weeks prior to our flights to Buenos Aires, we returned to Norfolk. I hadn't followed much news during the weeks away and catching up the next morning, over breakfast and coffees, it all appeared a bit doom and gloom. An estimated 80,000 fires were out of control in Brazil alone, with Bolivia and Peru also reporting unprecedented numbers. More concerning was learning that Ecuador had erupted in violent protests, over cuts to long-standing fuel subsidies. It could be over in a flash, but we would need to follow this turn of events, as only via Ecuador could we reach Colombia. South American news didn't often feature in European news, so to have two stories frequently covered was a little unnerving. Protests had a habit of spreading in South and Central America and it wasn't lost on us that Argentina was holding its general election the very day we were flying out of London!

With less than a fortnight remaining, to dropping the bike off in London, we had work to do. The new rear shock had arrived, along with the Continental TK70 semi off-road tyres we'd ordered. My head was in a bit of a spin tying up loose ends; seemingly, a host of silly things that needed addressing before we could leave. Almost a whole day disappeared setting up a new travel laptop, external hard drive and memory stick, backing them all up with my 'secretive' wedding plans and all the info for the trip. We both had our eyes tested, and even dental check-ups to last the possible year away. It was hard to fully enjoy the excitement of leaving; we were kept busy saying our goodbyes and continuously racked our brains to wonder what we might have forgotten. My parents came down for one last send-off, wishing us well and gifting each of us some money to take with us. Parents seem to have perceptive powers and sense when you're probably blowing your budget. In truth, I had no idea yet if Selly and I would be able to stay on budget. Selly especially couldn't know, as I had been engagement and wedding planning behind her back!

We made photocopies of all our important paperwork and joyfully poured over the various currencies picked up. Overall, these last weeks were becoming as stressy as they were exciting, though. I'd reached a point where I just wanted the pair of us to be checked in and sat in a bar at the airport. I was itching to get going, to be enjoying a pre-flight drink and knowing we had done what we could.

I dropped the bike off to get the tyres and shock replaced, collecting it again the same day. It was a different bike, I could tell just by sitting on it, but tomorrow I wanted to return once more. There was one final task and I asked if I could pop back in the morning, borrow their MOT machine and set up the lights properly. To cover the first months away, we were leaving Giulia a stockpile of cat litter and food, out in the garage, and that evening I delved into it. After the tent bag was bungeed onto the rack and the panniers were fitted, I weighed and filled each one with bags of cat litter. To each lid I strapped a sizeable bag of dog food, until the overall weight pretty well matched our touring weight. In the morning, I rode down and at the shop 'borrowed' the owner's young nephew, to sit behind me as the pillion whilst we set about adjusting the lights correctly!

"Are you planning on adopting some animals along the way?" queried the grinning mechanic, with a premonition my lack of hindsight failed to enlighten me of.

"You gotta be kidding, I'm still desperately trying to find room for coffee we brought back from Italy!" I replied, a little exasperated.

The ride there and back had been transformational; the shock was worth every penny and I felt confident we had that issue properly licked. Parked back in our garage, the bike was surely as good as we could get it and I happily told Selly so. She had good news for me, hearing on the radio that the protests in Ecuador had been resolved. That evening, we watched the news with almost disbelief as, yes, the protests had officially been discontinued in Ecuador, but a wave of new ones had erupted across Chile. A price rise in the Santiago metro fares had become the straw that broke the camel's back, and the capital's population was rebelling. It was shaping up to be an eventful trip!

The morning of Thursday, the 17th of October 2019 was beautiful, at least in Norfolk it was. By 6:30am, I had rolled the bike out of the garage, underneath clear blue skies. According to its dash, it was already thirteen degrees. It was the day I was riding to London and Selly would follow me down in the car, with her biking gear and some baggage we hoped to squeeze in the crate with the bike. We were both excited and even if we weren't flying yet, it felt like the adventure was starting. It had taken a lot to get to this point; research, planning, discussing, agreeing, saving, organising, compromising, emailing, phone calls and even worrying, or having doubts we could actually do this. But here we were, after a glorious journey down and hardly able to wipe the smiles from our faces, about to drop off all the results of these last two years' efforts. What could possibly go wrong? Well, the news, of course; with less than a week to our departure, the protests in Chile had spread to virtually all cities and large towns, violently. People were losing their lives and hundreds were getting seriously injured at the hands of riot police and additionally, the military's involvement. This was only the half of it, though; Bolivia had now erupted into protests over claims of election fraud. Borders were being illegally blockaded, and tourists were scrambling to find viable escape routes. All we wanted was a safe passage through the entire continent!

Chapter Two

We're Off

We felt like the scruffiest but happiest passengers checking in for the overnighter to Buenos Aires. Our last belongings, those not keeping the V-Strom company in a wooden crate somewhere, were packed into a strange mix of tired but colourful suitcases picked up in our hometown's charity shops. Like us, they were on a one-way journey. That pre-flight pint I'd dreamed of so many times was sat in front of me shortly after we'd cleared security. We toasted our trip and grinned like the kids we really were thirty years ago. There were a couple of screens we could view; one a flight departure board, we were on time, and the other a silent news channel, with headlines scrolling across the bottom. Nothing could dampen our childish exhilaration, not the Amazon still burning out of control and not the growing protests in Bolivia and Chile. As depressing as most of the news was, we were headed to Argentina on an eleven-hour flight and we were just relishing it!

With passports stamped, confirming at least the first country had been successfully reached, we recovered our cheap scruffy cases and cheerily headed out into the hazy morning sunshine. Along with the friendly and chatty taxi driver, thirty-degree muggy heat welcomed us to South America. Passionately political, Selly wasted no time enquiring as to how the election voting had gone and more importantly, were people generally happy. Apparently things had gone well and we could confidently cross off 'trip ruined by Argentinian protests'! It was just a twenty-minute journey, as the apartment we'd rented for ten days was in one of Buenos Aires' cheaper suburban *barrios*, out towards the airport. Our flight had landed early that day, but the apartment owner, Juan, had greeted us warmly and waved off our offer to pay for an early check-in. He showed us around our temporary home, putting on the air-con and pointing out that we even had a washing machine and small balcony; we liked the place. We were then passed over to his good friend and the building's maintenance janitor Daniel, who kindly showed us around the local area, pointing out bars and restaurants he thought we might like; it felt like a great start.

On this first morning, whilst purchasing a SIM card, we were introduced to the Argentine national drink of '*mate*' (pronounced 'mat-tay'). We had already noticed how so many people carried flasks and sat around with tall mugs, often sipping from metal straws. Frankly, from the glimpses I'd caught, it looked pretty disgusting, but I wanted to try it and see what everyone was obsessing over. In the phone shop, the chatty owner had his cup of soggy herbs already prepared and we were offered drinks too. Trying it didn't prove any more appetising, and my taste buds cemented the opinion my eyes had already come to. For me at least, it was no game-changing coffee substitute. Up close, the ground '*yerba mate*' leaves looked like weed but tasted similar to tobacco. Neither of us smoked and neither of us rushed out to buy any! Selly seemed to be enjoying meeting yet another Italian speaker. Everyone seemed to speak her language and just like her fellow citizens, Argentinians were both tactile and huggy. Maybe it was because Christopher Columbus was himself Italian and the Americas were named by another Italian, Amerigo Vespucci. In any case, she immediately felt completely at home on this new continent. Daniel proved super helpful; nothing was too much trouble and before he left us to settle in, he gave us his number, making us promise we would phone if we needed anything at all.

Back in London, I'd asked the shippers to try to get the bike flown over to us early the following week. We wanted a couple of days to get over the flight, acclimatise, sightsee and leisurely enjoy this first weekend. In any case, the city would be shutting down in just a couple of days for an important Latin American festival, 'El Dia de los Muertos', the Day of the Dead. Or so I presumed that was what it was. Buenos Aires is simply huge and over the next few days we travelled around it via cheap Ubers, ridiculously cheap trains and even cheaper feet. We bounced from *barrio* to *barrio*, a free tango lesson down El Caminito, in the heart of the colourful and arty La Boca *barrio*, an amazed stroll around Recoleta Cemetery, final resting place of Eva Perón, packed lunches in the smart Puerto Madero and street food enjoyed to street music in Palermo. For an added bonus, just about everything was cheaper than we'd expected; the exchange rate seemed to be swinging our way daily and nice bottles of wine could be enjoyed for just a pound, or two. Our first Argentinian steak was sublime, about as succulent as a steak could be, and we came to love and then miss them. The sun shone daily and indulging another of her hobbies, Selly happily photographed everything.

The weekend was upon us and in the hold baggage we had brought Halloween masks and face paints to dress up for the 'Day of the Dead' parades we had so been looking forward to. Without asking anybody, we turned to the ever-knowledgeable Google Maps, which displayed not only the lengthy parade route, but also the start and finish times. A full eight hours, wow, this was going to be something memorable. The Uber dropped us as close as he could get, apologising for the crowds already surrounding us and explaining that 100,000 people would be out drinking and celebrating today. It was only early afternoon, but glancing around, as we merged with the moving masses, nobody seemed to be dressed quite like us. Everyone was very colourful, but definitely not quite like us. The river of bodies spilled out into a huge plaza where the largest 'five-storey' inflatable rainbow greeted us, and realisation finally hit home. We had descended upon Argentina's largest LGBT festival of the year. Pride was all around, from scantily clad transvestites to a multitude of genders, all joyfully dancing to live bands and intent on drinking to excess. The atmosphere was fantastic, and we jostled through the partying crowds to get a front-row view of the wild and spectacular passing parade floats. Only later did we understand that we and our face paint needed to be in Mexico for the 'Day of the Dead', not Argentina! Even so, the city buzzed with street parties and live music long into the night and had more stamina than our now tipsy bodies could muster. We made our way back, laughing at the *faux pas* that had turned out to be just as magical.

The next couple of days were quieter as we shook off hangovers and waited for news of the bike's arrival. We had made an arrangement with a local agent in the city to help us clear it through customs, and I had emailed them to let them know we expected the bike as early as the next day. Sandra and Javier ran Dakar Motos, were avid bikers themselves and most importantly, had fifteen years of experience in navigating the ever-changing airport bureaucracy. For us, it was money well spent and conveniently, they also organised our bike's insurance, covering most of South America.

We were five hours behind London now and Tuesday morning I awoke early to check for any shipping updates. Over coffee, I opened my laptop and sure enough we had an email waiting. It wasn't good, though; in fact, it was a bit of a bombshell. Selly saw the look on my face.

"What's happened?" she enquired.

I summarised what I had read; the bike had flown out of Heathrow yesterday, with the intention of it arriving on time here today, but for some reason unknown to us it had landed in Canada, where it had then been offloaded. To cap it off, they didn't yet know when it would be put back on a plane or, of course, when we might eventually receive it. I felt deflated, Selly felt deflated and we were unsure of what to think, or how to respond. We had paid extra to fly the bike and avoid this scenario!

As a copy of the Air Waybill had been attached, I forwarded the email on to Javier, closed the laptop and sat back looking at Selly. She looked as bemused as I did. I guess to both of us this news just felt a little too early in the adventure to be having our first knockback. I took a walk in the sunshine, picked up warm croissants and dwelled on the turn of events. How we responded to this could set the scene for any future setbacks, so it was important to turn this into a positive. The easiest way to look at it was to accept that we had just gained an unknown amount of time, and there were definitely places we wanted to visit outside of the city, outside of the country even.

Over a late breakfast, we scrutinised the hardcopy of our trip's plan and saw we had listed two places in the 'if there's time' column. The waterfalls at Iguazu, 800 miles away and secondly, just a few hours away on the ferry, the Uruguayan coastal city of Colonia Del Sacramento. For us, Iguazu Falls was a must, but because it was a three-day ride each way, plus at least three nights spent there, it needed about ten days allocating to make it happen. These waterfalls considerably dwarfed Niagara, were truly something special to see and we desperately wanted to go. Always mindful of needing to be in Ushuaia before the weather turned against us, it seemed fate had now handed 'enforced' time on a plate to us. With the exchange rate still improving, we eagerly checked the domestic flight prices. They were cheap, affordable and the whole diversion could be completed in four days, instead of ten.

My phone beeped with an oddly comforting message from Javier: *So they used Air Canada then! Could be a few days, could be a week, don't worry, it will show up.* Clearly, this scenario wasn't as new for them as it was for us. I explained our plan to get away for a few days and enquired if that would be an issue. Apparently not, if the bike showed up in the next couple of days and we didn't collect it, we would just incur a daily storage fee. With that in mind and having no idea when we would see the Suzuki, we arranged flights to Iguazu Airport. Our spirits were lifted again, and it felt like we had just booked an adventure within an adventure.

Selly had also received a nice message; one of her backpacking nieces had just arrived in Buenos Aires and wanted to meet up with us. Taking the train once more, we made our way across to Palermo's bar street to meet up with Estelle and her friend Lidia. Over drinks, we eagerly listened to the youngsters' stories of volunteer working their way across South America. They had just arrived from Mendoza and highly recommended it to us for the vineyards and of all things, an apparently amazing Indian restaurant. It was a nice coincidence, to be in the city at the same time, and the tip for Mendoza later solved one of our dilemmas. The return train tickets for both cost about forty pence, with the journey including a noisy and mesmerising impromptu indoor market. Vendor after vendor hopped on at each stop and with ever-increasing volumes tried to advertise their wares, from bin bags to candies to *empanadas* and soft drinks. Often, the train was so crowded they couldn't physically move through the carriages. If your ears could handle the entertainment, three or four could be found hovering over you, trying to out-shout each other in the confined spaces. It might be cheap, but it was also bedlam!

The following morning, we had a more detailed email from London, one that shed light on our current plight. Yes, they had used Air Canada and yes, it was normal that the freight flights routed via Toronto. Once there, all cargo gets reassessed and prioritised, with perishable goods and larger companies, those that spend millions more than we had, getting immediate onward departures. As we had now come to realise, little privately owned motorcycles routinely get offloaded and deposited on the floor of a customs shed, until space again became available. There was a chance it could fly tonight, or tomorrow; they honestly didn't know.

Javier did, though. That afternoon, he messaged, stating, *See you at the airport 9am tomorrow, bring your passport, all your paperwork and don't forget cash for the customs fees, etc.* Wow, double excitement, it looked like we were going to see our bike before we flew to the falls after all. Informing Juan, he offered to keep the bike safe in the building's underground garage, and then went one better.

"The apartment isn't rented out so just keep the keys with you and leave whatever you don't need until you get back," he suggested.

Things were coming good and the following morning felt like an early Christmas. We got ourselves, helmets in hand, to the airport ten minutes early and were met by Javier. With a mop of hair, a full beard and weathered face, he looked like he could wrestle bears for fun and wouldn't tolerate fools easily. Already striding briskly towards the first building, he explained quickly what we needed to do and what would happen. Taking a short break from business, he enquired as to where we were staying.

"Monte Grande," I replied, whilst trying to stay within conversational range.

"Why there? It's dangerous, tourists don't stay there," he queried, clearly surprised at our choice.

Just to reinforce the gravity of my choice, he added, "Knew a Dutch girl who stayed there three years back, got pushed off her motorbike whilst sat at red lights, lost the lot, bike, luggage, everything."

I looked at Selly and saw her face mirrored Javier's, clearly because this was my idea to stay closer to the airport, rather than her preference to stay in the heart of the city. To cap off my ill-judged decision, Javier echoed and voiced her thoughts.

"Should have stayed in the city, much safer," he stated, before disappearing into the first building!

I turned to Selly, offering a 'we're alive, aren't we?' look and shrug, whilst simultaneously and bravely hurrying on after Javier. The next couple of hours were walk here, pay this, walk there and pay that, until I clutched enough receipts, sanitisation certificates and passes to be allowed airside. For this part, I was passed to Sandra, and introductions over, we made our way to my still-crated-up early Christmas present. I could see the crate but wasn't allowed to touch it, until both the customs rep and a police sniffer dog were present. Sandra enlightened me that the morning's rush had been to get to this point, before everyone snuck off for an early lunch. We passed the time chatting, mostly about our plans after leaving Buenos Aires.

"So, you're taking Ruta 3 down to Ushuaia. Be very careful of the winds. Javier and I have been south twice and it was bad both times." She had my attention; these were seasoned local bikers, so I pressed for a little more detail.

"We were on a bike each, both times, mine was light and either lifted in the air, or I was blown across the road," she continued.

I tried to picture a bike being lifted into the air and couldn't, but I think she read my thoughts.

"When it's bad, and it probably will be, you could find yourself riding a straight road leant right over. Then a strong gust hits you and it can lift the bike, it can be scary," she warned.

I totally believed her and didn't want to at the same time. At least we were heavy, two-up and carrying plenty of luggage. Maybe a little more steak and beer would help though!

With everybody now assembled, the crate was pulled apart by half a dozen hands, the bike rolled out and the luggage opened up and laid out on the warehouse floor. Everything appeared exactly as we had left it and the bike didn't have a mark on it. I wondered just how long that would last! Dogs sniffed whilst customs officers made cursory searches, more for the watching cameras, it appeared, and soon enough I was left alone to excitedly put the bike together. Selly couldn't join me airside and I knew she would be anxiously waiting for news, so I hurriedly refitted the screen, mirrors, rear storage rack, panniers and finally bungeed on all the luggage. The bike fired up instantly and I rode towards the exit gate, Temporary Import Permit (TIP) in hand to show the security guard and gain our freedom. With my helmet slid up my arm, Selly could clearly see my wide grin and instantly know all was well.

It wasn't, but I wouldn't find that out for another three whole minutes! With handshakes and 'good lucks', we said our thanks and goodbyes to Sandra and Javier and let them depart ahead of us. From our first contact with them, they had been fantastic, bikers helping bikers, and had undoubtedly saved us a bucket full of bureaucratic stress. Having said that, though, as we put our helmets on, I suddenly felt a little nervous. There really wasn't any reason to be; it was just a different country in a different continent, but no reason to have any doubts. The satnav would be guiding us effortlessly back to the apartment, so I should just be enjoying the ride. I knew we had somewhere between twenty-five and thirty thousand miles in front of us, but this first small step was niggling me for some reason. Selly jumped on and we pulled out and into the airport exit lane, coming across the first of several speed bumps. The bike grounded badly, on all three of them. Maybe I'd just had a premonition!

I couldn't quite believe it; the shock that had been so precisely set up, had felt so good back in the UK, was now unable to clear the first speed bumps we'd encountered. Once safely behind the two electronic gates and parked up, I could clearly see that somebody at the freight company had wound the shock completely off. For sure, it would have been handy to have been pre-warned, but I knew it was me I was annoyed at, for not bringing a peg or 'C' spanner away with us. I had been so chuffed with it that I never intended touching it again! Nothing could be done now, though; it was already late afternoon and it would have to be sorted after Iguazu. We had repacking to do!

Hoping for cloudless skies and exciting views, I had pre-booked our seats, thus ensuring my personal photographer was sat next to a window. The utter disappointment on finding her seat windowless was tangible.

There didn't seem to be any logic to it, but a third of the way down the aisle there was a seat row missing a window, that I had managed to book us into! The flight was totally full, no chance to swap and for the next twenty minutes I failed to find a plausible answer as to why this plane had a blank interior panel where her window should have been. I wasn't of course being blamed for the omission, but having previously worked on and around aircraft for many years, I felt I was expected to know why I had booked the only windowless seat, and why it was windowless. I swiftly ordered us drinks and pretended to read and understand the Spanish in-flight magazine.

Snatching glimpses out of other people's extravagant portholes, we appeared to be landing in a jungle strip and exited to even higher temperatures and humidity, but surrounded by lush exotic greenery. Colourful and eye-catching signs asked drivers to slow for jaguars, giant anteaters and the flightless rheas. In truth, we weren't even on the edge of the Amazon, but in our minds and with signs like these, we could have been square in the middle. Over the following two days, we explored the spectacular falls from both the Brazilian and Argentinian sides, with each of us competing for the most 'wows' gasped daily. Up to 300 individual falls cascaded 80 metres down to the Iguazu River below. They were simply mesmerising and held the distinction of being by far the widest waterfalls on the planet. Soaking boat rides took us under them, and a multitude of stilted walkways allowed us over them. The highlight of the falls is the mighty Devil's Throat, where half the entire flow cascades thunderously through one narrow chasm. Even after two full days, we had to drag ourselves away.

We managed to spare a couple of hours to visit Iguazu's endangered bird park, a tourist magnet masquerading as an animal rescue centre, or so it felt like. Mooching around, I was stopped in my tracks by a placard proclaiming I was presently looking at the last known five living 'Algoas Currassows' on the entire planet. Camera at the ready, I bent down to get a better look at these last few ground-loving jungle inhabitants. With a jet-black body and large red-hooked beak, they were a funny-looking bird. I leaned in to get a photo of the smallest and closest one and whilst distracted got stealthily but painfully pecked through the wire by the largest one. I just didn't know whether to feel proud, or foolish. Choosing both, I called Selly over to show off my ever-so-slightly-injured hand and proudly point out the incredibly rare offender.

On the first evening, we immersed ourselves in the national culinary dish of *parrilla*, the famous mixed meats charcoal BBQ. Evidence was all around that Argentinians loved their meat dishes. *Parrilla* BBQs lined the roadsides and the smells of roasting pork and steak would leave our mouths watering. Eager to try, we ordered and soon comprehended the challenge that lay ahead; you needed to be hungry, very hungry. Plate after plate arrived, offering chorizo and *morcilla* blood sausages (black pudding), pork ribs and fillets, sirloin and tenderloin steaks. There were further dishes of chicken, chips, salad and breads appearing that had us politely begging for no more! It was an unforgettable experience that we knew was just too over-indulgent for repeating; in the future we would stick to 'just' the sumptuous steaks! In the cooler evenings, we could stroll to the Argentinian tourist point of Hito Tres Fronteras, where the Paraná and Iguazu rivers converge. From this vantage point, huge flags of both Paraguay and Brazil could be seen proudly flying. It was a great break, but with tired legs and happy memories we headed back to Buenos Aires. If we had to choose and list only the top five highlights of the whole adventure, then Iguazu Falls is without any doubt right up there.

Monte Grande had a Suzuki dealer, a super friendly one it turned out. They fiddled with the shock for the best part of half an hour and wouldn't take any payment, not even a tip for a few beers. The mechanic told us to give it a try and bring it back if necessary and the manager gave us his personal number, telling us if there were any parts we needed shipping, anywhere within the country, then just call. We couldn't ask for better service and thanked them profusely.

Whilst flying back, we had hatched a small plan for testing out the bike, ahead of setting off southbound. We would ride it round to Uruguay, stay in Colonia del Sacramento for a couple of nights and catch the three-hour ferry back. Liking our idea, Juan came up trumps yet again.

"Keep the apartment's keys, leave anything behind that you want to and see you when you get back," he happily repeated to us.

We loaded just about everything and enjoyed a seven-hour ride in beautiful clear November skies. At nearly thirty degrees, we had to pinch ourselves Christmas wasn't that far off. The bike felt much better, but I'd take up the offer to have it tweaked a little more. The journey was broken up by several random police checkpoints, just a friendly document check and away you go. These became something we soon got used to as the weeks rolled by. At the border with Uruguay we had a fortunate meet with a truly inspirational German couple, Heike and Toshi. Heike was wheelchair-bound, so Toshi had built a sidecar, with her wheelchair mounted on the back, and this is how they had been travelling the world for several years! This chance meeting was warmly uplifting. How could I ever get apprehensive about what might lay ahead, after all they had achieved?

This border was also our first experience of cancelling down TIPs and getting new ones, something else we were to become very familiar and careful with. Toshi warned us they had just made this 250-mile journey to get the chassis number on his TIP corrected. This simple error was blocking their clearance to exit the Americas and continue their journey into Africa.

The colonial town of Colonia del Sacramento was beautifully tranquil and highly photogenic. Very old cars appeared to be popular here, parked in leafy cobbled streets, or in plazas lined with cafés and lively restaurants. After Argentina, everything in Uruguay was comparatively expensive and in truth we itched to be heading south and starting the adventure properly. After a couple of lazy nights, we caught the car ferry back to Buenos Aires and swung via the dealer. The shock now felt spot on, but again no payment could be forced upon them. That evening, we repacked everything and felt as ready as could be. One last sleep and we'd finally be heading south, bound for the wilderness of Patagonia.

Chapter Three

Patagonia Calling

After a mostly sleepless night, full of exhilaration, the day was upon us. The bike was packed early, followed by a light breakfast, enjoyed with anxious excitement and an eagerness to get out on the road. We had not only survived Monte Grande but thoroughly enjoyed its mix of authentic restaurants, artisanal craft beer bars and friendly locals. It had been a great start to the venture, but now we felt the pull of the south. Selly chatted outside with Daniel, who waited patiently for me to warm up the bike, ride up out of the underground garage and return all the keys. Using the key fobs, I opened both sets of gates and coming up the ramp I could see the satnav wanted me to turn left, against the one-way traffic and left again, just 20 metres up the street. I stopped on the pavement and started to explain to Selly that I would just ride along the pavement to make the left turn, but she cut me off, shouting an urgent warning I didn't comprehend in time.

The large metal gate was automatically shutting behind me and clipped the back of the luggage, by just a couple of inches, but effortlessly bowled me and the bike over. I lay there, half under the bike, not knowing whether to laugh or cry. I hadn't even made it to the road on day one! I eased out and asked Selly to take a photo of my embarrassment, before kind helping hands had the bike righted again. What a precarious start; other than the scraped sump guard, the Suzuki had collected its first proper scratches and unfortunately for me, they were on Selly's pannier. I would not live this down easily.

It was a comfortable cruise down to the coastal city of Mar del Plata, 260 miles south. The weather was just lush, a little cooler at twenty-six degrees, and with each passing mile we could feel the huge city finally slipping away behind us. We were looking forward to meeting a friend, actually the only Argentinian either of us knew prior to starting the trip. We had met Carmen on an island-hopping boat trip in Indonesia the year before and on learning we were due to pass by, she had given us her number. We overnighted and caught up with her in the morning, receiving more advice about our route ahead. Tomorrow, we would be crossing into northern Patagonia, and she added sporty truck drivers to the usual wind warnings.

Like the day before, though, the ride down was actually very pleasant and after the hectic capital, these roads felt both super smooth and relatively empty of traffic. We were heading for Bahia Blanca, another coastal city, and at a midway fuel stop we were approached by a jovial Londoner who'd spotted our GB licence plate. After a quick interchange of handshakes and introductions, Rob explained that he and his family were also road-tripping south, but in a car they'd bought and would eventually sell at the end of their vacation. It was the first British guy I'd met since our arrival and as we rode on, it had me wondering why beautiful, cheap and friendly Argentina didn't appear to get so many tourists from the UK. Was it the hangover from the Falklands dispute, still rumbling on, or maybe the language barrier? I had to admit I was guilty of some prejudice. I'd packed a spare number plate, in case mine was lost or broken, but I'd ensured this second one had no GB emblem on it. I was going to swap and fit it if we started receiving any negative attention. It was never needed and as our weeks in Argentina progressed, we only found more reasons to like its relaxed atmosphere and lovely people. What a shame, though, that there wasn't any roadside sign announcing our entry into Patagonia!

We had now picked up Ruta 3, the eastern coast road that would take us all the way down to Tierra del Fuego, the southern island shared with Chile. Ruta 3 has a reputation for being lonely, windy and often boringly straight, but so far, we just marvelled at all the birds of prey and wildlife we were beginning to see. A lot of the action was very close to the roadside, not at all traffic-shy, and upon seeing our first *guanaco* – members of the llama family – we couldn't contain our broad grins. Spotting new wildlife became a thrilling feature of the trip and played a sizable role in our shared love for the outdoors.

The next stop, the touristy Puerto Madryn, was a 400-mile ride and would be used as a base for exploring the Peninsula Valdes Nature Reserve. The notorious wind stayed away, the road stayed smooth and the miles ticked by effortlessly. If my backside numbed, then I'd unceremoniously stand up on the pegs and let Selly punch and massage life back into it. I wouldn't have to wait long; the quicker she did it, the sooner my bum was out of her face! At this stage, we weren't even looking for camping spots. We wanted to stretch out the riding days and if possible, claw back some of the extra days unintentionally spent in Buenos Aires. Wild camping wasn't looking too easy, though; Ruta 3 seemed to be lined with high wire fences along its length and many turn-offs had 'private property' signs. On the other hand, accommodation was easily affordable and allowed us to have an earlier start in the mornings. For ten dollars each, this particular one included air-con and a hearty breakfast, over which we now put together our peninsular wildlife excursion. The initial plan was to commute the 100 miles to Puerto Pirámides and start the day with an exciting whale watching cruise.

Day bags, with water, cameras and a packed lunch sorted, we rode happily away from the town under another clear blue sky and a quickly warming sun. The asphalt ended shortly after the park ranger's ticket office and we had our first lengthy experience of riding on dirt, sand and gravel. Everything seemed to be going well, and holding the bars loosely, letting them dance in my hands, I kept edging up the speed until the bike floated over the corrugations and bumps. Then from nowhere, typically on a bend, soft sand patches would grab a wheel and have us slewing sideways unexpectedly. It could be a little unnerving, but in this slide-and-ride fashion we safely made it, upright, to the little picturesque port. I knew I wasn't accustomed yet to the trickier surfaces, but I was enjoying these small challenges, feeling we were already gaining valuable experience and learning not to be too over-confident so early in the trip.

The boat was a welcome respite, though, and southern right whales with calves greeted us up close and playfully, too many to count in the end and seemingly curious of the camera-bedecked gawkers. Enjoying the novelty of an unloaded bike, we gave ourselves a mission to visit every viewpoint on the remote peninsula. At a total distance of just over 280 miles (including the round-trip commute back to Puerto Madryn), we'd be on the very limit of our fuel range. It would also prove a tad sporty time-wise; it had already swung past midday when we alighted from the boat. Doubling back and picking up the track to Punta Norte, we had our first rhea encounter. Two of the flightless ostrich-like birds suddenly appeared and raced alongside us, before crossing in front and gifting us a display of their crazy wing-flapping zigzag flee. Deeper into the headland, herds of *guanaco* roamed over the grasslands and at the road's side, quite happy to be photographed and admired from even short distances.

With the late afternoon sun beating down, we pulled into the sandy car park of the North Point and found armadillos scurrying around, oblivious to the noise of the bike, or our laughter. The highlight of this viewpoint is the possibility of seeing orcas, during high tide, attempting to catch sunbathing seals on the beach. We could hardly drag ourselves out of the car park, though, thoroughly enjoying watching the funny scaly-armoured mammals hurrying about their business. We had unwittingly missed both the high tide and the eight orcas that the teasing noticeboard proclaimed had been counted three hours earlier. It wasn't a great loss, to be honest; neither of us particularly wanted to witness the capture of any seal pups being dragged off to their untimely deaths, especially as these whales routinely dispense with a quick kill, preferring to toss and play with the unfortunate prey. Fat from the sea's bounties, there was no shortage of well-fed and contented seals to see, though. Despite the absence of hunting whales, the sea lions, elephant seals and fur seals weren't as undisturbed and happy as they could be. Clearly being harassed and annoyed by pecking seagulls, they jostled, grunted and rolled around, trying to shake off the opportunistic scavengers.

As the sun started to drop, we moved on to Caleta Valdes for its famous penguin colony. For company we now had huge hares bounding across the road, or racing alongside, comfortably matching our 40 mph. Parking up, we could already see dozens of the knee-high Magellanic penguins waddling around between their burrows. Wooden walkways allowed you to get amongst the funny characters, who seemed either oblivious or just used to being part of a selfie backdrop. We had the entire place to ourselves and only as the sun edged towards what would be a wonderful sunset could we drag ourselves away, quickly discovering we had left it a little too late. Mesmerised by so many sights, the day had run away from us and with our shadows lengthening out directly behind us, we rode into an ever-increasingly blinding sun. It was getting precarious; I just couldn't see any of the road in front of me, or more specifically, the sand patches in front of us!

Post-sunset, we progressed more carefully into a darkening dusk. In the twilight, the headlight was still useless and the flat light hid the soft patches perfectly. The temperature was also dropping fast, and not expecting to be out so late, we naively hadn't brought extra layers. I was beginning to feel a little stupid. Within what seemed like minutes, pitch-blackness enveloped us and scanning around, there didn't seem to be any visible vehicles or building lights across the flat 3,600-square-kilometre nature reserve. We were breaking one of our pre-agreed trip rules: not to ride at night-time, if at all possible. However, the feeling of being alone out here was both eerie and satisfyingly exhilarating. To add to the excitement, and as predicted, I was also beginning to get a little concerned about our fuel situation. We hadn't passed a petrol station during the 100-mile commute that morning and I could see we'd already nudged over 190 miles since the last fill-up. I'd underestimated the size of the peninsula and although I carried two fuel cans, they were just 2 litres each and good for about 50 to 60 extra miles.

We continued on in the pitch-black, picking out hares, guanaco and the odd grey fox in the now usable full beam. I watched the fuel range count down and then start to flash as we finally reached the comfort of the asphalt. We weren't home yet, but the tarmac came as a welcome relief. We could pick the speed up now and count our blessings that we hadn't actually fallen on any of the impromptu slides throughout the day. We cruised on back, numb and shivering; the temperature had dropped from twenty-eight to nine degrees. It was 10pm before we reached the outskirts of Puerto Madryn. Only then did I finally relax and knew we would actually make it home without resorting to the little fuel cans. The tank had lasted a respectable 280 miles, admittedly unloaded and mostly at slower speeds, but it boosted my confidence for the wilder stretches of Patagonia. Tired but happy, I reflected on some of the poor decisions we had made that morning and the lessons we needed to learn. For sure, it had been an awe-inspiring day; a mix of incredible wildlife and a dose of naivety thrown in!

Pretty much at random, we'd chosen a cheap and cheerful hostel for these three nights and midway through our breakfast the next morning, I heard my name loudly called out. Unbelievably, it was Rob from the petrol station a couple of days before! He joined us, introducing his wife and son, and explained they had their day planned very similar to ours of yesterday. We gladly passed over tips and mused at the odds of us picking the same accommodation in such a popular town. Remarkably and fortunately, we were to experience this kind of coincidence several times over the coming months. Breakfast over, I went through the morning ritual of checking tyre pressures, chain tension and additionally, giving the chain a much-needed brush and clean. Fuelled up, we headed off back down Ruta 3, for what turned out to be another 400-mile ride to the city of Comodoro Rivadavia. Following a tip from Rob, prior to departing, we decided to deviate to Punta Tombo, a famous penguin viewpoint.

Pulling off the highway, I'm sure I heard both the chain and myself sigh to find ourselves back on a dusty gravelly road once again, but this time with a fully loaded bike. It became another 75 miles of useful experience gained, and the inevitable slides weren't such 'heart-in-the-mouth' moments now; we were already getting used to them. In any case, Punta Tombo was a rewarding tip and detour, with hundreds of the Magellanic penguins filling both the hillsides and beaches. A Colombian couple, Santiago and Luciana, also riding a V-Strom 650 two-up, pulled into the sandy car park behind us. As we were riding in opposite directions, we spent the afternoon swapping useful information and sightseeing together. We gave them trivial fuel stop distances and the north's pleasant temperature ranges, and they told us of near-death experiences with the crosswinds! Just two days before, Luciana and been reduced to sobbing in her helmet, genuinely fearing for her life. They were the first Colombian couple we had met, and they couldn't have been any friendlier, even if their recent experiences and stories spooked us. Santiago wisely insisted we not only download the app 'Windy', but trust it and plan our riding days and routes accordingly. Luciana warned Selly of how much colder it was going to be on Tierra del Fuego and showed her a tip for keeping her hands warmer. Simple really, she wore latex surgical gloves under her biking gloves and kindly gave Selly a few pairs to get her through the colder days ahead. With mobile numbers exchanged and promises to try to catch up again in their home country, we parted company and went in our opposite directions.

If their warnings weren't sobering enough, though, at our very next fuel stop we were greeted by three Brazilian riders who, on realising we were headed southbound, wasted no time telling us their similar stories. Just the day before, two out of three had literally been blown off the road and crashed, but almost proudly, they nonchalantly showed off damage to bikes, baggage and hands, etc. It seemed nobody was exaggerating, or needed to; the damage was there to see and if we wanted to ride to the southern tip of this continent, then we also needed to get through these year-round infamous winds. I enquired how it was in Rivadavia, just 140 miles south of us.

"Oh, it was pretty bad earlier today, one of the windiest cities on the east coast!" one of them answered, in the same blasé tone.

Stood in just a moderate breeze, it was hard to believe, so we opened up Windy and sure enough it was currently blowing 50 to 60 mph there. I was beginning to really enjoy these petrol stations, though, with their pumps and café windows colourfully decorated in thousands of travellers' stickers. Fuel stops were typically 150 miles apart and so they became magnets for meal and rest stops, an easy place to meet and chat with people you could only normally nod to when out on the road.

Inside, we purchased our first pannier stickers of the trip, simple 'Ruta 3' stickers to accompany the Union Jack emblem on my pannier and the Italian flag on Selly's. We progressed into a steadily increasing crosswind, coming from our right and interspersed with sudden gusts, that would nudge us towards the centreline. Within 60 miles of our destination, we finally found ourselves in fairly strong winds and leant over to stay straight. It wasn't comfortable riding, but for now it felt manageable, a mostly steady wind and a mostly steady lean. Every time trucks came towards us, I'd subconsciously grip the bars and squeeze the bike that bit harder, in case a badly timed gust pushed us across the road. As they passed by, we were noisily thumped by a 'bow wave' blast of air, upsetting the bike and tensing us up. I was glad to reach the city, after our first loaded-up ride on dirt roads and with the last 60 miles in howling winds. It had been a challenging day; we ached from the constant buffeting and yearned for long, hot showers. I tried to fuel up and had to shout above the wind to be heard, as the attendant braced his back against the pump. Not realising the nozzle wasn't fully inside the tank, he managed to shower both me and the bike at the first pull of the handle, the wind whipping away the fuel I wanted to pay for!

"How do you live like this?" I shouted.

"It's all I've known, pretty much every day is like this, but today isn't so bad!" he offered, almost matter-of-factly.

There seemed no escape from the gale; it was noisy outside and it was noisy inside. I was concerned about what tomorrow would bring and cut our mileage back to a tad under 300 miles.

The following morning, we had been riding only a few minutes when Selly nudged me to a stop (we purposely didn't have intercoms, preferring to chat and catch up with each stop).

"Did you see that beach just then? I think it was full of seals!" she said excitedly.

We doubled back and sure enough, what my periphery vision had dismissed as boulders was indeed a beach packed with huge sea lions, and barely 30 metres from the roadside. It was an unexpected treat, a great start to a day that I frankly had been apprehensive about. The previous night I had lain in bed, wondering just how bad it could get and what if Selly gets too scared to continue, or what if I reach my limit of being able to control the bike safely? I just didn't know what lay ahead. The Windy app knew, though; with an easy-to-follow traffic light analogy, the app had most of our day's route squarely in the 40 to 60 mph amber zone again, with gusts of up to 75 mph. We weren't yet experienced enough to know what those gusts translated to out on the road, but seeing plenty of other neighbouring areas in Patagonia showing red, at 75 to 90 mph, we agreed to try riding down to Puerto San Julian. Sure enough, once clear of the city's protective buildings and out on the open road, we were again hit hard from the right side and leant over dramatically, trying to hold a straight line. Ruta 3 is so notorious that lorries are bizarrely and deliberately loaded lob-sided, depending on their direction of travel.

Ever-present is the camaraderie and though traffic continued to thin, every passing vehicle acknowledged each other with a flash, honk, or a wave. More than once, I had made the mistake of instinctively lifting my hand to wave back and now stuck to flashing my lights. I just wasn't strong enough, or brave enough, to hold the bike one-handed! Within a couple of hours, our necks were becoming painful again, from straining against the constant force on the helmets. We just weren't used to it yet, but I was already looking forward to and daydreaming of the west coast ride north, where everything could be blown and pushed back into place from the opposite side! My shoulders were getting sore from the unnatural grip of the bike and as the day progressed, the wind just steadily increased.

It had reached a strength where I didn't think it would be possible to make any kind of right-hand bend, let alone a right turn; luckily, there just weren't any! Forebodingly, we passed a flipped truck over on the opposite side, that had been blown fully clear of the road. Sometimes you could ride 10 or 15 miles without seeing another vehicle, but it was the oncoming trucks I came to be most fearful of. After several badly timed gusts, I now found myself just gripping the bars tightly and closing my eyes for a split-second as we passed by, thinking 'is this going to be the one?' Balanced by the wind pressure, I hadn't really noticed just how far over we were now leaning until, fortunately on an empty stretch, I felt the front wheel lifting and hovering as another strong gust hit us. I experienced a flashback to Sandra's warnings and needed to pull over. It had caught me by surprise, momentarily scared me, and aching from head to toe, I needed a rest. I eased off the throttle slightly and pulled into the next available fuel stop, 30-odd miles down the road. Over coffee, I asked Selly what she thought of it.

Her reply almost stunned me. "It's not so bad, my neck's sore, but I'm fine, don't worry about me."

I couldn't believe it; did I just need a can of 'Man Up' instead of the coffee? Was I imagining gripping the bike for all I was worth, knowing a wrongly timed gust, and one strong enough, could put us dangerously into the path of an oncoming vehicle? I wondered if she was just saying this to avoid me worrying about her. No, I dismissed this thought quickly; she was just too honest and was clearly having a different experience on the back, compared to mine on the front. Even as we battled on towards San Julian, Selly continued to cheerily tap my side and point out rheas, foxes and guanaco, etc. I, on the other hand, just hoped and prayed none of them ran across our path and required me to change the bike's direction suddenly!

Finally making our turn-off on the highway (thankfully a left one!), the road had one last surprise for me as we criss-crossed the town, searching for our hostel. Clearly having a surplus in the council tax budget, Puerto San Julian boasted speed bumps that could stop a medium-sized tank. Feeling pretty exhausted, I misjudged our speed over the first one and it nearly had us on our side. They seemed so over the top that I looked at every way possible to avoid as many of the others as I could, including forays along the pavements, or crossing to the other side of the road! Weary and hungry, we dumped our bags, showered and headed into town, to hopefully find a pub that would also serve us food. Harassed by a now bitter wind, we walked quickly to stretch our legs and see if the town had anything worth a photograph, before seeking shelter and warmth.

It had. Mounted on the seafront promenade was a full-scale replica of the expedition ship *Noa Victoria*, complete with cannons and birds' nests. Despite the original having the distinction of being the first ship to circumnavigate the world, from 1519 to 1522, to me it just looked like a pirate ship, and I stood waiting to see if Captain Pugwash himself would make an appearance! Spotting lights and hearing music, we tracked down sanctuary and just as our starters arrived, I heard again a now very familiar London accent; couldn't be, could it? Rob, his wife and son had walked in and as we were already seated, I got to accuse them of being the ones stalking us. It was a great, light-hearted and fun evening, one we all most definitely needed, with enough drinks enjoyed to ensure a sound night's sleep.

Feeling refreshed and full from a hearty breakfast, we loaded up in the chilly morning air. Windy anticipated a day similar to yesterday but forgot to mention the rain that would visit us soon. We both already had extra layers on and an hour later, waterproofs also, as the first rain we had experienced to date poured down. It had taken nearly three weeks to break them out, and in all honesty, the extra warmth they provided was gladly welcomed. Knowing how tiring the day was likely to be, we dropped the distance to just over 250 miles, which would take us down to Rio Gallegos. The wind proved just as testing, but with the rain came much cooler temperatures, a maximum of fifteen degrees, and the heated grips started to earn their keep, thawing my numbed fingertips. All our aches and pains from the day before were awoken and added to by today's hours of relentless buffeting.

It's hard to describe the experience; the noise is a constant howl in the ears and the wind pressure feels like someone's annoyingly leaning on your head and upper body. The rain just adds to the challenge, making the roads slippery and eventually finding its way through the protective layers. One of the cheapest purchases we'd made was the last-minute overboots, and they proved to be the most waterproof item we had! It was two wet and weary bikers that rolled to a stop at the first set of red lights, in an uninspiring and dreary Rio Gallegos. Glancing left and right, it appeared that two dejected dogs had taken it upon themselves to warn us of the town that awaited. Each was unashamedly taking a synchronised dump on opposite sidewalks. Their otherwise grim display had unintentionally captured both my feelings and the city's drab atmosphere quite perfectly. I couldn't help smiling, and thanked them for at least that.

Parking up outside the hostel, we just couldn't figure out if it was open, closed, or in the process of being pulled down. It really was looking that shabby, and I procrastinated about whether to even get off the bike and investigate. We didn't have the energy to replan, though; Selly was wet, sneezing and shivering and I was just soaked and shattered, so in we went. The first room was quickly dismissed. Having been in need of a pee for the last hour, Selly headed first to the bathroom and on flushing the toilet, she hurried out as it proceeded to empty across the floor. The second room was also turned down for smelling foully and nauseatingly of cigarette smoke. The third room seemed smaller than even our tent but was begrudgingly accepted out of the need for rest. After all, it would only be for a night, wouldn't it? Windy said 'no' and disappointingly advised us it was best to stay at least two nights in Argentina's 'Bates Motel'. For tomorrow, our planned route was showing red and Selly was also showing signs of a full-blown cold developing. As she rested up the following day, I ventured out on the bike, to find somewhere to get the first oil change done and a place to wash off yesterday's road muck. On successfully completing both tasks, I returned to the hostel to find my original parking space filled by two Colombian-registered Royal Enfield Himalayans. They were an amusing sight to see, looked at least ten years old and now appeared held together with cable-ties, duct tape and wire; they had clearly enjoyed rough lives. Hanging off the bikes, in no logical sense, were overly large water and fuel containers, BBQs and grills, lengthy machetes, hammocks and souvenirs of their travels. Underneath all of which were the rusting and dented motorcycles. On meeting the young French owners, the biggest surprise was to come.

"They're only one year old. We're students studying in Colombia and bought them new for this trip!" said one of them cheerfully.

The bikes were the epitome of a 'never-once-tidied' student's room, being replicated to perfection on two wheels, four in this case! I loved the character of these bikes and admired their owners' carefree approach to adventure biking. They were the complete opposite of my OCD packing and constant desire to keep our bike dirt free. Yes, I could learn a thing or two from these guys!

I coaxed Selly out of her restful slumber to be introduced and for her to admire the almost comical machines, adorned with their colourful appendages. She homed in on the large but partially hidden machetes, asking how they got them across the borders and why they needed them. Theo explained that as they hadn't really used many roads from Colombia down to Argentina, the machetes were mainly used for chopping firewood. As for the borders, nobody really cared, as everybody owned machetes up north.

Our journey so far had clearly been a tranquil and civilised affair compared to these jungle-loving explorers and I found myself pondering where we could strap and hide our own machete! As was often the case when you meet travellers coming from your future destinations, the conversation turned to borders and road conditions, etc. I eagerly enquired about the current political unrest and civil protests they might have experienced on the way down. Ecuador was fine and back to social order but Bolivia was still dogged by protests, with borders randomly opened and closed. It was still too unpredictable and dangerous to contemplate entering, even if it was possible. Chile was just a mess of ongoing violent protests and we were warned to avoid Santiago, if possible. Oh dear, that was going to be a problem; we had already booked flights from Santiago to Easter Island in the New Year. We had figured we would never be closer, and this would be the ideal opportunity for this once-in-a-lifetime visit. Oh well, it was still nearly two months away. Maybe it would be calmer by the New Year.

Poring over our maps, we could see our destination of Ushuaia was now less than 400 miles away and our confidence in reaching it had gone from hopeful to confident. Today, Windy agreed, was a riding day and after two nights here, both of us certainly wanted to see the back of the tired room and dreary town. We needed to catch a ferry, to cross onto the island of Tierra del Fuego and briefly cross borders into Chile and then back again to Argentina. Taking all this into account, we would break the remaining mileage up and overnight in Rio Grande, just 230 miles south of us. It felt like our coldest start that morning as we locked on panniers and bungeed on bags. Selly pulled on her latex undergloves and for the first time, we both wore our thermals. Even though it wasn't raining, the waterproofs went on, to act as windcheaters. As the bike idled to warm, I finally switched on Selly's heated seat and my heated grips. The dashboard said it was six degrees. It didn't just feel cold, it was cold!

The wind was less severe today and I could begin to relax more, again able to enjoy the beautiful wildlife and wilderness around us. The road itself may have been straight and featureless, but the fauna provided a non-stop kaleidoscope of colour and variety. Selly would never forgive me if I hit anything. I would slow every time we saw guanaco herds at the roadside. For sure, they had a habit of crossing in front of us, but worse, we'd sadly seen too many dead ones, trapped in the barbed wire fence lining the length of the highway. They were quite capable of leaping this fence and we could only assume they had been spooked by traffic not slowing and had misjudged their escape. In any case, me slowing down allowed Selly ample opportunity to photograph away. Red-backed and white-throated hawks could be seen circling overhead, and in the lagoons and lakes we passed, flocks of Chilean pink flamingos often shared the water with upland geese and ibis. Even this far south, noisy green parakeets could be found in most of the towns. Foxes and rheas became common sightings, but surpassing that and to her delight, Selly also spotted a skunk on the ride down to the Chilean border point. We couldn't know it at this stage, but they would become an uncomfortable pest in later months.

In comparison to our entry to Uruguay, Chile was a little more complex. We filled in entry forms and despite Chile sharing the island with Argentina, we had to declare we weren't crossing with fruits, nuts or any other foodstuffs. The bike received a cursory inspection and its chassis number was physically checked against the logbook, before the TIP was issued. A document I would only need for two to three hours, depending on ferry waits, before it was turned in again for the next one! Migration completed, we trundled down the last few miles to the Punta Delgada quayside, finding a ferry in the process of loading. We were promptly waved aboard for the half-hour crossing that thankfully turned into a much-welcomed hour as the captain waited upon more vehicles to fill the deck. As we crossed the narrowest point of the Strait of Magellan, our hands thawed out nicely on mugs of sweet hot chocolate. It felt exciting to be so far south and seemingly through the worst of the winds. As we crossed the border back into Argentina, I felt we were getting accomplished at the paperwork now. I'd given up producing our bike insurance; never once did it get asked for, either at checkpoints, or on the borders. If you were lucky and not arriving at the same time as any coaches, then you could be through both sides in half an hour. As we approached the city of Rio Grande, there was a new and exciting spectacle on the far-right horizon; just visible were white-capped mountains, tantalising hints of the Andes mountain range that lay over on the west coast. This mere glimpse would come to dominate the landscape for our next zigzagging 6,000 miles.

Although accommodation was proving cheaper than expected, we treated ourselves to a small apartment, nestled inside a large house. We craved some comforts after the forgettable experience of the last two nights, and it turned out to be a spot-on move. The host said we had the whole place to ourselves and showed us around a spotless modern apartment that was way bigger than the photos had portrayed. Later, she even popped back with a home-baked apple pie for us! I lightened one of our bags by opening a bottle of red wine and toasted the journey so far, for tomorrow we would be in Ushuaia; motto, *Fin del Mundo, Principio de Todo* – the 'end of the world and beginning of everything'.

Chilly air barely registered as we rolled on down those final 125 miles. The change in scenery, from straight, flat roads to fast sweeping bends, first through hilly terrain and then entering the mountains, was invigorating. We couldn't resist pulling over at a Lake Escondido viewpoint, the blue water shimmering beautifully below us in the bright sunlight. Also there taking photos was Sam, a young chatty Texan on a rental bike and like us, heading into Ushuaia for the first time. We were the first English speakers he'd met since starting his journey three weeks prior and we happily agreed to meet up in the Americas' most southern Irish pub later that evening.

Snow was up to the road's edge as we climbed and navigated the Garibaldi Pass hairpins, the last obstacle to reaching the city. Over many years, I had been inspired by the crazy and courageous exploits of British long-distance motorcycle adventurer Nick Sanders, and I couldn't help but think of him now. We had just very easily ridden up to the summit, but eight years previously, in tough winter conditions, this little pass had thwarted Nick's world record attempt by a mere few hours. Having just ridden the entire length of the Pan-American Highway in under twenty-two days (something we felt rushed covering in nine months!), the winter snow-jammed pass had cost him about five hours, rather than the twenty minutes it just took us.

With unconcealed grins, we dismounted at the large stone 'Ushuaia' pillars, erected either side of the road to congratulate and welcome visitors from around the world to the end of the world. It was the 21st of November, and we had arrived in sunshine, with a comfortable afternoon temperature of fifteen degrees and a healthy bike (with no new scratches added to it since Monte Grande's gate fight)!

That night, we met up and celebrated with Sam who, unlike us, was in the city just for one night, a tick in the box before he headed back up north again. Stories and drinks flowed easily; getting up the next morning wasn't quite so easy, but we had given ourselves a small task. The next day, we would ride 15 miles out of Ushuaia, to the very end of Ruta 3 in the Parque Nacional Tierra del Fuego. Only at this spot could we say we had officially reached the starting point of our PAH adventure. It was a sorry, fluffy-headed start. Reaching the park's busy ticket office, we were told we could get our passports stamped if we liked. We liked. I always had our passports with us when we rode, but this morning I had forgotten them and we turned back to retrieve them. Returning again, I parked on the gravel road and bought tickets for our entry, pocketing them as I cheerfully hopped onto the bike. As Selly climbed aboard, I lost my footing on the loose stones, realising too late there was also a dip below where my foot was trying to find some grip, and over we both went.

There wasn't even any wind or gusts to blame. Our unceremonious fall had been witnessed by two perplexed Spanish riders, who nonetheless sprang to our grateful rescue, picking the bike up before I'd even finished helping Selly onto her feet. Once we'd assured each other we were fine, I turned to the bike; it had new scratches! Thanking our helpers, we slunk off to the park's spacious café, to get our free souvenir passport stamps and two strong coffees! The wooden carved sign at the end of the dirt track had taken us 3,047 road miles to reach from Norfolk and proclaimed the opposite end of the PAH was 11,086 miles north of us. This was significantly less than the 18,000 miles plus our sightseeing route plan had added up to. Photographs taken, we headed back up the innocuous dirt track, leaving the most southerly point behind us and feeling, in some small way, that we were now adding miles to the northern leg.

Undisputedly touristy, we still found Ushuaia an easy city to like; modern, buzzing and plenty of tours to occupy us over the next couple of days. Taking a half-day boat cruise out into the Beagle Channel and around various islands offered us close-up views of sea lions, penguins and cormorants, by the thousands! As always, being out on the water leaves you peckish, and if it wasn't the lush steaks we were drooling over, we were now equally hooked on the delicious and filling Argentinian *empanadas*. Super cheap and tasty, they reminded me of Cornish pasties and we just happened to have a popular takeaway a minute's walk from the hostel. That evening, we discovered they also went rather well with red wine. We needed it, for the previous night (like almost every night so far on this continent), we had been kept awake and driven crazy by packs of barking dogs. Speed bumps and South American dogs were becoming my pet hates; excuse the pun! If they weren't keeping you awake at night then they were aggressively chasing the bike down the road, snapping at our heels.

With more stickers bought for the panniers and having sent postcards to Italy and the UK, we now itched to start the journey northwards. As we packed our bags, the weather abruptly turned to icy horizontal rain. After four sunny days, a cold front and storm descended upon us, dampening the excitement to be back on the move. Just prior to the check-out time, our host came to the room with cups of tea, telling us we could have the room all day if we wanted to wait out the worst of the weather. These kindly gestures were so typical of the overwhelming majority of Argentinians we had met. We accepted the offer, finally getting away in the middle of the afternoon. To depart the island we would take a different ferry route, Porvenir to Punta Arenas, which would put us more westward and on the Chilean mainland for the first time. Although the ferry ran daily, we were way too late to catch today's and decided to overnight, back in Rio Grande once more. The scenic miles were covered in cold but light rain, made more comfortable by the heated seats and grips. Thinking this could be our last night in Argentina for a while, we hit the supermarket, coming away predictably with succulent steaks.

Having scanned the ferry company's webpage the previous evening, I'd suggested an 8am start, to comfortably make the 3pm crossing. We'd seen on the map that the final 60 miles weren't asphalt, and after the previous day's heavy rains we didn't know what condition we would find the road in. Getting off the ferry, we were due into Punta Arenas around 8pm, so to avoid faffing around I pre-booked and paid for a night's accommodation there. Leaving Rio Grande, with the sun now shining brightly, I was feeling pretty smug and organised. We tracked across the island on now dry and wildly empty roads, cautiously turning onto the dirt track for the last leg. After about 20 miles and upon rounding a bend, we were presented with stunning views of the shimmering Strait of Magellan. Snow-capped mountains provided the backdrop, with their majestic peaks etched clearly by the bright blue sky.

It was turning into a wonderful ride. The road was entirely dry and quite compacted, easy-going by dirt road standards, and all the usual wildlife turned out to complement the landscapes. A few miles further on, we pulled over to chat to the only other road users we had met that day: two elderly Americans on their pair of BMWs. With few roads around, it was obvious where each of us was headed and they enquired if we were booked on tomorrow's crossing, to which I replied that we planned to take this afternoon's one. They looked a little surprised, saying they didn't think there was another one today. I knew differently, though, for I had diligently checked the night before. With the clock ticking, we wished each other safe journeys and left them admiring the views.

Entering the small and evidently run-down town of Porvenir, I filled up the bike, having come across a petrol station before spotting the eventual signs to the port. We rode through the town, wincing at the crumbling buildings and closed businesses. It was no Ushuaia and it seemed that hope and prosperity had already taken a ferry long before us. The road literally ended at the ferry terminal's car park, the completely empty car park, and dismounting the bike, Selly gave me that questioning look that required an answer. Maybe everybody just turns up last minute, I lamely offered, as we strode off into the small but equally empty terminal building. I went to the loo; at least that was open and clean, returning to find Selly staring at the wall-mounted timetable screens, before staring instead at me.

There certainly was a 3pm ferry, except it was from Punta Arenas and not to it. Evidently, I had been looking at the wrong timetable and hence, the wrong direction. The Americans had been too polite. Having come from Porvenir that day, I'm convinced they knew all too well I had cocked up but chose not to spoil our ride! The next ferry wasn't until early the following morning, and we were going to have to enjoy overnighting here. Using the terminal's internet, we resignedly checked out the three listed accommodations. It was a bloody rip-off but totally my mistake, and so I parted with more cash than I wanted to for our first overnight in Chile. To cap it off, we contacted the property in Punta Arenas to explain my *faux pas,* and weren't offered a single cent back.

After Argentina's warmth and hospitality, it was a rude awakening to the differences between these neighbours. It was early days, but so far Chileans were proving to be on the chillier side! To get a little exercise and leg stretching, we took a walk around what was left of interest to see in poor Porvenir. A few hundred metres up the street I was surprised to spot a sign for a disco, and we continued on out of intrigue. I should have known! It certainly wasn't the kind of disco for youngsters to dalliance and socialise the night away. A large red light, dangling from a pole to attract passing motorists, confirmed the venue's seedier wares. Driving rain arrived to save us from discovering further cultural delights and we scurried back to the extortionate extravagance of our mediocre abode. Beer, wine and views of the ever-closing mountains cheered us up, for tomorrow we would be amongst them!

Chapter Four

Into the Andes

Disgorged from the ferry's bowels, we quickly left Punta Arenas behind us, picking up Ruta 9 northbound. The east coast of Patagonia had been wild, rewarding and memorable, but it was essentially a transit route to our PAH starting point. The west coast was what we had really looked forward to, and the dramatic change in scenery filled us with excitement. After a whole morning spent in the comfortable warmth of the ferry's lounge, we planned a shorter ride of just 160 miles for the remainder of the afternoon, taking us up to Puerto Natales. As the road steadily climbed, so the temperature steadily dropped, quickly into single figures. The wind freshened and we pulled over to don waterproofs and switch on the heated seats, whilst looking ominously ahead at a twisting road disappearing into low, dark clouds. The timing wasn't a minute too soon; cars approached with lights on and windscreen wipers sweeping fast, pre-warning us of the bad weather we were about to run into. I could see hail bouncing off the road up ahead and glancing at the bike's temperature gauge saw it now showed just a couple of degrees. As the first of the stinging hailstones bounced off us, the 'ice warning' caption lit for the first time. We might have timed our entire trip between the continents' summers, but altitude has no respect for seasons. Seeing nowhere safe to pull over, we pressed on against the poor visibility, gusting icy winds and alternating hail and rain. It was a pretty miserable first west coast ride, and thoughts of finally breaking out the tent were quickly dismissed in preference of hot showers and a proper bed!

Like Puerto Madryn weeks before, Puerto Natales was going to be used as a base, but this time for the magnificent Torres del Paine National Park. It was out of our budget to stay within the park; even camping fees exceeded the cost of our ensuite accommodation (that also included a hearty breakfast)! So we opted instead for a base, with a daily commute of almost 60 miles to reach the park's ticket office. The town was busy with tourists and the accompanying tourist shops, cafés and tour offices. It didn't take long to find suitable pannier stickers each, something that would become an obsession following each new border crossing. With photogenic lakeside and mountain views, it seemed a pleasant town to stay for a few nights. With no obvious tensions, or visible signs of the protests being reported further north, it felt an easy place to relax and look forward to the days ahead. Shunning the pricey restaurants, we stocked up at a local supermarket to prepare both an evening meal and a packed lunch for the following day. It didn't prove much cheaper and we'd spent close to double for an equivalent shop in Argentina. Maybe that cosy pizzeria we'd passed would get a look-in after all!

Riding an unloaded bike to Torres del Paine the next morning was a welcome change, even fun, as the route eventually turned into a loose gravel road. We skirted beautiful lakes, caught glimpses of mountaintops amongst the swirling clouds and wondered at all the surrounding wildlife. It was an easy sell to purchase two three-day passes, enough time for our two-wheeled explorations, rather than the lengthier five, or even seven-day hikes available to the more adventurous visitors. Whilst inside the ticket office, we had scanned the wildlife boards, getting informed about what we had already seen and what we hoped to come across. Head of the visitor's wish list had to be the illusive puma, said to be abundant in the park and wider region. I didn't get my hopes up; according to the ticket-selling park ranger, they stubbornly stayed out of sight and we should pay for a guide to have the best chance of seeing one. Selly was an avid cat lover, for sure, but remarked that being on a motorbike wasn't her preferred way to come across a 100-kilogram mountain lion! The park also had Andean condors in healthy numbers, not that we had spotted any yet. Oh, and several glaciers. Back on the bike, we hardly knew what to get most excited about first!

Rounding the next corner, we were presented with one of the most memorable views the park has to offer. A long, straight dirt road seemed to disappear into the very heart of three iconic jagged mountains. The sky had momentarily cleared of clouds and Selly hopped off to capture lonesome pictures of me riding down the middle of the empty track, backdropped by these famous towers of Torres del Paine. She captured the isolation and serenity of the moment perfectly, and I think if we'd been forced to turn around, right there and then, the smiles we were wearing would have lasted long into the day. Of course, there was no way we were turning back yet. We wanted to see a glacier up close, and Lago Grey happened to have a huge one.

Something was blocking our path, though. The track was being repaired and worked on by a pair of formation grading machines. I was stuck behind them and riding (read: sliding!) so slowly that we were continually sinking into the deep, soft and freshly spread gravel. I guess the drivers probably had headphones on, listening to Andean melodies, as I'd been struggling for quite a while in their crawling wake, before being spotted and kindly waved past. It wasn't a simple manoeuvre, though; we were attempting to pass shoulder-to-shoulder with the two graders' carving blades, and the edge of the road was just super-soft spoil, pushed high on the side. Despite the bike being unloaded, I still didn't even fancy my chances, but now we had been acknowledged and urged on, gave it a go anyway. I upped my speed to a staggering 20 mph and with feet hovering low, we slewed our way past with the finesse of a happy drunk practising ice skating. We got past them in one piece, but I still had a lot to learn about riding in the squidgy stuff.

Several herds of guanaco later, we found the Lago Grey Hotel, perched by the shores of Lago Grey, of course. There must have been about twenty bikes parked up, all with Argentinian plates and all, bar one rebellious KTM rider, BMWs. I was proud to be the only GB plate amongst them, and also most thankful they hadn't witnessed my recent overtaking skills. Selly grabbed the camera as a grey fox (in the car park of the Grey Hotel, on the shores of Lake Grey, remember!) nosed around and happily posed just for us, or so it seemed. Walking through the hotel and down onto the beach, we were presented with the brightest blue icebergs either of us had seen. It was as if they were lit up from inside, just beautiful. Like a living kaleidoscope, the shoreline twinkled and sparkled with thousands of ice shards, lapping mesmerisingly against the stony shingle beach. The gentle rhythmic noise was equally captivating, a thousand crystal wind chimes soothing 'wind tortured' ears.

As dramatically enchanting as the whole scene was, the glacier itself was out of sight. It resided at the opposite end of the lake, around bends and several miles away; we needed a boat trip. The hotel could, for the equivalent price of a small mortgage, offer us afternoon tickets the day after tomorrow. Everything prior was already booked. I guess this way we would have more time to rob a bank, I mused. On second thoughts, the credit card came out and we happily left with two legally, if not immediately, paid-for glacier-spotting tickets. Could the day get any more exciting? We backtracked past the now silent and lunching – or was that laughing – graders, to pick up the alternative Y-150 track through the park. The views were breathtaking, and I could only imagine how frustrating it must have been, being here thirty years ago and having to change rolls of film every twenty-four or thirty-six photos. Selly never missed an opportunity, and other than when a passing vehicle sent up dust clouds, she hung over my shoulder snapping away like professional paparazzi.

We'd been looking for somewhere to have our packed lunch and rounding another bend, we came across a panoramic viewpoint, now being enjoyed by the twenty bikers we'd come across earlier. Pulling up, we engaged in conversation and learned they were all members of the same BMW club, but from various Argentinian cities, touring together on an annual pilgrimage to the park. They seemed incredulous that we would attempt a trip to Alaska on a 'little' 650. One asked if that was even possible with two of us on one bike. I didn't know, to be honest. We hadn't got there yet!

Lunch over, we photographed our way down the dusty road, passing a collection of small ponds glimmering in the late afternoon light. I was in my own world, admiring guanaco and their young grazing, when all of a sudden I felt Selly urgently prodding me.

"I saw a puma, did you see it?" she shouted over my shoulder.

I slammed on the brakes, lighting up the ABS symbol in my excitement. No, I hadn't seen it. She told me it was at the side of the track, just a metre or so off the road, and looked like it was about to cross. With a heart now beating faster, I spun the bike around, ignoring Selly asking if it was a good idea. Of course it was; she had seen a puma and I hadn't! We rode slowly back and then, with Selly pointing, I saw the sleek light brown body and sweeping tail of the big cat. For just a few seconds it watched us slow to a stop and then quite calmly but purposely crossed in front of us, disappearing all too quickly into the tall grass and bushes. The fleeting encounter had lasted mere seconds; too fixated were we to attempt photos, but we already knew it would be a memory that would stay with us forever.

We were still on a high two days later as we made our way back for the boat trip. The weather again graced us with clear blue skies, but it could have been a totally different story. Many visitors to the park are denied views of the mountains and glaciers, as only low clouds fill lenses, or strong winds keep the boats protectively moored up. We felt both lucky and exhilarated as we chugged out past shimmering icebergs and under watchful mountains. Barely thirty minutes later, safety briefs behind us, the guides had us straining skywards to see our first solitary condor, seemingly floating stationary high above us. At possibly 2,000 feet above us, I could only really tell that it was a big bird, too far to photograph, though most tried! The guide did his best to entertain us before the main event; mountain names were offered and quickly forgotten as all attention increasingly diverted to the growing white wall ahead. Strange how a large lump of slow-moving ice can be so moving; you could feel the excitement rising as we approached the first towering face. I felt lucky; Selly just loved having the camera in her hands. She was a good photographer and I knew that at all these tourist magnets I could sit back and enjoy the moment, knowing they would be artistically captured for us. Personally, I hadn't progressed beyond crayons, but Selly would magically turn some of these photographs into incredibly detailed and lifelike pencil sketches, or colourful paintings.

The Iguazu Falls 'wow' factor had returned as the glacier's spectacular colours, crevasses and moraines came into sharp relief. We couldn't get too close, of course; the occasional sharp cracks and deep rumbles forewarned of the random danger of calving ice. I think that's what kept us staring, the chance to see the birthing of a new 'baby' iceberg! The boat's speakers announced 'welcome drinks' were now available at the stern. I enquired if they were alcoholic, they were. Umm, I was riding the bike later, I explained.

"But, sir, the cocktails' ice has just been lifted from the water. They're 5,000-year-old glacier ice cubes?" remarked the bartender questioningly.

Oh, OK, if you insist, one won't hurt, will it? Quite the opposite actually! The couple of hours pacing the glacier's terminus passed too quickly and we vowed to find another glacier, one we could instead visit by road. Just a short ride back to Argentina would take us to Perito Moreno glacier, and after today's enjoyment we knew we couldn't miss it. It felt a little sad leaving Torres del Paine park behind us, but we knew it couldn't have revealed itself more beautifully, both the scenery and its wonderful wildlife. With heavy but happy hearts, we turned our backs and left the mountains to the soaring guardian condors.

At the border, we swapped from Chile's Ruta 9 to Argentina's infamous Ruta 40. Infamous for being terribly windy, lacking fuel stations and, in many places, having mile after mile of sand and fine dust where asphalt should be! Our introduction was an easy one, though; El Calafate, Perito Moreno glacier's nearest town and staging post, was just a couple of hours from the border. Even the brisk wind was tolerable after our east coast experiences. Being back in Argentina once again, we predictably sought out a local recommended steakhouse and washed down sumptuous fillets with a bottle of red, convincing ourselves it was almost free, as we were spending leftover *pesos*! We got on the road early for the one-hour ride to Los Glaciares National Park, guessing a morning there would suffice, followed by an afternoon's wander around El Calafate.

The park itself was a real treat; a perfectly smooth road guided us through a multi-coloured forest of blossoming trees and bushes. Lakes and rivers revealed themselves with each sweeping curve and even though it was a cold morning, I didn't want the beautiful ride to end too soon. When the glacier first came into view, I couldn't resist pulling over. How often can you photograph your bike with a glacier for a backdrop? Continuing on to the car park and with helmets locked to the rack, we descended to the various viewing platforms. This was a new experience and unlike a couple of days before, you now felt you could almost reach out and touch the ice. We were in awe of how close we were, and even more impressive were the sounds. This glacier, we came to understand, was never quiet, but delivered thunderously loud cracks, pistol shots and rumblings of deep imaginary earthquakes. It seemed alive before our eyes, cascades of mini avalanches – or full-on calving – were nearly continuous and had our heads spinning towards the next new noise. It was just too mesmerising, and the morning quickly rolled through into the afternoon. The only break we gave ourselves was nipping to the café for a sandwich and to use the loos. As glaciers go, this one is quite fast-moving, and it was easy to witness icebergs breaking away over the width of several miles. Before we knew it, the whole day was gone. Nine hours of wonder had slipped by and we had to leave exhilarated, before the park gates locked us in!

Over the next couple of days, Ruta 40 showed us its true colours. With winds again battering us, we twice rode well over 125 miles before finding any fuel. Usually, this wouldn't be an issue, but riding into 50 mph headwinds quickly emptied the tank. We were becoming desperate to camp but also didn't want to risk the winds wrecking the tent so early in the trip. Like Ruta 3 heading south, Ruta 40 had roadside fences penning us in and hampering chances to find somewhere suitably protected. We were convinced the winds would subside soon, but it was frustrating all the same. The second day proved even more challenging, as it included a notoriously bad 41-mile section where the asphalt disappears and gives way to a mixture of vibration-numbing washboard corrugations, loose gravel hills and large potholes. It wasn't a stretch to get into trouble in; we could count on one hand how many vehicles we'd seen in over 300 miles.

Like us, the bike was taking a pounding and at the tiny hamlet of Bajo Caracoles we pulled over at a well-known travellers' fuel & photo stop to check it over. There were just a couple of pumps sat out in the sun, completely covered in colourful stickers, hoses and pump handles included. We needed fuel, but the adjoining motel and café, like the pumps, were all locked up and quiet. I checked the bike over for anything loose or missing and cringed at the state of the chain. With nothing better to do, we sat out of the wind and worked our way through our packed lunches. After half an hour or so, a young schoolkid sauntered past and understanding our predicament, pulled a phone from his pocket and placed a call. Within ten minutes, we had filled up at arguably the most remote, photogenic and expensive fuel station to be found on Ruta 40!

The day had been taxing to say the least. Relentless buffeting winds and the challenging dirt road coaxed us into getting a neat little studio apartment for the night, in the small town named after the glacier, Perito Moreno. Selly was in heaven; the host introduced us not only to the space but also gave instructions for feeding and caring for the resident cat, Lola! She was adorable and both welcomed and tolerated our brief intrusion to her home. Overnight and over drinks, we shared the sofa with Lola and made plans to change direction, from north to west and cut onto Chile's Ruta 7, the famous 'Carretera Austral'. We wanted to visit Marble Caves, via a boat out of Puerto Rio Tranquillo, and would need to cross borders once more. Leaving Lola peacefully sleeping in her posh apartment, we rode to the Chilean 'Chile Chico' border, where the customs agent kindly but firmly asked us to fully unload the recently loaded bike and take the luggage inside for X-raying. The wind was still blowing a gale as we complied, and I tried to hastily eat all the oranges I'd forgotten about in the tank bag, rather than be forced to throw them away!

An elderly German biker had walked past and just as he entered the customs office we heard a loud crash behind us. Turning around, we saw his heavily loaded BMW had blown over and now lay on its side, up against a concrete kerb. Selly quickly retrieved him and the three of us righted the bike, helping move it to a more protected spot. We felt sorry for him as he inspected a cracked screen and a badly dented aluminium pannier. He shrugged off further help, though, and clearly didn't want to make a fuss of it, so we completed our paperwork, loaded the bike and headed into the wind for the mountain pass. The short length of asphalt ended as the town ended and we climbed a loose, boulder-strewn narrowing track that soon became our most challenging dirt road to date. Up or down it was steep, with sizable disconcerting drop-offs and no protective barriers. It wasn't a compacted road either, having mostly loose deep soil and gravel on the tight bends. I drew on all my nerves to mostly slide the heavy bike round blind narrow hairpins, finger-papping the horn and just hoping nothing was coming the other way. If we were forced to stop, either on the steep hills, or downhill, I just didn't know how we could safely get started again, so I bounced over rocks and through potholes, keeping the power on and hoping a slide wouldn't result in a fall.

The scenery, when I could snatch a glance, was of the beautiful lake Gral Carrera and surrounding mountains, but on such a narrow road I hardly dared to take my eyes off whatever was in front of us. Rounding another tight bend, I picked up speed quickly, so as not to bog down and to make sure we had enough power to tackle the next steep hill we were on. Halfway up, a couple on an adventure bike had precariously stopped on their way down, clearly daunted by the single-lane downhill hairpin and drop-offs facing them. They stared and waved, but I didn't dare lift a hand and so, with a pap of the horn, I powered past at a hefty speed, either looking like I knew what I was doing, or more probably, looking like a madman!

It was a short-lived relief, when many precarious miles later we eventually made the T-junction, signalling we had finally reached the famous Carretera Austral. Turning right and once more heading north, we faced a new challenge; it was a fast and busy gravel road. Oncoming tourist coaches, public buses and articulated lorries sent up billowing clouds of dust that could be seen well before the vehicles themselves. Passing these left you blinded for tense seconds and choking on the thick cocktail of sand, dirt and fumes. Locals drove mostly pickups, very fast and always in the middle of the road, it seemed. Stones would ping off the bike and sting our legs; it wasn't exactly comforting to know we had approximately 450 miles of this! The only slow vehicles were the motorhomes, or campervans, and as we plodded along behind them, covered from head to toe in thick dust and nursing a burning dry throat, I began to envy their protection. The saving grace being that in between the frequent dust storms, the Carretera Austral is an incredibly beautiful highway, with multi-coloured lupins lining the roadsides, lakes, meadows of wildflowers, waterfalls, rivers and mountains. It justly deserved its reputation as one of the most scenic roads in the world and overall, it really was a treat for sore, if dust-filled, eyes!

After three long and tough days riding, battling winds, sand, potholes and endless dust, Puerto Rio Tranquillo welcomed us with a neat, comfortable cabana and cold throat-cleansing beers. We had made it. Tomorrow, we would hang up the keys and relax on a boat for the day. As we sat on our veranda, drinks in hand, I half-heartedly scanned the bike again for anything missing, or looking out of place. The chain could be cleaned and adjusted in the morning; now was feet-up beer time! To complete the moment, a travelling Andean band, staying in the adjacent cabana, set up and started playing melodiously to their appreciative audience of two. The sky eventually darkened and then brightened, with a billion stars etching out the Milky Way. I couldn't hold back a smile; every bruising mile had been totally worth it.

Walking to the small quayside the following morning, we chatted with sixty-seven-year-old Livia from Sweden, also taking the marble cave tour. Our short conversation would totally change my Carretera Austral outlook. For the second time in her life, she was cycling its full length, on her own. Listening to her story, I was in awe. On this current trip, she almost spoke casually of being blown off the road twice and then wasting a whole day fruitlessly searching for her expensive Scandinavian tent. It had been ripped from its pegs and lifted so high into the sky that she lost sight of it and never saw it again. She faced the same winds, steep hills, billowing dust and careless traffic as we did, but alone on a pushbike, and I vowed to mend my ways. I needed to be utterly thankful for our seventy horsepower and just relish the challenges thrown at us.

Out on the lake, the sun shone down, and I remarked to Selly that we had only experienced rain when it didn't matter. Every non-riding sightseeing day so far had been blessed by blue skies and we felt so fortunate. There was an unexpected surprise before we reached the vast lake's caves; a pair of low-nesting condors was pointed out to us on a passing cliff face. As they soared much closer than those we'd seen at Torres del Paine, we could easily marvel at these huge birds, gracefully sweeping the waters and shore without a single wing beat to be seen. Leaving them behind, we idled engines and drifted into the first of dozens of marble caves. Polished and sculptured by the water's timeless touch, they were a beautiful sight and incredibly photogenic. The slightest movement of the boat opened up new vistas through weathered portholes in the caves' interior pillars and columns. Light reflected off the water, danced off the marble and above us, peacefully twirling the ceiling's shadows around. Cave after cave enchanted and captivated us; the guide's rehearsed patter and deft nudges on the tiller revealed all manner of animal-shaped marble formations. Some needed much more imagination than others, but it was a happy boatful of day trippers that returned to the harbour that afternoon. Selly kindly gave me another thousand or so photos to edit; she just couldn't bring herself to delete any of them!

The southern end of the Carretera Austral is mostly unpaved, snaking through valley after valley, alongside lupin-lined rivers and through inviting meadows. For hour after hour, we marvelled at the scenery, waved at fellow travellers and tolerated the dust and dirt. The cyclists we passed were held in a new high esteem. A family waved at us, their young children cooped into little trailers hooked onto their parents' pushbikes. I struggled to imagine how they coped. Some of the hills were just steep loose gravel, clogged by ancient trucks belching clouds of black fumes that mixed horribly with the road's billowing dust. The children were cocooned in fragile-looking bubbles of transparent plastic, wondering who knew what. This was no ordinary family holiday! In an old roadside bus, long since converted into a cosy café, we chatted with a Scottish couple cycling their way north to south. Despite all their pre-trip training, they were finding it tough going. As we couldn't give them any welcome news, of the gravel ending and turning to tarmac, we told them about the passing family we had witnessed, to try and spur them on.

Our adventures on the Austral were coming to an end and at the turning for the Futaleufu Pass we headed eastwards for Argentina once again. The lake district around Bariloche was calling, and so we needed to find another border crossing. The many hundreds of miles should have, but hadn't, prepared us for this particular pass. It proved as daunting as the Chile Chico pass days before. At some point recently it had been raining and there was more wet mud than stone on too many of the hairpins. Where the previous pass had been thankfully almost empty of traffic, this one was being used regularly by large trucks, heading across to Ruta 7. Selly had to hop off several times to check the blind hairpins and help push when we bogged down in the deeper, slippery ruts. It was becoming slow and exhausting work, and coming across a lengthy articulated truck stuck solid and blocking a hairpin gave us a grateful respite.

There was little we could do to help the stranded driver. The rain and heavy construction traffic had made some of the hairpins virtually impassable. We certainly weren't going back, and the truck certainly wasn't going forward, but with some begging and pleading the driver attempted to straighten the truck's angle just enough to provide us a small gap. It was a risky manoeuvre for him; the road wasn't barriered and the trailer wanted to go sideways more than it did forwards or backwards. At the point where the driver called it a day, we had been gifted barely a metre of slick, wet mud, sandwiched between the trailer's side and the edge of a sobering drop-off. As he jumped out of his cab with a shrug, it was clearly over to me, to either attempt it or bottle it. After the ordeal to arrive at this point, backtracking wasn't an option and forwards meant Argentina, with its lush steaks and cheap wines!

So, inch by inch, I edged, or rather slid, down the trailer's side. From safe distances, Selly watched through squinted eyes and the driver watched with curiosity, for one of only two outcomes. At the narrowest point, I had to lean my left shoulder against the trailer and try to keep my left foot on the ground. The drop-off on my right side was getting way too close for comfort, but inching along slowly and carefully I was able to keep from sliding sideways. It felt strange to be looking down over the edge, but leaning up against the trailer helped. In this fashion, I squeezed past centimetre by centimetre, finally getting the bike past and onto safer ground. We saddled up, waved to the hapless but helpful driver and pressed on.

Some miles, many actually, had been testing and hard-earned over the last few weeks, but highly rewarding at the same time, I reflected, as we navigated the border bureaucracy and collected our sixth Argentinian entry stamp. The road eventually ended at the small town of Trevilin, and we had a tip for a friendly and superbly run bed and breakfast hotel. Unlike us, it was immaculate, and I wondered if they would even allow us in! They did, and surprisingly we found an equally immaculate Ducati parked inside the spacious foyer that belonged to the owners, Luis and Rosana. I was again immediately all too conscious that we and our bike looked like we'd been dragged through a mud bath to get here. Well, we had!

With the bike unloaded and locked up, I could now walk, virtually fully clothed and much to Selly's amusement, into the shower for a scrubdown. Hand-washing our clothes was almost a daily routine, so for me, it just seemed easier to get it done whilst grabbing a shower. Who says men can't multi-task! With the pair of us feeling presentable, we could now have a good chat with Luis about bikes, routes and tips, etc. In the wilder parts of Patagonia, we had starved ourselves of news, too immersed in the beauty and remoteness to really care. Luis broke it to us that the Bolivian protests had ended the week before and that the borders were opening up again. That really was great news. We never needed much of an excuse to celebrate, especially when we had a biking sommelier hosting us, so 'wine not'?

After a comfortable stay in Trevilin, we pushed north on an admittedly paved but badly potholed road to rejoin Ruta 40, towards San Carlos de Bariloche and the famed lakes. By the time we reached El Bolson, the scenery had changed dramatically, from brown to green, and the hills and mountains around us were suddenly adorned with miles of yellow blossom. Much of Ruta 40 to date had been a windblown and dusty reddish brown, with the snow-capped Andes often a distant backdrop. That's not to say it wasn't enjoyable; we had come to love the stark remoteness of this road, with its rugged 'Colorado cowboy' mountains, the endless roadside guanaco herds and opportunistic vultures and falcons. However, the new fertile landscape hinted at the lakes ahead and was a welcome change. Even the road was now black instead of brown and gorgeously smooth; things were looking up. With fast sweeping bends, the last 60-mile stretch was just a dream, and all thoughts of the previous week's struggles were pushed aside by two beaming smiles. Heading out into town for an explore, we discovered that Bariloche had a bustling Christmas market and for the first time our thoughts turned to where we'd actually like to be for our Crimbo break. Argentina had so far proven to be cheaper and friendlier than Chile, and scouring the map, it seemed the tip Estelle had given us, back in Buenos Aires, about the Mendoza wine region was right up our street, literally! From there it would also be an easy hop across the 3,800-metre Uspallata Pass to reach Santiago for the New Year. Having her recommendation sealed it; we agreed we would be spending Christmas in sunny Mendoza.

Bariloche sits on the shores of the huge Nahuel Huapi Lake and is within easy reach of at least half a dozen more scenic lakes close by. Spanning the Nahuel Huapi National Park, together they form the area locally called the Lake District, and in every direction, it is simply stunning. With winter ski resorts and a full complement of summer mountain sports, you could be forgiven for thinking you were in the Austrian or Swiss Alps. Even the city had a Bavarian feel to it, boasting smart streets lined with cafés, bakeries and *konditoreis*. Colourful flower baskets and window boxes adorned fresco-painted buildings, and each evening the Christmas market lit up the atmosphere with bands, lights and candyfloss. For a couple of days, we rode from panoramic viewpoint to panoramic viewpoint, taking in the various lakes and enjoying clear, if windy, skies.

We actually cut short the stay, though, as back in Trevilin, Luis and Rosana enticed us with their own tip to stay at the opposite end of the lakes, in the prettier and quainter Villa la Angostura. As it was still on Ruta 40 and north of us, it made sense to check it out, and we weren't disappointed; it was everything they had said. Nestled under mountains and volcanoes, this pretty little tourist town was essentially one long street of skilfully and decoratively carved wooden bars, restaurants and shops. There was hardly a brick to be seen and the Alpine feel was reinforced tenfold; we loved it. On the second day, we had a nice surprise whilst out strolling and photographing. Having spoken so highly of the place to us, Luis and Rosana had then decided upon a mini-break of their own, and we bumped into them on the picturesque main street!

Just over the Chilean border from us was the start of the 'Volcano Valley', and as we sat cosy in the artisanal micro-brewery bar, conveniently under our room, we plotted another zigzag tour of Andean passes. If we crossed the 'Cardenal Antonio Samore Pass' early enough one morning, we should be able to take in five volcanoes in one day and even be back in time for a late dinner! So, with an unloaded bike and a full tank of fuel, we set off the next morning, carrying just the necessary border paperwork, cameras and a packed lunch tucked into the tank bag. The pass took us initially through the eeriest and most enchanted-looking forest we could ever have imagined. Thousands of leafless, grey dead trees stretched as far as the eye could see, seemingly rooted within a lifeless grey blanket. There were no birds or animals to be seen, and we later found out it had been this way since the eruption of the Puyehue volcano eight years previously.

The Argentine and Chilean borders were almost 20 miles apart, at opposite ends of the pass, and the 'no-man's-land in between was just spooky. Once more over the border and back in Chile, we passed between the Puyehue and Casablanca volcanoes. Unfortunately for us, they were mostly shrouded in cloud, and so we pressed on towards the city of Osorno, for it was the iconic and majestic Osorno volcano we had really come to see. All year round, it was beautifully snow-capped and resembled Mount Fuji's smaller twin; we kept our fingers crossed the clouds would eventually disperse. Our luck prevailed, and as we rode ever closer it tantalisingly revealed itself in fleeting moments. We couldn't get enough, though, riding dozens of miles to try to improve upon the views offered by the various vantage points. Eventually, we just sat under its unrestricted gaze, enjoying and sharing our packed lunch with a hungry 'round-the-world' cyclist, from Japan of all places!

The day was running away with us and, sadly, we just didn't have time to pull in the remaining two volcanoes, Calbuco and Shoshuenco. To be honest, neither of us really fancied riding back through the unearthly forest in the dark so, like a pair of scaredy-cats, we headed for the border in the already waning light. Luck was on our side again; on the way through that morning, we hadn't even noticed the borders closed daily at 7pm. We cleared the Chilean border just after six thirty and left ourselves a sporty twenty-five minutes to cross the haunted forest and pass (with the inevitable photo stops for Selly!), making it by the skin of our teeth. It had proved to be a long, tiring, but especially memorable day.

Mendoza was now a 1,000-mile trek, straight up Ruta 40, another sizeable chunk of its 3,230-mile length. However arduous this section turned out to be, we would have 300 plus vineyards waiting to welcome us. We could feel we were getting too comfortable in Villa la Angostura. Everything about the place begged us to stay longer, but Christmas was now looming and so we relented, loaded up and headed for fuel. Pulling into the gas station, I saw a Triumph Tiger with a UK plate, the first we'd seen in almost two months of touring. Steve and Janette's bike was the exact model and look I could have imagined us touring on and we happily put the bikes side by side for group photos, showing off the pair of UK plates far-flung from home. Over the next couple of hours, we swapped travel gossip and compared itineraries. Their tour of the Americas had lasted over five years, so far, and upon learning our schedule was ten to twelve months, they must have got the impression we were on a drag race! Feeling the road beckoning, we wished each other well and with paps of the horn headed off in our different directions.

With each fuel stop, the winds were noticeably dropping and the temperatures climbing. We hardly had to look at the Windy app anymore, but it did tell us Mendoza was basking nicely in thirty degrees. Sixty miles past Zapala, we slowed for yet another panoramic viewpoint, both of us needing water and a short rest. There was already a bike parked up and we pulled alongside to meet its owner, Dauri from Mexico. Every square centimetre of his machine was decorated in stickers, and Dauri himself was equally covered in biker patches. We thoroughly enjoyed all these chance encounters, and Dauri proved to be both instantly likeable and a pleasure to meet. We were both travelling north, but at a different pace. He'd sold a larger bike to buy this smaller one and help finance his trip. We swapped numbers and vowed to keep in touch. (Over the next 600 miles, I lost count of the number of times we leapfrogged each other on the road!)

It didn't take long to bump into each other again; having just passed the Ruta 40 midway monument near Chos Malal, we then found ourselves at the same fuel station. There and then, we made plans to camp together in the town of Malague. He'd been given a tip for the municipal campsite there, super cheap, but with great facilities apparently. We didn't need convincing; the winds had all but relented and the temperatures were comfortably in the mid-twenties.

Over a BBQ and shared drinks, we realised we had now crossed out of Patagonia. For Selly and I, a loop of over 6,000 awe-inspiring miles and memories to last a lifetime.

The evening had been so enjoyable that the three of us decided to stay and camp a second night, cooking steaks over open flames, drinking wine from cartons and swapping more tales from the road. Dauri was an excellent storyteller; almost his entire trip had been a whirlwind of being passed over from one bike club to the next, getting mostly free accommodation, non-stop parties and any help needed with his bike. This had gone on country after country and explained all the stickers and patches he had collected along the way. For him, having to pay to camp was unusual, even if it was just a pound per night! Whilst packing the next morning, we vowed to meet up at some point further north or, failing that, we were to visit and stay with his family once we reached Mexico. An absolute character and a gent; we looked forward to it.

Chapter Five

Crossing the Atacama and Altiplano

It felt strange to have left Patagonia behind us, almost as if we were starting upon a new adventure. For sure, the unknown, to us, Atacama and Altiplano, were getting closer, but our time in Argentina was also drawing to a close. Mendoza was our last planned stopover, albeit a lengthy Christmas one, but we knew we were going to miss this country; it had been kind to us and it would be remembered with a warm fondness. Of course, we would be saying goodbye to Ruta 40 also, but it gave us one last memorable day. Over the hundreds of miles, it had randomly stopped us at police checkpoints, bad sections of road, or closed gas stations, but today was different. Threading past queuing cars and trucks, we came to rows of burning tyres and wooden pallets blocking the highway. There definitely wasn't a way past and we doubled back almost 15 miles to find an alternative route, fortunately bumping into Dauri and managing to save him the wasted journey. Bouncing down dirt tracks, and more by luck than judgement, we rejoined the highway beyond the blockade. Except that the highway was again barricaded at the next town, this time with vehicles parked sideways and protesters filling the road as the police watched on. We looked for a road north that skirted Ruta 40 entirely and were rewarded with a scenic tour of beautiful vineyards and quaint wine-producing towns and villages.

The day had taken much longer than we'd expected, though, and realising we wouldn't make Mendoza, we found a campsite entirely to ourselves. With a borrowed hosepipe and bucket, I gave the bike a much-needed clean and check-over. Brush-cleaning and adjusting the chain, I saw it was missing some of the 'O' rings from the links. I had no idea why, but that couldn't be a good sign. I hadn't let the chain-oiler run dry and had kept the chain adjusted and cleaned regularly, so I was a little perplexed. I would just keep an eye on it for now and see how things went. As things turned out, we weren't quite so alone that night; five over-friendly dogs, four of them playful puppies, joined us for our evening BBQ. Selly being Selly carefully cut up the leftover meat, to ensure each dog had a perfectly equal portion. She then painstakingly taught each one to sit, whilst fending off the other four, to gratefully receive their treats. Five unruly dogs had been tamed by one persistent Italian, with a few bits of juicy steak. They had fallen in love with her and overnight did their best to get into the tent and kindly bark us a warning about every passing car, or passing anything it seemed. After a sleepless night, we couldn't wait to pack and then unpack in the Christmas apartment later that afternoon!

Francisco met us outside with his, coincidentally, Italian girlfriend, and Selly wasted no time reverting to her mother tongue. They were young, bubbly and with his long hair and collection of wristbands, he looked like a travelling musician singer. Turns out he was a travelling musician singer. It was his brother's apartment and whilst he was away for four months, Francisco had talked him into renting the place out. We had a secure garage for the bike and every mod-con you could want, including Netflix! It was a super find for the Christmas period and way too cheap, but you can't complain about these things.

They'd even filled a bowl with fresh fruit and left a couple of beers in the fridge for us. With a large mall on our doorstep, we soon had the fridge stocked and felt comfortably at home. We extravagantly planned three Christmas meals. Selly would cook Italian for us on the 24th, her traditional day; I would cook for the 25th and on Boxing Day we would hit Mendoza's bar street, Avenida Aristides Villanueva, for fish 'n' chips. So much for planning; none of that happened, at least not in that order!

On the 23rd, Francisco got in touch and asked if we would like to join his family the following day, for Christmas Eve. There would be two families, he told us, about fifteen in total, with each bringing some food and drinks, and he could pick us up and drop us back. It was exactly the kind of experience we had hoped for and of course accepted! Selly offered to cook a large lasagne to take, which happened to be my favourite. Being cheeky, I popped out and bought an extra oven dish, so she could also make a second one for us back at the apartment!

Being away on the trip of a lifetime, we had agreed not to bother with cards or presents for each other, but somehow that seemed a bit bah-humbug. I wanted to find something appropriate, something we could enjoy together and that wouldn't have to be carried on the already overladen bike. Back in Buenos Aires, I'd seen a billboard advertising Guns N' Roses on tour in Latin America, but hadn't taken in the dates. Searching now, I could see we could feasibly swing by San José, Costa Rica, for their mid-March concert and suggested it to Selly. Ten minutes later, we'd bought each other's ticket, as presents!

The following evening, the lasagnes were fortunately prepared and just out of the oven when the power went off in the apartment. The storm arrived out of nowhere, hitting hard, so suddenly that it was a shock, and along with the electricity, we had also lost our mobile signals. There wasn't any rain, or thunder, but we listened to the howling dry wind throwing bins and tree branches down the street. Francisco arrived, unavoidably late, and as we threaded our way carefully through the pitch-black streets, littered with downed trees, debris and damaged cars, he explained what was happening.

We were experiencing a random violent Zonda windstorm, peculiar to the eastern Andes and particularly the Mendoza region. Normally a high-altitude and high-velocity wind, it occasionally gets pulled down by warming air and can easily exceed 200 kph. Bizarrely, the Zonda had now departed as quickly as it had arrived, leaving behind a city-wide power cut and a thick layer of sandy dust over everything (even the bike tucked up inside the garage, we found later)! It was an eerie journey to reach his parents' house, but we were warmly welcomed into their home, cosily lit by dozens of candles. It was an Argentinian traditional and truly memorable evening. Going around the lengthy dinner table twice, each of us took turns to give short speeches on first what we had accomplished and remembered most from 2019 and then what we hoped for out of 2020. Not one of us around that table could have foreseen what a dire world 2020 actually had in store for each of us!

My second speech had to be on the vague side and slightly made up. I hadn't yet proposed to Selly and she had no idea about my Vegas scheming. Though I would have liked to do so, I just couldn't tell the truth and let the cat out of the bag! Our touring tales had captivated the enthused and attentive audience, but appreciative claps were soon followed by warnings of our next destination, Santiago. Mendoza is just a few hours' drive from Chile's capital, and it was evident they had much more up-to-date news than we currently possessed. The situation there had become much graver; the protesters were out daily, clashing with the police and for too many of them, paying with their lives. Francisco's father advised us to try to bypass the city completely, but our flights for Easter Island departed from there. On the back of that, we'd also pre-booked a city-central, but supposedly safe, bikers' hostel! To lighten the mood, Francisco grabbed his guitar and joined by his father, entertained us with self-composed songs and melodies. We felt privileged to have met such hospitable families and to be able to share this special evening with them.

With healthy hangovers on Christmas day, we cheerfully phoned around our families and friends. Due to the eleven-hour time difference with Australia, my first catch-up call was to Chris and

Caroline; 'Yes', they were fine and 'Yes', they couldn't wait to come and meet us at some point. Both were stockpiling their holiday allowances, to extend their vacation with us! I also got hold of Dauri, to see if he was in the vicinity and wanted to join us for a Christmas dinner. True to form, he was already staying with newly made friends, who happened to own a vineyard, and he was already way too refreshed to ride a motorcycle! I was almost relieved. Not really feeling capable of cooking the dinner I'd promised Selly, I instead convinced her into fish 'n' chips down bar street.

We sat outside in the cool evening air, simply enjoying people-watching and sipping our sundowner drinks. The throngs of partygoers kept us entertained, heading out to collect hangovers, or like us, topping up the previous night's. To complete the culinary tour, on Boxing Day, we found and ventured out to the Indian restaurant Estelle had previously tipped us about. It was a fab call; the Indian owners had nailed the décor and traditional dress. Hindi music played nicely in the background and a tasty authentic menu had us feeling like we were somehow in a posh part of New Delhi. In all, Mendoza had been an awesome break, far better than we could have envisioned, but before we could depart, we had a couple of things to attend to.

The bike received its second oil change and I sought a second opinion on the chain's missing O-rings. The gist of which was that it 'would probably be OK for a few thousand kilometres'! Not quite so convinced, I contacted a friend back in the UK, to ask why it might be failing so soon. His best guess was because I hadn't been switching off the chain-oiler whilst riding on the hundreds of miles of dirt roads. The oil, sand and dirt had most likely mixed into a grinding paste and started destroying the rubber seals. It looked like it was entirely my mistake and, further down the road, would prove costly in both time and frustration!

We decided to get some quotes for sending a parcel back to the UK. With a couple of months' touring under our belts, we realised we still had more stuff than we actually needed. It was all getting used now and again, but only because it had been brought along in the first place. Having a rinse-through, I made up a parcel that weighed just under 10 kilograms and took it to both the national post office and an international courier. The cheapest quote was over two hundred pounds. The parcel was promptly pulled apart and the stuff repacked!

It was a strange feeling riding out of such a great city, to head for one we'd been warned against entering. A few days previously, I'd checked in with the biker hostel, to confirm all was well with our booking over the New Year. I was assured the street they were on was trouble-free and we would be fine if we used a satnav. Apparently, many street signs had been torn down and traffic lights had been broken in many areas. We put this aside as we climbed the Uspallata Pass, stopping off briefly at the natural rock formation known as the 'Puente del Inca' – Inca Bridge. Cresting the 3,800-metre pass, we had an awe-inspiring view of the crazy hairpin road below; it was a rewarding ride and our first completely paved pass.

Like in many countries, it seemed more money was spent on the roads the closer you got to the capital. The western side of the Andes proved even hotter, and dropping down towards the suburbs, the bike told us it was now well over forty degrees. The traffic thickened until we were at a forced standstill in a lengthy tunnel. We could feel ourselves beginning to overheat. The claustrophobic tunnel was so long that it even had a couple of turn-offs inside it. That could be a problem; the satnav had lost its signal soon after entering it and we now sat dehydrated in forty-seven degrees, breathless on the fumes and getting dizzy. Mopeds frustratingly threaded through, but the narrower tunnel lanes and staggered rubbernecking drivers had us properly blocked in. I tried drinking some of the water we carried; it needed teabags! The top of the pass had been chilly, but now our layers were completely soaked through and we were wilting in the bad air. Finally, there was some movement ahead, just as I was beginning to think we'd have to walk out before we passed out!

The satnav sprung to life as we cleared the suffocating tunnel, and we followed its guidance towards the city centre. It was a bit of a mess to say the least, and nothing seemed to have escaped the anti-government graffiti. As warned, our biggest predicament was finding the majority of the traffic lights either torn down or their lamps smashed. We edged cautiously through what had become free-for-all junctions. Many businesses, hotels and shops had been closed down, with steel shutters literally welded over the fronts for protection. Despite trying to avoid it, we were riding on too much broken glass and it was a huge relief to finally find the street we were staying in.

Hostel Casa Matte is a mecca for overlanders and as the large metal gates were swung open, we were immediately offered cold beers. (We almost begged for cold water first!) Taking the place in was a treat, a little utopia compared to the mayhem outside. Overlander bikes were parked everywhere and came from everywhere. A fully equipped workshop doubled as the downstairs bar, complementing the second one, up on the rooftop terrace. It was basic but friendly, provided security for the bike and was seemingly of no interest to the protesters. Up on the roof terrace that evening, we met a few of the eclectic, mostly RTW, travellers that had chosen this iconic hostel for the New Year. Despite the drinks lightening the atmosphere, the darkening skies were never empty of police helicopters, or large military drones passing overhead. These in turn were being harassed by many laser lights from the protesters below, who we could hear quite clearly in different parts of the city. Orange glows would randomly appear from petrol bombs, or street barricades being lit like on bonfire night to hamper the riot police. It was all a bit surreal, and we began to wonder what we had let ourselves in for.

"Oh, it's not so bad," said a group of three Germans travelling together, "we've been all over the city, getting tyres and bits from the markets to repair our bikes, you get used to it," he continued as another volley of rifle shots rang out somewhere.

I had seen their battered bikes in the workshop, pulled apart, wheels off and balancing on blocks of wood. They had a lot of repairs planned and one of them drunkenly but proudly showed me a mixed assortment of Helicoil inserts he'd sourced that day.

"I was so happy to find these, now I can get rid of most of the wire and cable-ties holding the bike together!" he beamed.

For sure, we could hold out here, I mused, and my only real concern was whether we could safely transit to the airport and back. 'Sergei the Russian' came to our recue. Sober and of a more serious disposition, he was one of only a handful of legally licensed Siberian mammoth tusk dealers, something you don't come across every day! He told us we'd be fine if we paid for a private driver, and of course he knew of one and could easily fix this for us. He was staying at the hostel to haggle for one of the many bikes that had been left behind by departing nomads. Some of these were for sale and some could be talked into being sold. Sergei had his eye on one in particular and if successful, would find a way to ride it back to Mother Russia. Young and clearly successful, he was an interesting character to say the least, and then there was sixty-three-year-old Benjamin from Tel Aviv. He had been on the road for three years already, having announced to his shocked family, during his sixtieth retirement birthday party, that he was buying a motorcycle and was going to ride it around the world. He was now weary and sad, though, terribly homesick and missing his family so much he just wanted the trip to be over.

The next day, we ventured out to food shop and tentatively explore the streets around us. We didn't get far; the supermarket we'd been told about had closed up early and rounding the next corner we came face to face with running riot police, backed up by a water cannon. A small shop owner ushered us quickly inside, giving us a safe haven, until the hostilities passed by and we could retreat to the hostel's sanctuary. On New Year's Eve, we managed a clear run to the supermarket, stocking up on food for a rooftop BBQ and drinks to see in 2020.

It was a strange celebration; tear gas hung in the air and loud explosions echoed across the city. They certainly sounded louder than mere fireworks. The helicopters and drones were out, as they were every night, and we drank to the background noise of aggrieved citizens street fighting their government's police and security forces. It wasn't possible to enjoy the city, so we just ticked off the hours chatting away with the other bikers, up until the day we could escape to Easter Island. The hostel owners were looking after the bike and most of our gear for our week away; we just had to pack our camera and toothbrushes!

Finally, both the day and the 4am taxi arrived to whisk us the twenty minutes to the airport. The streets were mostly quiet now, but strewn with the debris of the previous night's battles. Glass and broken bottles lay everywhere and fresh graffiti seemed to cover everything. Once-beautiful statues and sculptures had particularly been singled out for wanton damage. As an artist, it was tearing at Selly's heart to see so much creativity reduced to mindless destruction. The people of Santiago, and of the country, were travelling to the city centre to tear it down; they had had enough. Many private businesses and private homes displayed pleading handwritten notices, begging to be spared damage, but often to no avail. We were thankfully and safely dropped at departures, with a mix of heavy hearts and excited heads. If flying to one of the remotest islands on the planet couldn't put this sad situation behind us, then nothing would!

Thankfully, our seat row had a window this time. Selly's excitement at seeing stone moai statues as we came in to land was infectious. Rapa Nui lies almost 2,300 miles from Chile's coastline and it had taken over five hours to fly there from Santiago. It didn't just feel remote; it was remote. From the quaint palm-thatched airport to the traditional Polynesian welcome of flower garlands placed over our heads, we refreshingly couldn't tell this island was at all connected to Chile. The capital, Hanga Roa, where we were staying, had the feel of a friendly village. There were no buildings over two stories high and just a few of the main roads were paved; we loved everything about the place. Avoiding the tours, we rented a Jeep for the duration, bought park tickets to enter the various symbolic sights and planned our own mini adventure.

The week was flying by in a whirlwind of scuba diving, trekking, cultural shows, exotic cocktails and sunrise or sunset visits to all the moai exhibits. With volcanoes to hike around, sandy beaches and ancient stone villages to explore, it was hard not to fall in love with this tranquil island. We were suitably wowed and moved by all we saw, a particular highlight being the Rano Raraku quarry, where monoliths in the making lay side by side, frozen in time at their various stages of being carved from the volcanic crater.

It was already an emotional day for me, the twenty-fifth anniversary of losing my only brother in a car accident. We had been close, both bikers, and both of us had served in the Royal Air Force, a camaraderie that ran deeper than the mere bonds of brotherhood. In time for dawn, we had traversed the island and lit a solitary candle at Ahu Tongariki, beneath the watchful row of fifteen solemn moai carvings. Seemingly at attention, the towering statues felt a fitting location for me to reflect and remember. Everything was just so peaceful, photogenic and heart-warming that it naturally lifted my mood. It didn't feel right to be sad, and I was pleased for that. I just wanted to ponder and remember some of the good times we'd shared, the bike adventures, the mutual friends we'd made, the pints and many laughs. Frequently, out on the open roads and confined within the helmet's sanctuary, my thoughts would drift to these youthful days, our collection of happy memories. Occasionally, I'd inexplicably feel his presence, sometimes a warning, or a thought I felt sure he'd engineered somehow to influence a decision. He might not be around to physically see anymore, but I don't believe he's completely gone either.

Each evening, Selly and I were treated to captivating Pacific sunsets and on the last day, as we walked amongst the 1,000-year old moai heads, with the sun dropping behind them, I picked my moment. I didn't have a ring; I didn't trust myself to choose that! In any case, I wanted Selly to have her shopping day in the Colombian emerald markets and be free to choose for herself. This woman was my rock, had polished my rougher edges and thankfully, kept the wayward Mark a little more grounded. For me, she was simply the woman I wanted my future entwined with.

With the sun gliding to the ocean's horizon, I tried to steer Selly to a stone bench to sit her down, but it just wasn't working. The camera in her hand and the unforgettable scene before her eyes were already marrying, and stealing my moment. I almost had to be forceful to get her to sit beside me, and knowing the competition I had from Mother Nature, I wasted no more time. Locking her eyes, I asked her for the second time in my life to marry me and was rewarded with an astounded 'yes'. She had no idea this proposal had been brewing inside me and I couldn't resist taking a quick selfie, to capture her sparkling eyes and beaming smile. It was a perfect and fitting end to an amazing exotic island adventure.

Sitting on the plane flying back just didn't feel like one week later; time had somehow condensed and we struggled to comprehend how it had all passed so quickly. The five-hour flight also passed quickly, as I could now divulge all the research, plotting and scheming that had been going on behind her back! Selly was pretty astounded to hear I'd already been in regular contact with the Bellagio in Vegas and listened with excitement to the information I had sourced on Colombian emeralds. Happy with both the venue and the practicality of a Vegas wedding, we next mused over a suitable date. Working backwards from needing to be in Alaska mid-July, sometime in early June made sense. Everything felt like it was falling into place and by now, that feeling alone should have been setting off alarm bells!

We were soon brought back down to earth, literally and figuratively, as we discovered Sergei's driver had forgotten to meet us. Welcome back to Santiago, I thought! We haggled for a new lift, whilst ensuring he knew exactly where we were staying. It was early evening and the streets would be busy, potentially dangerous. We got approximately halfway before we came face to face with running protesters, jammed into a one-way street. As they charged past, we then faced a water cannon, driving the wrong way up our street and powerfully soaking those too slow to get out of the way. Our driver slammed into reverse and managed to duck down a side street, only to be met by armoured vehicles and riot police aggressively baton charging another group of cornered protesters. It was an ugly scene, probably being repeated all over the city, and it was easy to believe the stories of so many civilians being seriously injured, even killed. Some quick thinking on the driver's part found us a way out and once back at the hostel we recalibrated, checked the bike over and repacked. Temporarily, these tasks took our minds off the surrounding dangers, but we vowed to get up early and depart early, whilst the city was hopefully still sleeping.

We had plotted a route out, avoiding known hotspots and which would lead us to the Pacific highway, Ruta 5. It was a relief to be leaving and to feel the injured city slipping further and further behind us. At times, the road swung within 100 metres of huge barrelling waves, or it weaved inland amongst beautiful sand dunes. Even with occasional stops and the time needed to extricate ourselves from the capital, the smooth surface allowed us to cover almost 300 miles that day. Deep in the 'old town', we sought accommodation in the coastal city of La Serena.

It had been a hot and sticky ride and needing to stretch our legs, we strolled a few miles around the beachfront and back within the vicinity of our hostel. Although we hadn't seen any troubles yet, this town had also suffered from a fresh coating of graffiti and general damage. The seafront connects to the old town most impressively via the wide tree-lined Francisco de Aguirre Boulevard. A mixture of thirty statues and monuments line the central walkways and at the eastern end sits an impressive marble portal. Sadly, all had been covered in graffiti and some were damaged. We settled into a pretty little square, sat outside in the evening warmth and ordered our latest favourite drinks: local *pisco* sours.

Connected to their internet, I could reply to messages from the Colombian couple we'd met in Punta Tombo and our Mexican *amigo*, Dauri, who fed us a constant stream of tips from his adventures. Following our diversion to Easter Island, everybody we had stayed in contact with seemed to be much further north than us now. Dauri had significantly leapfrogged us, initially continuing on up Ruta 40 towards Salta, before crossing Chile briefly to reach Peru, where he was currently enjoying cold beers with his latest newfound friends. It was handy for us to have these news bulletins trickling in, accommodation tips, weather reports, or road conditions, etc. I didn't expect us to cross paths with Dauri before Mexico, but it was something we both already looked forward to.

We barely had time to finish our first drinks before masked and balaclava-clad youths poured into the small tranquil plaza we had chosen. They were desperately seeking refuge as shots rang out and tear gas canisters rained into the square, followed by a charge from gas mask-wearing riot police. We niftily retreated inside the café's restaurant and took a 'viewing' table to wait out the confrontation. In fits and starts, this lasted a couple more rounds, until it eventually seemed quiet enough to make our escape. Within 100 metres of the café, we needed to cross a wide junction but discovered this was where the current standoff was taking place. We had unintentionally found ourselves on the fringe of a much larger group, of much better organised protesters. They were all ages and even had medics with first aid kits amongst them. Many had fashioned body armour of their own and seemed to be much better armed than previous protestors we had unwittingly come across. They far outnumbered the police, who stood back behind a variety of armoured vehicles. Very suddenly, I didn't feel we had left Santiago behind at all!

We spoke with those closest to us, asking exactly why they thought this was the best way to protest. It was the only solution left, they despairingly told us. The corrupt government had lied too many times, promised too much and stole even more. For them, it now needed to be a fight, a physical uprising. The road was blocked, to a degree, by burning fires, large rocks carted there in shopping trolleys and people, lots of people. The riot vehicles were pinned in place by dozens of laser pointers dazzling the drivers, and if one of them attempted to move, it was immediately bombarded by rocks and bottles. Amongst all this mess, I tried to assess our safest route out and realised we definitely had to get across this junction somehow, preferably at the bottom end and behind the main mass of protesters.

True to heart, Selly, bless her, had a more immediate mission. A couple of dogs had excitedly joined the action and were running around amongst all the broken glass. She couldn't bear to leave them like this and cornering one at a time, checked their paws for injuries and tried her best to entice them away with us. The atmosphere amongst the protesters was tangible, the air was full of nervous expectation and the two of us just weren't as interesting to the dogs as 300 people violently demanding justice. The dogs weren't going to be influenced by us and we needed to get away, retreat before it all turned ugly. It wasn't our fight, or our place to be here in this moment. What a different country we were experiencing after the sheer beauty of Patagonia and the recent serenity of Easter Island.

Like Santiago before it, La Serena could, at different times, be a place to linger. It had all the tourist trappings and very nice beaches close by, but we were now on the Atacama's southern doorstep and eager to press on. The hot, dry desert stretched north of us for 600 miles. We planned to cross approximately half of this along the coast, before turning north-easterly and climbing inland towards Bolivia. Knowing we hadn't seen La Serena at its best, we nevertheless gladly rode away and out onto Ruta 5, with its rolling multi-coloured dunes and now snowless high mountain peaks. It was a treat to be riding on an almost perfect surface, and apart from the sparse towns we encountered, there were virtually no potholes or speed bumps to talk of, just endless fast sweeping bends to enjoy.

Only the rising temperatures made the riding uncomfortable. Since leaving Mendoza, the mercury was sitting daily in the high thirties and occasionally over forty degrees. Our new tent was called an 'Atacama' and I was determined to find somewhere we could use it for our first night, in its namesake's desert. After almost 280 miles, we turned off the scenic desert road and headed down into the small tranquil resort of Bahia Inglesa. Appropriate for me, 'English Bay'!

It was comforting to be out of the cities and be beside the inviting blue of the Pacific. At the far end of the bay sat a lively campsite, hidden amongst the dunes of the beach. We could almost reach out and touch the clear waters of the bay; it was ideal, or so I thought. We set up the tent and a cooking area directly on the soft sand and hopping on the now unloaded and much lighter bike, I somehow managed to quickly bog it down. I really was an amateur at this off-roading! Giving it a handful of gas, I bogged it down even further, right down to the already suffering chain, and I temporarily gave up. As I stepped off the bike, it happily stood upright in its new 'bike rack', and turning my back to it, we strolled off into town, to explore and fetch supplies for dinner instead.

It was still sat upright when we returned, and with renewed optimism and Selly pushing, it released its grip on the Atacama. I subtly parked it a suitable distance away, pretending it was somebody else's. With the evening routines of exercise walking and hand-washing the laundry completed, we could now turn our shopping into a meal. The late evening air had cooled nicely, and we cooked tuna pasta to a waning sun, setting over the now restful ocean. It appeared the waves had lost their energy in unison with mine! Only camping can you truly appreciate a cloudless night sky, free of light pollution and lit only by the alluring stars. That first desert night didn't disappoint; we lazily finished our bottle of red, happily stargazing and meteor spotting.

Going through the morning bike routine, I was a little perturbed at how many deep cuts the rear tyre had picked up in Santiago and La Serena. They were lasting well tread-wise, but the rear had far too many dubious cuts in it for my liking. The chain's condition was visibly worsening. Slight kinks were appearing as the unsealed links slowly ran dry of their internal grease. I didn't want to risk crossing the Atacama and on into Bolivia with the bike like this, so a stop in the region's capital, Antofagasta, was going to be prudent and necessary. It would be another 300-mile ride, in close to forty degrees, and so we set off early, with full water bottles and a full tank of fuel.

For the first 60 miles we had the ocean for company, a sea breeze for comfort and were enchanted by huge dunes sweeping down to greet the surf. I don't think Selly took her eyes off the sea once, scanning the far-off waves for any signs of migrating whales. If we were lucky enough, we were in the right territory to spot blue, or humpbacks, and occasionally Selly would excitedly shout that she thought she had seen one. We were both very happy, me with the beautifully smooth scenic road and Selly with the Pacific at her side. Born on a Mediterranean island, she had an affinity with sand and seas. There was no shortage of either today!

We passed tiny fishing hamlets, somehow existing in sparse empty coves and comprising just a half-dozen simple wooden boats and a handful of single-room thatch huts. Pelicans and cormorants decorated the tiny vessels and dogs slept out the heat in the shade of the hovels, but there wasn't a soul to be seen. Against a backdrop of powerfully crashing waves, life here appeared as fragile as the fishing boats and shacks themselves. Unsuccessfully, I tried to imagine a life lived as harsh and bare as this, so remote and dry that the sea had to provide all. Eventually, the road swung inland and slicing between the towering dunes, it felt like we were suddenly riding into a hairdryer.

Mercifully, the road occasionally rose into cooler air and gave some respite. We marvelled at the morning fog clouds, rolling over the mountaintops and hugging the peaks. By the afternoon, they had evaporated away and as we continued northwards, on an almost empty and shade-less ribbon of black, we chased constantly retreating shimmering mirages. Our water had again become practically all but drinkable, certainly not pleasant or thirst-quenching, but we seemed to be on another 150-mile stretch lacking towns, gas stations, or shaded stops.

There was a prominent landmark on our route, though, one we were deliberately heading for and hoping to find uncrowded. Stretching over 10 metres in height, the 'Mano del Desierto' is clearly visible from Ruta 5 and has a dusty bumpy access road leading up to its base. A concrete monument of a hand, symbolically rising out of the desert's surface, attracts tourist coaches, travellers and the curious alike. As we ticked off the hundreds of scorching sandy miles, I was daydreaming, in my overheated helmet, of finding ice cream vans, or entrepreneurial sellers of frozen fruit and yoghurt drinks there to greet us. There was nothing, not even a cool box of chilled water! Amongst the few visitors, we patiently waited our turn to be able to park the bike, seemingly in the huge monument's palm, and have someone kindly take the obligatory photos of our passing. It was just one thirsty hour to Antofagasta now, where we had booked a 'cheap 'n' cheerful' apartment for a couple of nights, hopefully giving us enough time to find a rear tyre and a new chain.

The first litre of water was soon followed by an ice-cold beer, for we had covered half the length of the desert in a little over a day's riding. From dawn to dusk, the changing colours of both dunes and mountains had been stunning, but we had also been sapped by the harsh and unforgiving hot winds. We relished getting into the high-altitude desert's interior, and hopefully finding cooler air as we journeyed up to the popular town of San Pedro de Atacama. The eighth-floor apartment had a small balcony to enjoy the views, but as night fell, the now familiar sights and sounds of rioting reached up to us. Laser lights bounced and cut through the sky over the sprawling city, orange glows silhouetted far-off buildings and were accompanied by the rhythmic blue flashing lights of police and fire vehicles. It all seemed far away, until a short while later a noisy ad hoc band marched up the street below us. A mismatched collection of instruments and uniforms were loudly leading a hundred or so balaclava-clad protesters past our building. It was a spectacle to see and hard to turn away from, but in all honesty, we were genuinely fed up with it all. Pavements were being broken up before our eyes and backpacks filled with rocks and stones. A lot of the youths, the majority of the protesters we'd witnessed, certainly hadn't had their pensions or savings stolen by the government yet. They appeared to be out for the fight and to destroy for fun. We finished our drinks, skipped the usual night's stroll and instead, turned in early.

A Suzuki dealer was just a couple of miles from us and in the morning, despite feeling the need to save time, we opted to take a walk there, making up for last night's omittance. It was fruitful; they had a rear tyre I was happy with and could also fit it later in the day. There'd been another bike-related problem manifesting, albeit at a very leisurely pace, it seemed. The side-stand appeared to be ever so slowly bending, under the constant strain of often being parked up fully loaded. It didn't help that the aftermarket shock had raised the ride-height, but sometimes we needed to find a stone or piece of wood to put under the stand and I felt it was only a matter of time until the bike fell on its side! Along with the chain, I asked the mechanic if he could take a look at it.

In the meantime, though, we went on the hunt for something more permanent, something that would make a good prop and could live in my jacket pocket, preferably on a piece of string so that I could retrieve it once sat on the bike. Ambling around in the local vicinity, Selly pointed out a home department store, which I negatively dismissed as unlikely to be useful, but nevertheless joined her for a mooch around. Within minutes, Selly found me, triumphantly showing off a perfectly sized solid resin soap dish. To cap off its suitability, she pointed out how it was nicely scalloped to take the foot of the side-stand. I had to admit I wouldn't have thought of that and not to be outdone, sauntered off to equally and triumphantly discover some string-like string!

Dropping the bike in later, I pointed out the chain's slightly kinked links and missing O-rings to the mechanic. The parts manager weighed in, confirming they did have a chain of the correct pitch, but they didn't have any sprockets and the chain didn't have O-rings. Finally, it was also too long, so would need breaking, shortening and rejoining with a split-link. Bluntly, they told me my damaged chain was still the better option, rather than running their cheaper quality chain on my partly worn sprockets. I totally agreed, appreciating their honesty. They could have tried to persuade me to buy it and just taken my money!

We would try to nurse the chain until we could find a complete set. The mechanic confirmed my friend's thoughts; I needed to keep it oiled in the dry, but dry in the dirt, and it should last a few more thousand miles. This was all balanced off against a warning that if it didn't last, I probably wouldn't find one in either of our next two countries, Bolivia and Peru. There wasn't any solution offered for the side-stand, but with a pillar drill in the workshop, they put a neat hole through our new soap dish (all for my exceptional string find)!

The town of San Pedro de Atacama is a must-see desert stop-off for virtually all Atacama explorers. There's just so much of interest drawing in the visitors. The surrounding lands boast bizarre valleys, volcanoes, geysers and dunes, but for us in particular, it would also put us close to the Bolivian border we had chosen for our next crossing. We left the apartment early and figuring it would take us about four hours to reach San Pedro, hoped to complete most of the journey in the cooler morning air. Picking up Ruta 5, to lead us out of Antofagasta, we had our closest shave and another wake-up call to the current confusion out on the Chilean roads. Despite us coasting up a near empty two-lane highway, a car failed to slow for an intersection we were crossing. Being on the major road, I had assumed I had the right of way. Fortunately, we were both alert and slammed on, at speed, narrowly avoiding what could have been a nasty accident.

This was our last Chilean city. All had had either traffic lights or signs prolifically damaged, and I was happy to have survived them with the cost of just one rear tyre. The near accident was sobering but gradually put behind us as we steadily climbed into the beauty of the desert's interior. Our ears popped as the elevation rose to the 3,000-metre plus plateau, and we were rewarded with a new vista of salt flats, lagoons and ancient lava flows. Flamingos stalked the salty lagoons and guanaco could occasionally be seen nomadically searching for any greenery.

Turning onto Ruta 23, we felt and soaked up the region's remoteness. Little traffic passed us now and the seclusion of landlocked Bolivia beckoned to us. Its border was, according to our map, just 30 miles away. The whole scene was wondrous and otherworldly, and this was even before we had explored the offerings of San Pedro! The last few miles revealed tantalising glimpses of what lay magically in store for us. To the right sprawled 'Moon Valley', to our immediate left were crazy rock formations making up the 'Valley of the Dead' and behind the now visible town, several volcanoes towered up to 5,500 metres. It had been a beautiful but typically hot and sticky ride. The altitude and early start hadn't brought the relief of cooler temperatures we'd hoped for. We quickly learnt that after 9am, a switch gets flicked from 'cold' to 'hot', and back again shortly after sunset!

The altitude initially revealed itself as we breathlessly unloaded the bike, and then again as we ventured for an explore in the late afternoon's heat. Gentle hills had us breathing heavily, and energy seemed to get sapped far too quickly. Our planned route had us living between 2,500 and 4,800 metres for the next month or so. Acclimatisation would come, but we needed to ease it in sensibly. Over the first few days, we dropped all alcohol and switched to the local's remedy of either coca-leaf tea, or sweets made from the coca extract, combined with drinking plenty more water. The feeling of breathlessness never truly went away, but neither of us went on to suffer from headaches, or altitude sickness.

The town felt like a step back in time after the huge cities, or the high-rise holiday apartment buildings blighting the coastal towns. The first surprise was to find it so green, served by the Rio San Pedro, a river emanating from the easterly mountains and their volcanoes. It is a true oasis, flourishing within a bone-dry desert. Away from the main streets, many of the town's low buildings appeared to be either built of, or clad in, hard baked mud and echoed of passed-down knowledge and skills. It was another easy place to like and having booked to stay just three nights, we formulated a plan of what we wanted to squeeze in over the coming days. Tour companies tried to entice us with trips to dozens of incredible sights, from Bolivian salt flats to hiking up active volcanoes. Politely declining, it felt a relief to have our own maps, our own transport and our own timetable.

Moon Valley lay just a fifteen-minute ride away and the following morning we set off with cameras, water bottles and the now indispensable soap dish! It was refreshing to ride the bike unloaded again, especially as the road soon turned to dust and volcanic ash. I was beginning to really enjoy these challenges away from the asphalt. Beyond the ticket office, the road degraded to include sizeable potholes, crazy cobbled sections and then washboard corrugations for several miles. All was going well, until I heard a sharp snap. The combined screen, satnav and phone holder had dropped to a strange angle. Pulling over and investigating revealed that part of the front subframe had cracked through. The opposite side had a stress fracture running three-quarters through it, and if that went, we'd be in a bit of a mess.

We were on the verge of entering the first canyon and I wasn't for turning back! I pressed on at a crawl, receiving 'bonus thanks' from my rear seat videoing paparazzi. We had entered an unearthly landscape of craggy crevices running down from high peaks, dunes and lagoons of sand and salt. It's hard to put into words how the valley makes you feel. Sometimes you imagine you are part of a movie scene, sometimes just exhilarated and ecstatically happy to be experiencing it all so far from home. We climbed every marked path available, with the shadows, views and perspective wow-ing us as the angles changed. Tomorrow, we wanted to explore the Valley of the Dead and we puzzled over how this could possibly match what we had experienced today. They were just a few miles apart, yet said to be individually unique. Before we could enjoy that adventure, though, or any more for that matter, we needed to make some repairs.

Back at the hostel, by mid-afternoon, we first asked the owner if he knew any welders and he pointed up the street to one of his neighbours. That seemed too easy, and it was; nobody answered, or looked like they were even home. We hopped on the bike and took a wander to see what we could find ourselves. Initially looking for a hardware store, we chanced upon a mechanic working out on the street, fixing the electrics on an old campervan. I doubled back for a chat and asked if he had a welder, which of course he had, and he said he could get straight on it, once the van was fixed.

As he wrapped up the work on the camper, I set to, stripping down the front end and giving them clear access to the bike's broken sub-frame. In less than thirty minutes, the welding was complete and included additional bracing to both sides. Within the hour, the bike was back together and back at the hostel, all for ten dollars plus a healthy tip. I couldn't blame Suzuki for the failing; I had bolted a fairly heavy aftermarket accessory holder onto two small arms that ordinarily held just the plastic screen. It was all just too top-heavy with a satnav and mobile on it most of the time, and the couple of thousand miles off-tarmac had taken their toll. Contentedly admiring the ugly over-the-top agricultural repairs, I just knew this particular problem wasn't returning!

I woke Selly with fresh coffee early the next morning. I was being extra nice, for I had a plan I didn't think she would be too keen on but hoped she would agree to. Undoubtedly and unfortunately, it would involve getting proper cold, something she naturally shied away from. I explained that just an hour's ride from us, perched high at the end of a dirt track, sat the 5,050-metre ALMA observatory, and on the way to this we would pass very close to the near 6,000-metre Licancabur volcano. For a little sightseeing and a tick in the box, I wanted to ride to over a height of 5,000 metres and be back by lunchtime, for an afternoon at the Valley of the Dead. I think the volcano was the only attraction for Selly, but she agreed to placate my 5,000-metre tick-in-the-box and come along for the ride, excuse the pun!

We set off in the bright sunshine, wearing extra layers but not carrying the waterproofs. After 30 miles, the road steepened and Licancabur grew impressively in front of us, as did a bank of thunderously black clouds we couldn't previously see from San Pedro, now over 1,500 metres below us. Entering some slow hairpins, we came across our first llamas and it was so unexpected we just had to stop. To Selly's delight, the small herd was grazing right at the roadside. Each one seemed to be a different colour and had been individually decorated with bright ribbons around its neck. The volcano we were under straddled the Bolivian border and upon seeing the llamas, it felt like we had somehow unintentionally crossed it already. They were a joy to watch and for Selly this mini road trip had already been worth it. She could happily have turned back there and then.

I should have. Pressing on and under the blackened sky, we were beginning to shiver, having gone from thirty-three to seven degrees in well under an hour. Without warning, the sky suddenly unleashed pelting hail upon us and I frantically looked for a safe point to turn, but we were still caught amidst a series of hairpins! I was forced to continue on, until we reached a straight safe enough to spin the bike around. When I did stop, Selly asked suspiciously if I was still trying to reach 5,000 metres! I could hardly see the icy road ahead and assured her I just wanted to head down. She had had her altitude app running on the way up and informed me we were at 4,550 metres and 'hoped that would do for today'? Soaked, freezing and still being pelted by hailstones, I agreed it would definitely do for today and we gave up on ALMA!

Back again in San Pedro's heat, warmed up and fed, it felt like a different day as we headed out for sightseeing part two. In terms of being awed and fascinated, the afternoon's excursion to the Valley of the Dead panned out to be a similar experience, minus breaking the bike, to visiting Moon Valley. Within 100 metres of leaving the main road, we found ourselves within a narrow twisty canyon, on a track consisting mostly of fine powdery sand. The high red walls had us feeling that we had gone from a lunar to a Martian surface. It was just beautifully and hypnotically surreal. Wind and water-eroded monoliths rose out of sandy 'ponds', themselves bordered by caves, crevices and tiny slot canyons. Taken together, they formed a natural maze spreading out in all directions. It got a little more bizarre as we turned a corner to see dozens of people sandboarding down a huge dune, as others rode horses along the ridges and pathways. We couldn't get enough and again traipsed for several miles, venturing along trails from peak to peak, searching for ever more spectacular and unforgettable views. There was only one way to improve on all this, though. Our tickets allowed free entry to one of the panoramic viewpoints for this evening's sunset, and we weren't going to miss that!

That evening, we returned early enough to find an unobstructed viewpoint, having passed a snaking succession of small tour buses heading out to join us. It was a high vantage point and seeing the car park steadily filling up, we rightly guessed it was going to be a popular spectacle. The valleys below us were already carved by long finger-shadows, thrown down by the interlaced rows of jagged peaks. I heard Selly gasp, and as I turned around, she pointed out the Licancabur volcano. The storm we had encountered that morning had painted the last few hundred metres with a fresh coating of dazzling snow. Although dominant and impressive, the cap had been brown and dry since our arrival, but now it proudly stood out, as photogenic a view as a dormant volcano could be, or so we thought.

A smattering of clouds above the valleys added to the changing colours below us, and we romantically watched them turning from dark, to pink, to a deepening red. The minute the sun slipped gracefully below our horizon, the minibus drivers and guides promptly herded their guests back onboard. Minibus after minibus departed back down the hill and we felt a little sorry for the occupants. The sunset show was still producing its magic and the finale was yet to come. The sun might have finished setting on Moon Valley below us, but above and behind us the sun was now lighting up the higher peaks of the Valley of the Dead. The red rock formations looked like they could burst into flames, and the few remaining photographers were treated to a second sunset of fiery sky over unearthly brimstone. The grand finale, lasting less than a minute, arrived during the rapidly advancing darkness. In our neighbourhood, the sun had long since slipped below the horizon, but at over 5,900 metres, the volcano peak's snow was serenely picked out by the receding sunrays. It was a spectacular sight; all around was near dark, yet the fresh sprinkling of snow was briefly lit like a pure white shining beacon. Our smiles lasted all the way home, Selly hugging me for warmth as the night's chill grasped after us.

With hindsight, three nights weren't nearly enough time to exploit the region around San Pedro. We hadn't visited any of the geysers or other volcanoes in the vicinity, but what we had experienced proved magical and truly memorable. So, we found ourselves moving on from yet another place for which we could easily have found reasons to stay longer. It was already a theme running through the trip, and we understood how Steve, Janette and the Tiger had stretched their American adventure out to over five years, and counting. In San Pedro, we had connected and met up with a couple heading south, to exchange currencies with them. They had leftover *bolivianos* and we had left over Argentinian *pesos*, to swap and save us all a little commission. Chatting away, they gave us a tempting tip for a wild camping spot, right on our planned route and just 15 miles short of the Bolivian border.

It sounded almost too good to be true, a small collection of very old lakeside ruins, surrounded by mountains and volcanoes. They assured us there were some walls still standing and space enough to protect the bike and tent from the inevitable winds. The only road nearby served the border crossing, and after that closed, at 9pm, there wouldn't even be any passers-by. We were certainly interested enough to check it out and so, as we passed through the city of Calama, we stocked up on the necessary fuel, food and water. As we bore down on Bolivia, we couldn't help a little trepidation seeping in. A theme starting to run through the trip was being warned that every successive country was more dangerous, in some way, than the one we were currently enjoying! This started with warnings back in England, that the Argentinians would likely give us a hard time over the disputed Falkland Islands. This hadn't materialised, but now we were about to enter a country with a reputation for murderous truck and coach drivers, hell-bent on running us off treacherous roads. Apparently, if we survived Bolivia's drivers then we would find Peru to be even worse!

By late afternoon, we had lost count of how many lava fields and volcanoes we had passed, some with smoking fumaroles, which added a touch more excitement to the Jurassic landscape around us. Vehicles were all but absent and we watched the miles count down on the satnav, with eagerness to reach the lakeside ruins. We had steadily climbed throughout the day, from the 2,400 metres of San Pedro to over 3,500 metres and counting. It was another turning point in the trip; we were leaving behind the Atacama and heading up onto the Altiplano, our home for the next few weeks. At one point, the road sliced through the middle of a large dry salt flat, lined with 'salt mountains', waiting to be trucked off and processed. Within a few more miles, the lake we were looking for appeared both on the satnav and stretched out serenely in front of us. We'd found it.

We slowed to find the unobtrusive dirt track that would take us down to the ruins, barely visible from the road. The scrolling map married accurately with the narrow track and Selly spotted the low-lying stone walls, some 400 metres from the road. We instantly liked it and having plenty of daylight left, leisurely chose our spot and set up camp. Taking in our surroundings properly, we were awed at how simply breathtaking the views were. Herds of guanaco roamed around the lake's shores and in the shallow salty waters, flocks of bright pink flamingos trudged past us, all oblivious to their new neighbours.

The tent and bike were invisible from the quiet road, sheltered from the wind, and we had the place, as far as the eye could see, to ourselves. It felt wonderful and amazing to be here. Taking a three-sixty, we could only see either mountains or volcanoes, all snow-capped and majestic. Yes, we needed to say thank you for this tip-off. With the dinner cooked and the tent tidied up, we settled for what was shaping up to be another beautiful evening. Too far off to threaten us, a tight black storm cloud, spitting lightning, harassed a volcano and just to the right the sky was blue, but peppered with clouds turning to sunset pink. Behind us, the clouds were a bright yellow and Selly couldn't stop turning around to take in the bizarre and enchanting painting nature was gifting us. As the sun set, all the colours seemed to deepen in one direction and brighten in the other, before surrendering to the inky black of night. At almost 3,700 metres, the temperature was dropping quickly and so we retreated, sitting snugly in folding chairs, to sip *pisco* sours inside the tent's awning. Close to midnight, we turned off the tent light and stepped out to admire the sky. It was mind-blowing; at this altitude and with no lights in any direction, the stars were so bright, numerous and clear that you felt like it was an IMAX cinema screen above you. The Milky Way was thick across the sky, and we ended up stargazing for so many hours that we overslept the next morning!

Chapter Six

Bracing Bolivia

The plan had been to arrive at the Bolivian border by mid-morning at the latest, as our destination of Uyuni was served by an unpaved and uncared-for rough road, putting it kindly apparently. We eventually found the un-signposted border perfectly in time for the customs officials' two-hour lunch break. We were feeling so thankful for such a memorable last night in Chile, but not so thrilled at how our first day in Bolivia was shaping up. It was our fault for oversleeping, but the border guards sat around long after they had finished eating, seemingly taunting us as we baked in the unrelenting sun. There was nothing for it but to wait it out in any shade we could find! As the time dragged on past the posted lunch hours, Selly uncharacteristically lost her patience and gave the '*migración*' door a good pounding. Somebody was clearly woken from a post-lunch snooze and business returned to its normal, slow confusion of forms and photocopies of forms. As the passports gained a new stamp, the irritations and frustration gave way to feelings of exhilaration and curious expectation; we were through to our fifth country.

As pre-warned, the asphalt stayed behind in Chile and we bumped our way down a dusty broken road, replete with rocks, corrugations and potholes but devoid of signage and traffic. As if it was even possible, it felt remoter and wilder than Chile had. To our amusement, guanaco had been replaced by llamas and I had to agree, they were just so much cuter-looking. Selly would happily hug every one of them if they would let her! There's something so pleasing about seeing animals roaming freely. Llamas shared grazing ground with the occasional wild horses and drank from ponds popular with rheas and flocks of Andean geese. The abundant wildlife was heart-warming and made what could have been an arduous journey a surprising pleasure.

Although my eyes tended to be glued to the immediate road in front, Selly was forever searching for anything new to point out to me; fluffy baby llamas, a condor soaring above, or a fox prowling the plains. A hundred or so miles beyond the border, the road passed through some peculiar rock formations. They were reminiscent of the marble caves but carved out on the dry land around us. For sure, the soft curves and random shapes were enchanting but also fragile-looking, as many top-heavy formations sat upon time-weathered pillars. Disappointingly, a few had selfishly been carved with names and dates. For some people, sadly, a photograph just isn't enough. Our late start, delay at the border and many photo stops had stripped away the hours and we had to accept we wouldn't be arriving in daylight.

Asphalt finally greeted us at a lonesome roundabout, which led us falsely into the back streets of Uyuni. It was darker than it should be; no streetlights and no inviting restaurant or bar lights to guide us towards some civilisation. I stopped momentarily at a crossroads, looking left and right for signs of life, and was perturbed to see a line of soldiers, carrying automatic weapons striding purposely towards us. After the border guards, these were the first Bolivians we had come across and they were looking equally officious, but with a dose of menace thrown in for good measure. I thought we had left civil unrest behind us and was a little surprised to witness armed soldiers out on the suburban streets. The eight-man patrol passed us by without even a curious glance, walking just a couple of metres in front of these clearly lost and foreign overlanders. Wow, we had invisibility cloaks on; this could be fun!

Our fantasy crashed at the first hotel; we were both clearly seen and then denied a room, due to it already being full. The night manager kindly made a phone call to another hotel, which was also full, but then gave us the WiFi password so we could try searching ourselves. Finding very little available, it appeared we weren't alone in wanting to visit the popular Uyuni salt flats. Scribbled on a piece of paper, he then handed us a tip for the poshest hotel in town, adding convincingly that it boasted hot showers, and breakfast would be included. Well, beggars can't be choosers, can they!

Overnight, it rained hard, very hard, and as we finished our omelettes and coffee, we could see it was still drizzling under low grey clouds. It thwarted our eagerness to get out and onto the salt flats; they were so grand and the photo opportunities so iconic that if necessary, I was prepared to wait days for the skies to clear. Instead, we went in search of fuel, easing gingerly through flooded streets that almost certainly hid potholes. There weren't any culverts to drain away the muddy waters, just dips at the junctions. The depth varied from 'wetting the soles of my boots' to 'filling them completely'! As we threaded our way through the town, I could now see the fuel station across another flooded junction, which had a group of bystanders warning us against trying, but we were so close! Their morning's entertainment had obviously been provided by cars attempting, and then getting stranded in the deeper water. As I paused to take stock, Selly hopped off without a word and waded in to check the depth. Testing the middle and both sides, she found a narrow track, tight up against one of the invisible submerged kerbs. It looked like my boots would be refilled again, but passable all the same!

Despite denying them of any new drama, the onlookers were on the verge of applauding Selly for wading ahead and guiding me through the dirty brown floodwaters, almost up to her knees and as predicted, filling my boots. Now with a full tank of weak 85 octane, the highest they had, we found a circuitous slightly better route back to the hotel. Locking up the filthy bike, we grabbed umbrellas and walked the town from end to end. A drab town at best, exploring Uyuni in heavy drizzle wasn't a fulfilling experience. There wasn't any evidence that it had tried to capitalise on having one of nature's most spectacular locations on its doorstep. Tourists flocked here, but where had all the wealth gone?

The people were lovely, though, and we browsed through the street markets, chatting to stall holders and tentatively guessing at what the smaller cuts of meat being grilled on BBQs might be. Selly was an avid cat lover, and I think if she'd witnessed a cat being cooked before her eyes, her heart would simply stop. Our research had warned us guinea pigs and cats were still eaten in many South American countries, but one day I'd excitedly told Selly of a cat festival celebrated annually in Peru. Digging deeper, her excitement turned to horror upon discovering it was actually a culinary cat-eating festival. We wouldn't be attending!

There seemed to be a high indigenous population here. Many townsfolk wore traditional dress, men in their ponchos and wellington boots and the women with pleated skirts, colourful shawls and bowler hats. It felt like a step back in time after the more prosperous countries we'd passed through, but a pleasant one all the same. Bolivia was a country we had been so excited to visit, and we weren't going to let a bout of miserable weather dampen our enthusiasm.

With a brighter late-afternoon sky, we tried again for the flats and just a few miles out of the town, the roads promisingly started to dry out. The same couldn't be said for the salt when we arrived, though. The unpaved road leading to the flats looked like the magnified surface of a dimpled golf ball, with each dimple holding about 20 litres of thick muddy 'water'. We bounced along this for a good 6 or 7 miles, before we found ourselves surrounded by, and unnaturally riding on, pure salt. I felt reassured that the bike had recently acquired a semi-protective layer of filth and grime, with the salt being just another reason why it should be washed thoroughly at the earliest opportunity. In an ideal world, I'd hoped for a centimetre of surface water, thus allowing us to ride out into the emptiness and take a myriad of clever 'reflection' shots. The reality was closer to 10 centimetres, turned into a mushy and soggy sand-like texture by streams of tourist-filled 4x4 vehicles pressing on across the random tracks.

It wasn't quite how we imagined it to be, but nevertheless we rode out as far as we dared and then carefully parked the bike up, on its soap dish! I didn't want to spend the rest of the trip fixing electrical or corrosion problems, but we'd ridden a long way for this moment and wanted some nice memento photos. At almost twenty-five times the size of Bonneville's, Uyuni's salt flats are just staggering and beautifully surreal. They can turn any inept or amateur photographer into a genius, and we passed the time glued behind our lenses, playing with perspectives and the perfect reflections. I was so thankful now that we did have clouds drifting overhead; they made the photos so much more fun, adding depth and colours that a clear sky would have denied us.

It was easy to have a lot of fun and we walked miles soaking up the surrealness of the place. The reflections were so perfect that looking at the photos, it was possible to flip them upside down and you would be hard pressed to know it (us and bike photos aside)! We stayed out on the flats for the sunset and then backtracked to a roadside 'salt museum' we'd passed earlier. Outside, it displayed all sorts of sculptures carved from – you guessed it – salt, even including a full-sized car. The building was entirely made of salt blocks and in the gift shop we purchased a colourful llama doll, allegedly made from llama wool (not salt this time!) and with uncontained originality, I had to name it Salty. I had plans for it and immediately put Salty to work dampening the satnav 'bounce', by ramming him/her down between the screen and the back of the plastic dash!

There was only one other place we wanted to see before departing Uyuni: its hyped-up train graveyard. It was only a few minutes' ride from the centre of the town, but even so, we wished we hadn't bothered. The rusted collection of steam engines and carriages had received the worst kind of graffiti vandalism, nothing artful, just inane scribblings that left you feeling annoyed. Litter blew around within the open-air museum and it was clear the machines had been stripped bare over the decades by souvenir hunters. It was so sad-looking and derelict that neither of us even took a photo. Oh well, you can't win them all.

Bolivia was far off the PAH, but a diversion we were very happy and excited to be making. Compromises had to be made, though. As alluring as it was, we just didn't have the spare time to venture further east, to the Amazon and its indigenous villages. The narrow weather window for northern Alaska was never far from our minds and we had to pick and choose carefully the diversions we made. La Paz was a must for us and was now just 320 miles to our north. Unsure of the road conditions, we would break the journey up with an overnight stop in the city of Oruro. After the experience of the border road, this one turned out to be surprisingly good. None of the truck drivers tried to kill us, or even harass us, and we made good time, stopping only for a few more obligatory llama photos.

Our views of the Altiplano were hampered by intermittent rain, falling from the persistently low-hanging clouds, and with the altitude hovering around 3,700 metres, it made for a chilly ride. The accommodation promised warm showers, and reaching the outskirts of Oruro was a relief. Getting into the town wasn't! It seemed to be the epicentre of minibuses and trucks missing exhaust pipes, and we coughed and spluttered our way down choked (literally!) streets towards the centre. I couldn't imagine living in this polluted air; it was already thin enough and lacking precious oxygen. Making our way down a bustling main road, we were greeted by a strange sight. A shell of a car, propped on wooden blocks and masked off, was being sprayed within a single parking space, sandwiched between shoppers and traffic, who obliviously cruised by. The sprayer had on a head-to-toe paper suit and face mask, a compressor running on the pavement, and was filling the surrounding air with clouds of paint fumes, all as if it was a perfectly normal endeavour!

The receptionist checking us in assured us hot water was available and handed us both the key and a TV remote. It was a cheap but spacious modern-looking room. Clearly, more money had been spent on the large flat-screen TV than the hot-water system, though. Selly informed me from the bathroom that we only had cold water, and I guessed it was something we should start getting used to from now on. As she let the water run, in the hope of extracting a little more heat, I channel-hopped in the hope of finding something in English. Out of seemingly hundreds of channels, I dropped on CNN. It was the first news I'd seen in weeks. The headlines scrolling along the bottom of the screen, repeated every minute or so, gave the news that a new SARS-like virus had been detected in China. Specifically, there was a large outbreak being reported in a place called Wuhan. I hadn't heard of it and it seemed an awfully long way away. Today was the 20th of January and I had absolutely no idea how significant this news would later become. With Selly now out of the shower, I turned off the TV and pretty much forgot about it. Oruro couldn't hold us; with just 130 miles left to reach La Paz, we elected to turn in early and leave early.

Suburbia and its solid congestion started approximately 20 miles outside of the capital. It had been a similarly dispiriting ride to yesterday's. With the scenery mostly concealed behind the same low grey clouds, we weren't getting to see much of the Bolivian landscape. The traffic had steadily increased as we reached the outskirts, until the three-lane highway was choked with five lanes worth of traffic. Coaches now competed with minibuses, who competed with taxis and tuk-tuks for the pedestrian trade. Everybody got papped at by everything with wheels. Each set of traffic lights and every wide speed bump had been ruefully utilised as a vendor's opportunity to sell drinks, prepared fruits, or *empanadas*. Under less stressful conditions, I would have happily enjoyed all three!

Some of the speed bumps were so large they had their own potholes and I had to dodge those, plus the persistent vendors, whilst watching my mirrors for the traffic that didn't slow at all, for anything. At over 3,500 metres, we had arrived at the world's highest capital, but we weren't home yet. Sandwiched amidst the crawling traffic, we edged towards the rim of the huge bowl the city lies within. Thankfully, the satnav had found the street we were accommodated on, relieving me of the added stress of having to try and follow the mostly obscured road signs. It was hard work still, and we had gained just 10 miles over the last hour. As we finally reached the rim and looked out across the huge city, I was amazed to see it would be tight mountain-like hairpin roads leading the way down. It was steep, busy and the speed bumps had grown in both height and number to calm the crazier drivers. To make things a little more interesting, a storm unloaded on us with thunder, lightning and torrential rain, turning the twisting road into a fast-running river. It had already been a stressful ride in, but traffic still tried to overtake, or cut us up at all the wrong times. It was truly atrocious weather and I was getting anxious for the journey just to be over. The run down was so steep in places that I hardly believed we were in a city. Even with ABS, I found myself gingerly using the brakes over the wide slippery speed bumps.

To cap it off, I'd followed the satnav to the wrong street. Unbeknown to me, there were two with almost identical names, and I'd selected the wrong one, doggedly following the satnav, despite Selly warning me she was convinced we were headed in the wrong direction. The night before, she had downloaded offline maps for the city, found the accommodation on her phone and was rightly adamant the satnav was taking us the wrong way. Spinning the bike around, I was now fuming with myself, fuming with the unforgiving traffic and fuming with the dismal weather. I could sense she was annoyed with me being so obstinate, and so we continued in awkward silence (not that we had intercoms)! It wouldn't be anything lasting between us, rarely had we ever argued, and agreeing to disagree before raising voices was the norm. Nevertheless, I was content to have the traffic to curse and deal with rather than discuss my stubbornness!

It took a further two exasperating hours to backtrack and find the right street, but the heady relief we both felt upon parking up outside the accommodation had already cleared the air between us. What could we say anyway? Selly knew I could be stubborn, and I knew I could be stubborn. There was never any malice intended and I guess she just wished I would listen more often.

As if 3,600 metres wasn't breath-stealing enough, we were shown up to the twelfth-floor roof terrace! It was a pretty spectacular sight; the entire basin of the city spread out before us and we could clearly see the ongoing storm raging over on the far side. The Mi Teleférico cable cars fanned out, like a living web above the city's buildings, and even disappeared up into the clouds on one side. We couldn't wait to try them and give the riding a break. I felt like I needed a few days off, just to get over that journey in! From our vantage point, I could see the tight hairpins and the painfully convoluted route we'd taken across the city. The last few miles had involved coming back uphill again, with both the bike and myself struggling with the endless hill starts, caused by the stop-start traffic. This must be a great city to sell and fit clutches in, I mused, as I tried my best to protect ours! Thoroughly knackered, we managed little more than a walk to a supermarket and back, and then retired for lukewarm showers, food and a comfy couch. The day had squarely beat us.

Stretching over 20 miles and consisting of ten differently coloured lines, La Paz's cable car system is its crowning jewel. Subways might be quicker and more convenient but are dull compared to the feeling of floating silently and serenely above the hustle and bustle of a busy capital; it's just so very satisfying. With a bird's-eye view, you see everything, privacy having been stripped away as you curiously peer into once-hidden gardens, over rooftops and even into living rooms, now presented at eye level as you glide between the high-rises. The congestion and commotions down below, the confrontations at junctions and roundabouts had become an entertaining spectacle rather than the arduous grind imposed down at street level. Oh, those horrors of yesterday, owned today by those below!

The cable car tickets are ridiculously cheap and with a simple-to-follow map, we set out to cover as many lines as we could on that first full day, whilst hopping off at any intriguing stops. With ears popping, the Azul line carried us up a sharp 400-metre ascent, to almost 4,100 metres and up onto the Altiplano plateau once more. We had arrived at the neighbouring city of El Alto, famous for its lengthy indigenous street markets. We alighted and spent several happy hours nosing and scouting around the mile-long frenetic market. With its street bands, street food and eclectic mix of merchandise, it was all quite entertaining and fascinating. Car engines and truck axles sat alongside food stalls and pop-up bars. Parrots and llamas vied for attention amongst acres of cheap Chinese products, competing for sales alongside antiques, or myriads of beautifully hand-woven and hand-carved Andean mementoes. There were many nice artefacts, but our loaded bike would have to make do with the odd fridge magnet, or a pannier sticker.

The following morning, we ventured up early onto the roof terrace, for both the sunrise and another La Paz spectacle. There was a surreal and unique sight that could often be witnessed at this early hour and we were in luck. Before the sun had time to burn it off, the upper rim of the city was shrouded, like a halo, in ground-hogging cloud. Above us was clear sky, but we could watch the higher traffic and cable cars disappearing into the clouds hugging the city's rim. It was a memorable sight and a pleasing start to the day. You could feel the city awakening and watch the early commuters, mostly young army conscripts, fan out across the city on the silent cable cars.

After a light breakfast, we left the building to join them. The day turned into a repeat of yesterday, but on a selection of new cable car lines, and by the end of the day we had marvelled and enjoyed travelling on all but the shortest line. Never before had I felt like I had seen a capital so completely, and in just two days! Remarkable considering it's a sprawling capital so challenged by altitude and steepness. Our time had quite literally flown by and we found ourselves repacking to leave the world's highest capital for the world's highest lake.

To reach Lake Titicaca, we first had to extract ourselves from the city's gridlocked central streets and then up the steep, busy mountainside hairpins. I rightly hadn't looked forward to it and again felt anxious knowing that we not only had La Paz to exit, but also the sprawling traffic-choked city of El Alto, before we could reach the highway taking us out towards the lake. On tarmac, I would consider myself a fairly competent and experienced rider, but have to admit it was still a struggle to get the heavily loaded bike out of the capital. We were reduced to a slow-moving stop-start crawl, with the roads leading to El Alto being the steepest out of the city. I worried we were damaging the clutch, constantly hill-starting, and now wished we had left at 5 am instead of a lazy 8 am! Eventually, though, after several daunting hours, we had freed ourselves, left both cities behind and once again found ourselves on a surprisingly quiet highway.

The sun had reappeared just in time for our first sighting of the lake, lighting it up an inviting deep blue. We pulled over at a viewpoint and soaked in the unspoilt panorama of jagged shorelines, backdropped by snowy mountains and cultivated fields. From our vantage point of 4,200 metres, we could still only see a small portion of the Incas' supposed birthplace. It had tantalised us years before, when planning and researching this part of the trip. The numbers hint at how impressive the region and lake are. Sitting at an altitude of just over 3,800 metres and almost 125 miles long, its irregular craggy shoreline stretches over 700 miles in length. It was a heart-warming and enticing vista, especially after the cheerless experience that morning. We felt transported, from concrete to meadow, and it was hard to take in this feeling of seclusion, so close to La Paz. I was about to find out why this highway was so empty!

The road abruptly ended at the quayside of a tiny town, San Pedro de Tiqiuna, split in half by the 800-metre width of the Tiqiuna Strait. To reach the western side of the town, and our night-stop in Copacabana, we would need to cross the strait on one of the dilapidated wooden barges vying for the sparse trade. Approximately 20 metres long and about 6 metres wide, they sat low in the water and from a distance would look nothing more than floating planks, bobbing in the water. I was bemused; the deck of the one waiting to fill and leave was full of holes and gaps. A short coach was parked at the front, with a car behind that, leaving the stern sitting higher than the sloping loading ramp. I would need a run-up to bounce on board, avoiding the deck gaps, and then try to edge in beside the car. None of the barges were 'drive-on drive-off' and at the opposite side I would have to somehow get off backwards. It all looked and felt a little daunting.

A puntsman, 5-metre pole in hand, stood watching me watching him. I guess he was used to seeing the bemused looks on bikers' faces, or was it just my face, I wondered! Selly had hopped off to go and take a closer look at the step-up onto the barge and with confidence that I hoped wasn't misplaced, came back and reassuringly told me I should be able to get the bike on.

"What about getting it off again?" I posed.

"Well, there's a coachful of people to help. They won't be going anywhere until we're off!" she quite rightly stated!

The puntsman was still staring and I could delay no longer. With Selly guiding, I took a run-up and bounced the bike up onto the deck, missing both the car and a wheel-eating gap by mere centimetres. The puntsman wasted no time pushing us away from the ramp and into slightly deeper water where, thankfully, a small hidden motor took over for the crossing. With no chocks or ropes available, I had to remain seated on the bike to balance it. An easy task at first, but as we progressed out into the middle of the strait, the wind and waves picked up and a strange sensation emerged beneath me. My feet began to 'pedal' and looking down I could see each foot was firmly sat on different planks. Against the perpendicular waves, the barge was buckling and twisting along its length, exasperated by the gently rocking coach. My feet were pedalling up and down in a strange fashion as I also see-sawed from left to right. It felt like invisible hands were unhelpfully pulling at the bike and rhythmically pushing up on my boots.

It was a most peculiar crossing and I was quite relieved to finally feel the friction of wood grinding up against a concrete ramp. I hardly had time to react before dock and deckhands skilfully manoeuvred me backwards off the barge, and even uphill to a point where I could thumb the starter and park up out of the way. The drama of getting off had only existed in my head. It might have been my first crossing of the Tiqiuna Strait, but they were all dab hands and I gratefully tipped each one of them.

The rest of the ride to Copacabana was just wonderfully scenic and surprisingly hot, considering the altitude. We cruised along in sheer contentment, soaking up beautiful rolling views of the shimmering lake and surrounding mountains. Young boys waved as they shepherded herds of llamas and in turn, we gestured to the many locals we passed on carts drawn by ox, horse, or donkey. We eagerly embraced this rural transformation as a necessary stepping stone to our next destination: the agrarian Peru.

The two halves of the day's ride just couldn't have been more polar and we weren't particularly ready to get off the bike when we found ourselves already in Copacabana, and outside the B&B. Large wooden gates were opened up to reveal a cheerful and colourfully muralled inner courtyard, where we were directed to park up for the night. I'm not sure if I added to the cosy ambiance or brought the place down a peg or two as I strung our washing line from the bike to a nearby wall and hung out my newly hand-washed laundry!

The town is both a place of pilgrimage and a magnet for those wanting to explore the nearby 'Sun' and 'Moon' islands, with their own intriguing Inca ruins. We had arrived on a Friday, the 24th of January, and sure enough, another of the many festivals the town is famous for was in full swing. The plaza around the beautiful sixteenth century-basilica was full of stalls selling bags of petals, or coca leaves, flower garlands and other offerings for the Andean deity, Pachamama. Or was it all for the patron saint of Bolivia, and the shrine to the 'Virgen of Copacabana'? Turns out it was mostly for the start of a two-week long festival, celebrating the god of abundance, Ekeko, where people bought miniatures of items they desired in life. I don't think the people needed much of an excuse to celebrate here and I had the feeling, as we strolled on a carpet of fresh flower petals, that the pilgrimage stalls and businesses around the town were a colourful year-round festival in themselves.

Exploring down to the lakeside, we found the less religious tourists, drinking in cafés and restaurants, or scrutinising the many information boards, offering boat trips out onto Titicaca and its numerous islands. We settled to enjoy sundowner cocktails, people-watch and catch up on news flowing to us through the borrowed internet. An article caught my eye about China again. Just yesterday, they had locked down the entire province of Hubei, where Wuhan was the capital. A staggering eleven million people had been interned with no freedom to travel, all due to this new threat they were calling a coronavirus. The news conveyed a sense of full-on panic over there, with differing reports on the number of deaths. Again, it just seemed an awfully long way away from our sunset view of the peaceful lake and the majestic Andes. In that moment, I felt we were almost sitting on top of the world, one far away from its troubles and new viruses.

Chapter Seven

Problems in Plightful Peru!

Our more immediate thoughts were on crossing into Peru and what condition we would find the roads in. Dauri had warned us it had been raining a lot during his passage through the country and that we should stick to the main roads, if we could. A visit to Machu Picchu was at the top of our 'Peru list', but at that stage I didn't even know if the main roads would get us all the way there.

It was just a short hop to the border in the morning and upon parking up, we felt a now familiar mix of both excitement and restrained frustration. The procedures were never quite the same; sometimes we needed certain photocopies and sometimes not, sometimes photos of the chassis number would need to be printed off, and sometimes nothing more was required than a scrutiny of the original documents. Kasani proved to be a friendlier affair and after submitting to half-hearted inspections of the bike, luggage and our documents, I was led into an air-conditioned office, festooned with fellow travellers' stickers. The customs officer sat behind his desk, courteously preparing our import certificate as I perused the stickers of those that had gone before us, plastered all over the back of his computer screen and around the walls behind him. Formalities completed, we grabbed photos of the bike in front of the 'Welcome to Peru' sign and with new stamps in our passports, continued on around the lake towards the city of Puno.

Peru's landscape perfectly mirrored the last 50 miles on the Bolivian side and it was hard, so far, to distinguish the two countries apart. Every family here seemed to own pigs, though, and each little village we passed through had several of them tied individually on ropes, contentedly grazing either in yards, or at the roadsides. If it wasn't pigs then it was cows, horses, or donkeys, tethered a few metres apart and munching crop circles out of the roadside vegetation. Out on the hillsides, llamas had been joined by our first sightings of alpacas, who stared at us curiously, as we stared back likewise. Shepherds wore the same indigenous dress as in Bolivia, and I searched harder for the smaller tell-tale signs that we were indeed in a different country. Entering Puno revealed a subtle clue; a whole street seemed to be cooking guinea pigs. Sign after sign advertised 'cuy', alongside special roasting machines, slowly cooking half a dozen whole animals at a time. They were unmistakable as guinea pigs and as a famous national dish, this was something we would soon get used to seeing, if not actually get around to trying!

We parked up, leaving the bike conveniently outside of, and under the watchful gaze of, the main tourist police station and found a lovely courtyard café. Sitting for a spot of lunch, I just couldn't believe how warm and sunny it was. I had always imagined we would be freezing around this lake, but thankfully, it just wasn't so. A summer's day in England would struggle to be as pleasant!

In between hostels, we just weren't expecting to find WiFi so easily and freely available anymore, and thus, once fed and watered, we sauntered off into town to pick up a local SIM card and resume our journey. Prematurely resume our journey, that is.

I still don't know why I'd forgotten – there were enough tourists around to remind me – but we were supposed to stay in Puno long enough to take a trip out to the famous 'floating islands'. There's even accommodation available on some of them, giving you the opportunity to live and stay with local indigenous families. If I'd consulted it, I would have seen it was even highlighted within our plan! As it turned out, it wasn't until a couple of days later and hundreds of miles away that I realised I'd messed up, and it would be too far out of our way to backtrack. However annoyed I was with myself, the Uros islands, a chain of permanently inhabited floating reed beds, would have to wait for another time. We had inadvertently skipped them for a night-stop by the pre-Inca ruins of Sillustani, which lay roughly on our route to the famous Colca Canyon. When I admitted to Selly I had completely forgotten about the Uros islands, she was unperturbed.

"Mark, we don't have time to see everything, but everything we do see will be new to us anyway!"

It was the right attitude to have, and one I needed to adopt. Especially as it wouldn't be too much longer before I managed to engineer a similar mishap!

We had aspirations to camp that evening and before leaving Puno had stocked up on extra water, fruit and bread, etc. As the lake receded behind us, the roads became narrower with each successive turn-off, until we rode along a paved single-track route through the rolling countryside. Chocolate-box quaint stone farmhouses peppered the agricultural landscape, encompassed by neat stone walls and intricate arches. They were peculiar for two reasons: the tops of the perimeter walls and arches, like the farmhouse roofs, were often delicately thatched, and on every arch sat shiny ceramic bulls, cows, or chicken ornaments. We pulled over at one sitting close to the road and pulled out a camera as watchful alpacas grazed out the front. We must have been seen, as a bowler-hatted indigenous lady came out and beckoned us over with a cheery smile.

Selly was chuffed to be introduced to each of the alpacas by name. It was clear they were looked upon as the lady's pets and best friends. Having long ago lost her husband, she lived alone, a mainly sustenance lifestyle, selling alpaca wool and any excess fruit and vegetables she'd grown. Selly asked about the two ceramic bulls adorning the arch we were stood under, and we learned they had been 'good luck' gifts, given when the house was first built. With our eyes now opened, we saw them on almost every building we passed. Under the clear sky and lowering sun, we remarked what a beautiful house and setting the lady lived in, but as we said our goodbyes, I could only imagine how harsh it must be when the weather turns treacherous. We would have to wait a whole twenty-four hours to find that out for ourselves!

We continued on to another traditional farmhouse, one that advertised camping and was conveniently situated just a few miles short of the Sillustani archaeological site. The dwelling looked identical to the one we had just left, except the lady owning this one was much more entrepreneurial. Squeezed into her home was an interesting single-room working museum, exhibiting wooden looms, displays of authentic hand tools and wools in different stages of production. Leading off from this was a small gift shop, where the products of her labour could be purchased. Again, we were introduced to friendly llamas and alpacas, before being shown into the inner cobbled courtyard and a stone enclosure housing several scampering guinea pigs.

They were happily fattening up on vegetable scraps and somehow, I doubted these were being reared for pets. Selly agreed and wanted to buy them all and free them, but I think they would have run straight back to where they were getting fed and housed!

The light was waning and all our attempts to gain permission to put the tent up somewhere were being brushed off. Instead of a plot of ground, we kept being shown a bare mud-walled and thatched-roof room. It was certainly quirky, a compacted mud floor, gaps in the roof for stargazing and decorated with a single light bulb and plug socket. How could we refuse? We knew the tent would have been more comfortable, but this was going to be a unique experience and would put a little extra income into her pocket. We agreed to take it. I sat on the thin, prickly straw mattress, which smelt as if the animals had recently been evicted to make room for us, and scoured through the mismatched provisions we'd picked up earlier. A father to son handed-down delicacy, Selly declined sharing the banana sandwiches I proudly produced and instead dunked sweet biscuits into sweet coffee. Fearing what would in turn feast on us (and lacking any heating of course!) we fitfully slept fully clothed, drifting off listening to the noises of the various animals brought into the courtyard overnight.

Wanting to be at the ruins for when they opened, we rose early and got the host's permission to temporarily leave our packed belongings in the sty... sorry... room. It was a wonderfully peaceful ride down to Lago Umayo and the peninsula's already impressive ruins. Other than roaming animals, the road was completely empty, and we passed large glass-like ponds full of ducks, geese and other waterfowl enjoying the blue sky and warming air. We were directed to an empty car park, sold tickets and pointed past still-closed souvenir shacks to a footpath leading to the site's entrance. The strange towering cylindrical tombs could be spotted well before arriving, but now we were underneath them we could truly appreciate their size and intricacy.

Sillustani was effectively an ancient burial site, with upright tomb-towers tapering up to 12 metres in height. Despite pre-dating the Incan empire, the huge stones used to build each tower had been cut in an Incan fashion. No two stones were alike, yet so perfectly carved that you couldn't slide a playing card between the joints. Being totally alone on this symbolic hilltop was a magical feeling. It was just so tranquil, and we explored every pathway, marvelling at the scenery, nature and the dozens of tombs dotted around us. A hushed silence always seems to blanket places of burial and it was no different here, especially magnified by our solitary occupancy. Only by straining could we hear the distant squawks of the waterbirds far below us. As we descended hours later, the first of the minibuses were now arriving from Puno and we slowly crossed paths with eager tourists as we browsed the now open shops and stalls. Stopping to admire some of the beautifully handmade woollen hats, we had to point over to the bike and explain that, as nice as they were, we just didn't have the room to purchase and carry them. Selly settled on a miniature alpaca-wool alpaca, to accompany Salty, our llama-wool llama. I promptly rammed him/her behind the screen and nose to nose with Salty.

"Aah, look, they're kissing!" suggested Selly, suddenly feeling all romantic.

It was late morning by the time we were packed up and ready to say goodbye to the guinea pig farmhouse. The sky was a vast sea of blue, the temperature unbelievably almost thirty degrees, and both the satnav and the phone agreed it was 190 miles and just under five hours to reach our next Peruvian destination, Colca Canyon. Having already enjoyed an unforgettable morning, we set off in high spirits and high confidence that we'd be at the canyon well before sundown. As I dropped the bike into gear, I wasn't entirely sure which way up the road the maps were trying to point me and decided to just set off with my gut instinct and see if we were correct.

This seemingly innocuous decision would set off a chain of events that would dog us pitifully and punish us for the rest of the day. Within a few hundred metres, it seemed I'd bet on the wrong direction, but as the satnav screen flipped around, it was already offering to reroute us. The mobile was still showing a preference to double back, but as the satnav displayed an almost identical time and distance, I didn't see the point in turning around and pressed on with the alternative route.

By the time we reached the first turning, both maps had aligned and agreed to the new route and we found ourselves on a paved but less-cared-for minor track. Several miles down, at the next T-junction, the road degraded to an unpaved but compacted dirt track. Oh well, it is rural Peru, what else should we expect? The following junction showed only as a bend on the satnav, but the road deteriorated once more, to one of annoying corrugations and potholes that started to significantly slow our progress. We had been steadily climbing and in unison, the weather was also beginning to deteriorate. The blue sky was becoming overcast, with even darker clouds lining the horizon. As we started to feel colder and checked the app, our altitude showed we were now over 4,300 metres. A little further on, we lost first the 3G internet and then the mobile signal entirely. We were down to the map in the tank bag and the satnav, which started to do strange things, sometimes telling us we were riding in a lake, or were way out in a field, etc., and I was losing confidence in it. We were on some kind of mountain pass, not a main pass for sure as we hadn't seen a vehicle or a road sign for over an hour. It wasn't worrying at this stage, but not knowing if we were even headed in the right direction still was definitely becoming frustrating.

We pressed on in the hope the satnav would get a grip, or the road would improve, or we'd come across a reliable landmark we could use to cross-check against the hardcopy map. None of these materialised and instead things just went downhill, both metaphorically and literally! Arriving at an unsigned fork in the dirt track, we paused to best guess the way. Both seemed equally rutted and used, but venturing left felt like the general direction we should be heading in. It also looked to veer downhill for the first time in hours and so we set off down a muddy, rutted single track, skirting round boulders and potholes as best we could for mile after mile.

The clue to our destination should have been the amount of small streams, either crossing our track or sometimes running down the sides of it. I rounded a bend to be faced with a wide and fast-running bridgeless river, swelled by recent storms and with a makeshift crossing point now a quagmire of boulders and swirling eddies. It was a deflating sight and to add to our sinking feelings, lightning lit the sky across the far side, letting us know that if we did find a way across, we were going to get wet! I began to have flashbacks to when we had nearly got lost and run out of fuel, months before on Argentina's Peninsular Valdés.

I was still making silly mistakes, if new ones! Only yesterday we had purchased a SIM card, but I hadn't gotten round to downloading offline maps to the phone. As we set off earlier today and were being rerouted, I should have checked out the new route properly instead of being lulled by the great weather and the similar travel times. Instead, I had blindly followed the satnav. Our original route would have taken us through two towns, where I was confident we'd be able to find fuel in either of them. Rather than checking, I'd assumed that we'd still transit through at least one of these. We had filled up yesterday in Puno, had gone via the Sillustani ruins and now I wasn't sure where we were, or when we might find our next fuel! The final mistake: I was to set off that day with just water and a packet of biscuits! What had earlier appeared to be a four-to-five-hour ride in the sunshine, through towns in which we could surely find food, rest and fuel, had descended into something entirely different. Had I learnt anything so far on this trip? I wondered.

One thing was immediately definite: we weren't getting across this river just here and we would have to struggle back up the slippery track to the fork and reassess. Selly had to get off and help push us through some of the stream crossings. Coming downhill, I could just slip and slide, but uphill was far trickier as the rear lost grip and spun on the wet boulders. Finally reaching the fork, knackered, dirty and hungry, we discussed our thoughts over biscuits and water. Selly was for turning back, until we at least got a mobile signal again, but I was sure the right fork would lead us to some kind of bridge and convinced her to give it a try. It wasn't an easy option for either of us. Jet-black clouds and lightning continued to beckon us to find a way over, but we seemed to be losing more and more time. The cold and altitude were fogging our thoughts, our ability to make joint decisions.

"What makes you think a bridge is going to be down there?" Selly asked, looking dubiously down the fork's remaining track.

"All these old wheel ruts? When the river crossing's unusable, there must surely be an alternative close by, a bridge of some sort?" I could only instinctively guess.

Agreeing to give it a try, we descended the right fork and tackled similarly tight turns, slid through small tributaries and avoided wheel-swallowing muddy potholes. I rode on with fingers crossed we'd be mercifully rewarded and wouldn't have to struggle back up this mess once more.

It was there. Nothing fancy, but it was there! Spanning a narrow canyon, a simple strip of concrete masqueraded as a bridge and led the way to a steep-looking sandy bank. If I made it up the sandbank, then we'd be back on the dirt track, now visible beyond it. Buoyed up by the sight of the bridge, on which Selly was now stood, I gunned across it and used the momentum to slither up the sand and up onto firmer ground. I was suddenly exhilarated and beaming. We were still lost, cold, breathless and getting frustrated, but we were over the river and still in one piece.

With stubbornly numbed fingertips, I scrutinised the map. Unfortunately, the scale wasn't detailed enough to show either this bridge or the river. At least we weren't going back, though, and the clouds were so happy for us they started to cry with joy; winner. We hurriedly put on extra layers and over them, our waterproofs. What a day this was turning into! We pushed onwards and as the potholes brimmed with water and the muddy track became even more slippery, we were forced to slow further still. Looking down at the dash, I couldn't believe we had gone from this morning's thirty degrees to under ten (with the wind, it felt like five!)! We seemed to have finally stopped climbing, though I guessed we must be around 4,500 metres by now, and we were up on some kind of flat, featureless plateau.

As if things couldn't take a turn for the worse, the landscape ahead was now pure white. We soon found ourselves riding on a fresh thick carpet of hail that, floating on the water-filled potholes, masked them perfectly. We had risen high enough to meet the ground-hugging clouds and it seemed they just couldn't make their minds up as to whether they should be dispensing rain, snow, or hail. Currently, it was dense white hail, mini stinging non-transparent snowballs! The temperature on the dash plummeted to three degrees. We were truthfully freezing (still lost of course!), and having had just a few biscuits each, running out of stamina.

It was 5 pm and the low storm clouds had shortened the day, gifting us an unwanted early dusk. As we steadily pushed through and out of the storm, I spied a small motorbike. It was bouncing across the flat white ground, riding off-road and diagonally away from us. It was the first vehicle we had seen for hours and for no logical reason it lifted my spirits. I guess because we weren't alone for a minute, and it had to have come from somewhere! Sure enough, we soon reached a much wider road, invisible in the waning flat light, until we were literally upon it. Turning in the direction we felt sure was correct, we found ourselves on a larger scale version of the golf-ball dimpled road that had led us out onto the Uyuni salt flats. It was as if the large perfectly round potholes had been designed and planted in such a way that it was impossible to miss many of them. We bounced and zigzagged our way in the rain, until we were finally rewarded by a sign. What a welcome novelty! It told us we were on the 34A and headed in the direction of Arequipa, a sizable town we had actual knowledge of.

Finally, some good news, we were running late, low on fuel, cold and hungry, but we were no longer lost! A large truck awkwardly swayed towards us, at an uncomfortable-looking walking pace. I couldn't tell if the driver nodded at us, or if his head was just wobbling. As we passed one another, several of its twenty-four wheels emptied dirty potholes over us, but I could no longer care. We were getting out of this day, without having to resort to putting up the tent on this miserable frozen plateau!

We stuck with the Martian surface until an intersection pointed us towards Chivay and the Colca Canyon. Unbelievably, we climbed still higher and as we reached the paved and smooth highway 1S, we entered into more thick white clouds. It was such a shame, as this road is famed for its panorama viewpoints of the world's deepest canyon and the several volcanoes beyond. With better weather, the views could have turned our day around. We were now riding close to 4,900 metres, over 16,000 feet in places, and yet couldn't see 40 feet in front of us!

Not until we descended the hairpins into Chivay did we emerge from the shrouds and finally pick up the signs for our base town, Yanque. We were shivering, and had been for hours. Almost pitifully, the room had one small electric heater (that hadn't been plugged in), that had had the thermostat dial glued to number three, with what looked like bathroom sealant! We weren't going to warm up in here, especially as the advertised hot-water showers failed to reach 'warm'. Instead, we changed clothes and found a cosy bar in the small town's plaza. It was now nearly 9 pm and the five-hour journey had taken a full eight hours.

Unbeknown to us, it was also election day in Peru and alcohol sales were strictly forbidden, but the restaurant owner took pity on our dishevelled looks and served us drinks with our hot meals. We slowly thawed and satisfied our hunger as the drink mellowed us. What a memorable day it had been. The roads had been truly awful, as had been the weather, and our preparation! Sitting with our wine and beer, I just couldn't believe that in the morning we had been strolling, happily in T-shirts, amongst the ruins before it was even 8am. Our first full day in Peru would never be forgotten, though it would prove to pale in comparison to others still to come!

Our time in the Colca Canyon was thwarted by persistent rain and low clouds. Two days running we tried to reach the panoramic viewpoints, only to enter clouds well before we reached them. Overall, we had had so much good fortune with the weather along the way that I knew not to complain. We tried to make the best of it with trips along the canyon floor and visits to local ruins. Typically, the day we left, the skies brightened as we climbed out of the canyon. The ride was stunning and confirmed we hadn't seen the region anywhere near its best. It was Peru's rainy season after all. The road again climbed steeply to around 4,600 metres and we pulled over excitedly at the first designated viewpoint.

As if for our entertainment, a solitary condor glided effortlessly a hundred metres below us, circling long enough for Selly to dig out the camera and take some shots. It was the first time we had had this bird's-eye view of a condor patrolling and hunting in its serene territory. For a few minutes, we were captivated by the breathtaking scenery and the majestic bird of prey. I felt some of the last few days' disappointments melting away. Colca Canyon was a worthy diversion; until this moment we just hadn't been able to appreciate its raw beauty. Nevertheless, we rode on with broadening smiles and under brighter skies.

We wouldn't try to get there in a day but were heading north to the Incas' famous southern capital of Cusco. It was wonderful to be seeing Peru under a blue sky again, and the journey couldn't have been more uplifting, exactly what we needed. Volcanoes fought the mountains for dominance of the skyline, whilst misty green valleys took on Asian looks with steeply terraced rice paddies. It felt a step back in time as we watched oxen pulling ploughs and carts through the fields, and farmhands sat on wooden stools hand-milking cows. To Selly's delight, alpacas and llamas with their babies were everywhere, and we hardly knew which way to look for fear of missing something. It was one of those gorgeous rides, where the temperature was finally comfortable, the roads both empty and well paved, and the scenery just incredible. My eyes, soul and confidence had been thoroughly refreshed and rewarded. This was the Peru we had dreamt of and longed for.

San Pedro is a tiny town sitting under the gaze of the Quinsachata volcano. It doesn't openly bow to tourists and felt thoroughly authentic, to the extent that our meander through its streets, looking for a B&B, was hampered by horses, cows, or tuk-tuks abandoned on the narrow cobbled streets. We both immediately took to the place, having seen just about every little street twice, before finding a bed for the night. We were the only guests and the friendly hostel owner informed us she also ran a corner shop that could be opened up for us if we needed anything later. Assuring her that wasn't necessary, we had a rest before walking to the main road and flagging down a minibus to take us to a larger town nearby.

The idea was to either find a local cheap 'n'cheerful restaurant, or pick up some fruit and snacks to walk back to our room with. Exiting the bus, we soon realised the weather had other ideas and it set about launching a lightning show worthy of a horror movie. The air was paralysed and tangibly electrified, forewarning us of the advancing rain that would surely soon follow. We didn't dare risk walking around aimlessly and instead dived into the nearest shop, coming out with just bread rolls and a tin of tuna. The first overly large raindrops splattered off the ground around us and spying a bus shelter, we hurried up the road to join a dozen locals already taking shelter.

The curved, transparent Perspex gave us all unrestricted views of an enraged sky, lit up by an impressive array of purples or blinding whites. As the pounding deluge advanced down the main road, phones came out and we witnessed the tarmac rapidly turning to river. The noise on the roof became deafening as we succumbed to the downpour and, as inconvenient as it was, I was just thankful we hadn't been caught out riding the bike in this! A tuk-tuk, with no working lights, offered to rescue us and, diving in, took us back down the unlit main road to San Pedro. I didn't enjoy the journey one bit. As the enclosed cab slowly filled with muggy exhaust fumes, I just hoped every bus thundering up from behind could actually see us and wouldn't catapult us into the ditch, or surrounding fields. It was a relief to be dropped off alive and be warmly greeted at the hostel. And yes, we handed over a shopping list of wine, beer and snacks, to be bought from her locked-up corner shop!

The ride to Cusco was a short one, only 125 miles, but equally as stunning as the day before. It couldn't be classed as that adventurous to be on the well-maintained paved roads, but it was Peru all around us and we were loving it. People waved, wildlife was everywhere and the views were to die for. The country is so rich in culture, ruins, mysteries and folklore that you could ride in any direction and be amazed. Clouds may often shroud enormous mountaintops, but misty fertile valleys, raging rivers and deep canyons were sculptured throughout these lands.

With limited time, we had to again choose carefully what we wanted to see and do. As we approached Cusco, it dawned on me that I'd messed up once more on the sightseeing front. Back in the pre-trip planning stages, we had discussed diverting to see the famed and photogenic Rainbow Mountain. It was now far behind us and we should have headed there either before arriving in San Pedro yesterday, or when we left there earlier today. We were now on the doorstep of the Inca capital, and having already pre-booked an apartment there, were too excited to contemplate turning back now. Again, Selly wasn't too bothered we were going to skip the colourful mountains and suggested that as they were way over 5,000 metres high, we would probably find them hiding in the clouds anyway! I agreed, felt better about the lapse, and we moved on to Cusco's more comfortable altitude of 3,400 metres.

We couldn't wait to get out of our suburban apartment and into the city centre, steeped in history and treasures. Taxis seemed to be every second vehicle and it was a flat price to go almost anywhere locally, a nice change from dodgy meters, or prolonged haggling. We were dropped in the 'Plaza de Armas', as central as you could be, certainly tourist-central anyway! For the first couple of minutes, I felt rooted to the spot, taking in all the impressive buildings and exploring the lively square's hustle and bustle. Selly was already snapping pictures and pointing things out to me, like locals performing an indigenous song and dance, a tactfully discreet Irish pub on a prominent corner and the 'free walking tour guide'. Well, we shouldn't refuse that.

For just a voluntary tip, Miguel offered us a private two-hour tour and we happily accepted. He was young, enthusiastic, spoke good English and led us off down a maze of pedestrian pathways, pointing out the differences in Incan and post-Incan stonework. He turned this into quiz questions where, armed with the knowledge he'd bestowed upon us, we had to guess the architecture's origins. After having yet another wrong answer explained to me and by now losing three-nil to Selly, I gave up and wondered if they fancied the next round themed on 'beers sold in the Irish pub'.

Instead, we visited enough ruins to give me the feeling we were in one large splendid open-air museum, a smaller and quieter version of Rome. We photographed the famous twelve-sided stone and the nearby panther stone, noted the location of the 'Pisco Sour Museum', as we passed it twice, and ended up back in the grand plaza for handshakes and the passing over of a well-earned tip. The tour had left us a little breathless but given us our bearings on the city's layout. We retraced some of our tour steps, back to a ticket office we'd spied selling entrance tickets for Machu Picchu. As the overall number of visitors are capped daily and further split between either four hours in the morning or four hours in the afternoon, we wanted to choose and buy the passes in advance. For us, we preferred a morning slot and excitedly purchased two tickets for a few days' time.

Over the next couple of days, we explored all of Cusco's nooks and crannies, particularly enjoying the delightful large indoor market, with its tempting 'street food' aisles and colourful fresh fruit stalls. The city buzzed with tourists from around the world; no journey to Peru was complete without a day or two in this Incan treasure trove. Tiny, crammed souvenir shops tempted us with their handmade trinkets, and warm cafés provided sanctuary from the frequent showers, serving us excellent fresh coffee and pastries. We soaked in the lively, friendly ambience, people-watched and turned down the many tours being offered on almost every street corner. We had the bike and it was earning its keep, taking us where we wanted to go and at our timetable; it was a nice, satisfying feeling.

Ambling around, Selly discovered a cosy art supply shop and we ducked inside for cover as yet another one of the short and heavy rain showers rinsed the city. She was desperately missing painting and had, by now, hundreds of inspirational photos to choose from. As we waited out the downpour, she excitedly selected and purchased a neat compact watercolour set, pencils, papers and brushes. I wasn't sure where we were packing them yet but loved seeing her so enthused and happy.

Although it was officially summer, it was also the height of the rainy season; something we couldn't avoid if we wanted to reach northern Alaska before it turned too cold. Each evening, we had overnight thunderstorms and usually one good downpour during the daytime. We had scrutinised the routes to Machu Picchu and decided we would ride, via the Sacred Valley, to the town of Santa Teresa, ditch the bike and hike in from there. The nearby train station had a pathway running 8 miles alongside the tracks to Aguas Calientes, the remote town sitting in the gorge under Machu Picchu. Never once did it cross our minds to just leave the bike in Cusco, or somewhere closer, and take the train directly to Aguas Calientes.

I've still no idea now why it was never even considered as an option, but if we had taken the train, it would have saved us three stressfully painful and costly weeks! The ride to Santa Teresa meant navigating the 4,600-metre Salkantay (appropriately meaning savage or wild) Pass. Lined with glaciers and 6,000-metre plus mountains, the pass comprises over eighty hairpins and hundreds of bends, with steep barrierless drop-offs. In fine weather, it would be plain exciting, but in the rains, low clouds and temperatures we currently had, I imagined it could be challenging. We were assured it was a fully paved pass, with a good quality road and amazing views. I guess, for those reasons, we just never considered taking the train in.

Despite the charms and enticement of the city, after three nights we were packed up and ready for the next leg. Also on the move was this new virus apparently. We had just learned the World Health Organisation had declared, on the 31st of January 2020, that it was now being classed as a pandemic and worldwide emergency. On that same day, the UK confirmed its first two positive cases. That seemed to have gone from China's problem to everyone's pretty quickly. It was now the 2nd of February and we were heading to one of the remotest wonders of the world. It wasn't too hard to put this news on the backburner as we jumped aboard the bike.

The climb out to the north gave some lovely views and we paused briefly to look back down at the entirety of Cusco below us, knowing it would be remembered with fondness. Within half an hour, we had entered the green and fertile Sacred Valley, which would lead us all the way up to the start of the Salkantay Pass and beyond. It may be a valley, but one nestled high in the Andean mountains and it wasn't just the scenery leaving us breathless. Leading north-west, all the way to Machu Picchu, this Incan trail would be a dream to hike in the dry season, but on the bike, we just marvelled at the incredible scenery revealing itself with every bend. Agricultural terraces looked down at us from seemingly impossible-to-access mountain sides and above them, Incan ruins randomly dotted the peaks. We followed the roaring Urubamba River through quaint colonial villages, its power swelled by the recent storms. This river and its tributaries had carved a wide, flat valley floor, every inch of which was cultivated, or used for grazing. I couldn't ever remember seeing so many shades of green!

The previously smooth tarmac briefly turned to cobblestones as we rose to the hilltop former Incan town of Ollantaytambo. Rain had recently fallen and the steep entry, combined with tight turns, had the tyres slipping on the large polished stones. The picturesque colonial square appeared frozen in time and I parked up to admire the clearly visible Incan hillside ruins, nestled high on both sides. Restaurants, bars and cafés lined all four sides of the pretty square and before setting off, we discussed possibly overnighting here, on the way back from Machu Picchu. How prophetic this would turn out to be.

Exiting the town, the road immediately began a steady climb, with the first hairpins signalling our arrival at the beginning of the pass. Old and tired trucks crawled at a walking pace, belching black fumes as they struggled with the gradient. I'd managed to find 95 octane fuel in Cusco, for the first time since Chile, and the bike was feeling more responsive than what I had gotten used to throughout Bolivia and Peru. Selly called out the elevations as we passed through 3,500 metres and then 4,000 metres. The air chilled and the clouds seemingly descended to greet us. The hairpins were so numerous and tight that she began to suffer motion sickness and I slowed both for her comfort and to be able to take in more of the amazing views.

Even as we passed 4,500 metres, the mountains appeared dominating beside us, their snow-covered peaks disappearing into the clouds and hiding their true heights. Like a thousand slashes, waterfalls, too many to count, cut ribbons down the surrounding high grounds and as we summited we saw the Salkantay Glacier for the first time. It was a spectacular pass, the views almost allowing us to forget how cold we actually were. Dropping down the other side, we rode through several shallow waterfalls that, without culverts, cascaded across the road's surface and away down the drop-offs. I watched the temperature steadily climbing again; the valley on this side of Salkantay Mountain was almost 1,000 metres lower than Cusco's altitude and added a few extra welcome degrees.

We were nearing this journey's end, but Machu Picchu doesn't give itself up quite so easily. Turning off the main road for Santa Teresa put us back on a dauntingly rough dirt track for the remaining 12 miles. The heavy rains had turned the skinny track into a slippery quagmire, made extra challenging as it rose and fell above the now thrashing brown Urubamba River. Muddy hairpins had us hugging the gorge's walls and staying as many metres away from the steep drop-offs as we could master. We skittered and slid on the broken surface, hoping not to meet any vehicles in between the random passing places.

We'd passed only a handful of vehicles back on the pass, but this track now felt very remote and quite apt for the gateway to Machu Picchu. We negotiated our way around several half-heartedly cleared landslides, or rockfalls, and slithered down steep, wet sections fed by waterfalls. It was all heart-in-the-mouth riding; an oncoming vehicle driven too carelessly or a big slide could easily have us off. Huge rocks forced us close to the edge at times and I knew Selly would have had her eyes tight shut. It hadn't felt safe to either of us, and upon finally reaching Santa Teresa we collectively breathed sighs of relief. Once the bike was unloaded, the hostel owner's teenage daughter hopped on the back and, waving proudly at everyone we passed, directed me to the only fuel currently available, a paltry 80 octane! Next, she guided me to their second property, a nearby hotel where they actually insisted I park our thoroughly filthy bike inside the spacious reception, under a huge and beautiful wall mural of Machu Picchu. We had arrived!

Chapter Eight

The Way to Machu Picchu

With the bike and the majority of our belongings safely stashed in Santa Teresa, we had a taxi drop us at the road's end, the Hydroelectrica Train Station. To reach Aguas Calientes and the hiking trail to Machu Picchu, you either take a train or walk there, and so we set off alongside the tracks, carrying three days' worth of gear and a bottle of water each. It proved a lovely hike; the sun was shining, the temperature comfortable and we were surprised to find enterprising fruit stalls and jungle cafés were open to serve the passing trade. Even trackside accommodation could be had. As the gorge narrowed, the river grew louder and angrier. Occasionally, tree trunks could be seen in the turbulent water, flying past at crazy speeds. Several waterfalls and tributaries fed into the Urubamba and we would have to hop up onto the tracks themselves to cross these, ever aware we would never hear a train coming over the noise of the frothing river. Butterflies filled the air and iguanas, or smaller geckos, randomly raced across the path ahead of us.

A bright green steel bridge took us and the rails out of the tree cover and over the dirty brown water. If we had been looking up, instead of down, we would have had our first views of the Incan town perched high over us. After eight miles, we were rewarded by an incredible sight; an imposing sheer granite wall faced us and clinging to the opposite mountainside was the remote town itself, looking quite precarious and out of place. Slicing between these walls raged the river, barrelling over huge boulders lying in the gorge's bottom. A train line cut straight through the town and out either side. We paused to take it all in. Cloud and mist rolled down the rock face, parakeets flew over our heads and the distinctive yellow and blue 'Peru Rail' trains passed close by. It felt like a rich jungle setting, an unimaginable spot to find such a buzzing town squashed into a thunderous gorge. Being so remote, so precariously situated, it shouldn't ordinarily exist, but exist it did, and was wholly worthy of the trek alone. As a gateway to its world-famous Incan neighbour, it was perfectly apt.

Despite no roads serving it, the town had plenty of roads, plus a healthy fleet of smart Mercedes coaches, offering a comfortable air-conditioned ride up to the citadel. Transported in years previously on flatbed rail carriages, these were the lifesavers for visitors not able to, or wanting to, endure the steep hike up to the ruins. Yes, if money was of no consideration, you could alight from a train, step into a luxurious coach and be deposited at Machu Picchu's entrance with hardly a step taken.

In front of us, one of these trains was blocking the main crossroads and we marvelled as a bus driver, hanging out of his window, argued back and forth with the train's unruffled driver. Pedestrians and porters, ferrying the town's merchandise on wooden handcarts, threaded around the immobile stubborn vehicles and brazenly crossed the tracks. All of this unfolded before the eyes of a solitary frustrated policeman, who tried half-heartedly to untangle the congestion. It was a 'David and Goliath' duel and we had ringside positions, as did all the afternoon drinkers, enjoying the entertainment from the nearby quaint platform's many cafés and restaurants.

Unexpectedly, it was the train that finally relented, both backing down and backing up slightly, to let the coach and its thirty weary passengers go on their way. With smirks on our faces, we 'hiked' on to our accommodation and were nicely surprised to be given a spacious room, with a balcony looking down onto the tracks and fascinating street life below. We had been fortunate to get this room and views. Back in Cusco, our host there had recommended and booked this for us, obtaining a generous discount, due to a friend owning it. It was a treat; we could happily take in most of the town, see up and down the gorge and across to the misty mountains, all without leaving the room!

After a short rest, we dragged our aching legs through the streets, around the markets and up flights of stairs to discover our new neighbourhood. There was so much to like, and unlike Uyuni, which didn't appear to display a penny of the wealth brought in by the salt flat's visitors, this town was a prosperous pleasure to explore. Statues, murals, colourful signs and eye-pleasingly designed plazas greeted us at every turn. Musicians, entertaining the throngs of tourists, shared the pedestrianised backstreets with young children at play. With a lack of space to grow, facilities had become multi-purpose and we wondered at the small open-air stadium. In one corner, families picnicked on the artificial grass as close by a game of football competed alongside gym and yoga sessions. A tempting variety of busy food stalls lined one side and kept the various spectators fed and satisfied.

Happy-hour signs flourished, and we settled for *pisco* sours at an outdoor table, people-watching and listening to a three-piece Andean street band. It wasn't long before a couple of passers-by paused to dance, an impromptu display that encouraged others to join in, until we had an appreciative street party inspiring the band to play even louder. As our alarm clocks were set for 4am the next morning, we eventually had to tease ourselves away from the delightful cocktails, cosy ambience and comfortable chairs our bodies had sunk way too far into. Reluctantly trudging home, we were at least thankful that we'd booked up to stay for two nights. The town could again provide all the comforts we'd need after tomorrow's sporty hike up, around and back down again.

This was the day then, one we'd dreamt of for years now. Just its name inspired travel and had effortlessly lured us away from the PAH and into these misty mountains. Passing through the reception area, we were nicely surprised to see a line of packed lunches, prepared for those making the climb today. Selly popped hers into her large versatile fabric handbag. It had carried everything she needed for the three days away and would be her 'rucksack' for today's hike also. We were slight oddities in a town full of tourists clad mostly in expensive branded gear, walking sticks in hand and binoculars around necks. I popped my lunch into a thin day bag we had, which rolled up on itself into a small pouch. The only luxuries purchased for these few days were a poncho each, souvenirs from Cusco that neatly covered our mismatched gear!

A light drizzle welcomed us outside, plus a rather depressing sight of heavy mist reaching up to clasp fingers with the low, clinging clouds. Rolling lazily down the rocky cliffs and rising up from the roaring river, together they obscured pretty much everything. It was actually a beautiful early-morning scene, just not one I wanted to see on our long-awaited Machu Picchu day! Only 5am, we were surprised to see so many bus stop queues already full. Each stop was designated a departure time and the 7am through to 8:30 were full, or filling. Upon realising we were hiking up, I don't know if they thought we were crazy, or some were even envious, but certainly we were stared at as we trekked briskly past in our poncho tents.

We didn't get far, not realising the ticket office we needed was at the bottom of the hike rather than at the top and was still closed! We couldn't exchange our vouchers until 6am and so sat it out for the next twenty minutes, giving the legs one final rest. Only five other people, a young couple and an even younger group of three friends, joined us as we pocketed our tickets and followed the signs for the steep trail up. We graciously let them all pass, and never saw them again!

A long series of dirt road hairpins led the cocooned coach passengers to the top, and vertically up through the middle of this route is a mostly stepped path for the walkers. I can't imagine it's ever an easy climb; in just thirteen degrees and a cooling drizzle we were soon overheating and having to remove the ponchos. Covered in wet, moulding leaves, every uneven step had to be taken with care and we paced up, hardly able to take in the scenery. At each intersection with the criss-crossing road we'd pause to let any coaches bounce past, windows full of condensation and white faces peering out of small hand-wiped circles. These short stops were an opportunity to have a scan around and try to discern if the sky was just that tiny bit clearer yet; it wasn't.

Maybe we were a little fitter than we'd given ourselves credit for; after ninety minutes, we'd completed the signposted two-hour ascent, albeit breathless in the thinner air and in need of another rest! Clouds swirled below us and around us as we made our way up towards the high point of the Sun Gate, only to find the path closed due to recent landslides. Of course, just being here was a fantastic feeling, but we were becoming desperate to actually see something of the famous citadel! With ponchos back on once more, we backtracked in the drizzle towards the Inca Bridge trail. Far below us, the town of Aguas Calientes briefly appeared, before the merging clouds swallowed both it and our fleeting hopes up once more.

We had less than four hours total to explore the whole site, and we hadn't seen anything in the first hour yet! We ascended to a high terrace, facing the Huayna Picchu rock face, finding it crowded with expectant tourists, cameras poised patiently in what must be a popular vantage point on clearer days. The plateau below, containing approximately 200 Inca structures, was perfectly hidden under a white blanket laid neatly between the surrounding green mountains. There was light at the end of the tunnel, though; sunlight burned through the clouds above us in small patches. Blue sky broadened slowly, pushing back the drizzle and raising everybody's hopes.

We left the crowd behind and pressed on, settling beside the even higher positioned Watchman's Hut, built to overlook the steep agricultural terraces below. The timing was perfect; within minutes and before our yearning eyes, the misty cloak seemed to magically slide and roll down off the plateau, towards the Urubamba River below. We were suddenly presented with the classic postcard view of the six-hundred-year-old city, now bathed in beautiful sunshine. Having gotten used to the slab grey drizzle, the detail was now incredible, and we stared in wonder at the iconic sight before us, llamas freely walking amongst these legendary ruins, giving life to this timeless scene. Snapping away, worrying that the view could be snatched away from us, we felt thoroughly rewarded for the tough riding days we'd experienced, and the miles of trekking to reach this special place and moment. The remaining hours were spent happily exploring the streets and buildings, photographing everything that moved, or didn't, and thanking the weather for giving us this amazing opportunity. Back in the days of planning the trip, I could remember thinking if we made it this far, to this new 'wonder of the world', then we should be super happy, and we were.

The hike back down the steep trail wasn't any easier; our aching legs struggled to keep sore feet from slipping off the weathered or broken steps. I couldn't risk spraining an ankle; it would be a blow for the trip, especially knowing the road conditions to come, and thus picked my way down carefully. The temperature had climbed to a muggy mid-twenties and the humidity sapped at our remaining energy. It was also highly rewarding, though; the money saved on trains and coaches had nicely covered the accommodation costs, for both Santa Teresa and Aguas Calientes.

Back at our room, refreshing showers were followed by an afternoon's rest. Drifting in and out of sleep, but mostly just daydreaming, I played through the day's adventure, hoping to cement the memories. It was a magical experience and we'd enjoyed good fortune. At the height of the rainy season, and in between so many recent storms, we knew just how lucky we had been to have Machu Picchu reveal itself in the way it had. To press the point, that evening, lashing rain forced us off the streets and into a cosy restaurant for sanctuary, where we cowered and watched children continue to blissfully splash and play!

On checking out the following morning, we were again handed a packed lunch, or breakfast. Either way, it was unexpected and gratefully received. We set off back down the rail tracks, hoping the taxi driver that had dropped us would remember to pick us up. This time, at the large green bridge, we looked up to relish our last view of Machu Picchu, gazing down upon us from 1,200 metres above. We had picked up some company. A small brown scruffy dog followed at our heels, tail cheerily wagging and a glint in his eyes that guilted us into feeding him. Despite the number of times we and the bike had been chased by growling dogs on this trip, we both adored them. His was a polished act, and we didn't hesitate to take out our lunches and share them with the eager pooch. We retained a banana and a small carton of juice each, whereas he happily polished off all our sandwiches and biscuits. With his stomach full and loyalty now empty, he trotted off contentedly to find the next group of hikers!

Mercifully, our driver hadn't forgotten us, and we were soon reunited with the bike and the rest of the gear. As it was now approaching mid-afternoon, we planned to repack the gear and set off early the next morning. If things went well, we could put the Salkantay Pass behind us by mid-morning and potentially be halfway back to the Pacific coast. It had now been several weeks since we had seen the ocean and enjoyed its hotter climate. We had our sights set on another Peruvian marvel, the Nazca Lines, which we'd pass by not long after picking up the PAH again. Before retiring for the evening, I took some gear down to the bike and taking advantage of it being parked up in the warmth of the hotel's reception, cheekily adjusted the chain, checked tyre pressures and gave it a general once-over. I was looking forward to getting back on the bike tomorrow, even just to give the legs a bit of a rest!

Yet again, storms raged through the night and the rain was still falling heavily as I dressed and checked out the window. Selly wasn't hungry, so I went down to breakfast alone, feeling anxious about those first 12 miles of dirt track we needed to ride back to the tarmac. It was a dangerous stretch of road at the best of times, mostly single track with a few passing places. The tourist minibuses drove selfishly fast and with little care for two-wheelers. The tight hairpins had no protection from the drop-offs, and I didn't want to dwell on how flooded and slippery we would find it now. It crossed my mind to ask Selly if she preferred to jump in a taxi with all our gear, so that I could follow it and let him clear the path of oncoming traffic.

In the end, it wasn't necessary. With breakfast I was also served the news that the road, the only road out of here, was blocked by fresh landslides. Nobody was going anywhere until the graders and bulldozers had cleared a path through; it would be a couple of hours at the minimum. I slowed my eating to enjoy the breakfast and nurse the hot coffee. My thoughts were broken when I heard English and Scottish accents filter down the hostel's stairs. Moments later, two young chaps in muddy biker's gear and helmets in hands appeared before me in the reception area. Angus headed outside and left Charlie to introduce himself.

"Hi, I'm Charlie, 'Round-the-World Charlie' actually," he enthusiastically informed me!

He quickly brought me up to speed. At just nineteen, he was midway through a Guinness world record attempt, to be the youngest solo round-the-world motorcyclist. I had the unenviable task of breaking the news to him that we were currently stranded and frustratingly going nowhere.

"Bugger," he responded, summing up my feelings too.

He was supposed to be giving Angus a lift back to Cusco and then continuing his noble quest north. I left them packing their bike and popped back upstairs to bring Selly up to date on this latest news. We used the time to extricate our bike from the sister hotel's reception and load the remaining gear, before joining the lads to continue the chit-chat. We had all wanted an early start and with no news forthcoming, Charlie convinced Angus they should at least try the road anyway. We swapped numbers, said our good lucks and goodbyes, and watched them disappear up the street.

Half an hour later, they were back. The road was impassable and, from what they could understand, had been blocked by three separate rock falls, or landslides. The four of us traipsed into town, found a café and over coffees swapped biking stories. It turned out this wasn't Charlie's first round-the-world trip. Just the year before, he had completed the youngest solo pushbike around the world, narrowly missing an entry in the *Guinness Book of Records* for not having used an approved tracking device. He had to settle for a letter acknowledging his achievement but apologising that it couldn't be entered into the hallowed book. He was determined to make it this time round and I could feel his infectious enthusiasm to be back out on the road. He was instantly likeable, great company, and we were slightly in awe of how much he had achieved at such a young age. Via sponsorship for this record attempt, he'd managed to get hold of the second Yamaha *Ténéré 700* to reach the UK shores (the first predictably going to Nick Sanders!), so it was a pretty special machine he'd secured. Chatting about our similar routes up through South America, he enquired if we had bothered visiting Rainbow Mountain. I explained how, before realising, we had gone straight past it and on to Cusco.

"Oh, good move!" he replied, as I listened on curiously.

"I hiked up to nearly 5,500 metres and it was covered in snow and cloud, nothing to see and bloody freezing," he continued with a pained look on his face.

I didn't feel quite so bad now. We had unintentionally missed out on the floating islands of Lake Titicaca, but I now felt better for not having gone out of our way for a rainbow-coloured mountain blanketed in white! After a couple more hours of light-hearted bantering, his eagerness overtook his cautiousness and they geared up to try again.

"I'm hopefully meeting up with Nick Sanders, in Cusco this evening, by the way," Charlie announced matter-of-factly.

Apparently, Nick was heading south, on about his eighth trip down to Patagonia, and Charlie had been messaging Nick's wife to arrange a possible meet. How cool would that be? I thought, the first two UK *Ténéré 700s* meeting up here in Peru.

"Are you sure you're not his long-lost son, or prodigy?" I enviously teased.

We said our second round of goodbyes and vowed to keep in touch, feeling sure that somewhere further north we would cross paths again. If they didn't return within the next half hour, we would assume they had managed to get through and also set off.

They didn't return, so we pulled on our helmets and headed up the muddy track, leading us out of town. For sure, it was wet and slippery, but we skirted easily around several small landslides, before coming to a full stop behind a grading machine that spanned the full width of the road. It was struggling to push aside tons of loose soil and rock that had blocked approximately 40 metres of road. It must have paused to let Charlie and Angus through earlier but was now intent on making us wait as it made another pass to skim several more tons over the road's edge and down to the raging river below. Finally, our chance came and we rode up onto the soft rocky spoil; it was a nightmare! The tyres just wanted to sink in and hit rock after hidden rock, skewing the wheels left and right. At least I didn't have to worry about oncoming traffic, as a workman at each end controlled the few vehicles attempting the journey.

Once past this obstacle, we bounced along mile after mile, crossing deep, dirty puddles, fed by impromptu cascades and sliding our way around tight, hilly hairpins. Occasionally, we had to squeeze our way past huge rocks that even the bulldozer couldn't shift and then over fresh landslides that it had managed to flatten. My heart was beating faster and faster, as we were forced to skirt too close to the edge on too many occasions. The relief we both felt on safely reaching the tarmac an hour later was tangible.

Our plan to get halfway to the coast lay in tatters, but surely that was the hard part behind us, wasn't it? As it was already early afternoon, we decided to just get over the Salkantay Pass and head back down to the picturesque town of Ollantaytambo on the far side, and hopefully whilst still in daylight. We would lose a day's riding effectively, but in these conditions, it seemed like the most sensible thing to do. The rain had at least stopped as we started the climb. After a thousand metres more altitude, the bends progressively tightened until we were into the first of the hairpins.

Water gushed across the road at the first hairpin and I picked my feet up as we rode through, getting drenched all the same! It was icy cold, as was becoming the air temperature. At the next hairpin, yet another waterfall crossed the road. This one had dragged mud and rocks across with it and I slowed to give us less of a showering this time, and to be able to pick my way through, avoiding the larger rocks. We continued to climb, and it seemed that just about every other hairpin had water running across it, or the residue of debris.

Rounding a bend, we came upon a long line of stationary traffic and threaded our way apprehensively to the front, finding a coach stopped on another damaged hairpin. This one was a real mess. A large waterfall had caused a landslide, dumping several tons of mostly loose stone and rock across the entire road. The coach had grounded its front into the scree and almost ripped off its plastic front end. The passengers were out and trying to hand-clear the debris, as were many of the car drivers, also stuck on the far side. We were probably just a few hundred metres below the summit now. A glacier off to the right reminded us how cold it had become, and even the skies were beginning to darken. Several people tried to encourage us on, but I wasn't convinced we could get through yet. Water still gushed through the mess, had washed away most of the soil and left a slippery bedrock of loose stone behind. It was only about 30 metres from one side to the other and so very tempting to try. I really didn't want to turn around and head back again, so contemplated accepting the help being offered and try to get across. With helping hands to push, maybe two wheels would be much easier than four, I thought, as I watched a car try to unsuccessfully pass the stranded coach. It also got stuck and had to be pushed back out from where it came!

I was now positioned at the very front and before I had finished weighing the situation up, found the bike suddenly surrounded by eager bodies, kindly offering to push us across. I guess they just needed to see somebody get through this mess, but at that point I should have asked Selly to get off and then unloaded the bike. To my lasting regret, I didn't, and as I felt several pairs of hands start to move us forward, I dropped into gear and gave the task a handful of throttle. This carried us an encouragingly good few metres, before bogging down in the large loose boulders. With even more hands appearing on the bike, I let the clutch out and revved harder, but to little avail. Over the noise of the waterfall and enthusiastic shouting, I tried to feel what the bike was doing and, convinced the rear was just spinning on the wet stones, continued the attempt to power on through.

We were soon moving again and steadily making ground, but how much of that was the engine's doing and how much was from being pushed I just couldn't tell. I kept the revs up and was still convinced I was spinning my way forward, until I finally had a whiff of burning clutch. We were cheered as we cleared the last few metres, but my heart had already sunk. Had I just stupidly fried the clutch? As both wheels graced tarmac again, the helping hands melted away and I gingerly let the clutch out in first, with crossed fingers. Nothing, nothing at all. I was gutted, felt stupid and suddenly helpless. We were at least a dozen more hairpins from the summit, sat at 4,000 metres plus, in just a few degrees above freezing and with not too much daylight left. I had pressed on when I should have known better, should have unloaded the bike, should have helped clear a path, shouldn't have been egged on, and now we were stranded on an unforgiving mountainside, threatening us with fresh landslides.

I guiltily broke the news to Selly, that I'd probably destroyed a perfectly good clutch and that we were currently stuck.

"What can we do?" Selly said with a shiver.

"Let it cool down, cross our fingers and see what we can squeeze out of it?" I lamely offered.

The coach driver had seen us get through and, unaware of our fate, decided that brute force was also their way ahead. We watched as he gunned the engine and forced his way forward, ripping off the lower front plastic bumper and undertray, but he wasn't going to stop now and cheered on by the frustrated passengers, bounced over and through the remaining obstacles. It was almost painful to watch, but he succeeded, at a cost to his own vehicle's health.

After half an hour, I jumped on the bike and in first gear tried the clutch again. Just as the lever was almost fully out, I felt a little friction and the bike nosed forward. Wow, that was hopeful, we might actually be able to ride this out, I thought. Selly hopped on and we tried again. It was slipping, but we were able to gingerly get some movement. By 4,000 rpm, it had lost all traction and I dropped the revs and allowed the bike to slowly pick up a little speed, before attempting second gear. It was pitiful, but we were climbing the mountain once more. It wouldn't pull third gear and no more than 3,000 rpm in second, but we were at least moving.

The hairpins proved a tricky ordeal, dropping to first whilst trying to keep the momentum up as high as the tight turns allowed, then slowly regaining the speed out of the turn once again. If the gradient allowed for second gear, then the maximum speed we could achieve was about 25 mph; otherwise, it was half that in first. After a couple more dicey hairpins, we arrived at a waterfall with a fiercer, stronger-looking cascade running over the road and off down the mountainside. I picked up as much speed as the corner allowed us, just about everything the poor bike had left, and rode into the surge. Woah, I immediately sensed we were getting into trouble; it was so much deeper and more powerful than the others. In the flat twilight, I hadn't picked out that the V-shaped surface, on the bend's apex, was considerably deeper than the previous ones and that this water was moving much faster. The water rose up close to the top of my boots and instantly grabbed the bike and started to push it sideways, towards the drop-off. A daunting 'side of the mountain' drop-off. To make matters worse, it was a right-hand hairpin. The drop-off was on our right and to keep the momentum maximised, I'd turned in from the far left to apex across the right side!

Selly leant over my shoulder and screamed at me for more power. What power, though? Since I'd 'all but destroyed' the clutch, we were now hopelessly short of that. Above the noise of the waterfall, I clearly heard the seriousness in her tone, mixed with panic and fright. Things started to happen in slow motion. I tried to judge and work out if our forward motion would get us through before the waterfall won and pushed us sideways over the edge. If we panicked and jumped off, we would surely be swept over, but if I gave too much power, the clutch would just slip, and we'd lose what little traction we had. The day had turned into a desperate nightmare, a chain of events that had made both the roads and now the bike too dangerous to ride safely.

Had we pressed on earlier because we knew Charlie and Angus must have made it? The fried clutch confirmed we'd pushed the day too far and the trip might end right here, on this freezing cold mountainside. I leant the bike into and against the sideways current, whilst cautiously tweaking the throttle to squeeze a precious little more power, before the clutch gave in completely again. All the time, our forward motion was being harassed and closely matched by the inevitable creep towards the edge. Not until the rear wheel had crossed the hairpin's central 'V' and inched us into shallowing water did I start to breathe and dare to believe we might actually make it. It seemed to take an eternity to reach the other side. In reality, it had probably been under ten seconds total, but our hearts had been in our mouths and we had genuinely feared the worst.

We pulled over, shocked, and got our breath back. At 4,000 metres, it didn't come back too quickly! It was now just five degrees, but I was sweating from the scare we'd just had and knew we were now committed to continuing, come what may. There was no way we were attempting to go back through all of that again. Either we crested the pass and rolled down the other side or we found shelter for camping, or we hitchhiked. I knew which option I preferred; we were cold, wet and hungry. I'd had a little bread and jam for breakfast and Selly hadn't eaten at all. We really needed to get over and off this mountain. We pressed on, riding up roughly halfway to the summit, before taking another break to let the poor tortured clutch cool down a third time. A driver coming downhill kindly stopped to see if we were OK and gave us some welcoming news. There weren't any more waterfalls to cross, on either side of the mountain, and there were just half a dozen more hairpins left, before reaching the summit.

We were pretty elated, even if the smell of the burnt plates was a kick in the face! After the half-hour stop it was almost dark, but I was convinced that if we made the summit, we could roll down the whole 15 miles if need be, and still make it to Ollantaytambo. We both desperately wanted to reach the town to salvage something from the ordeal. There were bars and restaurants around the square we had passed through days before, plenty of hostels and maybe even a competent mechanic; we just had to get there tonight!

The clutch held out and we painfully crept around and up those last few hundred metres. Upon passing the summit sign, I'd never felt so happy to be emotionally drained, freezing cold and riding in the dark at 4,600 metres! We breathed a smug-ish sigh of relief as the bike quickly picked up speed down the other side; it was almost like it had been miraculously fixed. It was a joy to not be struggling and to feel the air temperature slowly rising as we descended. I didn't have to care about the hairpins anymore. We braked, swung round and let gravity pull us easily back up to 60 mph, speeds we hadn't enjoyed for quite a few hours! The last mile into Ollantaytambo was slightly uphill, though, and now the bike refused to pull even second gear as we crawled in and through the now lively square. Pulling up outside a random hostel, we checked a room out and agreed to take it. Tonight wasn't the night to be getting too choosy. The unloaded bike couldn't even be coaxed up the pavement and into the private parking area; it had to be pushed those last 20 metres. It had gotten us to Machu Picchu and back in some awful conditions, but it was now thoroughly done in, and so were we!

Chapter Nine

The Recovery

It was a Thursday night, almost the weekend, and as nothing could be done for the bike, we went out and got thoroughly drunk, celebrating the fact we had survived the day. A lively faux English pub attracted us inside, providing food, drinks and seemingly super friendly locals. We were the only tourists in the place and were invited first to share their tables and later to a house party, to continue on drinking and regaling stories of our troubles and adventures. It was the kind of night we needed, even if our heads didn't agree with us the next morning. Of course, we were in a bit of a predicament, but wasn't that why we came away, for an adventure, rather than a holiday? All had ended well. We had reached the town, found a bed, filled our bellies and drunk until the early hours. Tomorrow would be another day!

Ollantaytambo is a tourist town in its own right. Sitting within the Sacred Valley and boasting impressive Incan ruins, it was a quaint place to be broken down in. We weren't short of cafés, bars, or restaurants, but what we really needed was a competent mechanic.

The hostel owner suggested a local called Makuto, and on the Friday morning we took a walk to go chat with him. The tiny workshop resembled an untidy blacksmith's and the collection of dismantled small motorbikes, plus a tuk-tuk outside, suggested he might not have much experience of larger bikes. I wouldn't be asking too much of him, though, just to try and source some clutch plates that would fit and get us on our way, even if temporarily.

I felt convinced that if we could make the capital, we could find a dealer, or a distributor, that could sort us out. Lima was already on our intended route, via the Nazca Lines, but it was still a ride of over 700 miles. Makuto walked back to the hostel with us, looked over the bike and agreed to try to find some suitable plates. That afternoon he removed the burnt plates and scoured his disorganised shelves and parts boxes, to no avail. I don't know if the traffic and hills in La Paz had previously contributed, but the clutch was totalled, the six friction plates had broken up and the six steel 'driven' plates looked cooked; even the end pressure plate was distorted. Makuto offered to take the bits and try in the much larger city of Cusco, but it would have to be the following day now. As he knew far better than I where to try, it made sense to give it a shot and so we settled in for the weekend.

Late Saturday afternoon, we popped over to see how he'd got on with the Cusco search. It had been fruitless. Despite trying various dealers and repair shops, he now doubted anything matching our plates could be found anywhere in the city. It must have been a mammoth search as he'd actually gone the previous evening and cheekily added the cost of a hotel room to our bill! I was mildly surprised not to see half a dozen beers joining the tab. Looking over at our sorry bike, I was further perturbed to see the petrol cap was open and a dirty rag lay on top of the tank. Please, oh please, don't tell me he's been dipping the rag into the tank to clean bits up! There was only one thing for it; the bike needed rescuing, and I shot him a bewildered look as I removed the rag, locked the filler cap and pocketed the bike's keys.

My mind was made up; we really needed to get the bike and us out of here. Explaining this to him, we were enlightened to the fact he'd gone and left a chunk of our money, as a deposit, at a national parts supplier back in the city. They in turn had told him to check back in after the weekend, to see if they had sourced the plates nationally. It seemed worth a shot, and if by some good fortune that did happen, then I'd find a truck and get the bike to a proper workshop back in Cusco.

The downtime wasn't at all wasted, though, as we turned our heads to wedding planning and after several emails back and forth to Las Vegas, we pinned down a date and time with the Bellagio. Selly sent them a detailed and colourful drawing of how we wanted the chapel decorated and they organised video links for those that wouldn't be able to attend. Within a couple of days the contract was drawn up, signed and returned. Finally, we were booked to be married on Thursday the 4th of June, just four short months from now. It felt great spreading the news amongst family and close friends, a perfect distraction from the woes of the dismantled and broken bike. Chris and Caroline wasted no time confirming they would meet us in Vegas, amongst several other close friends. Over the coming days, we were thrilled to receive so many congratulations and then messages confirming flights were being booked to join us. It really was something for us all to look forward to. Oh, Mark, you really haven't learned your lessons about planning ahead, have you!

We passed the time catching up with Dauri and Charlie, both of them saddened to hear of our current predicament. Dauri was now in Colombia and Charlie had managed to drop Angus back in Cusco but unfortunately had missed the great adventurer, Nick, by just two days. Charlie confirmed having also had great difficulties with the many waterfalls and landslides but had clearly fared better than we had!

Arriving back at our hostel one morning, I saw another V-Strom 650, with Colombian plates, parked up. Peter and Sonia were packing to make their way back home to Bogotá, having also just visited Machu Picchu, but wisely by train. Clever people! On hearing of my clutch issues, they recommended a Suzuki repair shop down in Lima. They were headed there next, to get their bike serviced on the way through the capital. It was a promising lead and I noted down the details, thanking them and again swapping numbers to keep in touch.

Overall, it had been a pleasant and productive weekend but by Monday lunchtime I couldn't wait any longer and went back to see Makuto for any news from the parts distributor. It was a confusing and frustrating conversation that essentially boiled down to them not being able to find the parts anywhere in Peru, but in Lima we would probably be able to find them ourselves. I don't think Makuto totally understood what he was trying to tell us either, and asking if he had at least retrieved our substantial deposit just elicited a confused frown. Thank goodness we had managed to plan an entire wedding in the last four days and they didn't feel wasted on a fruitless parts search!

Other than paying for Makuto's little holidays (he had found it necessary to stay over in Cusco again the previous night!), we hadn't really progressed far at all. All the answers seemed to lie 700 miles away in Lima, and I got straight on to the internet to check for flights. A coach would certainly be cheaper, but it's a stomach-churning twenty-six-hour journey and the days seemed to be slipping through our fingers far too easily. We packed up the damaged bike parts and booked flights for the very next day.

Despite the mission we were on, landing back at sea level and enjoying thirty-degree temperatures was actually quite exciting. Makuto had given us the address of the main distributor's head office and we jumped in a taxi to try there first, straight from the airport. Frustratingly, he'd even got this wrong; we were at the main depot for car parts and were given another address that, naturally, was way across the other side of the city. We set off again, this time to a large smart motorbike showroom with accompanying parts desk. This all looked more hopeful. I gave the chassis and model number to the uniformed parts manager, even helpfully pointing out the six friction plates, six steel 'driven' plates and one pressure plate to him, as we scanned his on-screen parts catalogue. After a few minutes of keyboard-prodding, he pronounced, with a smile, that he could get all the parts we needed.

"The pressure plate will be available to collect the day after tomorrow and the rest will take approximately three months," he efficiently told us.

My shocked and dismayed look didn't even dampen his smile.

"Are you sure it could take three months?" I asked incredulously.

"Possibly four," he replied, at least a little bit guiltily this time.

Oh dear. Somewhat deflated, we nevertheless ordered the pressure plate and left to continue the journey in our patiently waiting taxi. Next up was the lead Peter and Sonia had given us which, of course, was in another way-off part of the city! Coincidentally, the pair of them were due to have arrived there that morning to get their bike serviced. Pulling up, the place looked positively futuristic compared to where we had left our poor bike, and I instantly wished we could just teleport it here. The owner introduced himself as Manuel and spoke pretty good English. He confirmed Peter's bike was booked in that morning, but he hadn't showed up and they hadn't heard from him. I would try contacting them myself, I thought, as I handed over our collection of damaged parts. Manuel turned to his desktop and pronounced confidently that he could get everything in three to four days. Wow, from three to four months down to three to four days; that sounded too good to be true.

I tested further, adding on a new front tyre and a chain and sprocket set. Again, that wouldn't be a problem. Out of curiosity, his mechanic had wandered into the office to inspect the damaged parts, and even my limited Spanish allowed me to understand his analysis. The pressure plate and friction plates belonged in the bin, but the steel plates could be cleaned up if really necessary. We just needed to get the bike down to them, and of course, Manuel knew a trucking company who could transport it from Cusco to Lima. We just needed to arrange moving it from Ollantaytambo to Cusco. So, a plan was forming on our first afternoon in Lima. Our return flight wasn't for another couple of days yet; we'd hopefully have enough time for a little sightseeing, catch up with Peter and Sonia, and check back in with Manuel before leaving.

We were staying in Miraflores, the tourists capital of the country's capital. Although it was full of trendy pubs and restaurants, we first hunted out and settled for a self-service laundromat, a small luxury. With no shame, we collected our fresh laundry and headed off to an Indian restaurant we'd spied earlier; it wasn't a cheap place, but some sort of minor celebration was required! Hooking up to their internet, I instantly had messages waiting from both Manuel and Peter. Manuel informed us we had missed their arrival by just fifteen minutes that day. Peter's messages were more sombre; his bike-mounted video had captured them crashing heavily, going down hard after taking a slide on black ice. It was painful to watch, seeing their bike spinning down the road, but that was only half the story. The day before, they had snapped their chain, battling through more landslides as they threaded their way out of the mountains and down towards the coast. He warned us conditions were pretty horrendous and implored us to truck the bike and get it fixed in Lima. I was happy to put their minds at rest and bring them up to date on our saga. As they had lost a day, they had asked Manuel to kindly stay open, complete all the work on their bike, and despite the aches and bruises, planned to leave early the following morning. They were too shattered and battered to meet up that evening and just wanted an early night. We bid them farewell and agreed to try to catch up again further north. I think Peru was dishing all of us up a little more adventure than we really needed.

Before we knew it, Thursday was upon us and we headed out first to collect the pressure plate, followed by a visit to the bike shop to deliver it. Manuel had already left for an early lunch but, wanting news on the other parts, and with a late-afternoon flight, we decided it was worth hanging on. Just down the street was a combined hairdresser's and barber's; another little luxury that we both needed! With my beard trim and haircut completed, I left Selly getting hers coloured and went for a beer with my new Venezuelan barber-friend. A few years earlier, he'd escaped the troubles of his country. Penniless and paperless, he'd made his way to a Venezuelan community residing, mostly illegally, in Lima's outskirts. Back home, he had worked for a small independent TV company, before the government destroyed the building and closed them down. Cutting hair used to be a hobby, now it eked out a living and allowed him to send some precious money back home. We enjoyed a couple of drinks, swapping stories of our lives, before I bade farewell and headed back to find Manuel behind his desk. Sure enough, the original forecasts proved a little too positive; only the front tyre had arrived so far. As for the rest of the parts, it wouldn't be this week now, but definitely should be by the end of next week. We could only hope and trust he came up trumps.

We had left ourselves a little short on time to reach the airport, especially as Friday rush-hour traffic was now clogging the streets. We arrived exactly one hour before the flight was due to take off, or put another way, half an hour before the gate would be closing! We had a bag containing the bike parts to check in and getting to the front of the queue seemed to be taking forever; and then the faff started. Apparently, I couldn't board the plane as I owed three dollars and a few cents. Selly received her boarding pass. Our hold bag was gone (even though it was under my name!) but I wouldn't be going anywhere until I paid this surcharge, over at the airline's sales desk.

It was irritating, as everything had been booked online at the same time, and I produced the paperwork to prove it. The clock was ticking and however much I challenged, they just dug their heels in and weren't budging until the three paltry dollars were paid! I was pointed in the rough direction of the sales desks and Selly legged it off through security, to find the gate and warn the boarding staff I was on my way. I had less than ten minutes before the gate closed to sort out the payment, go back and get my boarding pass, clear security and find the gate to rejoin Selly.

Without her help in translating, I wasn't feeling particularly optimistic. The queue at the sales desk was six-deep, with the guy at the front trying to purchase a flight ticket for later that evening. If I didn't intervene promptly, my flight would be lost. Oh, how I wished I'd picked up more Spanish along the way! I pleadingly asked if anybody in the queue spoke English. A young guy said yes, and he kindly translated my predicament to the others. After what still felt like an eternity, I was allowed up to the desk once ticket-man had finally departed. The surcharge was for an upgraded seat that I hadn't requested. After purchasing seats together, it seemed I was now paying to be split up!

Only concerned about making the gate in time, I hastily paid up, secured the valuable receipt and legged it back to the check-in counters, to find an even longer queue. My patience tested, I walked around the side and waited directly behind the person checking in with the now familiar attendant. In one last feeble attempt to show I hadn't been in the wrong, I handed over the new receipt along with the original invoice, showing the now different seat numbers. No explanation was forthcoming, of course, but thankfully I was handed my pass, along with the sarcastic (to my agitated mind anyway!) warning, "You need to hurry!"

Security was par for the course, rammed, but it gave me plenty of time to scrutinise the screens and find my flight gate. This was a little disparaging. *Gate 17 – Now Closed* was the welcoming message. I wasn't too put off. Firstly, I convinced myself that it probably automatically displayed 'closed' half an hour before the take-off time, and secondly, knowing I wasn't far behind her, Selly wouldn't let them; I was correct on both counts! Along with a member of staff, Selly spotted me hurrying towards her and both reassured me the plane hadn't yet departed without us, despite it now being ten minutes past the take-off time. The gentleman sat in my original seat readily accepted the roomier upgrade and I flopped down happily beside Selly, feeling very grateful I wasn't going to be faffing around rebooking any flights!

Upon landing, we found overnight accommodation in Cusco, figuring we had more chance of organising a truck here than in the much smaller Ollantaytambo. The plan was to enjoy the evening and tour the bike shops in the morning. At a cosy 'cheap 'n' cheerful' kebab restaurant, we received a message from Lima, another small setback. Manuel's truck contact had doubled his fee, to one I'm sure he knew we would have to refuse. I guessed he just didn't fancy venturing over 700 miles into the mountains, and back again, for some gringo's bike. We added this task to the morning's list and went to a bar instead. It seemed to have been a day of mostly one step forward and two back, the perfect type of day to cap off in a cosy pub!

With breakfast inside us, we left the hostel looking after our bags and ventured out in search of help. The sun was shining, literally and metaphorically. The very first person, in the very first bike shop, answered all our prayers. With two phone calls, he organised first a small truck, to collect the bike from Ollantaytambo, and then teed up a haulage firm to take the bike down to Lima. All for a fraction of the price quoted to us by the other end. For an added bonus, we could hop in with the bike and get a free lift back to Cusco, bags and all, that very afternoon. Being a Friday, the bike needed to be with the haulage firm by 6pm, to guarantee being on the weekend run down to the capital. Grabbing a taxi, we legged it back to Ollantaytambo to prepare the stranded bike and pack our bags. The road was barely recognisable from just a few days before. Fresh landslides had occurred in several places, all of them only partially cleared. The taxi driver told us this road had only been completed two years previously and after just a couple of rainy seasons had been shut so many times that the old bumpy route was still preferred by many.

Makuto seemed surprised to see us back so soon, and a little taken aback that our plan was to relieve him of our bike pretty sharpish and take it all the way to Lima. He quickly realised there weren't going to be any more hotel stays or pocket money coming his way. If anything, he owed us quite a bit as we were letting him keep the chunk he'd supposedly left as deposits on the non-existent parts. We reassembled what we could and pushed the bike out into the dirt lane, to await our escape vehicle. Almost on time came our truck and driver, minus any ramp, or way of getting the bike up into the back! The bike shop in Cusco had told us he usually delivered brand new tuk-tuks and that a bike would be easy for him. How did he get tuk-tuks in the back? I wondered. The driver gave us a look that said the problem was ours, definitely not his, and I turned pleadingly to Makuto. Surely he must have a ramp? No, he actually didn't have a ramp, just an odd collection of 'way too short' pieces of wood.

Having just experienced first-hand the state the road was in, I was already nervous about the bike surviving this short journey intact. Now I was nervous about how we were getting it into the back of the tuk-tuk truck! In searching around for anything that might be of use to us, I had evidently missed a Spanish conversation between the pair of them.

The driver had spied a low wall, on a nearby tight bend, and was now manoeuvring his truck up to it, albeit thoroughly blocking the road in the process. Makuto signalled to me to help push the bike to the other side of the wall and I guessed the collection of wood would be utilised to form some kind of a dodgy ramp. It looked worryingly promising; the height of the flatbed was only 20 centimetres lower than the wall and the gap between them 'only' about the same. On my side of the wall, the bike first needed to be lifted and bounced up onto a ridiculously high kerb. From there, it could be pushed up the loose wooden ramp and manhandled over the wall and across the gap to the truck's flatbed. Well, this seemed doomed to end in (my) tears then!

The blocked road had amassed a collection of taxi and tuk-tuk drivers, who would ordinarily be papping their horns with impatience, but now they just sat on bonnets and enjoyed their ringside seats. A passer-by offered the three of us help (Selly had long since departed on a mission of her own, to see if the hostel owner had, by some small chance, anything resembling a ramp!) and by brute force the bike was half picked up, half pushed up and mostly cajoled into the back of the truck. It wasn't elegant, but it was successful, and our driver redeemed himself by producing several sturdy straps, thus alleviating my next worry. I guess I was getting more attached to this little bike than I'd realised. My anxious thoughts were already in Cusco, wondering how we were going to get it off again!

With a handshake to Makuto and a 'thank you' wave to the patient, if slightly disappointed, onlookers, we awkwardly squeezed into the tiny truck's even tinier cab. As cosy and uncomfortable as it was, we were, after all, enjoying a free lift to Cusco, and if the bike did decide to have a lie-down, at least I'd be on hand to help pick it up. Improvised off-road diversions had hastily been constructed to skirt traffic around the segments still blocked by debris. The road was littered with boulders too large to be moved yet, some dwarfing our truck as we eased past. It was incredibly bumpy, forcing us to make frequent stops to check the straps and allow us to photograph the more imposing landslides. It felt good to be escaping Ollantaytambo, though, as lovely as the place genuinely is. After a week of frustrations, we had begun to feel trapped there. We hadn't expected to see Cusco so many times, but as we entered the city once more, we were feeling both grateful and optimistic.

As the haulage firm's security gates were swung open, I was brushed aside and half a dozen burly lads simply lifted the bike effortlessly to the ground. I'd never seen the bike look so light and decided there and then to stop bloody worrying about it. It was literally all in a day's work for these guys and witnessing how easy they made it look, I was finally convinced it would arrive in Lima trouble-free. They took photos, handed us copies of the completed paperwork, gave directions to the Lima depot and for a ridiculously small sum, assured me the bike could be collected by Monday lunchtime. I didn't envy the driver. Peter and Sonia had endured an awful journey out of the mountains and I guessed it would take a truck around thirty hours to complete.

With the whole weekend to transport ourselves to the capital, we had no excuse not to take the twenty-six-hour overnight coach and save some cash. Seats were booked for the following morning, giving us one last Friday night in the now familiar Incan capital. Surrounded by all this culture and local delicacies, I'm almost ashamed to write that I convinced Selly to come back to the Irish pub for 'fish 'n' chips' and a couple of pints. It had been a heady day and I craved some normality, something familiar and comforting.

"Fingerprints, please," stated the coach company's attendant as I tried to prematurely board.

On a seating plan, we pressed our thumbprints over our respective seat numbers. That's slightly ominous, I thought, as we climbed aboard and found our well-worn 'reclined' seats. To be honest, they were more broken than reclined. For sure, mine wouldn't stay up. Maybe that would be a blessing! We gathered coach accidents were fairly commonplace in this region of the world and my plan was to cowardly give Selly the window seat and try to sleep through the majority of the trip.

Assisted by a seemingly continuous stream of never-ending dizzy hairpins, I soon found travel sickness came much easier than sleep wanted to. The coach's elevated viewpoint offered us scrolling and unrestricted views of perilous drop-offs after perilous drop-offs. When we weren't actually lost in the clouds, we could look vertically down the mountainsides and convince ourselves we were actually flying rather than driving. It isn't a journey for the fainthearted, or those afraid of heights. This went on for a full sixteen hours as we wound our way out of the mountains. Oh, and a further ten to reach Lima! A small highlight was passing Nazca and actually seeing one or two of its famous 'lines' off in the distance. It wasn't quite the short flight we had hoped for to view them, but *c'est la vie*!

For a change of scenery, we rented an apartment in the almost equally tourist district of Barranco, just a few miles south of Miraflores. We had arrived feeling shattered, gave a pass to food shopping and searched the seafront for a restaurant instead. It was a Sunday evening after all, perfect for strolling along in the warm sea breezes, watching umpteen paragliders and kite-surfers skilfully master the winds and waves. A side street seafood restaurant, full of locals, beckoned us in for cheap prawns and cheaper drinks. It felt a big step forward; we weren't over the hurdles yet, but we had a plan, and the cold, harsh mountains had been swapped for the comforts of warmth and sea-level altitudes. We were back on track, our track anyway, the smooth black Pan American ribbon.

With renewed optimism, we made our way over to see Manuel, who'd assured us he could definitely organise the third truck we needed, to bring the bike from the haulage warehouse across the city to the bike shop. What I really wanted, though, was some kind of an update on the rest of the parts. We received a genuinely cheerful welcome, but then his expression changed as he broke the news there were problems finding the chain, sprockets and, more importantly, the plates. His initial source had let him down and he needed to widen the search, possibly up to Ecuador! I was convinced he was trying his best and settled for an appointment to meet his truck driver at the haulage depot mid-afternoon. It felt half like a setback and half just a reminder that we were on an adventure and not a holiday. I just didn't realise, at that point, how far this saga was eventually going to play out, and cost us!

The 650 and all our gear sat in the sun waiting for us, all accounted for and not a (new!) scratch on anything. The guys had impressed me. We knew first-hand what a journey the driver had had, and I gladly left a well-deserved tip. When our latest truck arrived, I was equally impressed. Operating like a skip carrier, hydraulic rams lowered a flatbed to the ground. We wheeled the bike on and at the flick of a lever it effortlessly and smoothly lifted the bike up onto the truck's bed, easy-peasy. Our work was done, so to speak. The bike disappeared off to Manuel's mechanics and we went our own way, to become tourists until our phone updated us of any new developments. It was only Monday and we weren't due to check out of the apartment until Friday. We could relax for a few days, with fingers crossed that the rest of the week would be long enough to fix the bike and get us on our way.

Lima was cleaner and more modern than I was expecting; at least the areas we had seen were. The Kennedy Park, named after President John F Kennedy, became an instant hit with Selly; it was simply overrun with well-fed, content and happy cats. Literally hundreds of them. Cat food was sold from stalls around the perimeter and cat charities were on hand to tend to any felines not yet settled in their 'life of fame' and constant adoration. It was a wonderfully relaxing place to wander and the cats seemed to have a calming effect within the bustling area. Ringed by restaurants and cafés, the large park had plenty of passers-by smuggling in leftovers to the grateful purring inhabitants. For our meal, Selly pointed out a roast chicken diner, knowing full well we'd be saving them plenty of treats.

Having heard nothing by Wednesday, I messaged Manuel for an update. Still no parts, but the new front tyre had been fitted. What I really needed was an honest answer, though, as to whether we were likely to get the bike back by Friday. Otherwise, we needed to try and extend the accommodation. Thursday morning, I contacted the host, to be told the place was already booked out. One way or the other, we were moving out tomorrow! It was time to take a taxi and see for ourselves what the deal was.

It was a timely intervention. Manuel was in a bit of a quandary and I was glad we had showed up when we did. The friction plates and pressure plate had arrived, neatly packaged in sealed bags correctly stating Suzuki DL650. As for the steel plates, he had no answer. Could be tomorrow (we all doubted!), could be a month. The chain he could get, but again, not the sprockets, until who knew when. It was my bike, my mess, and I needed to take the reins and make some decisions. Today was now a fortnight since we had burnt out the clutch and we were getting desperate to be back on the road, desperate to get the bike to a more developed country, somewhere we could be sure of finding the parts we needed. I had an idea forming but needed to get on the phone, and I told Manuel I'd get back to him before closing time.

Ultimately, our next destination, 1,800 kilometres north, was Quito, Ecuador's capital. I had a good friend living there and as we intended staying for a few days, I'd already researched the bike shops and found a highly recommended Suzuki dealer. I gave them a call, briefly outlining our predicament.

"Mark, don't worry, we have everything you could need. There is a chain and sprocket set here on the shelf for your bike, I'm looking at it. A complete factory clutch kit I can get in twenty-four hours, guaranteed," replied Sato, the owner, both confidently and in perfect English.

It was music to my ears. The call couldn't have gone better and thanking him, I had my mind made up. The decision about the chain was easy; I would rather 'nurse' it to Quito than change it without new sprockets. In my first discussions with Manuel, when we'd flown down with the damaged parts, I recalled the mechanic had said there was a possibility of cleaning up the flat steel 'driven' plates. I called Manuel and told him to leave the chain and sprockets as they are, try to clean up the steel plates and fit the new friction plates. This way, the bike would be ready tomorrow and we could just bring everything over to his in a taxi. It was a halfway solution, but it would get us moving again. Manuel finished the conversation with a fair enough warning:

"Mark, fitting the clutch like this, it might last 1,000 kilometres, or it might last 50,000. I just can't offer any guarantees, you know," he stressed, both truthfully and understandably.

This realistic assessment couldn't dampen our excitement as we set about repacking properly for the road, something of a novelty after the last fortnight's shenanigans. In some small way, it felt like we were starting the trip again as we made our way over the following morning. The sun shone, the temperature was north of thirty degrees and we were feeling rejuvenated for the ride ahead. The bike had been test-ridden and was drying out on the pavement after receiving a courtesy wash. Selly set about loading it up as I settled the bill. As the bike ticked over, we changed into riding gear and the whole shop turned out for photos and to wave us cheerily on our way. The saga was behind us, wasn't it?

Chapter Ten

Ecuador-Bound

It was a beautiful feeling to be moving under our own steam again, even if it took close to two hours to cross the congested capital and fully leave its suburbs behind. I couldn't stop myself from analysing the clutch, though. I guess I just needed to get my confidence back in it, but with each gear change I found myself listening intently to it. It did feel a little different. It wasn't slipping so I eventually put my thoughts to bed and enjoyed the riding. Despite the later start, we made it 280 miles up the PAH to the town of Chimbote.

We wouldn't stay any longer than necessary. Visitors were greeted to an all-consuming and nauseating stench of fish! The coastal town is one large seafood processing factory, with the repugnant smell starting several kilometres before you reach the outskirts. The deeper into the town you venture, the more pervading and gagging it becomes. Nevertheless, I fully unloaded the bike so I could adjust the chain. It needed it. Despite the automatic oiler, the chain links were kinking and seizing up in the hot, dry conditions and the chain had over-tightened. Today's ride had gone well, though, and wanting to be in Quito sooner rather than later, we planned stretching tomorrow's mileage out to 360. If we made the town of Piura, we'd be able to reach the Ecuadorian border early the following morning. Despite the length of the day, and having missed lunch, the smell had put us soundly off eating and we turned in early!

It's fair to say we were happy to be on the road early the next morning, without seeing anything the town might have had to offer. I didn't know if I should feel sorry for the people destined to live their whole lives there. I'm sure the factories provided many, otherwise poor, families a modest income and maybe they didn't even notice the whiff anymore. Like the Patagonian townsfolk of Comodoro Rivadavia, living in constant high winds, I guessed they just got used to it in the end. The sea breeze, a few miles north of the town, was literally a breath of fresh air and we gulped it in, along with views of the golden dunes and the deep blue ocean. Selly resumed her lookout for whales and I for potholes or speed bumps as we passed through sporadic towns and villages.

I was passing the hours, locked in the helmet's solitude, juggling dates and trying to work out the best way to make back the fourteen days we had lost. Having booked the Guns N' Roses concert in San José and now knowing the date for the wedding, we had given ourselves deadlines to keep to. In their own way, they served a purpose to keep us on track regarding the bigger picture. We had clawed back a few days by trucking the bike to Lima, rather than riding to and visiting Nazca, but we were still approximately ten days behind our 'loose' schedule. I had a simple solution to that, even if I was feeling reluctant to enact it.

As part of the original planning, I had researched and routed a ten-day Ecuadorian volcano and Amazon rainforest mini-tour. The idea was to leave the majority of our belongings in Quito and with a lightened bike, be a little more adventurous and get off the beaten track, so to speak. Now I was thinking we had already had quite a good dose of adventure, plus Dauri was pre-warning us that Ecuador was wet, very wet. I could postpone the plan for the mini-tour, save it for a dry season one year and instantly get back the ten days we'd lost.

Further still, we could eventually fly the bike over the Darién Gap and forget trying to find a cheaper 'container share'; that could easily save us up to another week. We might still make the concert in Costa Rica after all.

Once I'd kissed goodbye to the Ecuadorian tour idea, I began to feel better about our whole situation. That is until I started to notice the clutch was sounding and feeling different today. Not really worse, I couldn't say that, just different. I honestly didn't know what to make of it and didn't, at this stage, bother concerning Selly with my doubts. It wasn't slipping, so should I really care if it sounded a little different? After all, it was probably just bedding in, right? In my head, I saw the brand-new friction plates mating happily with the cleaned-up steel plates. It just took a while and that was why it all sounded a little louder today. But shouldn't they be getting quieter? I double-questioned myself. What the hell. We were riding, getting closer to another country and the chain hadn't snapped yet, let's stay positive!

We reached Piura in good time, if slightly guiltily. Our pre-clutch drama intentions were to head inland for one last diversion, to route through and explore Huascaran National Park. And we still could have, hence the guilty feelings! I just didn't think I'd relax by diverting into mountains once more, especially before we had made back the rest of the lost days. We settled instead for a lengthy stroll around the town, a half-decent meal and a few tentatively celebratory drinks. All being well, we would be in a new country tomorrow.

The last 30 miles to the border were a transformation; the scenery had gone from dunes and sunburnt brown to lush green. It was as if we had changed countries already. We took a break at a fuel station, filling up the bike and enjoying mid-morning ice creams in the sun. As we rested, a couple of small children wandered over to look at the bike and beg for some change. Looking across the road, we saw they had been sent over by a couple of families, carrying their worldly belongings in a collection of cheap bags. I assumed they must be Venezuelan refugees, hitchhiking south, and a few coins weren't going to make a difference to their day. I wandered over, confirmed they were what we had guessed and, keeping the coins, instead handed them all our remaining Peruvian notes. We had passed several trucks, with refugees riding on the roofs, or clinging onto the backs, even one truck with precariously under-slung hammocks. Travelling with children in this way was unimaginably tough for them and I really hoped they had a plan and found an easier life.

We parked up at the border and found a café to rest up. The leftover coins proved enough for a small bottle of cold water and a packet of biscuits to share between us. It was a quiet Sunday lunchtime and upon wandering across to immigration, to exit Peru, we found their only customer was a wild pig. It was right outside the main door, getting highly frustrated trying to bite into a coconut with his pretty useless tusks. It looked to be an impossible task, so I relieved him, or her, of the nut and found a large rock to smash it open. I received some threateningly stern grunts and squeals for my assistance, and left the pig to enjoy separating the shell from the prized coconut flesh.

The Ecuadorian side was even more memorable; the officials were the friendliest we had encountered. We were asked for travel stickers and I happily gave my last one. Formalities completed, the staff came outside, wanting photographs with us and the opportunity to wave us on our way. Ecuador's carnival week had started just the day before and we planned to catch up with it in Cuenca, in a couple of days' time. There's always a high when you first cross a new border, as if you're starting with a clean slate again. You can almost feel the whole country spread before you, offering to be explored and experienced. We passed fruit farm after fruit farm and roadside stalls overflowing with fresh produce. It wasn't long before we felt compelled to pull over and sample something. There seemed to be ten different types of banana for sale; I'd never seen so many choices. Trying to buy half a dozen, for the equivalent of fifty pence, gifted us a bunch of at least twenty-five!

It was a beautifully sunny afternoon, comfortably cooler than Peru's coast had been and one of those minority days when the weather, temperature, scenery and roads all came good for a memorable ride. I didn't know then it wasn't going to last but naively relished the few hours that it did! Every river we passed had dozens of cars parked up, and families picnicked to loud music as children played in the water. The towns and villages were full-on carnival crazy; it seemed everybody was taking part, young and old. Cars were double-parked, impromptu diversions set up as over-filled venues spilled out onto the roads. Bunting and flags decorated the streets as the revellers below danced and staggered their way from bar to bar. Most were wet, hosepipes lay on pavements and kids ran around with super-soaker water guns, claiming anything that moved as a fair target, including us. As we were quickly finding out, Ecuador's carnival was all about water. The atmosphere was infectious, though, and we received lots of friendly waves, amidst the odd soaking!

Shortly after the plantations and these first towns, the road started to climb steeply into thick jungle. Power lines were decorated with hanging mosses and even largish plants grew along them, like gardens in the sky! Though we were heading to the near-coastal town of Santa Rosa, we needed to cross a mountain chain to reach it. It became a significant and unexpected climb, and before long we were up into the clouds themselves. Low, thick and muggy, they obscured all but the 10 metres of road in front of us. Then the rain started pouring heavily, the rain both Dauri and Charlie had been warning us about. How quickly a day can change, I pondered, as we struggled into our waterproofs for the first time in weeks.

It had been so wet recently that Charlie had given up completely on exploring Ecuador. He was already in Colombia and we'd made a loose plan to fly our bikes over to Panama together, hoping we could haggle for a better price this way. He'd been riding alone for about three weeks now and was looking forward to seeing some familiar faces. As he'd had some bike issues of his own, I guessed we'd need more than one drink to catch up properly.

After the rain started, I don't think we made it more than half an hour before the chain started to slip going uphill. The deluge was lubricating the previously seized and kinked links, which were starting to straighten out and lengthen the chain. I pulled onto a short and narrow concrete bridge, the only flat few metres of road we had come across for a while. In the pouring rain, I unloaded the bike, adjusted the chain, reloaded and set off again. It held for another hour and started slipping once more. Nursing it to the next flat spot, fortunately under a tree this time, we went through the same routine and rode on through the dense jungle and enveloping clouds.

Even as the rain fell, I could see wisps of steam rising from the more protected but dampened forest floor. The trees and palms were so thick with vines that you couldn't see more than a couple of metres into the foliage. I wondered what lurked amongst the cover; there was very little traffic now and we felt almost alone with the weather and the forest. Maybe our passing was heard by jaguars, or pumas, but certainly fireflies as they danced mystically along the darkening roadsides. Bats flew up and down the road ahead of us, often in a tunnel, as the flora had grown completely over us, bringing an eerie early dusk.

It was a blessing when we had clearly passed an unsigned summit and started a descent in the direction of the coast. We came out of the clouds and thankfully, out of the rain. In dancing wisps, steam now rose off the fast-drying road. The chain also noticed how much dryer things were and started to slowly seize up again, getting louder and tighter, until we were forced to make a third stop. I knew, leaving Lima, that it was very much on its last legs, but now it really needed managing and I began to wonder if it would even get us the remaining 400 miles to Quito.

We pressed on, getting closer to the coast, and eventually picked up the signs for Santa Rosa. Forget the jungle 'tunnels', it was getting dark for real now! After all the photo and chain stops, we were again arriving later than planned, again riding at night. Just to finish our day off and with just 30 miles to go, the rain came back with a vengeance. I crossed my fingers that the chain would last until we arrived, but it had other ideas and for a fourth time that day I found myself unloading and adjusting it, just a few miles short of the coast. This time, we were caught out in the open. Rain streamed down my back and blurred my eyes as Selly tried her best to light up the adjustment marks with a torch for me.

A nearby shack of a bar had music blaring uncomfortably loudly; a collection of all-day carnival drinkers struggled to make themselves the centre of attention over the pumping decibels. It wasn't an attractive-looking place but neither was being outside in the rain, kneeling in puddles with tools spread out and trying to coax the poor bike on. I could almost taste their cold beers, but we were so close now I just wanted to get us to the hostel and dried out. Selly has never classed herself as a biker, contentedly describing herself as a pillion, but to her credit, I've met many a rider who would have been moaning and whining about moments like this. She just accepts, anticipates and gets stuck in with the unloading, tool passing and reloading. What needs to be done gets done, however bad the weather and without any negativity.

"How do you stay so positive all the time? Aren't you getting annoyed?" I shouted, above the din of rain and music.

"Mark, I'm a mum, remember. This is nothing to get emotional about," she replied, matter-of-factly for her, and reassuringly for me!

Rolling into a flooded town, we found the road to the hostel blocked. More precisely, the wide riverside promenade leading up to the hostel's entrance had been cordoned off for a huge ongoing music and drinking festival. This street happened to be Santa Rosa's carnival location, and it was still in full swing. Those not already passed out, in bus stops and under shop awnings, were drunkenly dancing, drink in hand, in front of a huge sheltered stage. Police randomly patrolled the cordoned area, but spotting my chance, I slowly rode around the bollards and onto a sea of mostly empty plastic drink glasses. At a walking pace, I threaded my way through the outer ring of dancers, avoiding the police and the occasional drunken gesture aimed our way. We sorely needed to reach the hostel and there was no way the bike was being left out on the streets tonight. It was a surprised night attendant that opened the gates and saw a motorcycle had made it there.

"Full, full," was his initial welcoming.

"We have a reservation, *reserva*," I countered authoritatively, with a little Spanish thrown in.

Although he still looked confused, he did at least swing the gate open enough for us to ride through and under some cover from the miserable weather. We waited patiently as he sauntered off to fetch his paymaster, an elderly lady who arrived to confirm they were indeed full. I produced my mobile and showed our booking. She produced hers and reminded me that I had indicated an 'approximate 6 pm' arrival. It was 8pm. We had been listed as 'no shows' and, due to the demand the carnival had generated, our room had soon been reallocated.

Whilst we pondered our good fortune, the two of them brainstormed what if anything could be done for us. There was actually a small room available, since some guests had departed unexpectedly, but it needed to be cleaned and there wasn't a cleaner available now. The night attendant stepped up and said he would sort the room if we could give him half an hour. Of course we could, and so we set about parking the bike up and getting our stuff out of the rain. Wanting to buy us something to eat and drink, I set off in search of an ATM. After half an hour of following drunken directions, I visited two that were already empty. I returned to the hostel unsuccessful and asked if there was somebody that could change some US dollars for me.

"You have dollars? That is our currency?" said our helpful night watchman and room cleaner.

I gave my brain a kick. Was I really so frazzled that I hadn't remembered that! I headed back out, amongst the obliviously soaked dancers, feeling both pleased and a little stupid. Oh dear, in the meantime, the police had finally reached their limit of drunk patients to attend to and ordered the stalls and bars to stop serving. People were still trying, but to no avail, and I really didn't expect to be treated any differently. I had no stamina left to join fruitless queues in the hope of a dodgy burger in the rain and so, on a thoroughly wet evening, we were going to have a thoroughly dry night, and empty stomachs! What a comically bizarre day it had been.

The weather hadn't improved by the morning and the barely dry waterproofs were needed just to get the bike ready. It would be a shorter ride, just a couple of hundred miles to the historical city of Cuenca, where we hoped to be celebrating the carnival for ourselves. Out on the road, we splashed our way from town to town, the scenery obscured by a drab blanket of low grey cloud. Guinea pig was a national dish in these parts too and could be bought at the roadside, frequently displayed on small BBQ racks. I was hungry; we both were, having shared just a small packet of biscuits throughout yesterday. A small part of me felt we should at least stop and try it; they smelled good enough! I knew I couldn't, though, they would always be pets in my eyes, and a pet is part of the family. We could wait. We were hungry, not starving.

The closer we got to Cuenca, the better the weather became. The rain gave up and even patches of blue sky broke through the grey. The chain was behaving, seeming to withstand the consistent damp conditions much better than wet, dry, wet. It would need adjusting after we'd arrived, but I would have the luxury of doing that in the choosing of my own time and weather. The hostel owner went one better. For security, he insisted we brought the bike inside the spacious reception area. Not bad for ten dollars a night, even a hot shower, something that was becoming a real rarity. Quito felt close now; we would stay just two nights. Tomorrow would be a day off, a day to experience the carnival in the nearby town of Paute.

That evening, I gave the bike a good check-over and adjusted the high beam, which had been annoying me since the welding work was carried out back in San Pedro de Atacama. It was hardly ever needed, but after the strip-downs and rebuilds, it had been pointing too low to be of much use. I adjusted the chain once more, as best as it could be anyway, and thanked it for getting us this far. Operating the clutch lever felt 'notchy', though. It definitely wasn't as smooth as a couple of days ago and I decided it needed to be opened up and checked over in Quito.

Back in the room, Selly had some disturbing news. A few days before, on the 21st of February, an Italian had been confirmed as the first European to die from the coronavirus, and dozens more were confirmed to already be infected. The government had been forced to implement immediate lockdowns, in ten towns across the Lombardy region. We hadn't heard of a single case in the Americas yet, but this definitely wasn't just a Chinese problem anymore. How it would affect us, or the trip, we just couldn't guess at this stage. I turned to the UK news and mostly it seemed to be deriding the recent Italian lockdowns, suggesting it was all an overreaction. At the very least, it was comforting to know almost all of Selly's family were living down in Sardinia, almost a thousand kilometres away from this outbreak.

The following morning, we jumped on a crammed local bus and headed out to Paute. It was a glorious day, a totally clear-blue sky and thirty degrees of sunshine. The carnival area had been set up down by a river; a huge stage and fairground were being enjoyed by thousands. Streets were decorated and everybody, except us, seemed to have water guns. We didn't make it far before the first hosepipe was refreshingly turned on us! Thankfully, we had dressed lightly, in clothes that would soon dry out before the next inevitable soaking! In the carnival area, kids ran around with foam and glitter aerosols and it wasn't long before we acquired the appropriate look, wet and sprayed from head to toe in foam.

Food stalls offered traditional dishes and we picked out *seco de chancho*, a tasty pork dish, and not a guinea pig in sight! The day passed quickly with cold beers under a hot sun, watching kids gleefully terrorising adults without repercussions. It was a day for fun and we eventually lost count of the soakings. Waiting back at the bus stop, we were caught once more as a pickup cruised slowly by, looking for victims. Stood in the back were three youngsters, armed with a dustbin full of water and plenty of buckets for launching it! We didn't stand a chance and it didn't end on the journey home either. It was too warm not to have all of the bus windows open and at every set of traffic lights, more kids would aim through and squirt us yet again! To dry off, we toured Cuenca's historical centre on foot, trying to see as much of the city as we could before heading off in the morning. We were tentatively excited about the next couple of days on the road, as the route to Quito was known as the 'Volcano Valley'. We just needed the weather to play ball.

We planned a 200-mile ride up to the city of Ambato that day. The weather refused to play ball and we didn't see even a hint of a single volcano. We didn't see a lot of anything, to be honest, but that's how it goes! Strangely, the chain seemed to have settled down and I didn't need to make any adjustment stops. However, safe in the knowledge that it would be getting replaced in a few days, I just kept it well oiled and ignored the strange noises it sometimes made!

Ambato was just a convenient place to stay the night. We hadn't booked anything and after finding the centre, rode around looking for something that fitted our budget. A small hotel offered us a room at an inflated price and we declined and departed, but only after I'd spied their internet password behind the counter. Outside, I got connected and found us a much better deal. We went for the usual leg-stretching walk, getting the steps in and perusing the town's meal options; there weren't many! A lively pizzeria grabbed our custom for the evening and once fed and relaxed, we could get excited about arriving in Quito tomorrow.

I was looking forward to introducing Selly to my friend Gabriela. We hadn't seen each other in years and she'd since married and now had two daughters. With a stroke of luck, Gabi had told us her mother happened to own a hotel in town and had offered us a room, with a discount thrown in! Tomorrow, she would try to meet us directly there and lay out the exciting itinerary she already had planned for us over the coming days. Bike dramas aside, we couldn't wait to get settled in there.

The promisingly dry day lured us into packing away the waterproofs, easily retrieved but packed away! We rode out of Ambato, not knowing, or caring, what it may be famous for. The road to Quito soon became a motorway and we rolled up to a row of toll booths. In the majority of countries so far, bikes could pass through for free, but not in Ecuador. We needed twenty cents. I had plenty of twenties, but unfortunately they were all notes and the attendant refused to take one, stating he didn't have change. With streams of cars passing through, I found this hard to believe and stepped off the bike to have a more thorough search of my pockets.

It quickly became a 'Mexican stand-off' as he took my dismounting as a sign of protest and promptly placed a bollard behind us to reroute the queuing cars out of our lane. My pocket search was fruitless, and I even scoured the floor around the booth for any dropped cents. I tried again to pay with the note and it was made clear we needed to go and get it changed somewhere. All this for twenty cents!

Selly wasn't for standing around all day and took one of the notes to a nearby administration building. They'd probably seen the lane closure on cameras, as she was given the coins for free! Not knowing how many more tolls there might be, we pulled over at the first gas station, bought coffees and kept the loose change handy!

Ambato to Quito was just a 100-mile ride, but a potentially exciting one. Two-thirds of the way there, we would pass the famous and iconic Cotopaxi volcano, the world's highest active volcano. At close to 6,000 metres, it was the second highest point in the country. So high that as we passed by the road signs for the Cotopaxi National Park, it hid itself entirely in the clouds! So much for Volcano Valley; we had been scuppered two days running. On clear days, and despite being 30 miles away, it could still be seen from Quito. We just had to be patient, and a little more lucky.

Our route took us onto the lengthy Simon Bolivar ring road, named in honour of the country's famous liberator, and three times I managed to take wrong exits. The satnav had gone on a 'go slow' and with so many 'spaghetti' junctions on top of each other I just kept getting it wrong. Spying a petrol station, with a 'free WiFi' sign, I gave up, parked up, and in we went for a frustrated coffee break. I downloaded some offline maps, retired the satnav and pulled up a route on the mobile instead. Both annoyingly and reassuringly, it pointed me to the exact turning Selly had been trying to tell me I needed. I had flashbacks to my similar antics in La Paz, I mean, how was she right so often? It's not like either of us had ever been here before!

We picked our way through the busy capital and at the very last roundabout, before reaching the hotel, I happened to glance left and saw the actual bike shop I'd been in contact with. Wow, that's only a ten-minute walk from where we are staying. I couldn't resist swinging around and calling in to introduce ourselves and let them see the bike, etc. Sato had remembered our phone chat and reconfirmed he could get anything we needed. I explained my concerns about the clutch, and he agreed to take a look at it and of course replace the chain and sprockets; that alone was worth celebrating! There was one last thing. I comically pointed out the string and soap dish under the side-stand; this had now been complemented by a small square of thicker wood, attached to the opposite end of the string. The stand still appeared to be bending and I'd had to add the 'wooden modification' to cater for different cambers! I arranged to drop the bike off the following morning. There was no great urgency; Gabi had insisted we stay at least four nights.

Arriving at the Hotel Walther, we were warmly greeted, shown the secure underground parking (mercifully served with a lift, as we were on the sixth floor!) and handed a key card to our room. The receptionist told us he'd contact Gabriela for us and we went off to find the room. Except it wasn't a room; it was a modern spacious apartment, with a full kitchen, living room and separate large bedroom. We were being very well looked-after and it felt wonderful!

I'd first met Gabi when she was working in the Maldives as the resort's restaurant manager. I was there on a diving holiday with an ex and we'd convinced her to give it a try; she loved it. That was ten years ago, and we hadn't seen each other since. Selly and I unpacked, showered and changed, just in time for a message letting us know she was now down in the hotel's restaurant. After hugs, smiles and all-round introductions, we got down to catching up on the intervening years of our lives. Selly and Gabi hit it off instantly and it was a pleasure to share a condensed version of our thirty-year story. Gabi explained she was running her own catering company now and offered there and then to organise our whole wedding, if we wanted to bring it forward to Quito. She wasn't joking either! Her husband was a gynaecological surgeon, but also an avid scuba diver and had trained in the USA to operate hyperbaric chambers. In fact, if he hadn't met Gabi when he did, he was destined to run a chamber over in the Galapagos Islands. I couldn't wait to meet him. After lunch, we were given a swift tour of the hotel, meeting one of her brothers, who was the hotel's manager.

"Anything you need, just give me a shout," he warmly offered.

I was liking this. Selly spotted the fancy espresso machine behind the restaurant's counter and Gabi immediately informed the kitchen staff that if Selly wanted to make her own espressos, day or night, she was welcome to! Having had the local eat-street, shops and ATMs pointed out, we were left to explore, settle in and collapse.

After Bolivia and Peru, Quito felt very modern. Most people spoke English, and spending dollars felt familiar. The city was easily likeable and I had the feeling we were in for a great few days. At almost 2,500 metres, we could feel the altitude once more snatching our breath, particularly after having spent most of the previous fortnight back down at sea level. Not wanting to waste any of our time here, I rose early and dropped the bike off promptly at 9am. See you when you're fixed and new again, buddy, I thought, as I turned my back and walked away.

Grabbing a taxi, we headed first to the former home of Ecuador's most famous artist, Oswaldo Guayasamin. Afraid that his life's work would be dispersed around the world, he'd turned his expansive home into a museum and donated it to the state. It was a gift to his fellow countrymen and was now crammed with his paintings, sculptures and personal Incan art collections. Selly was in her element; this was her territory and as the tickets included guided tours, we happily whiled away the entire morning.

Next on our sightseeing list was the number one attraction for most tourists: 'Mitad del Mundo', or 'Middle of the World' – the equator! Gabi had wanted to go with us but called to say she was going to be stuck in a business meeting.

"You should go without me. It's too sunny not to go today, it will be great fun," she advised.

"Look, we really don't mind going another day, so all six of us can go together," I countered.

"No, you have to go, most of the exhibits and games are outdoor. It's a perfect day to visit," she insisted, before hanging up.

Now we were intrigued, exhibits and games? The taxi dropped us near the official but inaccurately located equatorial monument. We bypassed this and trekked instead to the Intinan Solar Museum, as it truly and undisputedly is on the equator line. The official monument had been built some 300 metres away; on cheaper land was one story, the other being that they just weren't that bothered about complete accuracy!

At the Intinan Museum, we were given a friendly welcome and assigned a tour guide to a group of six of us. To get some mandatory photos out of the way, we were led first to a long terrace with a bold red line along its length. On one side were signs stating it was the Southern Hemisphere and the other, the Northern. We were willingly encouraged to have our photos taken with feet straddling the hemispheres and then kisses across them, all whilst leaning over a sign declaring our latitude as 00.00.00.

To prove the line was absolutely accurate, buckets of water were poured into a mobile 'sink' and as the plug was pulled, we could witness the water's rotation change, with just a few centimetres of movement either side of the line. With the plughole located directly over the line, the water ran straight down without any rotation. Yes, we believed them! Moving down the line, so to speak, we tried balancing an egg upright on a nail head, fairly easy when the earth's rotational forces aren't 'pulling' the egg to one side. Then, funniest of all, we each tried 'walking the red line' with outstretched arms and eyes closed. It was just weird, like you were balancing on a tightrope and continually falling off. Without the sensory input from the hemispheres, the brain really struggled to find any balance. We giggled away at each other's failed attempts to walk a simple straight line without looking like we were falling off a wall. Gabi had been right to send us on such a sunny day; it had been a great afternoon's fun and games. Hopping on a local bus to save money, we headed back towards the city. A very big city, and I'd put us on the wrong bus. I really was rubbish at navigating capitals and had to be rescued by a kind lady, who explained to Selly where we should get off and just hail a taxi. Oh well, we had tried!

As soon as we entered the hotel, my phone connected and a flurry of messages rolled onto the screen. Sato had been trying to get hold of me throughout the day. I sat down to go through the messages and

The magnificent 'Iguazu Falls', Argentinian side

Iguazu Falls, Brazilian side

Ruta 3's surprising
Patagonian wildlife!

Strong Patagonian winds at
'Punta Tombo', Argentina

Ushuaia, Tierra del Fuego – end of the southern PAH

Stunning 'Torres del Paine' National Park, Chile

*Guanaco and magellanic
penguins at Punta Tombo*

*Iceberg ice-cubes,
Grey Glacier, Chile*

Torres del Paine, revealing its best

The often dusty and challenging 'Ruta 40', Argentina

The mesmerising 'Perito Moreno Glacier', Argentina

Chile's Ruta 7 and the famous 'Carretera Austral'

The twists and turns of the 'Carretera Austral'

The enchanting
'Marble Caves', Chile

Lago General Carrera
and its marble islands

Argentina's Lake District, San Carlos de Bariloche

The 3,800 metre 'Uspallata Pass', between Mendoza and Santiago

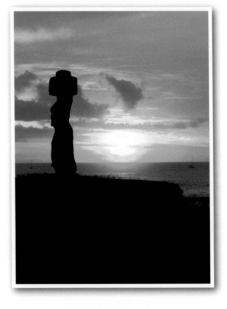

A diversion to the magical Easter Island

Remembering amongst Easter Island's Moia

Diving off Easter Island

The Atacama's 'Mano del Desierto', located 40 miles south of Antofagasta

Views of the snow capped Licancabur and Juriques volcanoes, San Pedro de Atacama

Bolivia's surreal Uyuni Salt Flats

Dodgy ferries to Peru!

Peru beckons!

Peruvian hospitality, the bike stays with the llamas and guinea pigs!

The modern day Inca!
Cusco, Peru

The road to Colca Canyon, Peru. Lost at 4,600 metres!

Machu Picchu reveals itself

Paradiso, Nicaragua. Mocha stretched out on the volcanic beach

Laguna de Apoyo, home for six months

*Mocha, the day
we all first met!*

*Commandeering my pannier
and enjoying a bike ride!*

The 'Almost Wedding' in Paradiso!

Mocha learns to paddle-board on the caldera's laguna!

Mocha chasing iguanas

to the bar's roof top

All dressed up

for the ride north

Taking a break, somewhere in Guatemala

Landing in London, home at last!

photos he'd sent. They had pulled the clutch apart that morning and found a mess. The brand new friction plates were chewed up, due to being too small for my model apparently. They were for a DL650, but an older model and significantly smaller than the plates needed for my XT Adventure model. The steel plates also looked wrecked. Either they hadn't been cleaned up very well or were just burnt again. I suspected they hadn't seen much cleaning, as the clutch hadn't slipped once to 'burn' them, and they looked pretty much identical to the last time I had seen them! Either way, they were toast, as were the new pressure plate and the basket end 'hub'. Sato had sent photos of all the issues. One clearly showed the recently fitted plates were too small for the clutch basket.

It was pretty depressing news, but something to absorb later. Sato needed responses and I fired off a message, hoping he was still at the shop. Apologising for my lack of internet and late reply, I asked him to please just replace everything that they found damaged. We were less than halfway through our trip after all, and I needed a bike we could have confidence in. His prompt reply showed they were ahead of us: *I guessed that, Mark. Everything that we don't already stock is on order and your new chain and sprockets are already fitted.* I thanked him and tentatively asked when we might get the bike back. The reply was spot-on: *The parts will come in tomorrow and your bike can be collected sometime Monday morning. Go and enjoy the weekend.*

Thoughts naturally turned to Lima, and my gut feeling was that the mechanic must surely have known the plates were the wrong fit. I somehow doubted he'd told Manuel, especially as he'd proudly unboxed the new plates to show them to me. Even I'd seen the packaging marked up for a DL650. I would sleep on it before contacting them.

Gabi messaged to say they would be over shortly to take us out for dinner; we had half an hour to 'turn ourselves around'! It was nicely timed to steer my head away from the bike's woes, and as a bonus we were finally getting to meet her husband, Ismael. To Selly's delight, they whisked us off to an Italian restaurant, Pavarotti's. This wasn't just any restaurant, though, but one owned by another of Gabi's brothers, Christian.

As the variety of dishes flowed to the table, Christian insisted Selly give him an honest 'Italian' opinion. He had absolutely nothing to worry about and the evening flew by with excellent food, fine wines and lively conversation. Ismael insisted we get ourselves back to Ecuador, for a group diving adventure to the Galapagos. A lifelong dream for both of us, we readily agreed and he vowed to organise it. Before being dropped back at the hotel, we were driven up to the top of El Panecillo Hill, upon which stands the world's tallest aluminium statue, The Virgin of El Panecillo. For some unknown reason, it wasn't lit up as normal, bit of a shame really as it is actually taller than Brazil's Christ the Redeemer and quite a sight. The city lights were spread far and wide, though, and it still made for a memorable view at the end of a wonderful night. I couldn't help thinking about how our fortunes had turned around since that first miserable night in 'wet 'n' soggy' Santa Rosa!

It was now a Saturday and Gabi had the weekend free, which meant it was about to get busier and more exciting for us. Ismael was stuck at the hospital with a patient, the wife of a friend, going into labour, but Gabi was on her way over to take us into the city for the morning. Whilst waiting for her to arrive, I sent Manuel a lengthy message rather than cold-calling. I wanted him to absorb the photos, particularly of the miss-sized plates alongside the correct ones, before we had a conversation over the phone. I also didn't want to put him on the spot before he'd had a chance to discuss things with his mechanic. I turned off the phone, putting the issue on the back burner for now, and headed out.

We drove into the city and parked up close to the historical centre and the famous Street of the Seven Crosses. This would be ideal for Selly, as her religiously inclined mum had been chastising her for never sending any pictures of churches or cathedrals! Although our own interest stretched no further than admiration for the architecture, or interiors, we figured we could fulfil all her mother's wishes with just this one street!

We didn't quite make it, though. Gabi's mother phoned, asking her if we were anywhere near the Presidential Palace, the president's private residence? Apparently we were, and so off we went for a rendezvous with her mum and some of her friends. The formal residence resembled a more ornate but miniature Buckingham Palace, complete with immaculately dressed guardsmen, stood to attention on either side of the main entrance doors. We mingled out the front with the inevitable city-tour groups, shepherded by shouting guides and faces hidden behind clicking cameras pointed at the grandiose building.

A lengthy second-floor balcony faced out onto the Grand Plaza, with a perfect view of its statues and fountains. To cap the scene off, an overly huge Ecuadorian flag flew proudly from the building's roof. It was all pretty impressive. The three of us had been spotted and Gabi introduced us to her mum, Alicia, the kind lady who was accommodating us! All of them dressed up; she was clearly with a group of influential friends. They were all connected through the travel and tourist industry and due to the president currently being away, had secured an invite for a rare private tour of the residency. Alicia, instantly likeable and persuasive, insisted Selly and I should join them!

"I'm sure that would be impossible, wouldn't it?" I blurted, half stating, half asking.

I could see the palace was accessed via a side gate, protected by tall barriers, scanners and several military police. We weren't on any invite list, had no identity documents on us and definitely weren't dressed for it.

"Nonsense," Alicia replied, full of confidence.

I clearly hadn't grasped just how influential our group of entrepreneurs were. Fifteen elegantly dressed ladies besieged the poor policeman, virtually telling him to stand aside and notifying him that we would be accompanying them on their tour. He did his best to push back, waving lists and trying to explain that without prior organisation it would be 'out of the question'. In front of his cowering subordinates, he received such a rebuke that I started to feel sorry for him.

"OK, OK, hand me their passports. I will see what can be done," he yielded, waving a radio with clearly ebbing authority.

Unhelpfully, we didn't have them or anything else of use really. It was all stashed in a zip-lock bag, tucked away in the tank bag. This small matter didn't deter the ladies for a second. Nothing remained impossible, and several insisted they would personally vouch for us. After a terse conversation on the radio, interrupted by further admonishments for making them late, the stubbornness prevailed and the security detail actually relented. We were ushered inside, scanned, patted down, photographed and begrudgingly issued passes.

We couldn't believe they had pulled it off. Gabi waved us off, knowing full well we were in the safest of hands, and arranged to meet up later. For the next couple of hours, we received a guided tour of state rooms, hidden courtyards, a private museum and were even allowed out onto the normally sealed-off balcony. We weren't exactly dressed to pose as VIPs, but this didn't stop the hordes of tourists from snapping away and wondering if they had photographed anybody important. No, they hadn't, but for a few minutes we could feel like they had!

Almost reluctantly, we left the palace behind and ventured off for lunch, in one of Quito's oldest and quaintest restaurants. Upon leaving, we were promptly accosted by two costumed ladies, who escorted us to a free cultural show. As they were draped in traditional dress, Selly had admittedly asked them if she could take their photos and in return, they insisted we join them at the nearby theatre. How could we refuse? This was a day of winging it after all. The seats filled quickly for a pleasant fun-filled hour of dance, drama and audience participation. Having a front-row seat, and much to Alicia and Selly's enjoyment, I didn't escape the mocking, not that I understood it either!

Time was now pressing on and we set off on a quest to photograph the length of the 'Seven Crosses', this time for Selly's mum's enjoyment. The street is so steeped in history, museums and religious buildings that it deserved a full weekend; we had just a couple of hours remaining. We made for one of the highlights, La Compañía church, with its interior lined in gold from floor to ceiling. We continued the sightseeing, having to duck into church after church as poetically the heavens opened up and forced us inside for shelter! With enough photos to satisfy the pope, let alone Selly's mum, Alicia kindly dropped us back at our (well, her!) hotel.

Sure enough, there were some messages waiting from Manuel. Initially very apologetic, the tone then became subtly defensive, as the hours had rolled by without hearing from me. He couldn't know we had been lording around as VIPs for most of the day! Predictably, he stated he'd bought the plates in good faith and had been assured they were for my bike. In all honesty, I did believe him but messaged back asking if he could explain why his mechanic hadn't noticed and told him the plates were clearly too small.

I put the phone aside; we needed to get ready for another night out. The day's excitement wasn't over yet. Gabi was meeting us at a prominent restaurant, sitting high above the capital and renowned for its views over the city. Ismael was tied up at the hospital and needing to drop the girls off with her mum, Gabi sent a car for us, to drop us off directly at the restaurant. Except there were three restaurants alongside each other, and neither we nor the driver actually had a name!

We took a guess and, of course, seated ourselves in one of the wrong ones. A very nice 'wrong one', it looked like the clock had been turned back a fortnight to Valentine's night. Either that, or they just weren't bored of the red love-heart balloons everywhere, or the fresh rose petals spread over all the tables. The view was incredible, though, and after we failed to explain we may have a reservation, they gestured any table was for our own choosing. Of course, we sat ourselves down at the one with the best view! Gabi eventually tracked us down, confirmed we weren't at her intended restaurant but loved the place anyway. For sure, it was a tad strangely decorated, but the interior was soon eclipsed by the grander spectacle of seeing the city lighting up below us. Like the evening before, it was another great night of fast conversation, hearty food, fast-flowing drinks and many a laugh. Gabi and her whole family were making us feel so at home and so comfortable. We'd been lucky to have seen so much already, but were also beginning to realise a month in Quito wouldn't do it justice.

Sunday was not to be a rest day, quite the opposite. Overlooking Quito is the TelefériQo gondola cable car, taking its passengers up to the Cruz Loma lookout, at 4,000 metres. We were having a proper family day out, as the two girls would be joining the adults. The weather couldn't have been better, and emerging from the gondola, we finally took in a postcard view of the snow-capped Cotopaxi volcano. Ecuador boasted nineteen volcanoes and from this one vantage point we could spy about a half-dozen of them. The entire narrow but lengthy city was spread out below us. There were even llamas to photograph as we walked around soaking in the spectacular panorama.

Ismael is a bit of an adventure sportsman and shunning the return gondola ride, had both run and mountain-biked his way back down in the past. He suggested the six of us should also try hiking back down instead. How could we refuse, when their eldest daughter, Luna, at just five years old, was quite happy to run down! The youngest, Sophie, would be carried and thus, we set off down the steep mountainside, with ears peeled for the speeding mountain-bikers that shared the same narrow path. At times, the track was a waist-deep rut, so narrow at the bottom that it kept threatening to jam and pull off my trainers. Ismael had set a fast pace, but the altitude was telling on Selly and I, and I took my time, not wanting to risk twisting an ankle.

Halfway down, I emerged onto a grassy bank and found him sat pondering where to go next. We had taken a wrong turn somewhere and the gondolas were way off to our left, almost on another mountainside! With some good fortune, a group of bikers appeared and provided us with a possible route and direction back to where the cars were parked. We set off again, through trees, down steep muddy banks and across fields of curious cows, until we finally reached a dirt road that roughly headed in the right direction. The gondolas guided us down the final leg. It had taken just eight minutes to get up and over ninety panting minutes to come down!

A well-known and popular restaurant resided in their neighbourhood. Apparently, it served up one of the best *ceviches*, a cold fish soup delicacy, in all of Quito, and we absolutely must try it. I wasn't expecting to like it, and didn't. It was absolutely delicious and I loved it. Surprisingly spicy, but so, so tasty, I just wished we'd discovered it earlier. Washing it down with a cold beer, we rested tired legs and chatted the time away... until Ismael could ignore his phone no longer; he was needed back at the hospital and with the bike due to be ready in the morning, we had to say our goodbyes. He'd been awesome company and we parted, holding him firm to a future Galapagos trip some day.

That night, we collapsed with our heads spinning from all we'd seen and experienced over these last few days. I was excited we'd soon be continuing northwards, but at the same time I didn't feel ready to be leaving Quito either. Let's get the bike back first, and hope it's fixed properly this time!

I woke early, fetched us pastries and pondered over the maps, wondering where we might get to that day. That, of course, depended on when the bike could be collected and how quickly we packed it up. I didn't want to bug Sato, but if I hadn't heard anything by 10 am then I'd take a walk, just to see how they were getting on. I had a message waiting from Manuel and opened it, already half expecting to be fobbed off. Sure enough, he had ducked shedding any light on why his mechanic hadn't mentioned the plates were the wrong ones. He just repeated that he'd bought them in good faith and what could he do about the problem now?

Very little at this point, I mused. The correct plates were getting fitted, or had been fitted by now, along with the other bits Manuel couldn't source. Yes, we were out of pocket, of course, but he had got us to Quito when we were desperate to be back on the road. It would have been nice if he had offered to refund us even some of the labour costs, but he hadn't, and I wanted to draw a line under it and move on. I sent a final message, saying his mechanic hadn't carried out honest work in my opinion and that I was disappointed to be paying out again, so soon after leaving Lima. I didn't get any reply, so the line was drawn, if a little uncomfortably.

I didn't need to take the walk; Sato messaged me to come get the bike around midday, which I took to be twelve, latest! We passed the news on to Gabi, who wanted to see us off, and then slow-packed the gear. I pored over the maps once more and decided to try for the border town of Tulcan, 160 miles north of Quito. If we made that, then it would allow us to be at the Colombian border nice and early.

I contacted RTW Charlie to say we should be in Bogotá in a few days and could he meet us there? It made sense for all three of us; the shipping company I was haggling with were based there but, more importantly for Selly, so were the famed emerald markets! He agreed to both meet us there and let me try to get a discounted quote for flying the pair of bikes over to Panama. Admittedly, shipping by sea was cheaper, and we both had budgets to mind, but time was pressing for all of us and containers could take over a week to organise. After a flurry of messages, I accepted the shipping company's best offer and we fixed a date to hand over the two machines.

At half eleven, I grabbed my helmet and took a stroll. The bike was already outside, drip-drying from yet another courtesy wash. I went in for a chat and settled the bill. Along with the genuine Suzuki chain and sprockets, just about the entire clutch was new. I enquired after the side-stand, but it had been forgotten about in the haste to have the bike ready. Not the end of the world; the soap dish would live on and continue its journey with us! I thanked them for what they'd managed to do in such a short time. Some of the parts hadn't arrived until late Saturday, just before they closed for the weekend, and by lunchtime, Monday, I was about to swing my leg over it. The short ride back to the hotel oozed new confidence and I couldn't get over how quiet it now was. I was beaming. Gabi and Alicia had arrived and insisted we lunch with them before leaving, along with Gabi's brother, Christian. It was a lovely way to be able to say thank you and goodbye to them all. It had been a wonderful chapter in our journey and we sincerely hoped to return one year.

Needless to say, we hopped on the bike later than planned but we were determined to make the border town for the night stop. With one final round of hugs, we pulled away, waving and papping the horn. If time had allowed, I know both of us would have loved to have stayed longer, but with excitement for reaching Colombia dispelling the sadness of leaving Quito, we headed north once more.

The chain was so quiet and smooth that I still couldn't stop grinning. Finally, I could relax and enjoy the riding again. The route towards the border was mountainous all the way, sweeping bends and series after series of hairpins. It was truly gorgeous scenery, now that we could finally see it properly. After a couple of hours, we skirted past the Cayambe volcano, which at almost 5,800 metres, was Ecuador's third highest mountain. Even now, it felt surreal to be riding our bike, brought from the flatlands of East Anglia, past these monstrously tall volcanoes! Llamas and alpacas were everywhere and above soared an assortment of birds of prey. I knew how excited Selly must be to reach Bogotá, I definitely was, but I also felt frustrated knowing our too-short visit to Ecuador had also been at the wrong time of the year. Today's sunshine was a rare day to enjoy. Not only had we sacrificed the ten-day Amazon adventure, but diving was meant to play a bigger role in this journey and it pained us to additionally be leaving behind the Galapagos Islands. We would have to make necessary but heavy-hearted compromises if we really wanted to see far-away Alaska.

An hour or so later, something very unexpected happened and I wasn't sure if I had imagined it. Passing yet another volcano, Imbabura, we were cruising up a fairly modest hill when I felt sure the clutch had slipped, momentarily, in top gear. I didn't want to believe it. Surely not, I pondered, as we crested the hill and found ourselves on a flatter road again. I wasn't yet over the joy of having a new chain, surely I could just have one day without any bike worries. We were probably over two-thirds of the way to Tulcan by now, so let's just see how this progresses. Over the next ten miles, the bike rode normally and I decided to press it and find out one way or the other. On another incline, I accelerated harder through the gears. This time, it slipped in both fifth and sixth gears, above 5,000 rpm. Undeniably and unbelievably, we still had a problem. Selly clearly felt and sensed we had an issue.

"What was that?" she shouted, leaning forward over my shoulder as I slowed down again.

"The clutch is slipping," I could only answer.

We retreated into our 'helmet worlds' to individually ponder this latest development and what it could mean for the trip. I tried to think of anything simple it could be, something we could sort ourselves, but nothing sprang to mind. The lever felt correctly adjusted and was 'biting' as soon as I started to release it. It was cable operated, so no fluid levels or trapped air to consider. What a bloody bore, though! With just an hour or so of the journey left, I wasn't going to turn back. We would continue to Tulcan, enjoy this fantastic scenery, find accommodation and get in touch with Sato for his thoughts.

Another cheap and easily forgotten hostel became our room for the night. The secure parking was a block away, or would have been three blocks if I'd not gone against the one-way direction to make it easier for myself on the empty street. The Ipiales border with Colombia was now just a couple of miles away and I really hoped we would still be crossing it early tomorrow.

The hostel was in some way affiliated to a nearby restaurant, one we had been given breakfast vouchers for, and we headed there for a bite to eat and to get an internet connection. I sent the message down to Sato, explaining what we had experienced riding up. He replied before our first drinks had been delivered. That was at least reassuring! He was apologetic and stated that as the mechanic had test-ridden the bike in the city traffic he doubted he'd even have gotten close to fifth gear. To be fair, they hadn't ridden the bike two-up and fully loaded either! He immediately suspected the clutch springs, admitting they hadn't thought to check their compression, despite knowing they had also been replaced down in Lima. It sounded plausible, and knowing we were headed to Bogotá sometime soon, he offered to phone me with a promising solution.

"Mark, one of my best friends runs Bogotá's largest Suzuki dealership. Let me contact him and arrange to have your bike checked out there. Anything they find I will cover the cost of," Sato promised.

I couldn't ask for better than that. It was a shame we needed to lose the bike again, so close to flying it to Panama, but I really appreciated Sato's commitment to get the bike looked at. These setbacks were starting to become a little too commonplace, but we were also handling them better, not letting them get us down. After Sato's call, I could at least sleep easier that night.

We arrived at the border early to find it was already chaotic. I couldn't see any signs for the immigration offices we needed to 'exit' Ecuador, and doubling back, I ended up on a one-way street, taking us all the way back to Tulcan! We retraced our route, more slowly this time, and pulled over where the first group of 'fixers' and money changers hung out. They were a feature at most borders we'd navigated, and usually we tried to avoid them, but today I relented and an unofficial 'parking attendant' was the quickest to grab our custom. He, of course, knew exactly where we needed to be and stopped traffic, ushered foot commuters out of the road and led us to a parking space closest to the correct building. With sign language, he indicated where we should go and that the bike and all its luggage would be safe under his watchful eye. He was also mimicking taking photos of the bike, but I didn't get this part, yet!

Armed with all our paperwork, passports and an assorted collection of photocopies, we walked around to the building's front. We were met by throngs of irritated and confused-looking people, stuck in two outdoor queues. From a distance, they just looked like a merged mess, but up close we could see they were arranged similarly to the annoying airport security queues. People were shepherded in tightly, snaking back and forth along the narrow lanes, and we joined the throng, tagging onto the back of one that appeared to lead to the passport office. Sure enough, we were in the wrong one! After approximately twenty minutes, a gentleman noticed we weren't in possession of the little green 'health-check' tickets we needed to get into the immigration building.

"You have to be in that queue first. It's a coronavirus checkpoint," he kindly informed us.

"Oh, thank you," we replied, thinking it looked more like a coronavirus-spreading initiative.

We started again and once suitably crammed in, shuffled forward painfully slowly for half an hour, to finally reach the front. A small banner proclaimed the checks were funded by both the UN and the Red Cross. We filled in a declaration stating truthfully that we hadn't experienced any recent fevers or prolonged coughing and that was it. Our first exposure to coronavirus checks was a bit of a joke, except the virus wasn't a joke. Regardless of our thoughts, a small raffle ticket was handed to each of us and we were instructed to go back to the queue we had first joined. Another half an hour of shuffle-dancing got us to the passport office's door, where a security guard controlled the entry via a 'one in and one out' system. He was clad in mask and gloves, his holstered gun backed up by a handheld thermal gun, now pointed in turn at our foreheads. I so hope you never get it the wrong way round, I thought, as he cleared us for entry.

We were stamped out of the country and showing my bike's import certificate, received directions to the next queue for getting that cancelled down. Finally reaching the window, I was told I needed photos of the frame number and licence plate, taken with their building in the background. This was to prove the bike was physically here, without anyone having to actually go out and check! Now I understood what our 'parking attendant' had tried to get over to us. I left the queue and found him where I'd left him, watching generally over the parking lot and giving me a knowing smile. I got the photos, went back and queued once more. This time, we were processed and declared free to exit the country. Now we just had to repeat the steps, in reverse, on the Colombian side. It was already nearly lunchtime as I tipped our 'helper' and moved the bike forward a whole 150 metres. I didn't even make that in one go, as we paused to purchase motorcycle insurance from one of the many roadside business shacks.

It's fair to say we were flabbergasted to find an almost identical 'health' checkpoint set up and run, again, by the UN and Red Cross. They were in plain sight of each other and I couldn't help thinking, why not just have the one, in the 100 metres of no-man's-land? Everybody still had to pass through, regardless of direction of travel. Wiser now, we first joined the lengthy queue to be coronavirus-checked for the second time in a couple of hours. This line moved twice as slowly, as there was just one desk and one nurse asking the questions whilst another took temperatures and blood pressures. The white tent we were squeezed into had only recently been erected and the floor was still being laid around us. Comically, we shuffled out of the workers' way, whilst trying not to lose our place in the disjointed line. We felt sure that if just one infected person was amongst us now, then the process was perfectly set up to ensure it was efficiently passed on.

It was getting muggy and in the cramped space it just wasn't possible to maintain any safe distances between the hundreds of us queuing, but worse was still to come. Finally reaching the front of the queue, we were pretty horrified to see that although two thermal temperature guns were on the desk, the nurse was using the same thermometer under everyone's bared armpits. The 'guns' were randomly picked up and played with, but it was clear they either didn't work, or they didn't know how to use them. Selly went first, filled in a form and had her blood pressure taken. The nurse took the thermometer and before she got the chance to get it near an armpit, Selly wiped it clean with her pre-prepared tissues coated with alcohol sanitising gel. I was up next, and leaning over the desk to look into the aluminium cup holding the thermometer, I was dismayed to see it was sitting in just a few centimetres of sterilising fluid. Only about a quarter of it was actually getting 'wet'!

As before, we now had our health tickets to join the next queue and gain entry to passport control. We emerged a half hour later with our entry stamps; now for the bike. Finding the right office was fairly easy, but the process here was a little different. They wanted us to take photos once more but then provide colour photocopies of the pictures for them. My Spanish definitely wasn't up to this and Selly set off to take the photos and find a copier service amongst the shacks. I took over bike-watch and mused over this first encounter of the virus catching up with our travels. I could feel the net closing on us. For sure, this was just for starters and who knew if border closures would soon follow?

Selly came back triumphantly and we made our way hastily to the office. We needn't have bothered. They had now closed for lunch and we ended up waiting two further hours before being processed. Six hours to move a total of about two football pitches; it was a new border record for us!

Chapter Eleven

Colombia and the Darién Gap

I felt like we should be patting each other on the back; we had made it to the last country of our South American leg. If we had to fly home tomorrow for some reason, then we would do so knowing we had already had one hell of an adventure. Of course, we dearly didn't want it to end here and instead took a slow enjoyable hundred-mile ride up to the town of Pasto. The views were staggering, much more rugged than Ecuador had been. Both countries were a biker's dream and beautifully scenic, but our route through Ecuador would be remembered for being swathed in and under its green jungle blanket. We were on similar hairpin passes, but the roads here in Colombia were narrower and the drop-offs into canyons considerably steeper. The high ridges were a jagged mountainous line from horizon to horizon. It was all beautiful, almost manicured, as we cruised down tree-lined roads, with their trees evenly spaced out and pierced by shafts of sunlight decorating the road ahead.

Every so often, the tarmac would abruptly end, though, and we'd be back to 'riding and sliding' Peru style. Signs for towns were just about non-existent and we were thankful not to have set too challenging a first day. It was Colombia after all, a country still shaking off its past murky reputation for being 'a dodgy country to get lost in'! Our only experience to draw upon was that every Colombian we had met, since the first one in Buenos Aires, had been incredibly friendly and helpful. We had looked forward to this day for a long time, I thought, as we slithered our way down another muddy section that cried out for a coating of asphalt. We stopped frequently for Selly to take photos, and for me to just stare and admire the scenery properly. Too much of my 'viewing' was still necessarily of the road immediately ahead of the front wheel!

It might have been a short bike journey, but it had felt a very long day. Riding up onto the pavement, we were amazed to find the cheap hostel could only be described as a very nice boutique mini-hotel. It was immaculate and, for its size, a classy looking place. The room was large and modern and within minutes of getting settled in, the door was given a gentle knock. With a smile, coffee and biscuits had been brought up to the room for us! I was offered a tour up to the top-floor breakfast area, essentially a roof terrace wrapped in glass and offering great views of the city and mountains beyond. After the faff at the borders and worrying they'd found an effective way of giving us this new virus, the hotel and its staff's hospitality were a wonderful end to the day.

Needless to say, we slept like the dead and I could happily have stayed another night, except we had appointments to keep. True to his word, Sato had messaged all the details I needed for dropping the bike off in central Bogotá. Today was Wednesday and the bike needed to be at the main dealer's by opening time Friday morning. We had two sporty riding days to cover about 530 miles, on roads that so far had proven to be randomly challenging. Not knowing what we would find, or how the clutch was going to behave, we had risen and breakfasted early. My hopes were that the closer we got to the capital, the better the roads would become. Friday was also the day we had arranged to meet up with Charlie, but that would be in the evening, and in a pub, of course! His messages enlightened us a little more as to his own predicaments over the last few weeks. Unfortunately, he'd taken a tumble, had crashed his *700 Ténéré* and damaged a few things, he'd lost the ABS and the suspension was also playing up. I guessed a few rounds were going to be needed, to fully catch up!

I think we were all starting to feel the pressure a bit. Charlie needed to find a competent repair shop in Bogotá and there were only five days remaining until we needed to drop the two bikes off with the cargo handlers. Once repairs were complete, both bikes needed cleaning properly and virtually emptying of fuel. At the top of Selly's list was making enough time to shop for an emerald stone and then have it turned into the engagement ring of her dreams. It was going to be a hectic few days. Yes, Colombia would be short, sweet and busy, but would it be successful?

We hadn't pre-booked any accommodation for that evening but planned on trying to ride at least 250 miles and reach a small town called La Plata. It was going to be a tiring and trying couple of days, with the dangling carrot being a decent hotel in the capital, for a whole five nights. One with hot water, we hoped!

As we exited Pasto, I found myself behind two Colombian police bikes. It was a twisty road they knew well, and they weren't letting things like speed limits or solid white lines hold them back. From a respectable distance, I stuck with them, feeling like we were getting a police escort and a free pass to overtake the crawling lorries holding back the traffic. I could see them checking their mirrors frequently, seeing if the overlander with his slipping clutch was keeping up, or were they adding up my misdemeanours to line their pockets? Eventually, they pulled into a lay-by (without motioning me to!) and I sailed past with a nod and a wave.

I was still finding my feet in this country, trying to shut the door on everything I'd read and heard in the past and just experience it for ourselves, judge it by how we found it. The scenery was amazing, for sure, the people seemed super friendly and our money was stretching much further. By late morning, we were ready for a break and had been looking for somewhere to pull over and get a coffee. The road had been testing, in a similar way to the day before. Without warning, asphalt would suddenly be replaced by muddy dirt sections up to 10 miles long. They had us struggling and I again found myself delicately balancing clutch 'grip' versus rear wheel grip. If it had all been dry then it would just have slowed us, but when wet and claggy, we had to really take care. We proceeded like this from hour to hour, but it soon became tiring and cumbersome, even if we were being treated to incredible scenery.

Shortly after finding ourselves back on a lengthy stretch of tarmac, we came across a lay-by with another panoramic viewpoint. It also happened to have a coffee and snack stand, just what we'd been looking for. The soap dish got slid under the side-stand and ascending the steps to the viewing point, we were hit with an unexpectedly surreal sight. Since crossing the border we had only seen a succession of rugged mountains, towering over deep valleys. Now we looked down on a wide shallow river, curving lazily around a huge flat plain that stretched to the horizon. All kinds of birds had made this their home and I half expected to see elephants, giraffes and hippos out on the grassy plain or wallowing in the sluggish waters.

Of course, this wasn't Africa and anyway, we knew by now we would have passed hippo signs! It was becoming a preoccupation of ours to slow and photograph the colourful road signs of Colombia, the majority of which were aimed at warning motorists of various animal types and we now had quite a growing collection. Some were easily identifiable, like giant anteater, jaguar, ocelot, iguana and even dogs (yes, really!), but some were not, one in particular being a giant rat-beast thing, with huge gnarly teeth. In reality, we mostly came across donkeys, pigs and oxen in the road, none of which had been afforded any warning signs at all! We pressed on through the changeable weather and as we hit occasional showers, I'd try to double-guess if they were worth breaking out the waterproofs for. Selly was beginning to feel cold and achy and had hers on for warmth and extra protection against the wind.

Although we were supposedly on a major road north, it was slow-going, with several sections undergoing repairs, or finally being blessed with asphalt. At the roadworks, traffic was usually allowed through in one direction at a time, so you could be sat waiting twenty or so minutes for clearance to pass. Occasionally, the road was just closed completely, for varying amounts of time, and I began to doubt we could make the 250 miles we hoped to. The phone-map had suggested the distance would take us ten hours' riding. (With the stops, it had eventually taken twelve!) Our breaks had mainly been thanks to the roadwork hold-ups, with one petrol and pee stop, plus a few random 'pulls' for paperwork checks. These police checkpoints had been common throughout all of South America, but never once had we been asked for any money or unduly held up. They just became part of a day's riding and we were content to stop and have a friendly natter over the paperwork inspection.

We'd been so determined never to ride in the dark, I thought, as we rode into La Plata, in the dark. The bike had been a handful to nurse again today; it just wasn't easy to try and protect the clutch and also get across difficult terrains. I was cold and knackered, Selly too, but she was also suffering deep aches and pains throughout her body. We needed to find accommodation for the night, preferably with heating that worked and a hot soothing shower for Selly. It sounded so matter-of-fact and something you could take for granted back in Europe but here they were luxuries many places promised but failed to deliver on.

Despite how we physically felt, there was justification for some self-congratulations. Today's twelve-hour struggle had put Bogotá firmly within our grasp. To give us something to keep us going tomorrow, we searched for, and found, a plush modern hotel in the capital, one that ticked all our boxes. These boxes had grown somewhat, but for twenty dollars a night we could have a spacious ensuite room, buffet breakfast, secure parking, lifts, heating and, of course, hot water! I booked up for the five nights we had left in the country. We turned in with high hopes; the worst of the roads were behind us and tomorrow's should improve all the way to the capital.

More out of habit, I still checked both the chain tension and the tyre pressures each and every morning. Very rarely did the tyres need a top-up and the chain was just sweet and dandy. What I really needed was for the clutch to hold out one more day, I thought, with a little *déjà vu*. It had deteriorated noticeably over the last 400 miles and would now slip in fourth gear also, if the revs weren't carefully managed. On the steeper hills, I tried hard to keep below 5,000 rpm and keep any slipping to a minimum. If it was just the springs that needed changing, I didn't want to increase any damage to the new plates. The problem was that on many of these hills, the extra crawler lane was so short you didn't have much time to get past the 'train' of labouring trucks. It was the safest place to get past them, but I didn't want this to be at the expense of destroying yet another clutch.

It proved another long, slow ride. Admittedly, we marvelled at the scenery, sometimes cursed the weather, tolerated the construction hold-ups and felt overall thrilled just to be in the country. The roads did improve the closer to the capital we got, but the volume of traffic appeared to have tripled as well. With Selly's phone guiding us, I concentrated on the congestion and let her shout directions over my shoulder. It worked and I think Bogotá, the sixth capital so far on the trip, was the first we didn't get lost in whilst trying to find the accommodation. It had been another twelve-hour ride and, just for novelty, we again arrived at our destination in the dark!

Selly collapsed onto the bed, with no appetite for venturing out, or eating. She was feeling worse than yesterday but we weren't sure if that was due to another lengthy day in the saddle, or if she was coming down with something. Leaving Selly to shower and rest, my hunger dragged me out to grab us some food and drinks. We seemed to have chosen an upmarket hotel, located in a very downmarket neighbourhood. Beauty meets the beast, so to speak. A strange mix of people, beggars and hustlers mostly, hung around the hotel and street corners. I walked purposely, pretending I knew where I was going, and followed my nose to a chicken takeaway. It wasn't a night-time area for exploring and, in any case, we had plenty of that planned for tomorrow. It was going to be a packed day, culminating with Charlie meeting us for the obligatory Friday night drinks!

I could have easily slept until 10am, if the alarm hadn't woken me at seven. I didn't want to miss out on the buffet breakfast before riding the ailing bike over to the dealers. I left Selly to enjoy a much needed lie-in as I threaded my way across the city and arrived, as requested, promptly at 9am. I was supposed to be meeting Sebastian, the manager of what appeared to be the biggest dealership I'd ever been in. He hadn't arrived yet, but that granted me a tour by one of the English-speaking receptionists. In a plush first-floor customer waiting area I was offered coffee and then led to the 'viewing gallery'. A wall of glass looked down into a workshop the size of a small aircraft hangar and I counted forty fully equipped workstations, all with ramps, airlines, toolkits and mechanics busying away. It was all very impressive, to say the least, and I watched with satisfaction as my bike was wheeled into one of the few vacant slots, awaiting Sebastian's arrival and input. The receptionist was clearly proud to be working here and showing me around.

"We have the contract for all the police Suzukis in the city and over sixty mechanics on our payroll," he stated and continued, "there are no fixed hours, they can clock in and out whenever they want between 7am and 7pm. We are never short of bikes here that need repairing, the city keeps us busy!" he finished off with a smile.

"What if all sixty come in on the same day and there's just forty workstations?" I enquired.

"They help each other. The police always want their bikes back, like yesterday, and they're always so bashed up," he replied and making his point, pointed out those that had clearly been heavily crashed.

Without even asking, a second coffee appeared and I was led down to meet Sebastian, who had now arrived. He greeted me by name (a great start, he knew who I was at least!) and retained the receptionist as a translator for us. Sebastian confirmed Sato was a good friend and that they had looked out for each other, with reciprocal aid to bikers heading north and south. The mechanics would inspect my clutch this morning and he would be in touch later to tell me what they found. I explained that I hoped to have the bike at the shipping agent Monday morning, as it was already booked on a Tuesday flight to Panama. I needn't have been concerned.

"Don't worry, we have enough parts and mechanics to build ten new bikes by tomorrow. It will be fixed, Mark," was the translation I most gratefully received.

I took a taxi back to the hotel and, despite wishing this clutch debacle had never happened, felt strangely comforted that the bike was getting some kind of thorough check-over prior to starting the next leg of the Americas. It was certainly doing well for oil and coolant changes; both had to be replaced every time the clutch was rebuilt!

I wasn't too surprised that, despite feeling under the weather, Selly was dressed and raring to go! This was her big day and I changed quickly out of biking gear, enthused by her excitement. We were off to the capital's emerald trading centre and nothing was going to dull this day for her. Outside of family and very close friends, we still hadn't broadcast the proposal back on Easter Island, wanting to wait until she at least had an engagement ring to show. The taxi dropped us as close to the four-storey building as he could. Armed guards stood either side of the main doors and as we passed through we were confronted by a large sign welcoming us to the 'one hundred and twenty individual emerald dealers under one roof'. We hadn't a clue where to start. Our 'game plan' of trying to look indifferent, or even uninterested in any stones Selly took to her liking, almost immediately went out of the window. Her eyes truly were the gateway to her soul, or heart anyway. The sellers were the professionals here and had seen this a thousand times. Our body language was being deciphered well before we had even opened our mouths and tried to convey a tone of 'just remote curiosity', honestly!

Try as we might, it was also impossible to guard our true budget; they had stones ranging from ten dollars to half a million and we didn't have the time to view a tenth of them. Within reason, I was now the pillion; this was Selly's day and only she would feel 'the stone' that reached out to her. Unfortunately, there seemed to be 'the one' in about every third dealer and so, after a couple of hours, we had to extract ourselves from the head-spin and go sit in a nearby café. She was dizzy from information and choice, we both were, but we didn't have an unlimited amount of time to spend here and it would only become more difficult to come to a decision the more we saw. She asked my opinion and I gave it honestly. I'd been watching her reactions, watching her face, and one stone had particularly stood out, even if it was over our pre-agreed budget!

"When you saw that stone on the third floor, your eyes lit up and you tried your hardest not to show it. That's the stone I saw you fall in love with and if we spend the whole day here, I doubt I'll see that look so clearly again," I offered to her.

"I know. It is my favourite, but I wanted to know what you thought," and after a pause, "isn't it too expensive?"

"I'm sure there's room to negotiate, especially if we can pay cash. Let's see what can be done!" I said, without any prior knowledge or experience of buying loose stones!

There was one more small snag; the stone Selly had fallen for was already mounted within a necklace pendant and we'd need it removed, independently laboratory certified and mounted in a ring. All within two to three days, and we would want a meaningful discount to conclude the sale!

Walking back to the centre, I spied a Western Union office and we popped in to see what time they closed and if they would release the amount of cash I suspected we needed. They had the money in stock and we had three more hours before they closed for the day. This would be our leverage for cash haggling and we threaded our way back through the floors, trying to avoid eye contact with all the other vying traders we'd visited. None had been 'pushy' in any way, but the dealer we were heading back to was a very pleasant lady called Diana, who just happened to have Selly's favourite stone. Our reappearance confirmed our interest was genuine, and so did Selly's smile, as the stone was presented for another viewing!

"We'd need the stone independently certified," I started with, followed by, "and then mounted in a ring, if there's time?" I asked.

"When would you need it by?" was Diana's first question.

"Within two to three days. We fly to Panama on Tuesday," I replied, hoping she would recognise and seize the opportunity for a quick sale. I added what I thought should be a sweetener: "We're willing to pay cash, for the right price".

Our timelines, requests and cash offer were quickly mulled over and Diana outlined a proposal I guess she knew we wouldn't turn down.

"I'll need to know the design of the ring and confirm this with my jewellery maker, but if he has everything today then I'm sure you will have your ring by Monday evening. This will also depend on the laboratory being able to certify and return the stone today. I'll need to call them straight away," she started with.

"I can design the ring now for you," added Selly, excitedly.

"As for the costs, I will round down the price of the stone and give you a twenty percent cash discount on the finished ring," Diana offered.

Wow, it was a better deal than I was expecting and took the wind out of my 'haggling' sails.

"I'll need a fifty percent deposit today, though, to allow me to remove the stone and send it to the lab," she concluded.

The artist in Selly quickly got to work, effortlessly producing a detailed design in white gold. The ring now sported a small diamond on either side of the emerald; it was gorgeous! Diana costed out the final price and we happily shook hands. Once calls had been completed, to her jewellery maker and to a certification lab, she confirmed the time frames were indeed possible. We were in business! The stone already had a reasonable grading, but without the lab's independent certification, both parties had taken a bit of a risk on the haggling. I just hoped our rounded-down price and further discount mitigated any screw-ups on our part! I connected to the shop's internet and, initially ignoring the flood of messages rolling in, logged into the Western Union app. It confirmed a transfer would be available to collect within the hour, and so I made the transaction from my bank and went back to the messages.

There were several from Sebastian. In all the excitement, I had almost forgotten about the bike's inspection. As I read through, my heart sank and my anger rose; none of it was good news. In fact, it was all pretty terrible news. Yet again, the clutch was destroyed, with more photos to prove it. He had copied to me a number of messages in Spanish that he'd already sent down to Sato. I translated these whilst trying to get my head around the broken-English ones that he'd sent directly to me.

Unlike my clutch plates, there was definitely some friction between Quito and Bogotá! From what I understood, the springs were fine, and all the other parts fitted in Quito were the correct ones for my bike. Apparently the issue was that they'd somehow both assembled and set it up incorrectly, resulting in the clutch spectacularly breaking up. Well, that accounted for it getting progressively noisier then. It appeared that Sato couldn't, or wouldn't, believe his mechanic had put the clutch together wrongly, and Sebastian wasn't rebuilding it until he'd received an assurance that someone was paying the bill at the end of the day! And so I found myself stuck between a rock and a hard place.

Then there was Selly's rock that still needed paying for, but I hadn't received Western Union's confirmation email, something I usually had instantly after making a transfer. I would give it a few more minutes and try to resolve, or progress, the bike drama first. My head was spinning as I tried to keep up with the conversation in the shop and positively inject myself into the spat between the so-called good friends. I phoned Sebastian and had his assurance that the clutch was one hundred percent assembled incorrectly. He even got his mechanic to send more detailed photos to me. I forwarded these to Sato and said I'd call in a few minutes, giving him the chance to confer with his own mechanic. In the pause, I checked my emails for something from WU, nothing, and looking at the app, it just said *Transfer pending*. I called Sato and he clearly found it difficult to believe they had messed up the rebuild, but in his heart he also knew his own friend wasn't one to be deceitful. He couldn't dispute the photos (Sebastian's mechanic had red-ringed the incorrect assembly), and I appealed for him to stand by his word. I just didn't have the luxury of time to faff anymore.

"Sato, our bike is due to be dropped off at the shippers on Monday. If it doesn't get fixed by tomorrow afternoon then I'm going to have to cancel our flights and be out of pocket again," I truthfully told him.

"Mark, I don't know how this happened, I really don't, but we will fix this, don't worry," he offered, and I closed the conversation with a plea that he confirm to Sebastian that the bill would be covered.

As a backup, I messaged Sebastian, politely reminding him of our tight schedule and that Quito had just confirmed to me they would be settling the bill. The message was read but not responded to.

I put it on the back burner. They'd have to sort it out between them; I had other problems looming. Still without an email or update from WU, we walked over and joined the queue for a face to face.

"Sir, a transfer can take up to five business days from Europe to Colombia," was the flat response.

I was transfixed to the spot. How is that possible? Surely, the point of the online app and transfers is to be virtually instantaneous, as the app declared.

"But the money has left my account and the app has sent me a transfer reference number. You must have it in your system?" I implored, probably a little too desperately.

"No, it isn't showing, and I suggest you either cancel the transfer by phone, or try again after the weekend," was her best advice.

Neither of these options was particularly palatable and I found myself rooted to the spot, taking in the implications of this twist. Realising I was also holding up the queue, we returned to the gem dealer's, to weigh up our choices and connect back to their internet. I tried calling WU, to see if they could hasten the transfer from their end and if not, kindly return our money. This met with a brick wall; a recorded message informed us that WU could only be called from a US registered number. We couldn't reverse the transaction even if we wanted to!

Sato had messaged, telling me everything had now been squared away with Sebastian. The bill would definitely be covered and Sebastian would have the bike ready by tomorrow afternoon. I couldn't fault him for keeping to his word, but this clutch fiasco had gone on long enough now. We wanted Central America to be a new chapter and a fresh start, without dragging any bike issues across the Darién Gap with us.

Whilst I had been distracted by the bike's misfortunes, Selly had repeatedly been putting the WU reference number into her own phone's app. After several *Transaction pending* responses, she excitedly announced to me, and the patient Diana, that she now had a *Funds ready to collect* message. Wow, the day was turning around, it seemed! Armed with this development, we virtually ran across the road and queued again, ever aware that they were due to close in a couple of hours. Faced with the same teller, Selly proudly held the phone up against the window, for the lady to note down and check the reference number once more.

"Sorry, there's still nothing on my system," she told us, with some sympathy.

I could almost feel her pain; it was nearly her weekend and we were going to be those awkward Friday afternoon customers, the persistent ones that weren't going to drop the bone. Damn right we were! Selly tried the female-to-female talk, along the lines of 'you just find our money, please, and I get to buy a ring across the road this afternoon'. Something struck a chord, as we were allowed to hold up the queue whilst she placed a call to her head office.

"We are trying to release your money today. Please come back in half an hour and I should know something more," she tantalisingly dangled, by way of explanation and placation.

Well, that was a bit more upbeat. We went back to the café and ordered black coffees, hoping they'd slow our spinning heads. Hooking into their internet, I received another piece of positive news. Sebastian confirmed a complete brand-new clutch was in the process of being fitted and that I could collect the bike tomorrow lunchtime. He'd agreed a price with Sato and it had already been paid. On a day of such disparate emotions, it truly was a weight off my mind and inwardly I felt confident this was third time lucky for both us and the poor bike.

Diana had been sympathetically following our rolling WU drama and taken it on faith that we would sort out the deposit by the end of the day. The stone had been carefully removed from the pendant and sent off to the lab. She would even stay open late, until WU closed, to give us the best chance of paying with cash and thus retaining the twenty percent discount. We were moving forward, hurdle by hurdle, but I could already taste that first pint with Charlie later!

Back in the line at WU, I tried to catch and read the teller's face, to catch any telltale indications we might be getting some positive feedback.

"There is a possibility of releasing your funds today, but I need printouts of your bank account, showing the money sent, and printouts of your WU account, showing the transfer reference number. I also need a photocopy of your passport, with a declaration underneath, stating the transfer was made by you. I will need to take your fingerprints and place it on the signed declaration. These will all be faxed off and if they get processed before we close, in one hour, I can let you have your money," she rattled off like a machine.

That's some process, I thought, for letting us have 'our money' and I wasn't sure whether I should be feeling happy, annoyed, or just overwhelmed. Accepting that we weren't hiding a printer, photocopier or ink-pad in our pockets, she provided an email address to send all this through to, plus a blank piece of paper to write my declaration. She even showed me her finger-printing pad, maybe to add some assurance that it was perfectly normal to be processed like a murder suspect!

In the meantime, the shotgun-wielding security guard pulled the shutters down halfway, locking us in and any new customers out. Along with continuously drumming his fingers on the side of his shoulder-slung gun, it was a stark if blunt gesture that it really was that close to his weekend starting and we should think twice before messing with that. The remaining interned customers were evidently less problematic than us and went off one by one, all happily served, until Selly and I were alone.

Not quite alone! Mr Shotgun made a fuss of noisily pulling the steel security shutters down to the floor. I assumed his brusque manner was aimed purely at reiterating the clock had now rolled past closing time and we had crossed a line. Trust me, we wanted our weekend to start as well! We'd presented our homework (adorned with my fingerprints!) some time ago and sat nervously as the helpful teller made a succession of calls and played with the antiquated fax machine. At twenty minutes past their closing time, we received a relieved smile and a wave to approach the counter.

"Everything is accepted. Please just complete these withdrawal forms," she beamed.

Even Mr Shotgun seemed happy for us, as he responsibly, or nosily, watched the cash being counted out for us. Selly stashed the bundles out of sight and into the depths of her Machu Picchu-hiking handbag and we wished the staff a great, if ever so slightly shortened, weekend.

Diana counted out her patiently waited for deposit and assured us she would let us know the minute the ring and lab certificate were ready to collect.

We made our way home, hardly believing the twists and turns of the day. It had been heady; we both needed a drink, wanted a celebration more to the point! Meeting up with Charlie was just the perfect tonic, poetic even. The pub was buzzing, pints and stories flowed easily and the three of us thoroughly enjoyed being back in each other's company after so many miles adrift and individual dramas. Our ongoing clutch saga fascinated Charlie, especially as it had kicked off within a few short hours of us parting ways a month ago. We were more in awe of him, though. He'd faced all his troubles alone and we had to remind ourselves he was still just eighteen! He regaled us with stories of bad roads, bad weather, getting lost, chance encounters and most recently, the crash that could so easily have hospitalised him. Fortunately, he had fared much better than his prized machine, which was also being repaired somewhere here in the capital. He had the same T-shirt on as when we first met, confirming he really did have just one set of clothes and a single pair of shorts!

"Did you hear someone in the UK died from the virus yesterday? What do you think will happen to the borders if it arrives here?" he asked, as the topics ranged far and wide.

We had seen it on the news back at the hotel. On the 2nd of March, the UK government had held a COBRA meeting and the following day revealed its coronavirus action plan. Just two days later, on the 5th, the first death attributed to the virus was announced. Italy was currently faring much worse, with almost 200 deaths and several thousand cases confirmed. The police had caught over 40,000 residents from the locked-down Lombardy region fleeing to the south of the country and taking the virus with them. The Italian government's hand had been forced; a national quarantine would be imposed in three days' time, the 9th of March. I guess returning to Sardinia isn't an option now then.

Poor Charlie, he could feel yet another Guinness record slipping through his fingers, through no fault of his own this time. I didn't really have an answer for him. None of us knew if it was going to be a problem here or not. Would the countries in South and Central America even admit to any infections?

"Let's ride together, up through Central America and see what happens," was all I could suggest.

The proposal was happily agreed to and cemented with the night's final toast. Three boozy musketeers were now flagging and needed their beauty sleep! It had been a top night, lots of banter, jokes and stories that we'd all benefitted from sharing. Laughter and a smidge of alcohol truly were our best medicines. Charlie was staying not too far from us, in a 'groovy' and ridiculously cheap hostel. We agreed to meet up there the following evening and compare bike repair stories.

We could afford the much needed lie-in, my first for what felt like weeks. We didn't expect to be collecting bikes, or rings, until the afternoon. Selly had powered through the last twenty-four hours on a high of emotions, but she was still feeling rough, had done since the border, and couldn't summon any appetite for breakfast. She had to try eating something, though. I ducked the buffet and brought the pair of us coffees and a selection of pastries to the room. If that couldn't tempt an Italian then I was facing serious problems. I wasn't, she ate!

It was nice to have some downtime, a chance to make only social calls for a change, watch the news properly and respond to emails, etc. We needed to recalibrate and try to take on board the possible implications of the virus. We didn't have a great deal of information to go on; we were double-guessing what may be in jeopardy and what may not. Was just the immediate journey likely to be affected, or was the whole adventure at risk, our grand dream adventure? I turned to the TV.

We had both CNN and the BBC World news channels and between them, a darkening picture of the pandemic's spread filled the screen. Dozens of countries now reported deaths and spiralling cases of infections. The uncertainty was ramping up everywhere, it seemed, yet none of these countries were in our immediate neighbourhood and it was hard to know what to make of it all.

In ten days' time, we were supposed to be in San José, for the Guns N' Roses concert, but the continued spread of the virus was rightly forcing organisers to cancel major events around the world. We searched the internet for any information, finding one webpage stating the concert was indefinitely delayed, followed by another that said it was still on. It pretty much summed up the vacuum of reliable knowledge throughout the whole of the Americas at that point in time. The situation over here lagged far behind Europe and nobody really understood, or grasped, what was coming for us, what was stalking us. Would our wedding be next?

What was clear to us, though, was that lockdowns of regions, or entire countries, were the primary defences and we realised we needed to have a plan. Hopefully, just a backup plan, but definitely a destination in mind. Somewhere we could hold out safely should any borders along our route temporarily close. We sat discussing possible options, noting what each of our concerns and preferences were. We had sound insurance; there just needed to be access to medical care close by. Ideally, we'd want to be somewhere not too heavily populated, definitely not a city, comfortably within our budget and very ideally, somewhere in the Caribbean!

In a few days, I hoped to be meeting up with a good friend, currently living in Panama City, and he'd already warned us that both Panama and Costa Rica were quite pricey. We could pass through these countries quite quickly if needed and on into Nicaragua, which was much cheaper, but I already had a grander idea in my mind. North of Nicaragua was Honduras, also relatively cheap, and it boasted a sizeable Caribbean island called Roatán. I put the suggestion to Selly.

"It's renowned for great beaches and diving. We can take the bike by ferry, and being a bit of a 'playground' for American and Canadian tourists, it has modern hospitals," I put forward, sounding like a tour guide!

I think Selly was pretty much won over at the mention of the Caribbean; the rest of the package was a superfluous bonus! We truly hoped it didn't come down to this, but if borders started closing in this part of the world, then we would make a bolt for Roatán. At least we had a plan, a pretty good plan, we thought.

I messaged Dauri, it had been a while, to seek his views on the whole situation. He wasn't taking any chances, had recently crossed back into Mexico and was heading for his home, in the state of Oaxaca. He didn't want to risk being separated from his family indefinitely but continued to insist that if we made it that far north, we must come join him and stay.

At lunchtime, I grabbed a taxi back to the Suzuki dealer. Even if my own wasn't ready to ride off, it was still a fascinating place to grab a coffee and watch all the bikes coming and going. I found the English-speaking receptionist and gathered the bike was out being test-ridden. Not too far, I hoped; the fuel symbol was already flashing! I'd purposely been running it down, ahead of delivering it to the shippers, thus avoiding having to drain the tank.

Sebastian found me, his hands full with the latest collection of plates and bits I'd destroyed out on the road. This time, though, I didn't have to empty my wallet, and he assured me the bike was properly assembled and good as new. I believed him and truly felt Panama was going to be the start of a new adventure for us. It would be, but not the one we had planned!

The bike was handed over and riding away, I tentatively pushed it through the first few gears; it simply felt great. An inner voice declared *this is sorted,* and on a short section of dual carriageway I spun the revs up quicker, without any hint of an issue. The bike was responding beautifully; we were back in business!

It was time to conclude Selly's business. Her gems were now ready to collect and at the dealer's we were met by both Diana and her husband, brought along to take some photos of the finished ring.

"I have some very good news for you both," she started with, in a voice that managed to convey half excitement and half resentment.

As Selly waited anxiously to see the finished ring, Diana laid out the lab's certificate before us.

"It's come back one grade higher than I'd estimated. This is very good news for you, and I can assure you nobody in this building would have sold you that stone at that price," she continued telling us, whilst keeping a grip on the box!

I produced the remaining fifty percent payment and offered it to her husband for counting.

He waved it off, rather gruffly, adding, "I don't touch the money, it's her business, her decisions."

Despite being amateurs, I was getting the feeling we had actually struck a reasonable deal. The box was opened and Selly gestured for me to slide the ring onto her finger. It was a perfect fit and the three stones simply shone in the shop's bright lights; she was over the moon. Diana's husband was trying his best to photograph it, but Selly was just too enthralled and couldn't keep her hand still! We happily departed with the cash and happily departed the building, but as thrilled as Selly was to wear it, her hand stayed hidden all the way back to the room!

Having got our bearings on the city, we grabbed drinks and took a walk over to Charlie's hostel. It really was as hip as he'd described, with a nice firepit blazing in the bar area and colourful murals across the walls. It seemed we had almost as much catching up to do as the night before. Although our day had ended swimmingly, Charlie's bike was still in bits and being worked on. It wouldn't be ready until at least Monday morning, and he naturally worried things were being cut too tight.

Another spanner in the works was his number plate of all things. Due to high air pollution, the capital had imposed temporary laws to halve the traffic on the roads. Odd and even-numbered plates could only be on the roads on alternate days. I had managed to drop lucky, as my 'even' plate was allowed on the road today, and again on Monday when we needed to drop the bikes off. Charlie's was odd!

"I'll just blag it!" was his happy-go-lucky response.

"I was warned at the shop they often confiscate bikes, and then you have to argue it out later," I said, adding, "I have a spare plate you could tape on, just for the journey if you like?"

"Nah, honestly, it'll be fine," he laughed, cracking another beer.

We were having too much fun. Selly loved having the fire's warmth soothe her aching body and the three of us cheerfully ploughed through our sizable 'carry-in'. Inevitably, it was cut short once the staff realised we hadn't any intentions of buying from their bar! Charlie's alcohol-fuelled efforts to placate them went down a treat.

"I do live here, you know, and I've always drunk my own beers," he reprimanded in a 'you do know who I am' kinda voice.

We were evicted. Charlie was dealt with first, having been invited to take his beers up to his room, like a naughty schoolboy, and Selly and I were simply told to vacate the premises! Oh well, all good things come to an end.

We tried messaging Peter and Sonia shortly after arriving in Bogotá. Today, there was a 'Sunday bike festival' in the city centre we thought they might like, but unfortunately we didn't hear back until we were already over in Panama. Instead, we took ourselves off to visit a museum and for a cultural walk. The plan was to meet Charlie later in the afternoon, enjoy the festival's bands and have a few beers in the sunshine. The morning had been so hot we'd dressed only in shorts and T-shirts, and promptly got caught out in a huge unexpected downpour. Despite running for cover, we were soaked by the cold rain in seconds.

A bunch of us stood shivering under the cover of a building entrance, hoping the icy rain would subside. It must have dropped twenty degrees in under a minute and typically, there were no taxis around. It was the last thing Selly needed, and she started sneezing just to prove it! We hopped from cover to cover, making it back to the hotel soaked and shivering. Where did that come from! There weren't going to be any festival meet-ups today. Charlie later told us he had just arrived as the heavens opened up and, likewise, rapidly legged it back to his own hostel as well.

Our altitude wasn't so high, but Selly was now struggling with her breathing, had developed headaches and still ached from head to toe. At just over 2,600 metres, Bogotá was high enough to give you altitude sickness, but we'd spent ten nights reaching here since last being down at sea level, in Ecuador's Santa Rosa. Many weeks previously had also been spent acclimatised at much higher altitudes. Neither of us believed this was the altitude hitting her, but with no fever, or loss of taste, it shouldn't be the virus either. The next day, she sensibly rested up in the hotel as I took the loaded-up bike and our paperwork to the shipping agent. Charlie planned to meet me there once he'd recovered his, hopefully repaired, Yamaha.

I was nicely surprised to find him parked up, smiling away, but anxiously trying to hand-wash his bike with a borrowed bucket and cloth.

"I didn't have time to clean it, and it needs to be as clean as yours," he stated, looking over at my shining black bike.

The shipping agent came out and introduced herself as Veronica. I was offered coffee with a smile, but after perusing poor Charlie's progress, she switched to a frown, telling him his efforts wouldn't cut it and he was going to have to find a car wash!

"Oh bugger, ah well," he laughed, throwing the cloth into the bucket.

There was a third bike there, an aging Yamaha XT600, with an enlarged tank and, coincidentally, also a UK plate.

"That's Mike's bike, great guy. Pop up and meet him," revealed Charlie.

I did and he was. The three of us had our bikes booked to fly on the same cargo flight and all three of us were generally heading north. By the time the first round of coffees were downed, it was already decided we'd ride together, up through Panama for starters, and Mike booked himself on the same passenger flight as us. The little gang was now four.

Mike and I bantered away, waiting on Charlie returning with a freshly spruced machine. Mike was a character, to say the least. Four years older than me and what I'd call an 'old-school biker', content with an ageing trusty steed and minimal kit. He'd managed to make Charlie's bike, with his one T-shirt, look overloaded! He could understand why I'd hung on to a ZZR for twenty-seven years and still cherished it. Best of all, though, he had a lifetime of travel stories to entertain us with. Working freelance, he took lengthy trips almost every year. Not your average ones either. Name a country and he had a yarn for us. For sure, the love of bikes weaved through his ventures, but he was also an avid and renowned climber. As an author, he had published books on both travel and climbing. You may even have read of him. On a cold November day, back in 2007, he made a daring 'protest' free-climb of the Eiffel Tower, wearing a 'Free Burma' T-shirt and making it up 720 feet before being arrested. It was fair to say all of us were going to get on just fine!

With Charlie now back, we rode out to the airport, trying to keep him sandwiched between our two machines, thus hiding his 'criminal' number plate! His luck held out and we submitted the machines to a thorough hound-sniffing and inspection by customs officers. With the bikes leaving Colombia, I was expecting to have to pull the baggage apart, but the dogs seemed to hold sway and we hardly opened up a thing. After the mandatory waiting around, for no discernible reason, we finally waved them goodbye, hopefully to see them on the other side of the Darién Gap in a couple of days' time.

It had pretty much taken up the whole day, though, and now I was anxious to get back and see how Selly was faring. I found her resting up in the room, still achy, but grateful for the day's peace and quiet. The last week had taken a toll on us both, Selly physically and me emotionally. She did feel up to tomorrow's flight, though; there just wouldn't be any partying, drinking or evictions on this evening's agenda!

So he could jump in the airport taxi with us, Charlie walked over to our hotel in the morning and I snuck him in for a decent breakfast.

"Blimey, this is awesome. I've just boiled the eggs I had left over and eaten four of them on the way here, but I'm not missing out on this buffet," he exclaimed, like the true skint student he was!

"Fill your boots, buddy. Selly won't be eating and it's paid for," I encouraged.

"That'd just be silly, Mark. I won't fill my boots, but I will fill my pockets!" he declared, and did. All of them.

We met Mike at the gate and with Selly introduced, we lapsed into the usual excitement of venturing into both another new country and a fresh leg of our journeys. Charlie and Mike really were epic guys to be around and Selly and I both looked forward to their company out on the road. Although we had different accommodations booked for that evening, we agreed to meet up for a beer, or few. I would be introducing them to my mate Bob, who'd recommended us a suitable drinking hole down in central Panama City, his local no less!

Chapter Twelve

Cornered in Central America

Flying over and looking down on the narrow strip of jungle, known as the 'impenetrable' Darién Gap, was both intriguing and captivating. Between the gaps in the clouds, there was just a blanket of green and I imagined a dark ribbon of black asphalt one day threading its way through and finally making the Pan-American Highway complete and continuous. For too many reasons, that just wasn't likely to happen, though, at least not in my biking lifetime. It looked pristine from 9,000 metres, but in reality it was controlled by drug gangs, human traffickers and lawless tribes. Neither Panama nor Colombia had desires to pay for, build and manage a highway. Especially one that was destined to be fought over and abused. A small handful of adventurers had made this notorious crossing successfully. I wasn't in their league and from the comfort of my seat, kicked back and, instead, enjoyed the banter between the four of us.

By 6pm, we were all enjoying our first Panamanian beers. Having initially introduced Bob, he then introduced us to all his friends, who'd kindly come out to meet and greet us. We didn't even have to worry about getting up to go to the airport the next day. Veronica had messaged to say our freight flight had been cancelled and we'd see the bikes the day after tomorrow, fingers crossed.

We soon discovered Panama has a very interesting expat community, and Bob's friends seemed to span the entire spectrum. As we all drank a little too much, they kept us entertained with their modern-day 'wild west' life stories and exploits. The bar owner got involved and in keeping with the evening's randomness, proudly let Bob show us his 8-metre-long rocket-fuelled drag car, that he kept in a room behind the bar. Nothing could trump that and calling time, we said our goodbyes as Bob reiterated a warning he'd aired earlier:

"Don't forget what I told you about the missing manhole covers, they're all over the city. I mean they're missing all over the city. Well, you know what I mean," he tipsily grinned.

Apparently, they were being stolen for scrap metal value and had caused many an accident. We wobbled back to the accommodation, heads already spinning but crossing the roads 'extra vigilantly'!

The bikes did indeed make the following flight and the three of us headed excitedly out to retrieve them. As Selly wouldn't be allowed airside, or in the customs area, she happily opted for the comfort of the room and another rest day. I nosed around, trying to get a glimpse of my own bike, suddenly wondering if the dodgy side-stand had caused any freight issues. All was fine, but before we could ride them away they needed to be disinfected and left to stand for forty-five minutes. Charlie was chuffed; two bike washes within a few days!

That afternoon, Selly and I refilled the bike and took a spin out to the Miraflores Locks, on the Panama Canal. Just before the tourist attraction's car park, a narrow bridge crossed a tributary, and looking down we saw a huge crocodile lazily swimming down the middle of the waterway. Our first sighting of the wilder Panama!

The whole 'canal' experience, with a 3-D IMAX show and lock-side viewing platforms, was enthralling. Impressive yachts, shrunk by dwarfing container ships, lined up together in the narrow lock, rose majestically to our platform height and headed off into the Pacific. The following mega-ship's crew looked like they had spent several solitary weeks on the open waters. They were out on deck, waving and, I think, smiling behind their brand-new face masks. Were they really afraid of being within thirty metres of us gawping tourists? If the Europeans were absurdly stripping their supermarket shelves of toilet paper and pasta, then I could forgive these seafarers for seeing us as a potential threat! We idled away the hours, fascinated by the expert manoeuvrings and safe passage of ship after ship. Half a dozen locos pulled them through and not one even glanced the lock's sides. Indeed, no precious yachts were harmed during the making of our videos! We couldn't resist a bit of crocodile spotting on the way out and were rewarded by the sighting of two more leftover dinosaurs.

It was Friday the 13th of March, and we'd all met up for the ride north. Charlie and Mike had some important news, potentially a 'game-changer' for all of us, and we waited with bated breath.

"The UK Premier League is suspended for the rest of the season," piped up Mike.

"No, not that news," interjected Charlie, "yesterday, El Salvador closed its borders, for at least a month," he dropped on us.

This certainly was news, big news for all of us. Although we could get around the country, directly from Honduras and up into Guatemala, this was most likely just the tip of the iceberg. It was a bit of a reality check; we hadn't even heard of any coronavirus cases being officially reported here in Central America. This became the first country, anywhere in the Americas, to implement border closures and a quarantine. Where was next? we all wondered.

The race was now on, and thoughts of any dilly-dallying and diving in Panama, Costa Rica, or Nicaragua were out of the window. Predictably, the Guns N' Roses concert had been cancelled, so all things considered, our backup plan, to reach the island of Roatán, had suddenly become a real mission. The desire to get as far north as possible, as soon as possible, was felt by all of us. To continue his record attempt, Charlie ideally needed to reach the USA, whereas Mike was in love with Mexico and would be content to make it that far. Selly and I were ultimately still aiming for the Arctic Ocean!

With all of us ready to hit the road, I gave a final reminder to keep an eye out for missing manhole covers and then nearly got hit by a taxi, swerving around a cover that was still there! It seemed the taxi drivers didn't trust any of them and just dodged round, whether they were there or not!

We left the city behind us and picked up the northbound PAH. Charlie quickly pulled ahead, setting a faster pace as Mike and I rode side by side and with Selly's help, managed to get some photos of each other riding. Our loose plan was to ride up as close to the Costa Rican border as we could, and then find somewhere to camp. After a few miles we regrouped, and then the stunts started.

Charlie came past stood on his seat, as Mike pulled alongside with feet planted on his rear pegs, laying flat on the tank, as if to squeeze a little more speed out of the big XT single. Having the benefit of a pillion, I responded by standing up on my pegs and letting Selly expertly massage my numb bum, as she so often kindly did for me. Can't do that now, can you, guys!

After nearly 300 miles, we called it a day and pitched tents at a makeshift campsite, beside a family's home. We were their only guests that evening and they looked after us wonderfully. The place had a pair of friendly dogs and several chickens that together, playfully invaded our intended campsite and generally got in the way as we set up. Having said that, we wasted no time pitching tents and jumping into the outdoor pool. A tame monkey curiously watched all the comings and goings from the safety of a nearby tree. There was a kitchen we could use and Selly kindly prepared dinner for us all. We loved the place; it had been a swelteringly humid day and the pool, cold beers and cold showers ended it perfectly.

Considering we were supposed to be in some haste, it was a bunch of hungover bikers who put a lie-in, followed by a homely breakfast, ahead of an early rise and any tent packing. It was early afternoon before we had all navigated our way through the two borders and into Costa Rica. We only managed 130 'hot and sticky' miles, before finding hostel rooms in the Pacific coastal town of Dominical.

Bob proved spot-on with his warning about Costa Rican prices.

It was the worst room we had stayed in, in the cheapest hostel we could find, and we'd had to haggle to get the price down to thirty-five dollars! For Selly and I, this would definitely be a one-nighter, with a run to the Nicaraguan border on the cards for the following day. Mike had decided to stay another night and the three of us said our goodbyes the following morning, promising to keep in touch 'from further down the road'. It all felt a bit hasty, but we all had our own goals in mind and the El Salvadoran border closing had spooked us, I guess. We all needed to be somewhere that little bit more urgently now.

I had been looking forward to riding the length of Costa Rica; it was the Central American country we had allocated the most time to. As we progressed north, it excelled our dreams. It was simply stunning and I already felt guilty that we had to abandon the plans we had for the country. Admittedly, the heat and humidity sapped and wilted us, but with the Pacific on our left, rich jungle on our right and wildlife all around, we were easily kept distracted. A pair of huge red parrots flew across our path, trailing long green tails, followed by toucans, and signs warned of sloths and giant anteaters. We just soaked it all in with wonderment and loved it all.

We were having to make frequent stops, just to take on water, but spying a Sunday chemist's open we pulled over once more, as Charlie ran ahead with another biker heading north. Selly had been putting a brave face on these last few days. In fact, we were both struggling just to stay hydrated in our bike gear. It was over forty degrees again and it didn't seem to matter how much you drank, it just poured out of you. We lingered a few minutes in the chemist's, letting the cool air-con revive us, before picking out flu remedies for Selly and rehydration sachets for the pair of us.

Sixty miles further on, the PAH crossed a bridge, with several people looking over. Slowing, Selly leaned forward and said she saw crocodiles, both in the water and out on sandy banks. Needing another hydration stop, we parked up and grabbed freshly squeezed fruit juices. Finding WiFi, I updated Charlie as to where we were and he responded saying he was already at the Nicaraguan border, and warned it was a choked, confusing scramble. Oh great, something to look forward to later!

We broke out the cameras and went crocodile shooting instead! Looking over the middle of the bridge, we excitedly counted twenty-three of them, either basking or lying submerged in the shallow river. It was quite a delight to see so many in their natural habitat, but hammered home just how much we would be missing out on by 'running for Roatán'. Our original hopes for Costa Rica included visiting a sloth sanctuary, diving in the Cocos Islands, hiking through jungles and, of course, the now cancelled concert in San José. To cling onto any hopes of reaching Alaska, we would have to breeze through this beautiful country in just a couple of days.

It was already dusk before we arrived at the border. Charlie was nowhere to be seen and I guessed long gone by now. We joined a queue of mixed vehicles, believing it was for the exit process. It was, but we should have stopped off to pay a Costa Rican 'exit tax' first and brought along the receipt to prove it. We started again, being bounced around from building to building and sent away for various photocopies until our paperwork was in order to leave the country.

Even when you have an idea of what to expect, it's usually a stressy time at the borders. There always seems to be too many people hanging around; the obvious ones are the money changers, drink and snack vendors, the fixers and 'helpers', offering to ease your way through the paperwork minefields, for a small price, of course. Added to these are the truck drivers, foot traffic and coach passengers, milling around with their assortment of multi-coloured bags. Then there's nearly always the shifty ones, who look out of place and make you feel uncomfortable having to leave a bike alone, loaded with all your possessions, whilst you disappear off to decipher the customs process. It didn't really help that there were two of us. Selly still had her own passport to sort out and invariably ended up having to translate for me, when sorting out the bike's papers. Despite receiving warnings, no tampering or loss had ever happened to us, though, and I often left the borders chastising myself for not being more trusting.

We still had a fair amount of Costa Rican *colóns* left over, but no Nicaraguan *córdobas*. Not knowing what Nicaraguan entry fees we might need to pay, I decided to break my golden rule of never changing money at a border. The problem was, I was changing blind. I had no idea of the exchange rate between these two currencies. The money changers circled like sharks, with wads of cash in their hands, sensing our predicament. I decided to change just a small amount to see us through the first couple of days. Like a pantomime, I loudly turned down the first three seller's rates, correctly anticipating each successive offer would be an improvement. Of course, they were all working as a team and I still got ripped off (I later realised), but at least we had cash for visas and bike insurance now.

Feeling smug with his lucrative transaction, the vendor at least pointed out where we needed to be next, at a carwash, it appeared. Sure enough, our boots and the bike duly received a mandatory disinfection, and when completed, I held out a few *córdobas,* hoping it would be enough.

"One dollar. Only dollar," he barked, in such a way as to make clear that *córdobas* weren't acceptable.

We left the bike trying to dry in the humidity and used the time to try to seek out an insurance policy. A tiny portable desk, set up and virtually hidden amongst the truck lanes, proved to be the insurance 'office'!

"Dollars only, twelve for one month, no change," she requested, upon seeing my clutched *córdobas* at the ready.

There seemed to be a theme running here, I gathered, as I stuffed them away and dug around for the right amount of dollars. The chaos we were pre-warned about greeted us inside the immigration hall. People, baggage and jumbled queues spun our heads, and nowhere was there a sign to guide us. We just didn't know where to start, but as we appeared to be in a queue by accident, shuffled forward regardless, whilst attempting to make sense of the commotion. Everybody in front of us had passports and forms in hand, so it seemed this must be to get our passports stamped. Selly located the 'arrival' forms for us to complete awkwardly as we inched forward.

They did have some free WiFi, though, and knowing it would be pitch-black by the time we escaped, I found and booked us a room for the night. It was only twenty miles to the nearest town of Rivas and I sent the hostel location to Charlie, in case he'd had a similar idea. If not later, then I thought we could meet up in the morning and chew over our options. Distracted by the phone, Selly nudged me to say we'd shuffled far enough.

"Passports and thirteen dollars each," said a stern-looking customs lady.

"How much in *córdobas*?" I wishfully tried.

"Only dollars," was all the reply I got.

Were our new *córdobas* Monopoly money? I was beginning to feel fleeced at every turn and we still had the bike to get through yet! From a vendor's stall that had popped up alongside our bike, I bought us bottles of water. Apart from quenching thirsts, I just needed to prove to myself our 'new' money was actually good for a transaction! We ploughed through more forms, queues, a cursory police inspection of our luggage and finally, a grand presentation of all the receipts and stamps at the exit barrier. We were free to go and cruised under the 'Welcome to Nicaragua' sign and into the darkness beyond, blissfully leaving the chaos behind. We had been given a three-month visa for ourselves and thirty days for the motorbike. Should be more than enough, I so, so wrongly thought!

There were no signs or streetlights to guide us and my fingers were crossed that our online map got us to where we needed to be. The excitement of being in another new country was tinged with a little anxiety. We were riding in a black tunnel, formed by the interlocking trees. Huge moths continually flew at the headlight and every so often, the bike's full beam illuminated pairs of eyes, off in the roadside's undergrowth. I never saw what any of them were and, instead, let my tired brain imagine what might lurk. Maybe just harmless fairies and unicorns, I mused. Surely not rabid dogs or nocturnal vampire vultures. There was virtually no traffic, just the odd person ambling along on the edge of the road, usually a machete in hand and dressed in shabby dark clothes and tired flip-flops. Even this was unsettling.

Why were zombies out with machetes, so far from anywhere? Silly me, to fight off the rabid dog packs, of course. Even zombies have their limits!

Just the day before, we were warned not to be out riding at night in Nicaragua, full stop. Do not even go out at night. It was that same theme playing through the trip; the neighbours are worse than we are! Bob's friends, back in Panama, had warned us about thieves being prevalent around Costa Rica's resorts and beaches, yet we'd all been OK. Then, in Costa Rica, we'd been warned about the dangers of being out at night in Nicaragua, but what choice did we have? We could hardly just pull up and pitch the tent.

Reaching the outskirts and lights of Rivas was a relief to both of us; I certainly wasn't in the mood for zombie slaying. Being late on a Sunday evening, there was little life in the town, but what we did see told a story. There were as many donkey-drawn carts and carriages as there were vehicles, with rickshaws and animals appearing to be the 'taxis'. The few places that were open, bars and corner shops, were actually closed off behind metal grills, with the odd customer being served through tiny security hatches.

Mostly, it was the men drinking, sat around on plastic chairs, either on the pavement or in the road itself. An oversized plug-in amp, out on the pavement, provided the entertainment. Everybody stared at us, not in a threatening way, just in a drunkenly curious 'why are you here?' way. Online maps don't make any effort to steer you clear of potentially dangerous, or poor neighbourhoods; however, after bumping our way around in circles, it was apparent this part of the town wasn't Rivas' best face. After Panama and Costa Rica, it felt we had gone back in time, to a much poorer time.

We checked in, to something resembling a room. It was an outdoor space that had had three wonky brick walls put up and a fourth wall, plus the roof cobbled together out of wood. I could clearly hear animals on the other side of the 'wooden' wall. Rather than using that modern fandangle plaster and paint stuff, sheets had been hung to hide the exposed and shoddy brickwork. I had excelled in finding this place, patted myself on the back and watched as Selly collapsed on the bed, vowing to sleep fully dressed. There would be no romance this night!

Despite having the audacity to call the place a hotel, the owner was a genuinely lovely and helpful lady.

"By any chance, do you have any wine, or beer we could buy, please?" I enquired, hoping to toast our first night in a new country.

"No, sorry, we don't," but with a smile.

I changed tack. "Is there any hot water for the shower?"

"No, sorry, but there is a shower," again, with a smile.

"Is the internet working?" I finished off, with fingers crossed for 'third time lucky'.

"Oh yes," she replied triumphantly, sensing I was somewhat placated.

Having passed nothing on the way here, I messaged Charlie, assuming he was also likely to be in Rivas somewhere. I didn't have to wait long for a reply, but I did have to read it twice and then out loud to Selly!

Me and the other biker are camping, we just pulled up and pitched the tents, followed by *We seem to be by a huge lake, it's full of mosquitoes and an insect hit me in the face. I can only see out of one eye.*

Crazy buggers. As amusing as it was, or dismal, I glanced around our digs and still felt envious!

Selly researched the internet as I poured over a hardcopy map. We might not be spending long in Nicaragua, but we should try to find the most scenic, even if circuitous, route up to Honduras.

"Have you heard of the Corn Islands?" she asked. No, I hadn't, and received an education!

"Nicaragua has two Caribbean islands, Big Corn Island and Little Corn Island. There's a ferry you can catch to Big Corn and from there you can hop on a boat to Little Corn," and just to make sure I was listening intently, "they're surrounded by coral reefs, have dive centres and the reviews are very good," she teased.

That put the cat amongst the pigeons. I was prepared for a circuitous route but hadn't considered one involving Caribbean islands and diving! We were supposed to be gunning for Roatán, admittedly for pretty much the same thing that the Corn Islands seemed to be offering. It would be something to sleep on, if the grunting animals allowed us to, and we'd see what tomorrow brought.

Well, the first thing it brought was Charlie, who looked like he had been boxing. One eye was entirely shut, and his cheek was sorely swollen.

"How you coping with the helmet?" I asked, attempting empathy whilst trying not to laugh.

"Bloody painful, and I keep getting flies in the other eye," he replied, grinning and proudly sporting his injuries like they were just normal adventure riders' trophies.

Hearing the commotion, a Dutch guy came out of our 'hotel' and enquired where we were all headed.

"You're heading north? Well, Honduras closed its border at midnight last night and Costa Rica closes its borders tonight, at midnight," he stated, pretty much flooring Selly and I.

So, it had happened then. Within another twenty-four hours we would be boxed in, unable to proceed north, or south.

"What about Nicaragua?" someone replied.

"Doesn't matter what Nicaragua does. The borders north are now impassable and at midnight, heading south will be the same," he logically pointed out.

Selly and I looked at each other, instantly realising Roatán was no longer an option and worse, with less than twelve weeks to go, surely our wedding plans were now in disarray. Was I ever going to marry this woman? We needed a new plan, and right now. The implications were equally dire for Charlie. His RTW record attempt was all but over and Costa Rica likely offered him more shipping options than Nicaragua could. He was the first to announce a decision.

"I'm going to head back to Costa Rica whilst I can. I'll try and meet back up with Mike," he said gloomily.

For a while, each of us became lost in our own thoughts, plugged into the hostel's WiFi and sat researching, formulising plans. The borders were closing initially for a month, but at midnight the following day, both Panama and Guatemala would also shut. The net was closing fast. I had messages waiting from Mike, confirming the same news. We didn't want to jump to conclusions, but it looked very much like a domino effect would ripple through the entire Americas. With hearts a little heavier, we hugged and reluctantly waved off the injured Charlie.

I was sorry to see him leaving us; he'd wanted to ride all the way to Vegas and be there for our wedding. I'd already imagined us riding up to Mexico together, meeting up with Dauri and continuing on up to the States. I'd miss him and his infectious cheeky smile. It was all a bit of a downer if we dwelled on it. Some of our friends had already paid for their flights and accommodation in Vegas, but still being nearly three months away, who knew what the situation would be then? We sat chatting with the Dutch guy, who, full of good news, told us a sad and potentially worrying story.

"The Nicaraguan government won't tell you if the virus is in the country. This hotel owner's German father died two days ago, couldn't breathe," he went on.

Selly and I had seen a black ribbon tied to the doorway, but hadn't intruded upon its meaning.

"Was it unexpected?" I queried.

"Oh yes, he lived here, I chatted every day with him. A few days ago, he felt ill and the next day he died, from breathing problems. I'm leaving today for Ometepe Island," he finished off.

It was sobering news all round; it looked very likely that we were going to be stranded in a developing country, with a dubious government and 'wanting' medical facilities. We didn't know a single person here and there wasn't even a British consulate based within the country! Our decision to stay put was accepting we'd now be trapped in Nicaragua for the foreseeable future.

Chapter Thirteen

Escape to the Caribbean

After a little deliberation, Selly and I made our minds up to try for the Corn Islands. The port was a two-day ride across the country, over to the east coast and then requiring a six-hour ferry crossing. The rider Charlie had crossed the border with had left us with an intriguing tip, for a hostel tucked inside a volcano crater, of all places. It was offering discounts for longer stays and could be just what we needed. As tempting as it was to head straight there, the Caribbean was irresistibly luring us.

It was nice to be riding in daylight, in the sunshine, and the road conditions were surprisingly good. What little traffic existed was incredibly law-abiding, speed limits were rarely broken, solid lines weren't crossed and stop signs were actually obeyed. I was impressed; it was easy to relax and unlike the unlit roads of last night, it felt very safe to ride here. Maybe the compliance was because there were so many more random police checkpoints, or handheld speed-traps in Nicaragua! They seemed to be about every ten miles and occasionally we were asked for our papers, but otherwise left alone and just waved on.

It was another sweltering day as we made our way eastwards, over forty degrees again, and the terrain around us was bone-dry and scorched brown. Not expecting the roads to be this good, we had planned on a relatively short ride, just 160 miles, to the city of Juigalpa. It appeared to be one large building site and midway through having all its streets dug up at the same time! Searching for any accommodation, we melted at stop sign after stop sign as JCBs and bulldozers went about their carnage. The first three places were fully booked and only in the far outskirts did we strike lucky, with a hotel that had a nice frontage hiding tired and dilapidated rooms. They did have cold drinks, cold showers and cold air-con, though. Everything we needed right now!

"There's a great steakhouse just up the road and we can hand-wash your laundry if you like," said the receptionist, who was also the cleaner and the laundry girl by the looks of it.

"That's great, but could we swap our room, please?" I enquired, after finding fresh rat droppings across the floor and on the bed.

"Oh dear," she exclaimed, as I pointed out the gnarled holes in the sagging chipboard ceiling.

The taxi dropped us at a much nicer-looking hotel cum ranch, wrapped around an inviting steakhouse and bar. The food, service and atmosphere were terrific, and I felt myself relaxing, properly warming to this country. The bill had been so cheap that we'd already decided to stay a night here, if we had to pass back this way. Returning to our slightly less posh abode, we were greeted by the sight of all our laundry flying in the dusty air, tied to the car park's chain-link fence! I couldn't wait to get moving again.

A strange sight occurred when we left Juigalpa that morning, within just one or two miles; the entire landscape turned from scorched brown to a lush green. We had crossed some imaginary line and even the harsh temperatures we had been riding in, since arriving in Panama, had subsided to a more comfortable mid-thirties. It was a wonderful if unexpected transformation and added to the joy of the day's riding.

To catch the ferry, we needed to reach the former pirates' haven of Bluefields, on the Mosquito Coast. It should have been another comfortable 160-mile dawdle, on a brand-new road, but the satnav had other ideas. It took us in a plausible but ultimately wrong direction to the city of Rama, where the road turned to dirt and didn't end up anywhere near the coast. We'd wasted several hours, had gotten ourselves filthy and dehydrated, on a series of muddy roads we shouldn't even have been on. Soaked from the humidity and pondering our next move, I felt all the hotter, just for having to admit I no longer knew where we were.

The new road wasn't on any of our maps and it took some questioning to get an idea of where we were meant to be. Nobody could understand why we were in Rama if we wanted to be in Bluefields, silly foreigners! Our ferry to the Corn Islands wasn't leaving until the morning, so there really wasn't anything to get stressed about, but it did pain me to admit I'd messed up, lost us several hours and we'd have to double back most of the way again!

The transformation in the scenery was a sight for sore eyes, though. The barren brown truly was gone for good and all had been replaced by fifty shades of green. Vehicles were easily outnumbered by meandering animals and foot traffic. Hand in hand, groups of uniformed schoolchildren, as young as five or six, walked remote miles to the various schools. No such thing as a 'school run' here. We were getting used to pretty much everyone, even children occasionally, brandishing machetes, as they went about collecting firewood, or fending off packs of starving dogs. Occasionally, we'd be chased aggressively by a snarling stray and it could be intimidating, but overall we just felt pitifully sorry for them. Those that were 'owned' fared little better, permanently tied up and serving no more purpose than alarm clocks to warn of visitors, or warn off intruders.

We might have had our rabies jabs but didn't enjoy being startled out of the blue and chased down the road! Another randomly common sight was iguanas being sold, for food, at the roadside. Usually, they were thirty to forty centimetres long, trussed up and held up as motorists passed by. I so wanted to stop, buy one and free it, but the mood these mini-alligators were likely to be in, I very much doubted I'd successfully set one free before it feasted on a finger or two!

The unintentional diversion had added a hundred sweaty miles to the day's journey, with the final sixty on the much-hyped about 'new road'. It had been meticulously and entirely constructed out of 'driveway' paving blocks. The story goes that the company producing these little blocks is owned by a government minister, and this is how many of the new roads are now painstakingly built!

Our arrival in Bluefields, tree-lined and empty, had felt like we'd just ridden through some huge and sprawling private estate. There wasn't a pretty mansion at the end of this road, though. We'd been warned Bluefields was a rough harbour town, and it certainly hadn't lifted a finger to try hard to hide it. However, the hostel had a secure garage and the owner was happy to look after the bike, for the duration we'd be away on the islands. They lay forty-two miles off the coast, a full six hours if the crossing was smooth, or a lengthier stomach-churning ordeal if it wasn't!

It had been a testing day and Selly was feeling washed-out, aching and exhausted. It had now been two weeks since she'd first become unwell. A sore throat had developed and mucus continued to cause her breathing difficulties. She looked, and was, poorly, with the only consolation being she didn't have a high temperature, or experience loss of taste. There wasn't anywhere in Nicaragua to take a coronavirus test yet. In fact, the government weren't admitting it was even in the country.

We needed to fix this ourselves and Selly started a course of antibiotics, had a rehydration drink and got her head down. During this same fortnight, I'd felt 'off' for about three days, but quickly recovered and other than being dehydrated too often, had felt mostly fine since. We really didn't know what to make of any of it, but hoped the antibiotics and a week away from the road would go a long way to getting her well again.

Around 6 pm, I took a wander out to find the ferry port and to see if I could secure our tickets for the morning. It soon felt a mistake; Bluefields was already a ghost town. Almost all of its inhabitants had retreated behind metal shutters and I stuck out like a sore thumb, ambling around with my wallet, passport and phone bulging in my pockets. It's a hard place to write about without sounding unkind; I'll let your imagination paint the picture!

On the ride down, I'd been thinking I'd feel a little more at home here, as it is pretty much English-speaking, albeit a mixed-up Afro-Miskito-Creole English. The city was named after an infamous Dutch pirate, had been a buccaneer stronghold for one hundred and fifty years and still felt haunted by its past. Throughout the Corn Islands and certainly in Bluefields, pirate surnames are commonplace to this day. I was sharing the darkening streets with a motley collection of drunks, hustlers and beggars, a scene unchanged in centuries, I was sure. I was too easily sized up as being quite out of place at this 'late' hour and I gave up on the tickets and slunk back to base with a handful of snacks!

In the room's sanctuary, we plugged into the WiFi and caught up with our online world, 'admin' time, so to speak. I'd hoped for something from the Bellagio, anything we could pass on to those wedding guests that had already booked flights, etc. They'd gone stubbornly quiet and I guess we'd need to prod them. Mike had updated us, though. After a lonesome second night at the Costa Rican hostel, he'd decided to ride north and join us all. Fortunately, Charlie had bumped into him at the border and turned him back before all five of us were trapped in Nicaragua. They hatched a plan to share a shipping container, get their bikes back to the UK and find flights home together. I couldn't blame them; with the RTW record attempt crushed, Charlie needed to return to university life and Mike had a patient and loving partner awaiting him.

The ferry was bigger than I'd expected, could take a couple of hundred passengers and if needed, about ten motorcycles could be manhandled on at the rear. As the vessel rhythmically bobbed around, I was quite content ours was staying behind. On an island that could be walked around in two to three hours, it just wouldn't be needed. So, with seasickness tablets already taken, we boarded and paid the hefty eight dollars each for our 'cruise' to the Caribbean. I have to say it all felt quite exhilarating!

Our fellow passengers were an eclectic mix, carrying everything from smart suitcases to bundles of cheap merchandise and chickens.

Six distinct ethnic races and tribes make up the autonomous Miskito Coast, and all seemed represented here. For some unknown reason, we had attracted the attention of one peculiar and spaced-out woman, who took it upon herself to stare menacingly at Selly and draw her hand across her throat. This would be the first of many 'strange' people we would come across in the Corn Islands, as we later learnt drug and alcohol dependency was all too commonplace, unfortunately. I say unfortunately, but for a sizable proportion of the tourists we met, it was their main, if not sole, reason for being in Central America!

Rum and beer is cheap and as for drugs, well, they were everywhere. They were in a tripping heaven, where many of the norms were reversed. For those on a budget, wine and most spirits were expensive luxuries, but psychedelic mushrooms could be handpicked, local rum bought for a pittance and so much coke flowed north from Colombia that it was freely offered around like cake at a kid's birthday party. It wasn't our cup of tea and not our place to judge, but it did bring us into contact with some interesting characters!

As Big Corn island came into view, it was everything we'd hoped to see. Swaying palms stood taller than any building, waves broke over submerged coral reefs and the sun bounced off white sandy beaches. Little Corn was out of view, nestled behind its bigger brother, and would require another half-hour crossing, by speedboat. Maybe we would visit, but for the next eight nights we planned to just chill, hope Selly fully recovered and react to any developing border news.

The hostel couldn't have been built any closer to the water's edge. The crystal clear waters gently lapped up against our ground-floor balcony wall; no relaxation tapes needed here! Sitting directly across the road was a diving centre, how convenient. There was an honesty system for the drinks fridge. Grab a beer and put a tick against your room number, I liked that. Hot showers were advertised, which were lukewarm, of course, and finally, a request that we cancel our online 'card' booking and pay upfront in cash. That seemed a little fishy, but we were here now and so I wandered off into town, to find the island's one and only ATM.

Before I made it, I was accosted in the middle of crossing the road by Terry. Sporting long hippy braids, rags for clothes and bare blackened feet (that matched his remaining teeth), he was a bit of a local legend.

"Hey mister, you need any coke?" he said uncomfortably loudly, whilst snookering my move to the other side.

"I'm good, thanks," I tactfully replied, in what I hoped came off as firm but friendly.

"What about some grass, or shrooms, man?" he pressed, shuffling a large dirty cotton bag from shoulder to shoulder.

"Honestly, I'm good, thanks. I don't do drugs actually," I admitted truthfully, hoping to curveball any more illegal offerings.

"Well, what about seashells then? Got a bag of them here, conch shells and everything," was his final pitch.

This was desperation. Shells were everywhere you looked and even in my ten-minute walk to find the ATM, I'd seen so many conch shells lying around that walls were routinely built of them.

"Thanks, but I don't need anything right now," I finished off, conscious we were stood in the middle of the road still, and next to a bend!

"My name's Terry, everybody knows me. I can get anything you want, just ask," he offered with a mischievous grin, but finally allowing me to get off the road and be on my way.

From what we'd seen so far, the island looked beautiful. It shared the same sea, sunsets and palm trees that all the other Caribbean islands had, but these two were arguably the cheapest you could visit. Big Corn just wasn't particularly developed for tourism, which also made it attractive, if you could deal with witnessing a chunk of the poorer population all too often drowning their plights in cheap booze and even cheaper drugs. Despite the natural beauty of the place, it did tarnish the overall atmosphere somewhat, and we couldn't get away from the feeling of being tolerated rather than welcomed. Many islanders had an air of abandonment about them; the seas were no longer quite as bountiful and the vast majority of tourists they relied upon just transited on through to reach Little Corn. In hindsight, we probably should have joined them!

The hostel's reception and breakfast area were upstairs, giving lovely views across the beaches and we could enjoy a coffee looking down on the various exotic fish, darting about the shallows. Ali, the manager, came in, prompting me to go downstairs, grab my now flush wallet and settle our accommodation bill. Except it wasn't where I'd left it. I popped back up, to ask Selly if she had moved it by any chance, but she hadn't, and together we turned the room upside down, before alerting Ali to its loss. It was a little strange, as the wallet had been out of sight, hidden under my small rucksack on a chair that doubled as a bedside table. The wallet was gone, but the bag, containing cameras, etc. was still on the chair.

Ali came down, saw the sliding patio doors were slightly ajar and looking out onto the balcony, saw a large black machete lying there. It looked like the door had been prised enough to get an arm through and Ali immediately went to question the neighbours, who'd been outside sunning themselves. They gave a description of a guy that had been on the balcony and appeared to be chatting away to somebody inside our empty room. I guess stealing the whole bag would have been a little too obvious and the thief had settled for the wallet. I most likely spooked him when I'd returned for the wallet, and he'd promptly legged it, leaving behind the machete. In any case, Ali jumped on his pushbike and with a description in hand, went off in chase. Another of the hostel's workers called the police, followed by several of her friends. She kindly asked them to keep an eye out for anybody flaunting more cash (about three hundred dollars more!) than they looked like they should have and let her know.

Things started to escalate quite quickly. Ali returned, totally out of breath, at exactly the same time as the police arrived in a battered black Landcruiser. After the room was photographed and the machete bagged up, we all piled in for a lift to the police station. We gave a statement and Ali provided a more detailed description, having only been stopped from catching the guy by the thick undergrowth his bike and bulk couldn't push through. The thief might have escaped through the deeper thickets, but it was still a small island!

We'd been there about an hour when Ali's phone rang, to say a known toe-rag, matching our description, had changed a large sum of dollars and bought himself a mobile phone and some new flashy bright red trainers. This seemed too much of a coincidence and he asked his friends to discreetly follow the guy whilst he brought the police up to speed. I had wondered if this was something the police really cared about, some tourist's lost wallet. I'd kinda doubted it and to mostly speed things along, had said I'd be happy enough with a copy of the police report, letting the insurance company handle it. I didn't really have any higher expectations than that.

Ali was getting frustrated; he was convinced this was 'our man', yet since telling the police of his whereabouts, they had all disappeared without a word. We paced around for a few minutes until the Landcruiser reappeared, plus a collection of motorbikes, all loaded up with shotgun-toting police pillions! There was a posse of eight armed police on five motorcycles, and Ali was asked to place another call and find out exactly where 'our guy' was now. The update revealed a chunk of our money had already been exchanged for drugs and some new clothes and was now rapidly disappearing over the counter of a bar. Wow, this guy was living it up and not hiding it! Ali was ushered onto the back of one of the motorbikes and the commander turned to Selly and I.

"Are you coming? Get in the Landcruiser if you want to come," she offered.

Too right we did, you don't get many offers like this, and so in we hopped and off we went. It seemed the entire police station had turned out for this little raid and we'd been invited along. I'd already written off the lost cash; you couldn't pay for excitement like this, I thought, as we raced across the island. Ali had stayed on the call and kept his phone to his ear, getting regular updates as he bounced along. The guy had got suspicious of his tails and had now run to a nearby family member's house, within a tiny ghetto.

We had arrived at a small clearing amongst the palms and filled with a dozen or so wooden shacks, perched on stilts. The motorbikes piled in first, surrounding the property, and we followed up on foot, staying behind the assortment of guns and batons. After a few shouted exchanges, the guy came out fast and threateningly, a large knife gripped in one hand. Faced with an array of pointed pistols, rifles and shotguns, he quickly saw sense, threw the knife to one side and allowed the handcuffs to go on. That went well, I thought, as they laid him down in the bed of the Landcruiser and we hopped back in the front.

At the police station, he was frogmarched past us and into a forced confession, I mean, interrogation room for a cup of tea, probably. Within a minute, he'd agreed to show them where he'd dumped my wallet, thus providing all the proof they really needed. As the adventure played out, we were beginning to feel like actors, caught up in the makings of a B-movie. We moved to one side as the police plonked him, handcuffed to the grab-rail, onto the back of a motorbike and shortly returned with my wallet, minus the cash and cards, of course. He was taken back into the cup of tea room and moments later I was presented with a bag.

"These are all the new clothes and trainers he bought with your money. These are yours now, plus some cash remaining. Sorry, but there wasn't much left," said the policewoman apologetically.

I mean, granted I'd recently 'paid' for them and he'd only worn them for half a day, but I didn't want them back! I couldn't help imagining him being stripped naked and another unnecessary confession being forced out of him, just for practice, of course. We were free to leave, with our bag of sweaty new clothes and about fifty dollars in *córdobas*. The following morning, we needed to be available at the hostel, though, to sign the typed-up statements. That night, we took the four people who'd been instrumental in helping us out for a meal and as much to drink as they wanted. It had been a heady but exciting first day; we needed a few drinks and these guys deserved them!

First thing in the morning, I introduced myself at the dive centre. It was a real shame that Selly was most unlikely going to be well enough to join me during our time here, but she was excited for me anyway. I enquired about their next outing.

"Tomorrow morning, we have a couple of divers. See you around 9 am," they responded.

We settled in the hostel's communal area, sent off an email to Vegas and waited on the police arriving with their statements. My query to the Bellagio bounced straight back, with an autoreply stating they were now closed indefinitely, due to the coronavirus. Wow, we hadn't even had a heads-up from the wedding planners; that seemed like pretty poor service. There was a free-phone number to call and I tried that, getting a recorded message stating exactly the same thing. Having paid deposits and swapped contracts, we felt as if we'd been left hanging. So much for it claiming to be one of the more prestigious venues on the strip! We didn't really know if our wedding was on, or off, but we both felt let down and it subtly changed how we felt about spending our money there. With a sizeable team of planners working in the office, or from home, a short courtesy email would have made all the difference. Maybe I'm just old-fashioned, but I was already thinking stuff 'em!

My thoughts were dragged back to the present; the police had arrived. Our statement and the accompanying police report had been typed up and required our signatures on each page, except our statement had been changed, almost beyond recognition. None of the 'locals' were named or mentioned. Not Ali, or the other hostel workers, or their friends who had tracked down and tailed the thief for us. The statement now said Selly had spotted the thief on our balcony, had given the description to the police and additionally identified him upon arrest! The island was just too small for any of them to get involved, explained Ali. So, with some reluctance, we signed the reports, thinking that would be the end of the matter.

Later that afternoon, we got a call from the police station, wanting to know if we had plans to leave the island, as the judge wanted to see us sometime this week. We had discussed venturing across to Little Corn Island for a day or two, but I guess that could wait. Selly was expected to tell the judge her side of the story, or more to the point, tell him the police commander's version of her story! Apparently, as the victim, I got a say in the thief's punishment, for the judge to consider.

There seemed to be a lot hanging over us now, considering we'd come here for a dream break! It was Friday, the 20th of March, and back in the UK it had been announced that pubs, restaurants, cafés and a host of other venues were being ordered shut. It all felt somewhat surreal; practically everywhere in England was closing and yet I felt compelled to cling onto a small tradition. That night, we went out for 'Friday night fish 'n' chips' and a few drinks!

After breakfast together, I wandered over to the dive centre, to make sure the diving I'd been looking forward to was still on. It wasn't.

"The boat captain is ill. Come back tomorrow at nine again," was the curt explanation.

Before I could tell Selly, she had news for me that seemed more important. The judge's assistant had called her and requested we meet the judge at, you guessed it, 9am tomorrow morning. Oh well, it was going to be one of those weeks, and I jokingly considered squeezing my size ten feet into the miscreant's size nine red trainers, laundering the bag of clothes and wearing them all to meet the judge and thief face to face!

We opted for a walk around the island's perimeter. Clearing our heads and collecting some 'Caribbean' photographs. Midway around, Selly hit on the perfect 'punishment' proposal. Like every shoreline the world over, the beaches here were blighted by washed-up plastic debris.

"Why don't we ask the judge to have him litter-pick the beaches for a couple of weeks?" was Selly's idea.

I liked it, a lot. We needed to have something prepared if we were asked tomorrow morning, and this was definitely a worthy suggestion, one that we both believed to be fair and beneficial to the islanders. Back at the hostel, I asked Ali if I could settle our bill by card, to save us several cashpoint trips and the withdrawal charges. Stubbornly, and despite knowing our plight, he was still insisting on cash. Well, he'd have to wait a couple more days then; we didn't have a lot of cash to hand anymore.

There was a buzz of nervous activity around the hostel most days. Nearly all the guests were either discussing the implications of the virus's spread, or were already dealing with airlines, trying to make their escape. Some had had their flights cancelled and were struggling with refunds; others were engaging consulates, trying to find out if repatriation flights were on the cards. It seemed everybody had a story to tell, us included, of course. We were trying to get a refund on our concert tickets and trying to find out if our wedding had officially been cancelled.

The Foreign and Commonwealth Office had now advised all UK residents to return, and out of prudence, I messaged the British consulate in Costa Rica (it turned out they had responsibility for Nicaragua), just to let them know of our whereabouts. Next up was a call to our travel insurance provider. We needed to know if our policy was still valid. I put the phone on speaker, for Selly to hear their responses.

"Yes, we will continue to honour your cover, as the virus emerged well after the commencement of your policy and your UK departure date," said a pleasant lady, after first consulting her manager.

That was a relief. Several fellow travellers had told us their providers had terminated their cover and strongly suggested they should return to their home countries. In truth, we felt safer staying put, rather than cramming onto packed long-haul flights and returning to a locked-down Europe. Having the backing of our insurance company helped bolster our decision to stick around and see how things played out. Only time would tell if we were making the right decision, but it felt right, to both of us. Nonetheless, we felt the frustrations and anxieties of those around us. Flight prices were rocketing, and once booked, they were all too often either cancelled or delayed. The tension it was causing, just in our one hostel, was palpable.

The taxi dropped us at something resembling a shabby primary school, but which was, indeed, the courthouse. In the end, I couldn't bring myself to don the gaudy clothes, or trainers, and instead went in shorts, T-shirt and flip-flops, the island's apparel of choice. We waited an hour, to be eventually told there wasn't any police escort available to bring the accused a whole hundred metres to the court building. I was convinced we were being fobbed off, which would have been fine if they'd cancelled earlier. I could have gone diving!

We left, having been asked to await a future call, one that I very much doubted we would get. Walking back, we took an unusual shortcut across the middle of the island's runway; it was the done thing here! Although short, it divided the town in two, and in between the few daily flights, it provided a convenient if unnatural shortcut. I swung via the dive centre and confirmed there was another 9am excursion planned for the next day.

I couldn't tell if the island was particularly more prosperous than Bluefields, or just more presentable for being all the prettier. The islanders seemed proud of their piracy ancestry and dozens of Dutch and English pirate surnames survive to this day. But like their past lost riches, the present bearers of these names hadn't held onto much of the wealth currently being generated. From what we learnt, these Caribbean islands' resorts, hotels and hostels were, in the main, owned by overseas investors. An Australian bar owner enlightened us to the islands' true plight.

"Everybody around here calls the islands 'Big Coke Island' and 'Little Coke Island'. Don't be fooled by the beauty, it might as well be snowing with the stuff," he summarised glumly, having spent years living here.

We'd been told Nicaragua was the 'land of opportunities' and we were beginning to see it and believe it. Property and land were extraordinarily cheap, business opportunities and start-ups were plentiful and were mostly unencumbered by the red tape with which Europeans had to comply. Of course, the country was randomly plagued by revolutions, earthquakes, erupting volcanoes, both hurricanes and even occasional cyclones and then actual plagues. Not just the current coronavirus plague, but dengue fever, coffee plague and plagued by poverty.

Adding fuel to the fire, one of the hostel managers warned us of her experience in the capital, Managua, whilst studying there at university. She had been robbed of her mobile phone twice, at gunpoint, and she also knew of people similarly robbed outside supermarkets, just for their groceries! The overall situation seemed pretty dire, not that we'd made any plans to visit (cue 'silly me')!

It was just so hard to take all this in as we soaked up another beautiful sunset beside the shimmering, flat sea. For those that wanted, or needed, them, the 'highs' were varied and plentiful and the two islands swayed to the old tunes of 'supply and demand'. We were still happy to be here, knew we could comfortably co-exist between the beauty and the beast, especially if diving was on the cards.

I made my daily excursion and received my next fob-off.

"We have two students making a shore-dive. You can join them for thirty-five dollars," she said with a straight face.

"But you quoted me twenty-five for boat diving?" I queried.

"Yes, that was because the boat was already going out. Today is a course," she explained.

"But why would you charge me more for a student shore-dive? It might only last half an hour," I politely enquired, to a continuous blank stare.

"Well, it's thirty-five dollars for a shore-dive across the road, or twenty-five if we take the boat out," came the nonsensical offer, wrapped in a meaningless shrug.

Umm, I really wanted to dive, but not here in the shallow bay. I could see most of the fish from our balcony! With a final sliver of perseverance, I asked them to please let me know if a boat trip materialised. The next day the centre closed, with a notice proclaiming, 'Due to coronavirus measures'. That ended that saga; everyone's diving hopes were sunk!

Selly was slowly but surely on the mend. The antibiotics seemed to be kicking in nicely, along with the break from riding, of course, and day by day she visibly improved. It certainly hadn't been uneventful on the island, but we could feel its remoteness and tranquillity seeping into us, relaxing us. It wasn't yet midday, but it still felt perfect for grabbing a cold beer, putting our feet up on the balcony and catching up with Mike and Charlie. Even if they hadn't, I had plenty of gossip to pass on!

Turned out they'd been busy boys, having already dropped their bikes off for shipping, and were now in the Costa Rican capital, San José, hoping to fly home the following day. Unlike our experiences to date, coronavirus restrictions for them had been plentiful and strictly enforced. The police had raided their hostel and taken away all the pool cues and table-tennis bats. Like naughty schoolboys, they'd been photographed and given a stern telling-off, for daring to venture out on a walk. Yes, it was fair to say they couldn't wait to return home!

Despite us refraining from day-tripping (or any 'tripping'!) over to Little Coke, the judge never did call back. Instead, we idled away our time taking beautiful walks, indulging in cocktail sunsets and devouring fabulously fresh seafood. Selly had religiously taken her week's worth of antibiotics and had dramatically rebounded. It was so good to see; after almost three weeks of struggling to get her breath properly, the sore throat, constant headaches and generally feeling weak, she was back again. I don't think we'll ever know if she had actually caught the virus back then; I just knew what a relief it was to have her 'back'.

Before we knew it, though, the sand was through the hourglass and our mini-island escapades were over, nearly! We'd made up our minds not to extend the stay. It had been quite the adventure, but we wanted to check out the volcano hostel next, and had booked a couple of nights with them. I finally handed over the cash Ali desperately wanted paying in and with our small bags packed, we headed for the return crossing. Like a flight home after a wonderful holiday, it felt like we'd only been on this ferry yesterday. Nothing had quite gone how we'd imagined, I pondered, as we picked up speed across a flat blue sea. Not that we had anything to complain about, though. On this very day, the UK population, already deprived of its pubs and restaurants, was now being placed into a strict lockdown and deaths attributed to Covid-19 had just surpassed one thousand. The following day, Boris Johnson would announce that both he and his health secretary had tested positive.

Our Corn Island experience had certainly been memorable, and maybe if we had had more confidence in the medical facilities there, we could have looked harder for a longer-term option. Instead, we reunited with the bike and made our way back to a certain very nice hotel and steakhouse in Juigalpa.

The island caught up with us one last time. Out of the blue, I had a message from the Spanish hostel owner, asking if we'd actually visited the Corn Islands and stayed at his hostel. It turned out Ali was cancelling bookings and pocketing the cash. He'd actually robbed us (the owner, to be correct!) of more dollars than our balcony-burglar had.

Chapter Fourteen

Finding Paradise

Melting inside our riding gear and finally nearing the city of Granada, we made a fuel stop and took a much-needed water break. I was busy resetting our route, to take us the final leg to the crater-lakeside hostel, when Selly spotted its name.

"Paradiso? That's perfect. Italian for 'Paradise', you know?" she said approvingly.

"Well, let's hope it lives up to its name then. Soon find out, we're only half an hour away!" I replied.

We turned off the main road and onto a smaller rustic one. One where small kids energetically played ball together and skinny dogs lazily sunbathed on the tarmac, oblivious to the infrequent traffic. This became an even narrower road as, following the signs, we turned a corner into the Apoyo Laguna Nature Reserve. We really were entering the rim of a large extinct volcano. Spread out below us was a four-mile-wide water-filled caldera and the old volcano's walls were thick with jungle. Under a clear blue sky, the flat, calm laguna shimmered like a mirror; it really was an awe-inspiring first view.

This was the only paved road in and out of the crater and looking down and around, we couldn't see any buildings, nothing manmade at all. It looked pristine. Life was hidden down there somewhere and we eagerly descended the bumpy road to find it, bouncing around corners and people. Despite its steepness, we passed several rural folk, struggling uphill with hauls of bundled firewood, balanced skilfully on heads and shoulders.

The popular tourist destination of Granada might be just half an hour away, but we were already feeling so wonderfully isolated. The descent ended at a T-junction, and leafy lanes, hugging the laguna's contours, headed off in each direction for just a few short miles. This was where the waterside resorts and private villas were nestled, hidden mostly by the exotic overhanging jungle. Even with the bike's engine running, we could hear various birds loudly squawking as we crawled along searching for the 'Paradiso Hostel and Resort'.

"There it is," Selly pointed out for me.

We had found it and were ushered through secure gates to an internal parking area, surrounded by mature mango trees and tall lush coconut palms. The ride had been another forty-degree scorcher and I craved a cold, refreshing shower and a cold, refreshing drink! Nicaragua was now in the latter stages of the dry season and the trees were dropping their fruits and leaves in abundance. We hadn't really seen anything yet, but already loved both the setting and the noisy tropical nature.

"Yes, I have your reservation for two nights. If you want to extend, I'll have to swap your room at some point, as the family owning the resort are going to occupy this upper terrace soon," said the friendly receptionist.

That was promising news; the owners were French apparently (not quite correct, we later learnt!), and whilst everybody else seemed intent on escaping, they were choosing to stay here, which meant the resort was unlikely to close on us. Online, we'd already seen a rash of worrying evictions, as hostels and campsites were forced to close down in some of the countries we'd passed through. Further restrictions in road travel had made it almost impossible, for those evicted, to find any new accommodation. There were just so many travellers now trapped, in so many different locations and circumstances. So far, it seemed fate hadn't been at all heavy-handed with us. We quite liked Nicaragua, and we quite liked Paradiso!

Showered and refreshed, we went to explore the resort. A picturesque pathway, consisting of several flights of stairs, descended through an assortment of terraces, private rooms, dorms, seating areas and gardens. The roofs were thatched with dried banana palms, nicely blending the resort into the jungle's background. Bougainvillea and tropical flowers were in full bloom, being tended to by hummingbirds and numerous butterflies, as bright green lizards scattered across the pathways.

Just reaching the crater's shore had been a wonderful nature walk. Paradiso had its own natural volcanic-ash beach, and being a Saturday afternoon it was fully occupied with paying day guests. The more adventurous were out on the clear water swimming, kayaking, or paddleboarding. We couldn't stop smiling as we absorbed the view. Almost the entire circumference of the wide caldera was visible from the water's edge and exactly opposite us, the skyline was dominated by our nearest volcano, the semi-active Mombacho. A wooden platform was anchored about twenty metres out, with half a dozen sunbathers enjoying drinks and the bar's music. Lying in the middle of the beach was a solitary cute-looking dog, with front legs poshly crossed and seemingly keeping a watchful eye over everyone enjoying themselves. Almost predictably, we gravitated to check out the bar and restaurant area.

Wow, eight large and colourful menu boards were strung high across the back wall. There seemed to be every cuisine catered for and the prices looked very reasonable. This was mirrored behind the bar also, but for cocktails, shots, spirits and an assortment of beers. We grabbed drinks and scanning around, could see even the tables were split up on several terraces and levels. It was busy now, but virus-wise, it was still easy to find your own spot and social-distance, so to speak. Choosing one of the 'out of the way' tables, I again soaked up the enchanting view.

"How long do you think it would take to get bored of this?" I asked.

"It truly is a paradise, I love it!" she let out.

"I'm thinking when we go back upstairs we should extend for a week and see how we feel then. I'd hate to find out they're fully booked," I suggested.

She nodded and I knew we were both feeling comfortable here, safe here. The atmosphere was holiday-like, there were plenty of afternoon drinkers, lots of chatter and laughter around us, yet all spaced out and set in such a tranquil environment. In addition to the kayaks and paddleboards, there was a pool table, table tennis, darts, *pétanque* (boules), a well-stocked library and a new separate kitchen for the guests, where another couple of dogs greeted us.

"These two are Blacky and Canela. They have to be tied up mostly, as they bark a lot and intimidate the other guests," explained one of the volunteer workers.

At this early stage, we hadn't a clue who the day guests were and who was actually staying here, but it all felt impressive and I really couldn't imagine struggling to find things to do around here.

"See you at six for welcome drinks?" said the departing volunteer with a smile.

Umm, 'welcome drinks'. Turned out the room rate included a free rum cocktail each, every evening, plus unlimited fresh coffee and free use of all the sports equipment. Due to the pandemic, an ensuite private room was currently available for three hundred dollars a month, or put another way, about five dollars each per night! With a revised plan, we headed back up to see the receptionist.

"Can we book for a month, please?" I enquired, with fingers crossed behind my back and binning the idea to extend by just a week.

"Of course, and you will benefit from a twenty percent discount on the bar and restaurant prices," she offered with a smile.

So, that was it, we'd found our longer-term refuge and committed to a full month, all within a few hours of arriving! We had the city of Granada close by, the capital an hour away, both of which had large hospitals, and maybe a month would be long enough for Honduras to think about reopening its borders again. After all, only a few cases of infections were being reported so far, in the whole of Central America. There was some speculation that the high temperatures here didn't particularly suit the virus. We couldn't really feel much safer, certainly not the way things were back home in England and Italy. It might not be Roatán, but it felt pretty special all the same.

As the evening progressed, the day guests melted away and revealed there were about twenty full-time guests staying here. They certainly looked close-knit and seemed to get on great together, as they collected welcome drinks and congregated around the largest wooden table in the bar. A table that would later become known as 'the survivors' table'. We were a diverse bunch. As far as we could tell, it consisted of Aussies, Swedes, Germans, French, Dutch, three Brits, one Canadian, one Russian, a Kuwaiti and three Nicaraguans. Apparently, they all quite liked to party!

The names we'd pick up over the coming days; for now, it was just great to see everyone thoroughly enjoying themselves and getting a little 'Saturday Night' drunk together. The laguna hadn't had a ripple on it all day and it was still stiflingly hot and breezeless. Day or night, the view remained exotic and dreamy. Across the far side, though, chimneys of smoke rose up and there appeared to be fires burning amongst the trees. Our barman enlightened us.

"They're hunting for iguanas, smoking them out the trees," he told us.

"Do the fires ever get out of hand?" I asked, knowing the trees and land were bone-dry.

"Sometimes, yes. It's illegal, but people are hungry and nobody stops them, it can be dangerous," he finished off, leaving us to our imagination.

With the drinks helping, we fell asleep with the room doors open wide and the fans on. It wasn't long enough, though, nowhere near long enough! It woke us both around 5am, forty minutes or so before sunrise. We lay mesmerised, listening to the loudest uncoordinated cacophony of a dawn chorus either of us had ever heard. It was interspersed by occasional heavy thumps on the roof, or pavement, outside, and loud low grunts, which I wrongly presumed were wild pigs out in the bush. We knew we were living in a nature reserve but hadn't expected such an exotic and lengthy wake-up call.

I pulled on swim shorts and took a peek outside. Half-chewed mangos lay around on the ground (and I guess our roof!), and the pathways were littered with several more, along with some impressively large fresh 'droppings'. A defensive 'poo hat' would be needed before exiting the room! Scanning the trees revealed we had a mixture of squirrels, huge dark green iguanas and large black birds, sporting bright yellow tail feathers, feasting on the ripened mangos. The trees were so full of the fruits that I just knew this was going to be a regular morning occurrence. The chorus lasted a full hour, before subsiding and allowing us to doze off in relative peace, in between the sporadic wallops raining down on the corrugated tin roof.

A desire to test the water temperature, plus a little hunger, enticed us down onto the beach, where I promptly scorched my bare feet on the hot, dark sand and had to run cowardly down to the shallows. It was only 8am, but already the sun was plenty high enough to burn you, and entering the laguna was like easing into a hot bath. For sure, the water was over thirty degrees and swimming out, I had to dance my legs around to try and stir up some cooler water. It was basically the largest outdoor heated pool you could wish for. No wonder the platform was so popular.

We sat with coffee and pancakes as one of the hostel's volunteer workers came over for a friendly morning chat.

"How are you settling in? Have you seen any of the monkeys yet?" she asked cheerfully.

"We didn't know about monkeys being here, but we heard the wild pigs grunting this morning," I answered knowledgeably.

"Oh no, that is the monkeys! They're howler monkeys making that noise. Be careful not to stand under them, or they might pee on you!" she helpfully schooled us.

We had another guest at the table. 'Posh beach dog' had laid down beside us in a very subtle 'I might become interested in what you're eating' kind of way. I was still slightly wary of her, as unlike the other two, Blacky and Canela, this one had no collar and appeared to be more of a stray, albeit a very cute and gentle-looking stray. Selly offered a little pancake, which was gratefully accepted after a precautionary sniff.

"She's fine, her name's Mocha, kinda lives around here," offered Lea, before sauntering off to tend to other guests.

A little later in the day, we hopped on the bike to ride over to Granada. A spin around the town centre revealed beautiful colonial buildings, surrounded by bustling markets, and we could see why it was a tourist destination in its own right. It was nice to see the vast majority of people were wearing face masks and using sanitising gels at the shop entrances. The population of Nicaragua appeared to be taking the virus seriously, even if the government was keeping schtum.

Granada is the largest city on the shores of the hundred-mile-long Lake Nicaragua. Linked directly to the Caribbean Sea by rivers, even this city was once a pirates' haven, along with the lake's dominating Ometepe volcanic islands. The city boasts its own impressive 'island' tourist attraction, though. After an ancient eruption of the Mombacho volcano, a maze of over three hundred tiny 'islands' was deposited and created close to the city's shore. Many of these were just big enough to have a solitary luxury house, or villa, built upon them. Others are inhabited by monkeys, and 'booze cruise' trips offered tourists daily excursions amongst and around them.

We were surrounded by several volcanoes and just fifteen miles away stood the very active and photogenic Masaya volcano. After just a few days at Paradiso, we couldn't resist a sunset trip over to it. For a few dollars, an entrance ticket allowed us to ride our bike up to the crater's rim and, due to the nauseating fumes, spend just thirty minutes there. This crater was wide open, allowing you a surreal view straight down into the bubbling red-hot lava. I could hardly take it in, that we were watching a fiery display only normally seen from the safety and comfort of your couch. It was an awe-inspiring spectacle, seeing the molten lava change colour from bright yellows to vivid reds and releasing plumes of white smoke. Clouds would be more accurate.

In the clear blue skies, Masaya created clouds that could be seen from many miles away. It was another unforgettable chapter of the trip, right up there with the Iguazu Falls, Torre del Paine's mountains and several of the glaciers.

In those first couple of weeks, we spent a lot of our time on one of the quieter upper terraces. It wasn't entirely down to 'social distancing'; we had since moved rooms and this beautiful terrace was just so much closer and more convenient. Even so, we were the newcomers and weren't feeling quite ready to switch into full-on party mode. It was so pleasant just, well, just relaxing! Everybody else seemed to have known and lived with each other for some time now and were quite comfortable dispensing with any social distancing.

For us, Europe was never far out of our minds and by the end of this first fortnight, the UK had now reported surpassing ten thousand deaths and Italy twenty thousand. Boris Johnson had spent some nights in intensive care and was trying to run the country from his hospital bed! It was just impossible to compare, or even relate, our near-utopian surroundings to the fear and restrictions being experienced back home. We could take the bike out whenever we wanted, shop where we wanted, and the only restriction was having to have our temperature taken and wear a face mask to enter the supermarkets and banks, etc. The masks we had already purchased before the trip, thinking they would be useful against smog, or dust storms, etc. We couldn't possibly have guessed just how much use they would be getting now.

Selly's birthday loomed at the end of the week. I'd dreamed the pair of us would be celebrating it somewhere in Belize, or Mexico. Nicaragua hadn't crossed our minds, but it's not often you can have a day out exploring volcanoes, craters and jungle tracks, all rounded off with steaks and cocktails on a volcanic beach! To be fair, there never seemed to be a dull evening in Paradiso. Activities were planned almost nightly and our circle of 'stranded' friends started to grow quickly. The volunteer staff would dish out the nightly welcome drinks and happily organise quizzes, movie nights, games and BBQs. Just a few days after Selly's birthday, we had the full moon, dubbed the 'supermoon' and it was all the excuse needed for a boozy beach BBQ, ending in late-night dancing on the beach.

The owners, Matteo & Iulia, had settled in with their two young children and they both proved to be a match for anyone up for a celebration. Young at heart and laid-back, they were the perfect hosts. Matteo strutted around in his trademark fedora hat, and if he discovered nothing had been planned for the evening, would grab a drink and shout, "Come on, BBQ time, let's get the beer-pong going," or "Welcome drinks out on the platform, everyone, let's go swimming." They were the life and soul of the resort and rarely missed joining all of us in the evenings. Past 6pm, the twenty or so of us pretty much had the place to ourselves, and later, when the bar staff needed to go home, they'd leave us buckets of ice to go with bottles of rum brought down from the rooms. There was never much of a reason needed to enjoy a drink in such an exotic setting.

Usually, because of the dawn chorus, we were getting up very early and going out on 'monkey spotting' walks, of which there were dozens, or strolls down to the beach to enjoy the sunrises. It was a great time to watch the kingfishers, herons and the odd cormorant fishing off the platform. A scan around the beach and bar, at the empty bottles and items of clothing often lying around, told stories of the late nights we'd retired early from. Occasionally, somebody would still be cosily sleeping it off in a deckchair or hammock, having not made it back up the flights of stairs to a room, or dorm. We were hardly ever alone, even at five thirty.

Mocha could usually be spotted laid out somewhere on the sand; it was her quiet time. A chance to enjoy the sun's early warmth, before the niggling sandflies woke up and harassed her. If not the insects, then Blacky and Canela would sometimes be off their leads and playing together. Mocha was something of the underdog, though (excuse the pun), and would often be excluded from their fun and games, even chased off into the water. In the evenings, though, after spending her days quietly alone, she would appear at our sides, gazing up lovingly at Selly. It was impossible not to have a soft spot growing for her, the gentle princess.

Having developed a habit of cooking us morning pancakes, I'd frequently be in the kitchen early. Blu, a young Aussie volunteer, could often be found on the beach for the sunrise and then in the kitchen herself, messing with my body clock. I didn't yet know what had come first, her blue hair, or her nickname, but seeing her with a cracked beer in hand skewed whatever time of day I thought it was.

"Starting early, Blu?" I ventured.

"Kind of, this isn't the first, you're just a late starter!" she digged.

It wasn't yet 9am, but that's how she rolled. Her job, prior to the pandemic scaring off the customers, was running the Granada 'three hundred island booze cruises' by day, and bar-street pub and club crawls by night. She was basically paid to drink and make sure all the customers left the boat, or clubs, happy and drunk. I guess she was just keeping her hand in; can't have the customers showing up the rep! A true Aussie, she told it how it was and didn't suffer fools. We liked her immediately and the three of us were soon to become lasting friends. Mocha had also worked out my morning culinary routine and joined us in the kitchen.

"She's a proper snob, you know. Barks and chases all the fishermen, or anyone that is dressed too poor for her liking," warned Blu.

"Maybe she's trying to earn her keep around here?" I offered.

"Oh, you'll see. She's a bit of a racist and a snob. Anybody dark-skinned gets chased off the beach, but if a couple of tourists walk by, she's perfectly fine," expanded Blu with a laugh.

She looked so gentle, maybe just needed some decent food, love and attention. Something had happened in her past, though. Just a stump remained where her tail should have been and she refused to let anyone touch or stroke near it. There was just enough left to waggle the hanging lock of hairs and let you know when she was happy!

It had gone by so quickly, but it was fast approaching the end of our first month in the country. Since arriving at Paradiso, we hadn't yet seen a single cloud, and found we had sublimely slipped from 'on the road' bikers to relaxed holiday sunbathers. It wasn't in the plan, but it wasn't unenjoyable either. It was a pretty amazing place to be; the jungle never quietened down, night or day. In competition with the dawn chorus, the evenings were filled with the sounds of frogs and toads, calling out across the still water. After dusk, fireflies danced in the greenery and huge moths explored the bar's lighting. There was also the odd scorpion and snake wandering through to keep us on our toes. Neither of us was squeamish about the creepy-crawly guests, and Selly happily photographed them all, big or small. We were warned to make the most of these sunny days; the wet season was just a few weeks away now and we'd be in for a transformation.

Our thirty-day bike insurance and temporary import certificate needed renewing. There was only one place to sort this; we would be visiting Managua after all, and it proved to be unlike any other capital we'd experienced so far. This city had had a tough paper round, to put it mildly. Flattened by a devastating earthquake in the seventies, hit by a decade-long contra war throughout the eighties and then badly hurricane-damaged again in the nineties. It had just never fully recovered, and riding around gave no hint or feeling that you were in the country's centre of administration, centre of government. If anything, it felt turned inside out. The suburbs had some nice new malls and recreational developments, but the central areas were just frankly shabby. The original cathedral lay in ruins, along with several government buildings, and destitution was pretty much everywhere to see.

Hordes of vendors stalked a sale at traffic lights and beggars hung around the entrances of shops and banks, or anywhere vehicles had to stop. Even bare-footed children chanced the traffic, juggling balls in the road for a few coins. Horse-drawn carts shared the roads and slowed posh SUVs on the roundabouts. Even riders on horseback trotted along, or worse, loose horses could be found grazing on the greener central reservations. It all felt a bit incongruous, a clash of two worlds and a pretty depressing city at first glance. If we didn't need to get our paperwork in order and avoid the fines, I would happily have turned around and left.

However, after a few bureaucratic hours at the customs HQ, followed by a bank, to renew the bike insurance, we were free to depart. We had asked for longer but could only extend by another thirty days. As I rode out of the city, I had the distinct feeling we would be back visiting at least once more.

The resort had its own fifteen-seater minibus and along with Matteo and Iulia's 4x4, we had enough space for a group weekly outing. The first one we had a chance to attend was a trip to the beautiful natural freshwater springs of Aguas Agrias. Blu had boarded the minibus with her third beer of the morning and upon stopping for fuel halfway, promptly ran off singing to find a toilet. She didn't want to leave drunk; she wanted to arrive drunk! Thankfully, the ice and beer-filled cool boxes had been strapped to the roof; otherwise, there might not have been much left after we'd parked up and excitedly debussed!

Hidden under a shady tree canopy, the cool springs were just perfect for escaping the heat of another forty-degree day. Of course, to complement the refreshing streams, we'd also taken music, a gas BBQ and flagons of mango cocktails, etc. I quickly fell into conversation with a couple of fellow Brits, Steve and Jess. If Matteo ever needed a right-hand man, Steve would perfectly fit the bill, encouraging the evenings to start with rounds of shots and, if he was successful, later descend into drunken laguna skinny-dipping. In his early forties and a London fund manager, he appeared to be our very own 'Wolf of Wall Street'. Full of confidence and always hungry for a laugh, you couldn't help but have a good time in his company.

Almost the oldest amongst our group, Jess was a little more reserved. He was an absolute gent and would happily regale us with stories of his travels and exploits until the beer, or his energy, ran out. Throughout his life, he'd worked as a freelance shop fitter and found that with just a few months' hard graft each year, he could cover his travel costs for the rest of the year. He never boasted, or exaggerated, but had just simply spent the majority of his life travelling and exploring. Like with Mike weeks before, it was so easy to just pluck a random country out of thin air and ask Jess to tell us a story. It was almost guaranteed he'd not only been there but had a worthy yarn to listen to.

This outing's hangovers had just about withered before Matteo's birthday was upon us and the shenanigans kicked off, with some afternoon *piñata* bashing. Well, slashing, to be truthful. Once blindfolded, he insisted upon being given a machete rather than the traditional stick, and proceeded to endanger the lot of us, kids and dogs included! Only the sweet-filled *piñata* seemed immune to his mayhem. As the staff feared having to clean up a massacre and parents raced to pull their children away, Matteo was prudently relieved of his sword and led away for an afternoon and evening's attempt at drinking his own bar dry. By 10pm, the hostel's main kitchen had been raided for a drunken messy eggs, flour and mayonnaise fight. The bartop, tables and pool table became dance floors and were weight-tested for how many revellers they could support. Departing early, at 2am, we staggered back up the stairs, before any ambulances or police were summoned.

We had a nice surprise the next day; Mocha had discovered where we lived and was lying contentedly in the open doorway. She'd done well to find our room; there were five flights of stairs to climb from the beach, where she usually hung out. Her stumpy tail was wagging away and I'm sure she could just sense that we were out-and-out dog lovers. We were sure the poor girl had experienced some mistreatment but had chosen to reach out and trust us. With a little encouragement, she settled on the floor beside the bed, out of the sun and enjoying the room's cooling fans.

It didn't take her more than a couple of days to then work out our schedule for early-morning walks. She routinely began appearing at our door, in good time to accompany us. She would follow us out onto the road and excitedly trot ahead for just a few hundred metres, until reaching the edge of her comfort zone. We were soon to discover she'd been hiding another quite embarrassing trait, to add to the snobbery and racism. She just couldn't let a motorbike or moped pass without turning into a barking, growling sprinter. Yes, she was also a dreaded bike-chaser, and we were going to need a collar and lead for her!

We'd often seen her taking herself off for walks, away down the shoreline. She'd disappear up through the rich undergrowth and come back an hour later, covered in sticky weed and, unfortunately, often ticks. Selly would remove any she found and Mocha would run off into the laguna's water, followed by a vigorous roll in the sand, to remove most of the jungle debris. She just loved to explore, but with so many territorial, or wild, dogs around, she wasn't comfortable straying too far from Paradiso, or either of us now. Everybody was starting to notice her attachment and joked that we had been successfully adopted.

"You just need to find a sidecar for the bike, Mark, shouldn't be difficult in this country," teased Jess.

Blu added her two pennies' worth. "Sell it and get a camper," she smirked, knowing how attached to two wheels I was.

"Mocha's too much of a free spirit. She doesn't even like bikes," I countered.

She might be a free spirit, but just to undermine my argument, she was currently imploring Selly to go on a forage with her. Curious to know where exactly she went on these lonesome walks, Selly stood and beckoned her on. Mocha instantly understood, and over the next hour she proudly and excitedly took Selly on a tour of her favourite iguana and squirrel hunting spots. She would dive into the thickets, like an arctic fox into deep snow, and bury her head to listen for any movement. When a squirrel was spotted, she would be rooted to the spot, excitedly watching its every move, before attempting to climb the trees. They both came back happily covered in green sticky buds, and Mocha knew she had at last found an exploring playmate.

We fell into somewhat of a regular schedule, starting with taking Mocha on early-morning monkey spotting, bike-chasing walks, and Mocha later taking Selly on iguana forages. In between, we spent a lot of the daytime at an 'out of the way' table that three of us had commandeered down by the beach. Timo, a web designer, was half-Dutch, half-German and joined us daily with his laptop. With volcano views, a palm roof over our heads and Mocha invariably at our feet, the three of us had inappropriately nicknamed our retreat 'the office'.

As Timo toiled away on his laptop, I started to make notes and early drafts for this book and Selly contentedly painted pastels of the surrounding wildlife. It was a nice routine for all three of us. 'The office' was unofficially a 'dry' table, and helped encourage us not to start drinking before the 6pm welcome cocktails. Not that Timo drank very often; he was just a genuinely nice and well-liked guy, who had the time of day for everyone. It wasn't always easy, though. Not too many metres away sat the survivors' table, and that was never short of temptation, conversation and rums, whatever the time of day or night!

The following weekly excursion was upon us and the minibus filled up for a run out to the Pacific Coast. Mocha tried desperately to climb aboard and we had to reluctantly persuade her not to jump in. I felt quite guilty as we drove off, and just to ensure that we all did, she ran down the road after us, only stopping when we were almost out of sight. It was all a bit of a rerun of the previous week's outing, except we had a deserted beach to ourselves this time around. All the usual crowd had come along, with the addition of Timo's uncle and family meeting us there.

His uncle just happened to be the Dutch Honorary Consulate General, covering both Guatemala and Nicaragua, and a lovely guy at that. Roberto and I hit it off immediately and as the drinks flowed, it suddenly seemed a great idea to snort a whole tin of snuff between us. Not that I particularly like it, but it just seemed rude not to! Just a few years older than myself, he hailed from a tiny southern Dutch town that, coincidentally, I just happened to know very well. Once (many moons before!), when I was stationed just across the border in Germany, we had, in our youth, frequently drunk in the same bar, which happened to be owned by a good friend of his. In fact, for many years, both of us considered the place 'our local'! Selly and Roberto's partner, Lucélia, got on like old friends, and a new lasting friendship was born.

On the way to the beach, we'd stopped off in a tiny fishing village and to the locals' delight, bought all their freshly caught red snapper. This was BBQ'd amongst the dunes and washed down with homemade mango shots, beer and rum. Never quite knowing what, if any, coronavirus restrictions were about to be imposed upon us, these outings were great fun and an opportunity to see a little more of the country. As we said our goodbyes, Roberto and Lucélia promised to come visit us all in the crater and, having stayed for the sunset, it was 9pm before we returned to Paradiso. Mocha was waiting at the gate for us, looking like she hadn't moved the whole day!

After several weeks of failed attempts to connect with a wedding planner, an email arrived, out of the blue, from the Bellagio. It confirmed what we had found out for ourselves: that the hotel was currently shut down until further notice, but that they hoped to be open in time for our 4th of June ceremony. Now just six weeks away, it all felt very pie in the sky. I replied, initially explaining we were stranded 3,000 miles south of them, but that overall, we felt let down by their lack of communication. I ended by asking for a cancellation and refund. We didn't want to spend the next few weeks stuck in limbo, not knowing if it was on or off. Coming to that decision, despite knowing it was the right one for us and our friends, was still a disappointment. What a year to have planned a wedding!

We'd kept Chris and Caroline updated along the way, but for them it was more than a wedding invite; it was the starting point of their own mini Pan American adventure. From day one, I'd been looking forward to this part of the trip and knew they would feel as disappointed as we did now. I was inwardly beginning to doubt North America was still going to be on our itinerary; hardly anything was going to plan anymore!

Demonstrating much better communication skills were the British consulate staff, down in San José. I'd received several messages from them, keeping me aware of any flights leaving the country and in turn, I passed the news on to Steve and Jess. I couldn't fault them; even though I had stated our intentions were to stay, they continued to make sure we knew of any developments, or repatriation flights.

It was time for another 'pick-me-up'. Matteo and Iulia had organised a private 'Paradiso only' pool party, followed by a booze cruise down in Granada. The minibus filled up and we descended on the pool, cranked up the music and enjoyed an afternoon of tapas, sangria and inevitable dive-bombing! Despite losing count of how many previous trips she'd hosted, Blu was persuaded to join us on the booze cruise and be our guide. To be fair, we were all pretty drunk, and expecting something semi-professional from Blu was asking a bit too much. I mean, she'd only been here eight months after all, but had us crying with the following inspirational knowledge.

"That's Bird Poo Rock, that's Bird Poo Island and that's Monkey Poo Island!" was about all we got, after she'd fallen into her polished tour-guide mode.

It's a good job it was a cracking trip out; it proved to be the final one.

Chapter Fifteen

Almost a Holiday!

The restrictions had been fairly informal up to now. Outside guests were still allowed in at the weekends, though not for overnight stays. Us 'permanent guests' had been encouraged to use the taxis working solely for the hostel rather than public transport, and a few hand-sanitiser bottles had been placed around the resort. Other than that, we couldn't honestly say we were in any kind of a lockdown. There was nothing in place to stop Steve and Blu heading out on the odd Friday night, to pub crawl Granada's bar street. This Friday night happened to be the night after the drunken pool party and early the following morning we were greeted by one of the Germans.

"I heard about the two prostitutes coming to your room last night!" she hit us with, walking on past and wearing some kind of knowing smile.

Selly and I looked at each other, confused and curious about this bizarre revelation. Reaching the bar, we were surprised to see that both Blu and Steve had beaten us to breakfast coffees and were in the middle of trying to recall all of the previous night's exploits.

They'd painted Granada red and were comically attempting to jigsaw the night together, through foggy memories. We told them of the revelation we'd just had, resulting in Blu rounding on Steve.

"Didn't you get into a taxi with two girls last night?" she quizzed Steve.

"They weren't prostitutes," defended Steve.

Matteo conveniently arrived, to throw fuel on the fire, of course.

"So, Mark, I was woken at 3am by the night-guard telling me two prostitutes had arrived in a taxi for room two," he mocked, and continued, "I don't judge, but it is always the quiet couples you have to watch."

He was thoroughly enjoying himself and I had to admit to coincidentally being up around that time. Our cat back home was unwell and being six hours behind England, I'd set my alarm to get up at two thirty and call the vet's for poor Giulia. Due to the heat, we still slept with just curtains pulled across the open doors and if the night-watchman had just let these girls in, Selly might have had unexpected visitors waking her!

Blu threw another intriguing nugget into the unravelling mystery.

"Steve, you used to live in room two, when you first arrived. Maybe you were too drunk to remember your room number," she teased him.

Whatever the story, for Matteo, it was way too good to drop so quickly. He happily spent the next few days giving Selly and I 'knowing' nods and winks at every opportunity!

The following evening was another quiz night. In general, Selly and I were usually crap, but on the music rounds we were especially crap. Shame really, as the winning teams, from every round, got free shots on the house. It was often just the two of us, against larger teams, but tonight we had been split more fairly, even if the various nationalities had gravitated to each other. The music rounds were the forte of the two young Swedes. They were such masterminds that they had to host these rounds, or they would be guaranteed to win them outright. It came down to a tiebreaker, between the predominantly British and German teams. The Brits raised an arm quickest, answered correctly and won the tiebreaker. The Germans promptly complained, quite bitterly.

"We had our hands up first," they fired at the Swedes, whilst sending us death stares.

Before the Swedes could counter, Matteo overruled in his own style.

"For God's sake, Germans, get your arms up higher. You didn't have any problems eighty years ago, did you?" he cheered, whilst sending the winning team's shots over to our table.

I couldn't believe it; the first time we had enjoyed free shots on a music round, and we'd gotten one over the Germans into the bargain! It was another typically fun-filled night and, compared to some of the lockdown horror stories we were hearing about, our small resort was akin to a lively Butlin's holiday camp.

Steve's forty-third birthday was coming up after the weekend and in anticipation of a heavy night, Selly and I actually declined the sundowner cocktails and detoxed for a few days. Timo's birthday was just three days after Steve's, and as it fell on a Thursday, the weekly outing was skipped in favour of a shindig in the resort. Unbeknown to either of them, Selly had been working hard to produce portrait gifts for the pair. When Steve's portrait was finished, Selly collected everyone's birthday greetings, to adorn the reverse side, including Timo's. He was bowled over by the finished gift and it was written all over his face that he would love one too. He was just too nice a guy to even drop a hint and, of course, had no idea his was almost complete too!

On the evening of Steve's bash, Paradiso emptied for a hundred-metre stroll up the road, carrying cool boxes of beer, ice and spirits. With a limited menu, a local family's wooden shack served as a basic and rustic restaurant. They could put a simple meal in front of us but didn't have any alcoholic drinks to serve. The whole country was experiencing hard times and eating here a couple of times per week put some money the family's way. The tips invariably doubled the bill and, in turn, kept food on their own table. Hardly had we settled when Canela and Mocha breezed in excitedly to join the fun. I guess they had ventured into Paradiso's bar, found it strangely deserted and decided to come out looking for us. Steve was made up; he had a soft spot for Canela he couldn't hide if he tried, and swept her up for besotted cuddles. The affection was reciprocated in a strange way; despite being female, Canela tried vigorously 'humping' Steve's leg as a thank you!

The meal devoured, Selly presented him with his portrait. He was floored and couldn't put it down, switching between his portrait on one side and all the cutting banter on the back. What a nice way to remember these strange times and close-knit friendships. An emotionally charged speech was cut short by kidnapping the birthday boy back to Paradiso. The night was moved up a gear and in a similar fashion to Matteo the month before, he soon found himself partially stripped, wrapped up like a 'mummy' and ritually treated to a ketchup, mayonnaise and flour shower.

The Swedes dug out some of their crazier music and cranked up the volume. Nobody was holding back tonight and Iulia, who we'd since learnt hailed from Moldova, mesmerised us with some bizarrely fast robotic Moldavian moves that none of us could hope to match.

Despite the late hour, Steve dumped several bottles of rum on the 'survivors' table, signalling the night was still young. The bar staff had seen enough, leaving us a healthy supply of ice and calling it a day. Blu was suffering; she'd started a little too early and was being coaxed awake by Steve with cajoling drunken hugs.

"I love you, Blu. You're not going to sleep this early, come on, stay with us," he'd tell her, as they sat with arms wrapped around each other.

"I love you too, I never expected to meet someone like you on this trip," sobbed a drunken Blu, failing to hold back her 'happy' tears.

It was super cute, and if Blu wasn't gay, we'd be telling the pair to 'get a room'! Irma had packed away her timid side for the evening and upon discovering she shared the same birthday as Giulia, hugged Selly enthusiastically whilst bouncing up and down.

"Oh please, can I be your daughter too? That would be super, super exciting," she squeaked excitedly, as if to prove it.

I seriously hoped we weren't still stuck here in nine months' time and celebrating hers also! The numbers inevitably waned as the rum disappeared and forced people into dormitory retirement. Matteo swaggered around still, with his fedora perched on his head, an unlit cigar in one hand and a cocktail in the other. It had been another epic night, and a birthday Steve wouldn't easily forget. So much for being stranded abroad; at times like this, we had to pinch ourselves there was even a pandemic going on around us. Mocha had watched all the antics from afar but was relieved Selly and I were finally calling it a day. She followed us up the stairs and plonked herself down, half in and half out of the room.

Although we didn't find out until the morning, on Steve's birthday, the 4th of May, the UK surpassed even Italy for total numbers of Covid-19 deaths, almost 30,000. At the time it seemed a staggering number, sobering and too unbelievable to comprehend. We still had no real idea of the situation here in Nicaragua, and within our Paradiso microcosm, we were carrying on like it was Glastonbury! The lockdowns and stripped supermarket shelves back in Italy and England might as well have been news from Mars; it was just too surreal to relate to.

Dwarfing the car park was a new addition. A huge and expensive-looking motorhome now hid the bike from view; it appeared we had newcomers. Walking down for breakfast, we were caught by Matteo.

"Mark, Selly, these are your new neighbours, Cedric, Jeniffer and their two lovely daughters. They're staying a couple of nights and are from Switzerland," he informed and introduced us.

"No, they're from Belgium. They just live in Switzerland," corrected Iulia!

Wow, they had just missed one hell of a party, I thought, as we greeted them and continued on down to check out the state of the bar. We found Steve peacefully sleeping on the beach, where it looked like he'd spent the remainder of the night. For company, he'd had Canela beside him and various other bodies, who'd made it no further than the nearest hammocks! The state of the bar was to be expected. It was trashed!

Steve's 'feather and tarring' had left ketchup and flour over walls, tables and floors. Empty cans and bottles were everywhere, and items of clothing lay on the beach and on the backs of chairs. Timo was looking a little anxious at the mess and, ahead of his own birthday, in just three days' time, had actually stopped drinking ten days prior. The German side of him had tried to take control of how his birthday would be celebrated. He wanted just a quiz night and kindly offered each of us three welcome drinks. That could work, alongside the ideas we already had in mind!

On his big day, he proudly announced he hadn't had a drink for two whole weeks (and was promptly handed a shot of tequila). It was mid-afternoon and the perfect temperature for kayak racing. This happened to be a forte of Timo's, something he liked to get competitive about, particularly with Jess. At twenty-seven, Timo had over thirty years' youth on our ageing Jess, and we'd figured more tequilas would even things up a bit. This was England versus Germany once more. The platform had been turned into a floating bar and lined with several shots to slow down each of his passes.

"But I have volleyball at 4pm. It's not possible to start drinking now!" he protested, having switched from a softer nuanced Dutch accent to a more authoritative German one.

The course was set and once pushed out into the laguna's 'handicapped' course, four furious laps and four large shots followed. With just 'a little' assistance, Jess had it in the bag, but Timo was the birthday boy after all and an amicable draw was declared. With the three Germans split into different teams, Steve hosted a quiz entirely made up of German-related questions. All of these questions having been selected to be just obscure or tricky enough to embarrass them on their levels of national knowledge. The questions proved pretty sporty for the rest of us too, but wrong answers from Timo earned him a drink, of course. True to his mickey-taking form, Matteo gave up and answered 'prostitute' to most of the remaining questions, getting two correct!

As the quiz was finalised and the beer-pong table was about to be set up, Selly found her moment to bring Timo out and finally present him with his own portrait. He was moved to give a lengthy heartfelt and teary speech. He probably should have turned it over and read some of the comments first! Like three nights before, the evening descended into drunken fun and games. As the clocked rolled past midnight, Steve went around insisting platform skinny-dipping was in order. He had the bit between his teeth and eventually had his way. We laid out on the moonlit platform, horizontal star-gazing and counting shooting stars, Selly dripping in her dress and several of us with drinks we'd swum across with. It was proving another magical evening.

Back on dry land, Timo was nowhere to be seen. Concerned for his whereabouts, Selly asked if anyone had noticed him leaving. Nobody had seen him in the water and so she popped up to his dorm, finding it locked.

"Irma, you share with Timo. Do you have your key, so we can go up and check he's OK?" she asked.

"Oh yes, but I'll just have a cigarette first," she said with a smile, completely unfazed Timo could be passed out, or worse, actually missing!

Selly ignored her nicotine needs, took her by the arm and propelled her up the stairs, where they found the star of the party snoring blissfully in his bunk!

The following afternoon, I was woken from a doze by Matteo's urgent-sounding voice and a commotion outside the room.

"Fire close by, any volunteers?" he called out.

Iguana hunting must have gotten out of hand, I guessed, and headed out to see if I could help. Steve, Jess and a few of the workers were already bringing water, shovels and palm brushes up to the 4x4.

"Have you got long pants and trainers, Mark? It's going to be hot underfoot," Matteo warned.

Squeezed into the 4x4 and shadowed by a half-dozen small motorbikes, we followed our noses through the smoke-thickened air. Matteo was glued to his mobile, getting updates and instructions from the local park rangers. During the dry season, fires were a constant threat and the crater's residents banded together to bolster the limited resources available to the rangers. This fire ran narrowly up from the dirt track we were now on to the crater's rim, a few hundred metres above us. The rangers would tackle the fire from the top down and we would try to work our way from the bottom up, beating out the flames and dampening the ground with our limited water. We parked off to one side of the fire and set to work. Just being fully clothed felt warm; I'd been living for the best part of two months in not much more than swim shorts and flip-flops!

With our hands already full, carrying water containers and straw brooms, it soon became exhausting work to climb the jungle's steep sides. The carpet of dry loose leaves proved slippery and it was randomly on fire! In the smoke, we soon lost sight of each other, self-absorbed in the burning patches grabbing our attention. The heat from the fire was causing strong drafts and every so often I was getting caught up in suffocating, twisting smoke 'chimneys'. For sure, we were making headway and thankfully more vehicles and volunteers were continuing to arrive. As we beat and doused down the flames, we also had to keep climbing higher and returning further for more water each time.

The smoke was stealing both my visibility and breath as I made my way up once more, only to be stopped in my tracks. A large flaming 'boulder' bounded erratically down towards me and I froze, trying to decide how best to get out of its way! Strangely, small flaming pieces seemed to be breaking off with each bounce and starting new fires along its path. At the last second, I leapt out of the way, and it finally came to rest against a large tree trunk ten metres below me. Gingerly backtracking, I found it was a huge old circular wasp nest, burning quite ferociously and needing all my remaining water to put it and the now burning tree trunk out!

Eyes and lungs stinging, I made my way back to the vehicle to refill. Just as I reached the 4x4, I heard a series of invisible but urgent shouts and a loud crashing from above. The noise rapidly increased and sounded how I imagined a landslide would. For the second time in minutes, I felt rooted to the spot, ears straining to make sense of the growing commotion and my brain scrambling to compute a safe escape. With last-ditch desperation, I ran behind Matteo's vehicle, just seconds before three large boulders burst out of the undergrowth. A shower of debris had been dragged down with the boulders and once the dust had settled, I could see the 4x4 had missed being hit by less than a car's length!

It took the next couple of minutes to pass the word around and ensure everyone was accounted for and uninjured. We struggled on until dusk arrived to relieve us; there was no way we could risk continuing once the light had left us. We were all shattered anyway, and the water we had brought along was just about gone. After just three hours away, blackened and dishevelled, we called it a night and headed home. I think we were barely recognisable as we climbed down from the truck, to be greeted by a concerned-looking Selly and Mocha. I polished off all the water we had in the room as Mocha sniffed me all over, seeming to understand what we had been up to. She gently licked my grubby fingers and was clearly unsure if she should still be worried, or just happy I was back. It had been a memorable night, one I hoped I would never have to repeat.

Another month had caught up with us; we needed to make the paperwork run to Managua once more. Having gone through the process already, I felt better organised this time, though. Silly me.

"You need to write a letter requesting an extension and stating why you need it," said an official at the door to the customs building.

"Well, the borders are closed and we can't exit the country," I replied, dumbfounded.

The obvious didn't matter; it had to be a grovelling letter, with all the bike details and my details in it. We begged a sheet of paper, struggled to write it up in understandable Spanish and queued up.

"I also need a photocopy of the letter, and of your passport's photograph and your entry stamps," said the next manufacturer of bureaucracy.

"Really? You didn't want any photocopies last month," I wasted my breath challenging.

We left, found a copier place and came back, just as the entire office departed for lunch. I was getting good at predicting the start of these breaks. Several hours later, paperwork completed, we returned to Paradiso and found an excited Mocha patiently waiting by the room. She bounded over before we could even get off the bike, jumping up and panicking me that she'd burn herself on the exhaust, or engine. This was a turnaround for a bike-hating, bike-chasing dog! Here she now was, clambering all over us and not the slightest bit put off that the humans she'd adopted were actually bikers!

That same day, a friend of Blu's arrived from Little Corn Island to join us until she could get a flight home to Calgary. Taylor had been volunteering also and, knowing a few of the Paradiso crowd, fitted straight in and showed the boys how pool should be played. I declined to be shown up anymore; Selly had only recently started playing the game and was now regularly beating me. The table was the worst I'd experienced, but by far the most interesting. Before setting up, the larger bugs and insects first had to be relocated from the table, then the cloth and balls had to be brushed free of gecko poos.

The table couldn't be levelled, due to slowly rotting feet, and the game was played knowing the balls would all end up down one side and usually in three out of six pockets. Mid-play, more poos would fall from the palm ceiling and a variety of insects, or huge toads, would arrive ringside, along with the odd snake, to spook the players. I can never say a game was dull; the cue tips were bent or, worse, missing, and Selly pushed past all this to pull off some cracking games. It was clearly more than beginner's luck and I unceremoniously gave the game up.

The next day, we had another new visitor to the laguna. Clouds. Other than those the volcanoes produced, these were literally the first we'd seen in two whole months. Sure enough, late that afternoon, they darkened the skies and a distant rumble could be heard. We all awaited the rainfall that must surely follow. The advancing storm clouds cast an eerie glow across the laguna and eventually a white sheet descended, blocking the view of the far rim as it marched across the water towards us. People actually ran to grab their cameras!

"Welcome to the rainy season, folks. Don't worry, it'll be over sometime in November!" announced Matteo, with a hint of sarcasm.

Cool, refreshing air reached us a few minutes before the tropical downpour. The advancing wall of water seemed so out of place that even the three dogs stood with us to welcome its arrival. The thunderstorms became an 'every other day' occurrence, dropping the temperature overall and alerting the jungle that spring was finally here. Thankfully, it also put an end to the fires.

Late one night, it was still raining hard as we got back to the room. Mocha had followed us up, but as we needed to close the doors, couldn't sleep 'half out' on the path, as was her usual choice. She looked up at us questioningly. We weren't going to shut her out, were we? She needed no encouragement to settle down by Selly's side of the bed and slept peacefully through the night. Over the coming nights, even though the doors were often open, she continued to come in and make the room hers also. And so it transpired that day and night, she was now constantly by our sides, and we couldn't deny we were falling in love with her.

She would even follow me into the water when I went paddleboarding, and one day I asked Selly to gently lift her on. She contentedly stayed aboard and I paddled out to the platform, to show her all the fish hiding in its shadows. She was pretty enthralled, peering over the board with her ears up and stumpy tail wagging. On successive trips, we went further out, and I turned back to give her a view and perspective of 'home' I doubted she'd seen before. Reaching the shore, she ran forward excitedly, pushing the board backwards and sending me off into the water, much to the delight of those up in the bar.

"It will break her heart to leave her behind," I said, knowing full well we had both been thinking this for a long time.

"It will break ours," replied Selly, more truthfully.

It seemed ridiculous; we were here on a motorcycle, not in a comfy motorhome like Cedric and Jeniffer's. We still had hopes to resume travelling, slimming hopes admittedly. The thought of 'rescuing' Mocha did seem outlandish, but not as outlandish as allowing her to get attached to us and then just leaving her behind. We went to see Matteo, who unsurprisingly laughed at us.

"Told you she was going with you!" he cracked.

We couldn't let our thoughts run too far ahead without trying to learn something more of her background. We were full of questions. How did she end up here? Where did she come from? Who looked after her before us? Can anybody claim that they owned her? Back home in France, Matteo was a dog lover, but here in the resort the dogs were barely tolerated by the wary Nicaraguan guests. In turn, this made the dogs more of a headache, for both him and the resort.

"Come on, take her. She won't be the first to leave, two went last year," he offered.

As they had been here the longest, we started to ask around the volunteer workers and the Nicaraguan staff, and a common story emerged. Mocha was thought to be around three years old and had been turned out of a nearby house a couple of years previously, when the lady had had a baby. One of the bar staff had found two dogs on the beach one day and brought them to Paradiso. They were both underweight and one needed care for its wounds; he named this one Scarface and the other Mocha, a Nicaraguan nickname for 'short-tail', or 'stumpy'. Scarface was one of the dogs Matteo referred to that had already been rescued and taken back to Germany. For at least the last year or so, Mocha had mostly hung around Paradiso, living off her wits and the kindness of the staff and guests passing through. Nobody believed there was anyone who could legitimately stake a claim on her and as the news spread, that we were considering taking her back to England with us, so did the excitement. We had absolutely no idea how to make this happen but were thrilled by the thought nonetheless!

Chapter Sixteen

Heading for Lockdown

On Sunday, the 17th of May, we all woke to a comprehensive set of lockdown rules, put out on the Paradiso group chat. Some possible measures had previously been discussed, so this wasn't a huge surprise to any of us. For sure, our freedoms would be curtailed, but also Matteo and Iulia's finances would be taking a hit, just to keep us all that bit safer. For the foreseeable future, there wouldn't be any 'day guests' allowed in, or any new guests admitted and allowed to stay at the resort. Our individual shopping needs could be submitted weekly and this would be carried out by one member of the staff. There would be no more use of public transport permitted, and any cashpoint or visa runs would be conducted via Paradiso's subsidised and sanitised taxi. It all made common sense and was designed to try and keep the virus out. Our resident Russian immediately renamed the resort 'Paranoia', and vowed to leave!

In general, everyone else seemed happy going forward with the rules, up until the various consulates put the cat amongst the pigeons. Lately, it seemed they had started working overtime, and a rash of potential repatriation flights were popping up in email and social media alerts. It looked like there would be flights either at the end of this month, or in early June to France, Spain and the UK, in addition to the States and Canada. Combined with the lockdown rules, it started to generate an atmosphere of unrest and a lot of talk now gravitated to the possibility of leaving Nicaragua. The Swedes wanted to get back to Gothenburg, the two French girls now wanted to get back to Paris and Timo had been busy sending off job applications and needed to get back to Germany. Steve and Jess were both undecided, and only Irma, Blu, Selly and myself said we would definitely skip any upcoming flights and stick it out a while longer. There still wasn't any reliable news coming from the Nicaraguan government, so none of us could truly judge where we would be better off but, undeniably, there was a feeling of change in the Paradiso air.

Timo started the exodus, having signed up for a repatriation flight heading to Germany. He would be missed by all of us, but with his uncle, Roberto, living just down the road, he said his goodbyes and headed off for some last-minute sightseeing. A couple of days later, the Russian said his goodbyes also. He was the oldest amongst us and had rarely joined us in the evenings, so I had wondered if we'd all been a bit too loud for him. Over a coffee on his last morning, he surprised me by saying he 'really needed to get out and party more'!

That evening, Blu fell ill with a temperature, coughing and struggling to breathe. She also had severe stomach pains and a doctor had to be called for. Appendicitis was ruled out, and with no Covid-19 tests available in the country, all we could do was isolate and monitor her. The following day, the other Aussie also fell ill, again with a high temperature, and both stayed in self-isolation. Things were starting to get a little too ominous.

Taylor managed to hop on a flight home to Canada and we really started to feel our numbers dwindling. The usual evening's fun and games just seemed to be overtaken by a succession of 'leaving bashes'. As the repatriation flights firmed up with dates, several more of the 'lockdown' crew announced they were reserving seats. Steve and Jess remained steadfastly undecided, feeling the lure of England but still loving their temporary home and friends here.

Within days, one of the German girls fell ill, announcing she also had a high temperature and had lost her sense of taste. Things were spiralling down quickly and Matteo was forced to introduce further measures. Specific showers and toilets were allocated to those in the dormitories and rooms without ensuites. Anybody with any of the Covid symptoms was asked to immediately self-isolate.

We needed some confirmation of what we all now suspected, and it seemed to come a couple of days later. Taylor informed us that after returning home to Canada, she had gotten tested and was positive for Covid-19. Unless she had caught it during her transit through the airports, or during the flights back, it seemed likely the virus had finally caught us up and was now amongst us.

With so many people now leaving, or planning to, it brought home the need to start preparing Mocha. Whether she actually left with us in the end, or not, we wanted to get all her inoculations up to date and have her microchipped. Putting her in a taxi for an appointment, she made it almost all the way before getting carsick! The vet confirmed she was still a little underweight, gave her a rabies jab, gave us a bottle of anti-tick 'drops' to treat her with and took a swab, to test for worms or parasites. She seemed a little annoyed that the intriguing escape from the crater had resulted in some pain, but now sported a smart bandana collar and a new lead. Unsurprisingly, the parasite swab test came back positive and we returned later in the week to get Mocha the necessary treatments. Again, she got carsick, this time over my pre-prepared microfibre towel!

Blu finished her week's worth of antibiotics just in time for the next round of send-offs. After a week off the drinking, combined with rest and the antibiotics, she'd made a sound recovery and was back to her old self. Even the remaining 'patients' were picking up again, after just a few days, and importantly, nobody else had since fallen ill. The three of them continued to wear face masks and social distance around the rest of us, but it was wonderful to see them on the mend so quickly.

Although we had used the drops to help rid Mocha of any ticks, we booked a third appointment. This time for a blood sample to be taken and tested for any tick-borne diseases she might already have picked up. She wouldn't thank us, but she was also getting a general multi-vaccination! This appointment fell on what should have been our Vegas wedding day, the 4th of June. I came down to the bar that morning and joined the now fully recovered Blu, plus Steve and Jess for a coffee. I couldn't help feeling a tad down. I didn't want to bore anybody but spoke up anyway!

"We were supposed to be getting married today. Instead, we're off to the vet's again," I stated, a little solemnly.

"Don't worry, I'm sure it will happen soon," replied Blu, smiling at me and then the other two.

Already my second attempt to marry Selly; I guess I was now resigned to third time lucky!

We got Mocha to the vet's, and for the first time she wasn't sick inside the taxi. She made it as far as the street's gutter instead. Oh well, that's something of a minor celebration! She loved these trips out, trying to get her head fully out of the window and watching everything with a keen interest. Once on the vet's table, though, all curiosity was swapped for suspicion and we had to be on hand to soothe her. After the first appointment, she had been a little annoyed with us for a day or two, but now she just took it out on the unfortunate vet and saw us as her rescuers.

Once home, she followed me back down to the bar and settled under the table as I joined Blu once more, for an early afternoon drink. Selly was intercepted and diverted away to give a drawing lesson, up on the top terrace. Unusually for Blu, she stopped chatting and drinking after just one beer and with Selly still occupied, I retreated to our room, followed by the loyal Mocha. Later in the afternoon, we'd hardly reunited before Matteo appeared at our door.

"Come on, you two. Early welcome drinks today, 4 pm, and it's a smart dress day," he informed us, looking unusually dressed up himself, in jeans, a white shirt, blazer and the trademark fedora.

Something for sure was going on; it was thirty-seven degrees and

Matteo wasn't in shorts and flip-flops. He'd given us twenty minutes to shower and make ourselves presentable, but for what? The only top I had with a collar was black with long sleeves, last worn as an under-layer in a chillier Patagonia. That would have to go with the one and only pair of cargo pants I'd brought on the trip. Selly fared better; she had a couple of lightweight dresses packed, pulled on a deep blue one and even had a pair of strappy lightweight high heels to wear. She was just finishing off fixing her hair, when Matteo returned again, to hasten us along.

"Enough, you two, it's gone four already and nobody is allowed to start drinking until you pair come down!" he chimed.

"Italian, Matteo, don't forget she's Italian!" I joked.

He walked us down the first flight of stairs, where Iulia was patiently waiting for us.

"Mark, please go with Iulia. I need to borrow Selly," he instructed, taking Selly by the arm and leading her away in the direction of the bar.

Iulia escorted me away and down a flight of stairs that led to the resort's thatch-roofed 'temple', the girls' yoga area by day and our movie venue by night. Poor Mocha hadn't a clue which one of us to follow, but with the kitchen being closer to the temple, followed her stomach!

I was floored and rooted to the spot. Within the last couple of hours, it had been transformed. Everybody was present and seated in rows, dressed to the nines. A bamboo pagoda, draped in flowers, lights, white linens and ribbons had been erected, complete with a decorated lectern. Jeniffer had a movie camera set up on a tripod and the Swedes had musical instruments at the ready. One of the Germans was poised as the photographer and Steve was stood patiently smiling by the lectern, papers in hand and a bright sash round his neck. He confidently kicked off his intro.

"Welcome to your 'almost' wedding, Mark. I'll be conducting the service today. Don't worry, I've already written both sets of vows for you!" he pronounced, with a wink and a cheeky grin.

"Do you need a beer?" grinned Blu, skipping any reply and returning with beers for us both, plus an extra shot for me!

"Wasn't sure what you wanted, got you both. By the way, your 'almost' wife might be late. She's drinking shots with her 'borrowed dad' and getting flowers stuck in her hair," laughed Blu.

I was gobsmacked that they had gone to all this planning, for a day we thought we'd lost. Despite the recent departures, there were still twenty of us, including the four youngsters, and they had all been organising away without us having the slightest clue! I looked around in amazement. For so long we had all lived day and night in swimwear, and here was everyone not just fully dressed but properly dressed. Blu had put a collared shirt on and the rest of the girls all had dresses or long skirts on. I had to double-take to recognise everyone. What a turnaround. I had started the day quite down and now, as the musicians started up, I was on top of the world!

Around the corner from the bar came the two daughters of Cedric and Jeniffer, scattering petals ahead of Matteo, who led a beaming veiled Selly by the arm. She clutched a white bouquet, had flowers in her hair and a reaction that mirrored mine. As the music fell away, Steve turned minister and asked Blu to give a comical reading, reminding us all of some of the recent Paradiso-antics. This was followed by a set of highly sarcastic but hilariously funny vows and an exchange of garlands, in place of the rings we hadn't gotten around to buying yet!

Having been pronounced 'almost husband and wife', we kissed, had a photo session and retreated to the equally transformed bar. All of the tables had been put together in one long line, decorated in red tablecloths, flowers and candles, etc. A sumptuous three-course dinner was interspersed with speeches and the cutting of a beautiful cake that Iulia had made for us all. Selly got to throw her bouquet for the ladies, which was grabbed by an overly enthusiastic drunken Blu, who ran off proudly to celebrate with it. Down on the beach, there was even a fire show organised. They had thought of everything and we couldn't thank them enough. The least we could do was announce a free bar, guaranteeing the night would be a late one. We might be locked-down and not legally married, but these amazing new friends had given us such a wonderful collection of special memories. I'm sure the 4th of June will always remain special to us.

The following day, we were eager to share our experience with family and friends. The only question was how to exactly, without sounding like we were rubbing it in! We seemed to be living on a different planet; the UK had now been in a truly miserable lockdown for over ten weeks, parts of Italy even longer. Whilst Italy's death rate was still under 30,000, the UK had now surpassed 40,000. I couldn't understand how that had even happened so quickly. Even so, we spent most of the day making video calls and one friend summed up how we hoped most felt: "Don't come back, you pair have won the lockdown lottery, keep enjoying yourselves!"

The coming days were consumed with discussions around the various repatriation flights. The London-bound flight was fast filling up, due to it making additional pick-ups in both Guatemala and Costa Rica. Steve had made his decision and booked a seat as Jess, bless him, continued to dally, changing his mind with each passing day! It was now the 6th of June and the Swedes wanted to celebrate their National Day. They had also booked flights and would be leaving us the day after Steve (and possibly Jess). For the Swedes, it had to be a music quiz to kick off their night's celebrations, but with a twist: they weren't allowed to host this time. Steve organised the rounds of questions, loosely revolving around tenuous links to Sweden and aimed at thwarting their usually solid knowledge of both music and country. Shots flowed, of course, and the night descended into another epic party.

Jess had drunk through the entire night, torturing himself weighing up the pros and cons of leaving. He was still in the bar when Selly and I went down in the morning, though he announced to us he'd had some kind of overnight epiphany. He'd made up his mind to accompany Steve back to London and had finally booked his escape. In honour of them departing, yet another fitting send-off was organised. We wouldn't be the only ones missing these two. Steve regularly walked Blacky and Canela, who doted on him. She rewarded Steve by cornering a passing skunk at their leaving party and getting herself thoroughly sprayed. For weeks to come, she stunk terribly, as did the whole bar area!

It was a very hungover pair of Brits we waved off in a taxi the next morning. Steve must still have been drunk, as he happily swept the badly stinking Canela up into his arms for a loving last cuddle. Jess could hardly keep his eyes open and with a fixed grin on his face, hugged us all twice. We were truly sad to see them go, knowing the atmosphere wouldn't be the same again.

Our feelings took a further knock that day, with news from Giulia back home. Our poorly cat had sadly passed away during the night. The vet had found advanced kidney disease and nothing more could be done for the poor girl. Giulia had been up the whole night, comforting her and hoping for some kind of miracle. It was a heavy day, one of those when you wished you could hop into a tele-transporter and be where you needed to be. Every long trip has days like these and however much you want to be, you just can't always be in the right place at the right time.

Another send-off knocked us out of our gloom. A couple of days later, we had our goodbye drinks with the Swedes and one of the French girls, followed soon after by two more. Other than the lovely Belgian family, still living out of their motorhome, only Irma, Blu and us two remained a week after our almost-wedding day.

Cedric and I shared a taxi into the capital, to renew our vehicle import paperwork.

"We managed to find a flight back to Belgium in a couple of days' time, Mark. We're going to leave the motorhome here in long-term storage for the time being," he told me.

Wow, there really was just going to be the four of us left then. The party felt well and truly over. It had been a blast, but it felt like a new beginning was upon us. I was quite glad of the opportunity to be sharing a lift with Cedric; we'd had so many heavy rainstorms that the bike had refused to start that morning. It hadn't been used throughout the lockdown and I'd carelessly gotten used to its reliability. Once back from Managua, I whipped the plugs out, cleaned and reset them and with a short push down the hill it fired up easily. From now on, used or not, it would get started regularly!

Selly convinced Blu and I to start Spanish lessons, and for my part, it was something well overdue. The three of us began to fall nicely into a much healthier daily routine, one that no longer ended in nightly parties. We would meet up early in the mornings, for forty minutes of stretching and exercises, followed by dog walks, Spanish lessons and ending with lengthy chats over coffees. It was a new, proud Blu we were getting to know, swapping those breakfast-beers for weights and even knocking drinking off during weekdays. She was looking great for the changes; the weight was noticeably dropping off, she had more energy and even had her eyes on a potential relationship looming!

Out of all those who had been tested on returning home, only one more had tested positive for Covid-19 and it left us with a mixed-up picture. The UK were only giving tests to people with symptoms, so Jess and Steve went into a fourteen-day self-isolation, without tests being available to them. With no idea where infections had been picked up, we continued rolling with all the usual precautions.

Over the weekend, we said more goodbyes to Cedric, Jeniffer and their two girls. Jeniffer had painstakingly edited a nice parting gift for us, an 'almost wedding' video! Not only did the resort now feel empty, but the car park looked it too. Walking into the bar and not seeing all the usual faces would take some getting used to, not just for us but for the confused dogs also. They became noticeably clingier and suspicious of our every move, clearly wondering who might be next to desert them. It didn't stop Mocha sneaking off on her daily wanders, but all too often she was coming back moody, even grumpy with all of us. Becoming ever more curious, Selly had tailed her on a couple of occasions and observed her seeking out a particular plant to chew on. However unusual, there seemed to be a connection and we set about identifying it.

Oh dear, poisonous 'white snakeroot', potentially fatal to both humans and animals. The plants contained trematol-alcohol and even small doses cause neurological disorders. She was getting high! So our motorbike-chasing, racist, snobby dog was also drug addicted; what were we taking on! We would have to supervise her walks closely from now on, and try to wean her off the plant. In his unique way, Matteo lightened the mood.

"Hey, guys, have you taken your poo to Granada yet?" he asked, as I waited for a punchline that didn't come. Scanning our confused faces (not faeces!), he added, "You've all been here over three months now. Need to get your samples down to the lab for worm checks," he elaborated.

A taxi fetched the sample jars and having another vet's appointment in the morning, Selly and I offered to return them. I'd wanted an excuse to give the bike a run, and even couriering poo samples to Granada was fine by me! The following morning, we were missing a sample. Irma couldn't 'go' without her morning cigarette and had lost her lighter at the previous evening's BBQ. To be fair, she had been quite tipsy and rather 'German' the whole night. Somehow the discussion swung as to whether we should even be helping the various dogs around the laguna when there were families living close by who were struggling to feed their children properly.

It was a valid point for a discussion, apt pub-talk. Selly and I were guilty of feeding any starving dogs we came across, but we had also given out a number of micro-loans. We had no real expectations, or desire, to see them repaid, but we felt a loan rather than a handout left the recipients with their dignity. Young Irma saw things a little differently and was adamant that the animals came first and that if anybody mistreated her dog back home, she would simply kill them!

"So, you would kill somebody if they killed your dog?" baited Matteo, sensing Irma was about to dig her own hole, and she didn't disappoint.

"Of course," and then with way too much afterthought, "actually, no, that would be too kind. I would watch that person's family and then kill somebody they loved, but only a bad person, and that is why I would watch them first," she squeaked, seemingly proud of her alcohol-fuelled solution.

It was too much for Matteo to let go and for several days he replaced her name with "Hey, dog killer killer," or "Morning, killer of dog killer's best friend," etc. Anyway, I digress, the lab kindly handed over the results and sure enough, the medicinal alcohol had scared the worms off, or plain killed them!

We'd found a new vet, one who spoke English and specialised in arranging the paperwork and certificates needed to allow Mocha to leave the country. As we chatted away with him, he made an offer we jumped at. He could arrange an 'emotional support certificate', allowing Mocha the chance to fly in the cabin with us rather than in the aircraft's hold. Only a few airlines would allow this, but it was certainly worth a try. Checking over the previous vet's paperwork, he realised we'd made a glaring error. Mocha should have had her microchip inserted prior to the rabies jab, administered the month before. To return to the UK quarantine-free, Mocha would need to have the rabies jab a minimum of four months before we returned, but this had to be administered after the microchipping. We had just lost a month and if she was definitely accompanying us, we wouldn't be seeing Europe before the end of October at the earliest now.

Blu swung by our room with some interesting news.

"Lockdown's over, we can do our own shopping again," she excitedly told us.

So, we were about to get some extra freedoms. After six weeks and with just the four of us 'guests' remaining, it was decided to end the Paradiso lockdown. Limited numbers of day guests would be allowed back in over the weekends only, and we would be allowed out, to do our own shopping and run errands again. The next morning saw Irma, Blu, Selly and myself piling into a taxi and celebrating with a day trip to one Granada's bigger supermarkets.

It was a good day to be out; we returned to find the power had been knocked out by an overly adventurous monkey, trying to cross the overhead lines. The accumulation of vultures spoke of the poor animal's fate.

Chapter Seventeen

The Family Grows!

It was still sinking in that we had come away on a lengthy bike trip and had allowed ourselves to be adopted by this beautiful dog. The ramifications stretched beyond altering this trip. All our trips, for the foreseeable future, would be reshaped! Today marked a big day and a turning point in our travels. Mocha was going to the vet's to be microchipped and finally registered in one of our names. After today we could proudly be responsible for her future, give her the love and care she so deserved, and we honestly couldn't be happier about having met her. The taxi arrived, but unusually, we couldn't find Mocha, and Selly had to make a search of the resort as I chatted to our patient driver.

It was a sorry sight that returned from the direction of the beach. She'd taken herself off for an untimely swim, followed by a good roll around in the dark volcanic sand. She was wet, dirty and must also have been hunting lizards in the thick greenery. She was covered in little green sticky buds that were knotted and tangled up like Velcro in her fur. Strangely, her nice bandana collar was also missing, but there wasn't time to look for it, or clean her up as we headed off, already running late for the appointment.

The chip was successfully inserted and Selly and I glanced at each other as the vet asked whose name and passport details were going to be registered as the owner. We wished it could be both of us, but to her delight, I happily handed Selly's passport to the vet. Tomorrow, Mocha would have the rabies jab again and after a thirty-day wait, an antibody titer test. Without a good result from this test, she wouldn't be going anywhere, but it meant couriering a blood sample to an official lab in the States and waiting another month for the results to come back. We were becoming quite knowledgeable in the art of transporting animals (or so we thought!), as we diverted the taxi to pick up a new collar. Mocha wasn't carsick, hadn't even minded the vet injecting her, and we were just so chuffed to have her registered that it felt like a great day. It didn't last long.

Deciding to give the three dogs a lunchtime feed, I picked up their bag of dried biscuits and felt a stinging pain in the palm of my hand. Dropping the bag, I watched as a small transparent scorpion defensively scuttled off and down a crack in the patio. It wasn't the first time I'd been tagged by a scorpion, but this one got me good. A burning sensation ran through my body and I went both light-headed and woozy within minutes. With the unsympathetic dogs fed, I sat and let my head settle as the initial sharp pain diminished to a burning throb. The soreness was definitely receding, but red and white rings appeared around the sting and the palm swelled up and tightened.

After a bit of a lie-down, I decided a late-afternoon walk with the three dogs would be nice. And it was, until we were almost back home. As usual, Mocha was off the lead and running up and down the quiet lane, exploring every nook and cranny. As we passed a gate near to the resort, a young woman made a grab for a confused-looking Mocha. She called her by a different name and then remarked that 'Lassie' had a new collar on. (My Spanish had progressed enough for a limited conversation by now!)

Was she responsible for Mocha's recently missing collar? I wondered. To my disbelief, she tried coaxing the clearly stressed and reluctant dog through the gate of her property. I stepped forward, explaining she lived at Paradiso, had done for many months, and took the frightened Mocha back gently by her collar. A blunt conversation ensued, with the lady claiming ownership and telling me she only let her out for a couple of hours per day.

This had to be the lady that had turned Mocha out years before. I couldn't believe what I was hearing, though. Mocha had been cared for by the staff of Paradiso for over a year and she had been sleeping inside our room for at least the last two months. I was trying to stay calm as I listened to what I knew to be mostly lies. Whatever she now thought her connection to Mocha actually was, it was clear this woman must have been tipped off that we were planning to take her to England, and that some exchange of money was potentially in the offing. For sure, times were tough in Nicaragua, but I needed to get nearer to the truth of the situation, before things escalated out of hand. I invited her to walk the hundred metres down to the resort, where I could get assistance with the translating. I needed it; my heart and head (and hand!) were pounding. The 'ownership' we so recently felt after the morning's vet visit was in jeopardy of slipping through our fingers. This needed to be handled rationally, calmly and amicably. And quickly!

I managed to find both Selly and Iulia, and as word spread through the resort, we were soon joined by several of the concerned staff. Mocha cowered behind the safety of the resort's gates, seemingly understanding the seriousness of the discussions. I felt hopeless; my Spanish was elementary compared to Selly's and I struggled to follow the twists and turns of the unfolding story. The lady claimed she'd been given Mocha as a puppy, to protect the house, but had turned her out after having a baby over a year before. That bit of her story tied up with Diego's, the barman who had found Scarface and Mocha on the beach years before.

The previous evening, she believed somebody had tried to steal her chickens and she now wanted 'her' dog back. Almost an hour passed, where her story of Mocha sleeping nightly at her house and being cared for daily changed several times. I was convinced there were dollar signs in her eyes and that she was making things up as she went along. Even the staff were getting annoyed that their long-term care of Mocha was being denied.

She had no answer for the missing tail but persisted in stating that she fed Mocha daily, cared for her and insisted the dog had been sleeping overnight in her house. We were going around in circles; Mocha had been with us night and day for weeks now! On all the walks we'd taken, Mocha had not once ventured near her house. If anything, I now realised she usually crossed the road and passed by at a distance. She had been fed daily by us for at least two months and before that, she was looked after by Diego and many of the other staff. It was hard to hear the lies and not let our anger rise. The vet's blood tests had shown her to be deficient of iron, suffering from parasites, needing basic vaccinations and treatment for ticks.

To me, it seemed a farce was being played out and I just felt relief when finally she 'named her price' of forty dollars. It was ample enough for her to purchase a more suitable guard dog, if that was what she really wanted the money for. I couldn't blame her for the ploy; times were difficult and I suspected (and hoped) the dollars would be used to better feed her family. We exchanged the sum for a receipt and all parties seemed quite relieved to draw a line under the saga. The young lady left smiling and without even a glance towards Mocha, who suddenly refound her composure and followed us, tail-stump furiously wagging all the way down to the bar!

I was still feeling dizzily lightheaded and I couldn't tell if it was the emotions of the day, or the toxins from the scorpion sting. Either way, Diego, not just a barman but also our resident witchdoctor, made a rum-based potion, infused with medicinal jungle and lemon leaves. The flora around us was alive with dangers, but he had spent his lifetime learning what could instead be used for healing. The man was a genius and within twenty minutes my head was wonderfully clearing.

The curious and explorative Mocha needed nine lives to live here. She was at much more risk than myself, and not just from snakeroot. She liked to taunt the venomous snakes, scorpions, tarantulas and hairy caterpillars. She played with poisonous frogs and sought out the dangerous but mind-altering snakeroot. If this wasn't enough to worry us, then there were the careless drivers, aggressive stray dogs, drunks wielding machetes and finally, we could now add attempted kidnapping to the list! I poured myself another large 'medicinal' potion.

The following evening, it was us that needed a guard dog, though. We still slept with a door open and I awoke with a start, to a noisy kerfuffle inside the room during the dead of night. We had a visitor, Butch, an adept scrounger and scoundrel of a dog we knew well. He was happily raiding our food table and clumsily made off with a bag of dried pasta and a packet of biscuits! He's a large muscly dog, strong and stubborn, but one we also had a soft spot for and occasionally gave a good meal to. Stealing from our room crossed a line, though. Not a line he, or Mocha apparently, recognised, of course, as he returned late the following night to try his luck again. This time, he succeeded in waking the three of us up and without so much as a growl from Mocha, relieved the table of a box of nachos. Wearing just a pair of boxer shorts, I chased him theatrically out of the room, shouting so loudly that Matteo appeared to see what the commotion was.

"More whores, Mark?" he enquired, as Butch flew triumphantly and proudly past him!

Mocha clearly declined to get involved in guard dog duties. Butch was neither black nor now poor (or on a motorbike!) and I suspected she secretly fancied him. She preferred to act out the 'gentle princess' role rather than be bothered by these late-night dramas. Instead, we elected to go shopping, for a large plastic storage box with a securely fitting lid!

Saturdays generally didn't need a reason for celebrations in Paradiso, but as it was now the 4th of July and labelled by the UK press as 'Super Saturday', how could we refuse? After fifteen long weeks, the nation's pubs were finally being allowed to reopen and of course it was our American friends' Independence Day. We could even add to that our first month's anniversary of being 'almost married'. Whatever, the BBQ was lit, the rum flowed freely and the following morning's hangovers were joyfully manufactured. The Spanish lessons were moved to Mondays!

On the Sunday, we took a tearful and sobering call from Giulia. With no ambulances available, she had taken a taxi to A&E, with pains so strong she thought she was going to pass out and had suspected appendicitis. After scans, she was informed she had a sizable kidney stone and sent home with painkillers. Only the previous month she had dealt with our poor cat dying in her arms and again we felt the weight and downside of being so far away from home. It's inevitable, of course; the buzz of an amazing adventure has to be tempered against the times you wish you could be in two places at once. We had missed Selly's mum's ninetieth birthday and in a couple of days it would be my mum's eightieth.

Feeling a little sad and frustrated, I sat dwelling it all over. There just isn't a perfect time for lengthier adventures. You can try to pick a window, plan and replan, but you never know what's around the corner. Reasons pop up why 'this isn't the best year', but they'll pop up every year and ultimately you just have to go as soon as you can make it happen. If you dilly-dally over it for too long, it really will become that long-lost dream.

Yet another month had slipped by and it was time for the Managua run again. Bureaucratic hassles aside, we didn't mind these trips too much anymore. Nobody had pulled a gun on us, stolen our phones or shopping! It was an opportunity to hit the malls, have a decent ice cream, and Selly could stock up at the art supplier's. We were leaving early, in the cooler air, and Mocha followed the bike out to where we paused, to pat her and assure her we would be coming back. A full seven hours later, we found her lying down, virtually on the spot where we had said our goodbyes. She sprang to her feet and the second our helmets were removed, we were rewarded with enthusiastic licks. The gate security man told us she had kept him company throughout the day, only leaving to get the odd drink of water, but otherwise she'd waited patiently for our return.

Our days were melting into weeks that too quickly ticked off the months. Selly had complemented the Spanish lessons by additionally taking German lessons from Irma. She continued to sketch, draw and paint as I dog-walked, swam and paddled. How naive we were, back in the Corn Islands, thinking a month or two and we'd be back on our way again! The borders remained steadfastly closed and the airport had just sporadic flights to Mexico City, or occasionally Miami. None of these airlines could take Mocha, though, and we felt as trapped now as the day the borders first closed.

We hung out mostly with Blu, who was still flirting with her potential girlfriend. It had been an on-off rollercoaster for some weeks, not helped by the lovely Roxana having to both live and work over in Managua. She was great fun and could definitely be a positive influence on the new Blu, if only one of them would ask the other out! Foxy-Roxy was energetic, liked to party, dance and keep fit. Exactly what Blu needed to continue her own healthier lifestyle. We tried to stay out of any matchmaking, but not too hard, mind! It all came to a head one Saturday morning, after Roxana had made an unannounced visit to surprise Blu in Paradiso. It had been a lengthy journey for her and all to no avail; she had missed Blu by just ten minutes.

We had to let her know Blu had left on a bus for the weekend. She was heading to the coast, for a change of scenery and to clear her head. It became the turning point they both needed and after this missed opportunity they soon became inseparable. We couldn't be happier for the pair of them and finally, Blu didn't have to play gooseberry to us pair of lovebirds all the time. The weekends again became livelier, as the four of us frequently got together. The flipside was that thoughts of ever making it to Alaska drifted further from our grasp.

We often sat and debated our options, mulling over the 'what ifs' and trying to guess the future. If we persevered to try continuing the trip, we would now need a 'Mocha' sidecar, trailer, or a change of vehicle! Even if the Honduran border opened up sometime soon, other borders further north were solidly closed, and for good reason. The USA had now recorded over four million infected and nearly 150,000 dead. For several months, non-essential travel through Canada, to reach Alaska, had been banned. Even if we could cross the borders and reach Canada, transit corridors were in place, restricting us to certain roads and rightly denying us any diversions for sightseeing. It began to cement in our minds that the dream of pressing on, for the sake of completing the trip, was the wrong approach, and even selfish.

There were no signs that the pandemic had passed its peak in Mexico, or the USA, but every sign it was a worsening situation. It was the middle of July and although the UK and Italy were presenting a more positive picture, of emerging from the 'first wave', here it felt very different. Living in a void of reliable information, Nicaragua seemed to be in its own bubble; not one we were prepared to trust but evidently not too dire either. Many of the remaining countries on our route had varying restrictions, or places of interest to us were simply closed. Overall, our feeling was that it just wasn't the right time to be thinking of pressing on. We vowed to just live in the moment, enjoy Nicaragua and review our options again in a few months. Who knew? Maybe a vaccine would come along, or the infections would taper right off.

We don't know if Butch had tried poaching from our new food container. If he had, he'd most likely slunk off disappointed. However, that night, we were both suddenly roused by something much worse: the foul stench of a skunk. So strong and putrid that I was convinced it must be inside our room. I dived out of the bed to check and stuck my head out around the curtain. There it was. I could see it clearly in the moonlight, scampering away across the grass. It might as well have been inside; it had scent-marked our doorframe and with the doors wide open, it just became unbearable and unbreathable.

Even Mocha couldn't bring herself to stay in, or near, the room and in the morning Selly and I jumped on the bike for a day's escape. We tried all the recommended tricks, washing the area down with vinegar and tomato juice, but it persisted for days. Workhands fruitlessly inspected the roof cavities for signs of any nesting. Looking back, I think this was a turning point for us. As much as we loved the setting, our wonderful hosts and the wildlife, we had had four months of living out of a fairly small room. This was shared with Mocha, bike gear, spiders, ants and all sorts of other insects, big and small. We needed some kind of a break, or a change of scenery, or at the very least, another long-overdue reason to throw a party!

Conveniently, Roxana was down to see Blu for the weekend, along with Silver, another one of the original Paradiso 'Lockdown Crew'. Also of convenience, everybody seemed to both want and need a drinking weekend. Matteo, Iulia, Irma and Ramon (our super patient Spanish teacher) joined the five of us to once more nostalgically fill the 'survivors' table'. The rum flowed endlessly for two days and two nights of reminiscing, fun and games. Silver had moved to the coast some six weeks previously, but it was great to have her back amongst us again, even if it was just for a couple of nights. She had one of the loudest, most infectious laughs and joyfully contested Matteo for the position of life and soul of the party. I couldn't drink a drop of alcohol for the next three weeks after that weekend; it was that needed and that epic!

Something was wrong with Mocha; she was occasionally limping and having to hop to get up the flights of stairs. Once, on the beach a few months before, she had dropped to the sand yelping in pain, holding a hind leg up in the air. As it had quickly passed and she'd been sprinting around at the time, I'd put it down to a simple bout of cramp. But now, seeing her struggling to walk, we called a taxi and took her to the vet's. It would kill two birds with one stone, so to speak, as a month had now passed since the last rabies jab and she could have some blood drawn off, to courier to the States. A physical exam revealed nothing out of the ordinary, but after taking the titer test sample, he advised we took her for an X-ray, to check for rheumatoid arthritis joint damage.

An appointment was secured that afternoon and we hopped into another taxi to take the three of us to the capital. With the X-ray in our hands, Selly had to carry the still heavily sedated Mocha out to the waiting car. The poor dog was out of it, tongue hanging out and eyes vacantly staring, leaving us feeling guilty and sorry for putting her through this. Once back at the room, I left Selly looking after the dopey dog and jumped on the bike, to get the X-ray over to the vet's.

With the plate hung up on the backlit screen, he scrutinised bones and measured critical joint angles. There was nothing at all amiss, no sign of trauma and no rheumatoid arthritis. Thankfully, all was fine and dandy. Mocha had most likely just pulled a muscle on one of her over-zealous foraging trips. I jumped back on the bike with a sense of relief, and a prescription for a seven-day course of anti-inflammatories.

Month number five in the country was upon us and I warmed up the bike for another visa run. As we slid on helmets and straddled the bike, Mocha deftly scaled a low wall and tried to step across, onto the pannier and Selly's lap. She was making it quite clear she wanted to come along for the ride and I had to lift her gently down, whilst assuring her we would be returning later. Travelling into the city, I couldn't stop pondering how we might be able to travel around safely with her. We had seen her climbing trees and the high thatched roof of the bar, and to the delight of other guests, she happily came out kayaking and paddleboarding with me, but now she wanted to join us on a motorbike! Her adventurousness amazed us and now it seemed it was our turn to step up. We may be complete novices at this, but we had to find a way for her to join us.

We wanted to see how she'd react to being away 'full time' with us and came up with a compromise. We would hire a car for a week, take Mocha along and go off exploring the country. It would give us all a change of scenery, let us see some more of the sights, but most of all, we could show Mocha the ocean! A holiday within a holiday, I guess, and with excitement we loaded up the car and the ever-curious dog. For once, she would be enjoying a car journey that didn't end at the vet's!

We drove north for three hours, to the usually vibrant Pacific beach resort of Las Peñitas. To our knowledge, Mocha had never seen the sea before and we couldn't wait to let her run wild on a huge beach. Bags dropped in the room, we eagerly walked her down, removing the lead as our feet touched the sand. There literally wasn't another soul to be seen, but it didn't stop Mocha crazily running up and down, exploring anything and everything. Every piece of driftwood got inspected, birds were scared off and crabs were chased down their sandy holes; she was loving it. These were large surf waves, though, rolling in and crashing noisily along the shoreline. Mocha became mesmerised and tentatively trotted out to follow the receding waters, only to be caught out and drenched by the next advancing wave. This wasn't the gentle laguna she was used to. She was a little spooked by the speed of the waves, and the fact this water was disappointingly salty and undrinkable!

The fun lasted a full hour, before a storm rolled in, parked up and had us running for home. We endured the longest overhead thunder and lightning show either of us had ever experienced. A full forty-eight hours of nonstop vertical heavy downpours. We couldn't go anywhere, as all the town's roads quickly became rivers. Day had turned to night and we were just thankful that we were here with four wheels, instead of the usual two. Even the car looked as though it was parked out in a pond, as the water rose up to the sills. The noise of constant thunder and rain, on a corrugated tin roof, had us packing up and escaping after only the second day.

Backtracking south, past Granada and down towards the closed border with Costa Rica, found us at the small lakeside port of San Jorge. Halfway through the drive, the rains had finally given way to light broken clouds and as the evening ferry took us over to the twin volcanic island of Ometepe, we found our blue skies at last.

The island sits out in the vast Lake Nicaragua and is dominated by the highly active 1,610-metre Concepción volcano. Just a couple of miles away, its slightly shorter neighbour, Maderas volcano, reaches up to an equally impressive 1,394 metres. Despite both having erupted within the last decade, it truly is a beautiful and recommended destination, if a daunting sight! Almost 30,000 people have made Ometepe Island their permanent home. We would brave the risks for just three nights!

Arriving at our accommodation, in the pitch-dark, having crawled along tiny roads scattered with free-roaming horses, cattle, pigs and dogs, we found the gates closed and padlocked. We had booked online, received the confirmation email, but were now confronted by a startled and confused-looking security guard. He explained the grandish-looking hostel had been shut for many weeks and he couldn't understand how we had managed to even make a booking!

There was no point contesting the issue at this hour. We thanked him anyway, put it behind us and rejoined the narrow coast road, in search of life and a bed for the night.

"We just passed a nice-looking place set back on the right, seemed to have some lights on," Selly announced as we entered the tiny town of Moyogalpa.

I spun around, parked up and with fingers crossed went to find a reception, getting intercepted before reaching it. Quickly summarising our homelessness, we were given a warm and friendly welcome.

"We're actually closed, there just aren't enough tourists, but don't worry, we can soon have a room ready for the three of you. Would you like dinner and a drink out by the pool?" asked the lovely host!

Compared to ours back at the laguna, the room was huge, even had air-con, and after so many months with just a fan, it felt an exquisite luxury. Three days of beaches, sightseeing, swimming and trekking followed, but alas, it all flew by in a whirlwind. On the final morning, whilst breakfasting by the pool, I opened an email from Granada. Mocha's rabies titer results had come back from the USA. She had passed with flying colours and one more hurdle in her 'escape' had been crossed.

It was an uplifting start to the day; we didn't really want to leave the exotic Ometepe, but the road trip wasn't quite over yet. Silver had been living in a rented apartment on the nearby Pacific Coast, and had invited us to stay the night. We headed over, with Mocha taking up her usual pose of front paws on the centre console and her head between ours, giving her clear views of the road ahead. She had mastered the movements of the car, even bracing for speed bumps, and she could happily keep her balance hour after hour. Nothing escaped her; dogs and pigs usually received a token mini-bark, Nicaraguans brandishing machetes were regularly growled at, and we received the odd random lick on the cheek.

We headed first for the beach, letting Mocha have a good run and leg stretch. Pelicans skimmed the barrelling waves, or adorned the fishing boats bobbing out in the bay. San Juan del Sur was Nicaragua's Benidorm. Currently, only the permanent expats and a few dozen stranded tourists remained, but it was still evident that in normal times, this was a surfers' party town. It had a laid-back arty-hippy vibe, bars around every corner and a picturesque, lengthy restaurant-lined beach. It was an easy place to like, with its diverse cultures providing a mix of French bakeries, patisseries, ice cream parlours, pizzerias and much, much more. No wonder Silver had made this town her new home.

Her apartment was as modern as anybody could want and in the current climate, great value for money. As the drinks flowed, I could tell Selly was thinking the same as me: we could use a slice of this! Silver added her penny's worth, reiterating the town was pretty empty and it was a renter's market. Our trip home was dominated by conversations weighing up the pros and cons of moving. These thoughts evoked both excitement and some sadness. We still loved Paradiso but had to admit we were outgrowing our room, and with the lockdown crew dispersed around Nicaragua and the wider world, the resort somehow felt different, 'emptier' now. We vowed to do some research and line up some viewings for the following month.

We lasted a week! Our Paradiso room seemed to have shrunk whilst we had been away. Everywhere we had stayed had outsized it, and our minds were set on finding a place on the coast. Discussing our thoughts with Blu, she imparted news of her own.

"Roxana and I want to get a place together, we want to live together," she excitedly told us.

This was big news from Blu, a turning point in her life. The now month-long relationship was her longest yet. In just a few weeks she had found love, cut back the drinking, kept up the exercising and was looking great. She wasn't recognisable as the '8am beer-drinking Aussie' we first met five months ago. This was the new and happier Blu, getting all grown up on us!

With viewings arranged, we jumped on the bike for a stunning ride back to the coast. Mocha had again tried to jump across from the low wall and once more left us feeling guilty as we pulled away. Sometime soon, Mocha, sometime soon. The wet season had brought an explosion of greens, with backdrops of volcano after volcano dotting the horizons. This was no longer the parched brown Nicaragua we had first encountered months before. Cattle and horses grazed out on the pastures and you could be forgiven for thinking you were back in a European spring. There were always plenty of huge vultures around, though, to bring us back to reality. Flocks would suddenly fly up as we passed the scenes of ill-fated road-kills and with a 2-metre wingspan, it was a tad more intimidating than dodging the odd pigeon or pheasant back home. The daytimes were mostly dry and fortunately for us, the waterproofs rarely had to venture out of the otherwise empty 'shopping' panniers. Even with the nightly storms, the temperatures remained in the low thirties, a biker's dream.

Despite several apartments to see, it was the very first that bowled us over. Housed inside a securely gated resort and set in manicured grounds, it had an enticing pool and gym luring us in. For the bike, there would be an underground parking bay and for Mocha, a lengthy fence wrapped around the grounds, allowing her to run free. It was ultra-modern, totally desirable and now that we knew the rent, totally over budget! We plodded on to several other locations, meeting hopeful landlords and helpful letting agents. There really wasn't anything wrong with any of the subsequent apartments; they just weren't the first one. All of them had internet, air-con and hot water, but only the first had a picture-postcard balcony view, overlooking the entire bay. Oh, and that infinity pool. I was already tasting those sunset cocktails and suspected Selly was too.

We had plenty to mull over on the ride back, both full of our own thoughts but feeling a tad deflated that the trip hadn't been conclusive. Strangely, Mocha wasn't outside to greet us when we got back that evening. We were taking it for granted she would be there and rode into the gravel car park a little concerned. It was unnecessary; there she was, sleeping peacefully outside our room, snuggly up against the closed doors.

"I have an idea. Let's remove one of the pannier lids in the morning, put something in the bottom and see if she will sit inside. Maybe take her out for a test ride?" I suggested.

And so, the following morning, Selly lined the lidless pannier with one of our towels and helped Mocha to sit in it. She didn't budge, seemed to understand what was happening and let us repeat the exercise with the pannier fitted back onto the bike's side. For her size, it was roomy enough and as she calmly waited, we warmed up the bike and set off for our first outing together. It certainly went better than her first few car-sick journeys, except she kept wanting to climb up onto Selly's lap! Not even a dog with his head stretched out of a car window could be happier. Her nose worked the scents and her eyes sought out everything of interest. She seemed proud to be taken along and never missed an opportunity to announce her presence to the foraging strays and lazy street dogs. This inaugural trip couldn't have gone much better.

The next day, we improvised a short restraining chain, hoping it could just be a temporary training aid, and headed out again. With a couple of breaks, we went all the way to Managua and rewarded her with a visit to our favourite ice cream parlour. She couldn't be happier and I wondered what we had let ourselves in for. She would be expecting to go everywhere from now on!

With a vanilla cone dripping down my front, I told Selly of a plan I'd been thinking about on the ride in. Not having anything to lose, I wanted to make a low-ball offer on the 'posh' apartment, test out this 'renter's market' theory!

"What should we offer?" queried Selly.

"What we can afford, they can only say no," I reasoned.

The price we could afford was lower than what I felt the apartment was worth, which of course was much lower than what they were hoping for, but it was also sitting empty. We sent the offer in and saw that the message had been read almost instantly. No reply was forthcoming, not that day, or the next. Maybe I had offended them.

With Mocha aboard, I was keeping the speed down to a modest 40 mph. She seemed to love the wind on her face, but any quicker and she was having to squint. It was fine for now, but if we needed to go any distance, we would have to rig up some eye and ear protection for her. Everywhere we went, she was attracting attention. Cars would slow alongside us, papping horns, and children would point and wave from the pavements. I could clearly see her head in my mirror and I swear she was grinning away! Yes, she was comfortably lapping it all up, only flinching as ancient lorries gunned tired engines, or taxi-minibuses flew by a little too close to us.

To everybody's delight, we now had a bike-chasing biker dog. Surely even she could see the irony in that and stop embarrassing us on the walks! That evening, we had a clear sky and to round off a great day, Mocha came out with me for some midnight full-moon paddleboarding. On a glassy-flat laguna, I paddled us far out, chasing the moon's dazzling reflection and wondering if she had any fears or limits. It took just a few days to find the first one.

September's visa run was required by the end of that week and we pre-booked the car for this trip. Whilst having the ice creams a few days before, we had spied a grooming parlour, something Mocha was desperately in need of. She would be coming with us again, to get a good scrub, groom and trim of her unsightly dreadlocks. The hair around her backside had become so long she couldn't really pee without getting some of it wet, and the smelly dreads needed to go! As we tried to drop her off, she made it quite clear this wasn't her cup of tea. She didn't like the look or smell of the place and definitely didn't take to the kind gentleman whose job it was to groom her. To say she really didn't look impressed with us as we headed out of the door would be a solid understatement. Sorry, dog, but this is all part of the transition from stray to pet!

Yet again, we were caught out by more process changes and additionally, we both received a lengthy grilling from separate immigration officers. On top of the usual questions, we were asked how we could afford to stay in the country, where our income was from, could we prove it and a little ridiculously, why we were even still in the country. Profiteering from the closed borders, the monthly visa renewal fee had more than doubled since last month. We left with the worrying impression we were no longer welcome in the country and that visa renewals shouldn't be taken for granted any longer.

It was all a bit of a kick in the teeth, but overshadowing their negativity, we had some good news. Some great news really. Out of the blue, we finally received a reply to our rental offer, and it had been accepted! Having been 'left hanging' for a few days, I'd taken the silence for a resolute 'no'. I was wrong, the only condition was that we stayed at least two months and paid up front in cash. Wow, that was awesome news; we were going to be moving then. The excitement was further added to by collecting the beautifully scented and freshly groomed Mocha. She seemed overjoyed to see us, or overjoyed to realise she hadn't been abandoned in a nauseatingly sweet poodle parlour!

Over welcome drinks, we mulled over the best date to move. Paradiso was paid up until the 26th of September, a total period of exactly six months. It felt apt, I could have my looming birthday amongst friends and we'd be giving Matteo and Iulia nearly three weeks' notice. We sat with them and over a meal announced our plans. They couldn't believe we had lasted this long and were genuinely happy for us. Blu said she would start house shopping and Mocha trotted off to carry out some scheming of her own. I guess she felt the need to clarify to us exactly what she really thought of posh 'pink 'n' fluffy' poodle parlours. Having taken herself off down the shoreline, she had come across some rotting fish and had a good old roll-around. To our disbelief and everybody else's delight, she proudly returned looking and smelling disgusting!

"Well, that was a waste of twenty-five bucks. At least she doesn't smell of skunk. We couldn't use the bar for three nights after Canela's fight," stated Blu, trying not too hard to cheer us up!

Dismayed at Mocha's show of gratitude, I turned the conversation to my birthday, which fell on the coming Saturday.

"Told you months ago you would still be here for your birthday, Mark, and for Christmas," prophesised Matteo, with a grin.

Since arriving in the country, we had so far avoided Granada's very lively pub street, Calle La Calzada. In fact, we hadn't allowed ourselves a pub-night out since meeting up with my friend Bob in Panama City over six months previously. Of course, there would be pre-going out celebrations at Paradiso, Matteo wouldn't have it any other way, but we fancied a proper night out.

I woke to a surprise card that Selly had hidden since leaving the UK, plus a selection of new clothes, to replace those now falling off my back. Iulia very kindly presented me with a voucher for an hour's massage in Paradiso's recently re-opened spa, and Matteo kicked the afternoon off with cocktails for both of us and an open beer-bar.

His mission was to not only give us a fantastic day but have us half drunk before we hit the town! It was indeed a tipsy pair that met up with Blu, Roxy and some of their friends. The street was inside out, the bars empty and the pedestrian boulevard slammed. It was eye-opening, no hint that a pandemic was raging across the world. Escaping the cacophony of competing Latin street music, we retreated into the void of a colourful but vacant pub. Shots and beers flowed, we could hear ourselves talk, we felt safer. This we repeated a few more times, until the clock swung past midnight and my birthday was officially behind me. I might have felt younger than my fifty-five years, but we easily resisted the peer pressure to go clubbing with the youngsters. As if it was possible, it was getting even busier outside, a 'coronavirus factory', and Selly and I quit whilst we were ahead, whilst we were still walking!

Since Timo's departure, Roberto and Lucélia had visited us a few times at Paradiso but now insisted we stay at their house for a weekend. He enjoyed a relaxed and enviable life. Consular staff ran the embassy's day-to-day stuff and he was rarely called upon. After our move to the coast, we would practically be neighbours, living just half an hour apart. They took us, the only gringos present, to a 'finca' farm, a farm with a difference and the type of place we could never have found by ourselves. Amongst roaming horses, cows and pigs, there existed a makeshift restaurant and bar, complemented by an overly loud local band enticing dancers onto the bouncing wooden floor.

The farm owners had rescued an orphan spider monkey and a young leopard-mottled ocelot. Selly was instantly in love and I had visions of both panniers filling with animals! The beautiful cat was now quite used to being around people but still as wild as could be and wanted to play-fight continuously, with sharp claws and sharper teeth! Irma had come along for a daytrip and swept up by the cat's beauty, allowed it to tattoo her arms and hands with dozens of scratches.

"This is the best day of my life. I'm so in love, it's super super exciting," she squealed, as the cat tried to remove her eyes once more!

Thank goodness we'd left Mocha back at Rob's; she wouldn't have survived this little leopard. With our own fingers and arms still in one piece, we retreated to the bar, where a dozen of us filled a rickety table. We merrily drank, sang, danced and ate away the afternoon, receiving a bill of a hundred dollars, for all twelve of us!

Our six months in Paradiso were up, the day of departure was upon us and it required a hire car to load all our burgeoning belongings, well, ours and Mocha's! The previous day, Iulia had the kitchen produce a full English buffet breakfast as a late brunch, and Matteo and myself started the day with potent 'pirates' cocktails' that I'd dreamt up the night before (rum, vodka and tequila, topped up with fruity sangria). A dozen of us piled into the hefty 'stomach-lining' brekky, before continuing the afternoon and evening's drinking and games.

Irma, still proudly sporting her leopard-scars, soon rounded on Matteo for having not yet proposed to Iulia. Despite them having two beautiful children and several businesses together, that just wasn't enough for the rum-powered German. To our amusement, she threatened a laughing Matteo with having his 'eggs' chopped off if he didn't marry Iulia by 2001. Despite being reasoned with, she just didn't see that it was already 2020, a year destined never to be forgotten. Not to be outdone, she instead refocused on having a shot-drinking contest and that evening, to her credit, outlasted every one of us. What a fitting last night!

Chapter Eighteen

Hitting the Coast

Of course, we knew we would all see each other again soon enough, but hugged and said our heartfelt goodbyes anyway. It had been a truly amazing six months and of all the places we could have found ourselves locked down in, I just couldn't imagine fate, or luck, landing us anywhere more special. The resort was perfectly named and Matteo and Iulia couldn't have looked after us any better. We were taking so many happy memories with us, and all down to their hard work, personalities and love for Paradiso. It would be a whole day before I saw them again, as I returned the car and rode the bike down to the coast! Of course, everybody turned out to say their farewells to Mocha also, who waited suspiciously by the hire car, determined not to be left behind after surveying the room being packed up and haphazardly thrown into it.

Once on the road, she took up her usual inquisitive pose between us, surveying the scenes ahead and offering quiet, meaningless growls for each dog we passed. With the luxury of having the car, we attempted a monthly shop, squeezing everything onto the back seat for an excited dog to sneakily unpack and sniff through. Once the unloading was out of the way, the kettle was put to use and the three of us relaxed into this new space. It was initially bewildering to be able to spread out; a storage room for all the bike gear, our own small laundry room, even a spare bedroom and bathroom for guests to come stay over. Selly wasted no time jumping into the ensuite, for her first truly hot shower in seven months. Sitting high up on a hillside, the balcony faced directly west, and centrally over the town's Pacific bay. Mocha wasted no time sprawling out on it, soaking up the heat and seemingly approving of the day's upheaval. That first mesmerising sunset confirmed the apartment was going to be worth every extra penny.

We soon began to get a stream of visitors, starting with Silver, who lived just a walk across town, followed by Roberto and Lucélia, and of course Blu and Roxana. In view of our balcony lay the communal infinity pool and clubhouse, as perfect a place as any to enjoy the sunsets. Despite keeping the fridge party-stocked, I'm convinced the pool was the main attraction for our visitors! Flocks of green parakeets would dive-bomb its surface, skimming between our heads and screeching crazily, only relenting as the sun slid beyond the horizon. As the sky glowed with pink and orange hues, the pool's mood lighting would come on and silent darting bats took the place of the squawking birds. They'd weave amongst our night-time swims, deftly plucking insects from the water's surface. Hardly a day passed without the pair of us plunging into the pool for the sunset show and an end-of-day swim.

Following an invite to a BBQ, we were able to meet and be introduced to a few more fellow stranded bikers. A French couple, Didier and Nelly, travelling southbound on an identical pair of BMW 1200GSs, were adamant they'd wait out the pandemic, however long it took. They just wanted to sell their bikes and swap to something much smaller and lighter for their South American leg. A solo-riding Russian girl had temporarily set herself up as a fitness instructor and was also prepared to sit things out. Months before, in South America, she'd been attacked and was currently rearing and training a young pet rooster to be her travelling alarm clock and bodyguard. Vasilisa took the bird everywhere, either tucked up asleep in her cleavage or perched guardingly upon her head!

I did admire these fellow bikers' resolves, but realistically, Selly and I just couldn't see the global situation improving, not within the next six to twelve months anyway. In fact, the thought had even crossed our minds to see if it was possible to send our bike home! With everything now within walking distance, the bike just wasn't being used much. It was all wishful thinking, mind. Nobody we'd met seemed to have any leads on shipping and the bike was no less stranded than the three of us were! Three months previously, we had vowed to live in the moment and just enjoy the country we found ourselves trapped in. Now, as we reviewed the situation once more, we had to accept the second half of our road trip, and reaching Alaska, just wasn't going to happen. Not this year and most likely not next year. Accepting this realisation stung; it's tough closing a lid on a decades-old dream.

2020 just wasn't the year to be frolicking through different countries with wild abandon. Adding to the woes, our insurance company was boxing us into a corner, refusing to extend the cover past twelve months. Scrutinising our policy booklet, I found a clause that covered being unintentionally stranded abroad and after several calls and emails managed to negotiate an extra two months of medical-only cover. It bought us a little more time, but nobody was offering any new policies, not whilst the government was still advising travellers to return home. We tried to get insurance locally but, as non-residents, were declined.

It was all understandable, Mexico had so far recorded over 80,000 victims and infections were rapidly on the rise. Deaths in the US were north of 200,000 and since George Floyd's death, back in May, the USA had seen growing protests in all fifty states. The White House had announced the president himself had tested positive, along with eight million citizens and with their elections looming, bringing more rounds of rallies and protests, America just wasn't that attractive to us or the insurance companies anymore!

Having said all that, it truly wasn't easy to let go. We would sorely miss catching up with Dauri in Mexico and meeting up with Chris and Caroline in the States. Coming to this decision was one thing; getting us all out of here was another matter entirely. The land borders were closed still and there were no flights operating out of Nicaragua that we could take Mocha on. When options did present themselves, our resolve would be to get us all safely back to the UK. Right now, though, we had a new location to explore and it soon became apparent we hadn't left Paradiso for the quiet life!

Our social circle quickly grew; adding to the bikers we had met, Selly was introduced to several Italians who'd made San Juan del Sur their home and life. We traded visits with Didier and Nelly, Roberto and Lucélia, Silver and visitors from Paradiso. Over the weekends, Blu and Roxana bagged first dibs on the spare room and we'd hit the street-food markets and live music nights. Mocha came everywhere with us and just loved having the lengthy beach to run on. She'd chase iguanas around the resort and to her delight, had even found another damn snakeroot plant to chew on! We thought we'd seen the last of those.

She was also making her own acquaintances. One too many, it turned out, as the bay had a potentially nasty surprise waiting for us. Heavy rains combined with high tides often resulted in the beach being dissected by the Escondido River. With no bridge, you could either wade or, when deeper, take a small wooden ferry boat across. Compared to the sea's waves, Mocha preferred this shallow river for frolicking around in. However, a riverbank sign had recently gone up, warning of the presence of crocodiles. As we were practically in a town centre, I'd pretty much taken the sign with a pinch of salt and was foolishly, if happily, paddling with Mocha in the cool water.

"Mark, get out, there's a crocodile heading for you," shouted an alarmed Selly.

Sure enough, with just eyes and nostrils protruding, a sizable croc was stealthily gliding diagonally across the current and straight towards the pair of us. As it was amongst the debris, slowly drifting downriver, neither Mocha nor I had noticed its proximity and I hastily caught hold of her and retreated out of harm's way. Chatting with the boatman, we learned five crocs had been swept downriver and now resided close to the mouth. Several dogs had already disappeared.

Word on the grapevine was that the turtles had arrived in great numbers, to nest on a beach half an hour south of us. Well, that sounded like a much less riskier venture, and so we grabbed Mocha and made our way down to the Playa La Flor reserve. Hiring a guide, we learned the rangers had counted over 20,000 Olive Ridley turtles emerging from the surf, in just a seventy-two-hour period. Our jungle drums had been slow; we saw just five! Making up the numbers, though, were hundreds of black vultures, and they weren't shy. As we watched the turtles laying their eggs, the vultures gathered just a metre or so away, awaiting their chance to poach the fresh nests. It was an enthralling spectacle, but now, as dusk fell, the guide led us off on a bird-spotting tour of the mangroves and swamps. Mocha found a playful stray to run along with and they soon made their way over to one of the ponds.

"Better get the dogs back, full of crocodiles and snakes," warned our guide.

Slipping Mocha back on the lead, I was beginning to think dogs should be the endangered species here!

A heavy weekend loomed. Blu's birthday fell on the coming Saturday and coincidentally, she shared it with another friend, who lived here in town. Individually, they were both characters. Together, they were plain crazy. It was going to be as much a laguna reunion as a birthday bash. Matteo and Ramon, our old Spanish teacher, would be travelling down from Paradiso, with Blu and Roxana coming down from Granada. It was a triple celebration really; the pair of them had found a house and finally moved in together. Since leaving Paradiso, our intentions had been to try to lead a healthier life, but it just wasn't panning out that way, I mused, as we brimmed the fridge once more!

After the inevitably high-spirited Friday night 'apartment party', Selly and I opted to take Mocha out with us all for the birthday night. It was unashamedly a cop-out, knowing that if things got out of hand, or just way too busy for our liking, we could make our excuses and leave early. Not that Mocha would want it any other way; she still deciphered being left alone as some kind of punishment. I guess it served us right that our plan backfired. Mocha's appetite for staying out happily surpassed ours. It's a wonderfully dog-friendly town and she lapped up the welcomes everywhere we went, settling at our feet to curiously watch over the drunken antics. Eventually, we had had to plead with the pooch to let us go home, at 2am, leaving the rest to enjoy a private 'lock-in'.

Barely recovered from the weekend, we had a little celebration of our own to mark. On the Tuesday evening, we cracked a bottle of red, to toast our full year away. Despite having met numerous 'overlanders', out enjoying the open roads for several years, this still felt quite an achievement and a milestone for us to raise a glass to. Skipping back through our photos and videos, we marvelled at the many highs and winced at some of the lows, all those ingredients of a memorable adventure. Despite our previous motorbike trips together, we had left the UK feeling like a pair of novices to this kind of longer-distance endurance. My dirt and gravel-riding experiences had been limited to just the odd few days, and we'd certainly struggled at times, but we hadn't fallen (whilst riding!), hadn't lost or broken anything, yet.

We'd made the classic mistake of packing too much, overthinking it and trying to cover-off every eventuality. Looking back, though, there were just a handful of times we'd disagreed on anything, usually something trivial, and very rarely had we needed to retreat into our 'own space'. For sure, we knew each other's strengths and weaknesses, and rather than turning them into something to gripe about, we'd simply chosen to look out for each other. I once asked Selly why she hardly ever queried my decisions (navigating aside!) and her reply was uplifting: "Because I know you must have good reason, and I trust you." I really do love my life, and definitely my life with Selly. The whole journey had been incredibly rewarding. Not only had we deepened what was already an inseparable relationship, but we'd managed to grow our family. As we gazed across at Mocha, safely and peacefully sleeping, we knew the pandemic had allowed our paths to cross and our bonds to cement. However difficult it became, or however long it took us to get out of the country, she would be coming with us.

We had pre-planned to combine November's visa run with a stopover at Paradiso, a chance to catch up properly over drinks with both Matteo and Iulia. This would be followed by a night staying at Blu and Roxana's new place in Granada. We had been looking forward to this trip away, but subsequently learnt it's best not to make too many plans. Ours were now being disrupted by a miniscule bacterium, a skunk and a hurricane, all in that order. We were overdue the three-monthly stool check, for the dreaded Nicaraguan worms, and I'd picked us up some sample containers from a local laboratory. On returning the samples, I was asked if I also wanted tests for the helicobacter pylori stomach bacteria. I hadn't a clue what this was, but it seemed prudent for a few extra dollars. Within the hour, we had the results confirm both of us were again worm-free, but both had become infected with this troublesome bacteria.

An internet search revealed it was easily picked up in developing countries, usually from infected water, or salads simply not being washed properly. A doctor's appointment followed and we walked away better informed and carrying a large bag of medications. These were tough cookies to eradicate; we had been prescribed a ten-day course of three different antibiotics each, an antacid to be taken twice daily and lastly, a course of probiotics. For a fortnight, there wasn't going to be any alcohol allowed, not even any coffee. I wasn't sure which I was going to miss most; it was definitely going to be a bit of a bore! For all we knew, this could have lain undetected from our years of travelling, but if left untreated can lead to stomach ulcers, and even cancer. We wouldn't avoid the treatment, but we could delay starting it, until after our couple of days away in Paradiso and Granada!

We messaged Matteo to confirm we were coming over and got a strange response: *We had to close the resort, but don't worry, there's always a room for you two, come on over.* This visit was still nearly a week away and he gave no details as to why they'd closed. Surely it had nothing to do with the hurricane we were hearing about, way out in the Caribbean? Two days later, Hurricane Eta strengthened to category four, headed straight for Nicaragua and pummelled the north-east coast. Fortunately for us, we were the best part of 300 miles away, on the south-west coast, but as the gales strengthened and the rain poured down, sandbags came out to defend against our rapidly flooding town.

The roads soon turned to rivers and we could only imagine the awful devastation being wreaked on the other side of the country. The rains were horizontal, the apartment sprung leaks and as the noise of the hurricane increased, Mocha refused to venture outside. As night fell, the town turned inky black from the inevitable power cut. Thank goodness for the bike's underground parking bay and the resort's generators! From our vantage point, we could see the angry ocean had claimed the entire beach, with seawater rising up against the restaurant fronts. Palm trees were doubled over and flailing in the gales; less fortunate trees were snapped like twigs and blown down across roads. There was no let-up for four days and neither of us could find sleep over the howling noise outside. Whenever we sensed a lull, usually around 2 to 3am, we'd take Mocha for a short walk, but staying close to the apartment.

It was an unnerving experience and even though we planned to hire a car, we juggled whether we should risk making the trip to the passport office and back to Paradiso. Not going would just result in fines and extra red tape, for not renewing our visas and the bike's paperwork on time. A small price to pay if it meant staying safe. Days later, however, on the morning we were due to set off, we woke to find the storm had subsided to persistent rain and the winds had backed right off. Selly fired up the Windy app and we could see Hurricane Eta had tracked north, passing into Honduras. Managua's weather and wind strength were showing as identical to ours. We would hire a car and if conditions worsened, we could always turn back.

There were signs of damage everywhere, plenty of trees down and widespread flooding, but we made the city and after too many hours of bureaucracy managed to renew the passport visas. It was still getting tougher, though, more and more questions, more and more faffing. For some unknown reason, they took our passports away and made us wait until closing time. It was incredibly frustrating to see everyone else coming and going and we just sat there, not knowing if their previous threats not to extend our visas anymore were about to become reality. We'd been told that we should be booking onto one of the few flights leaving the country. Explaining we had both a dog and a motorcycle didn't seem to make one jot of difference. The stamped passports weren't returned to us until the staff were walking out the door and the lights were getting turned off! They'd left us no time to sort the bike's paperwork; we would have to return and run that gauntlet tomorrow.

As we drove down into the crater once more, a skunk passed in front of the headlights, skittering across the road with tail held high. Turns out this was a prophetic sighting. Exiting the car, Mocha seemed confused as to why we were back at Paradiso and after gazing at each of us for some kind of explanation, trotted over to the doors of our old room. I half expected her to disappear off to find Blacky and Canela, but instead, she glued herself to us.

The resort was indeed without guests, bar or kitchen staff. The BBQ was ablaze, though, and as the rums were poured, Matteo explained that Gabriel, one of the bar staff, had cornered and killed a skunk behind the bar a week before. The smell had been so awful that the bar and restaurant area were completely unusable, and they had had to take the decision to temporarily close whilst they tried to deal with it. Poor Gabriel had been trying to capture the skunk for weeks and finally triumphant, he now reeked so badly that his wife wouldn't even let him back in the house!

Within a few days, the hurricane had arrived and the weather deteriorated so much that they had been forced to remain closed. Despite all the downpours, the smell was still stomach-churning and every time the wind changed direction, we all picked up drinks and comically moved to a different area. Gabriel's escapades had given us a memorable if queasy night! Things weren't so dandy back in the UK either; today was Thursday the 5th of November and England had just started its second national lockdown.

Almost having to beg, we managed to get another extension on the bike and legged it back to Blu and Roxana's place. Granada was another washout, literally. They tried showing us around their new neighbourhood, but most of the town had shut down and braced for the hurricane. Before departing the city, we called in on Mocha's vet, asking him to please start preparing Mocha's certificates and exit paperwork. After a fair bit of research, we began to understand how difficult it was going to be to get us all home. Only one airline would allow a dog of Mocha's weight to board with us, and the nearest airport they flew out of was San José, Costa Rica. Teasingly, it was less than a two-hour journey from us, but the border remained stubbornly closed. Shipping enquiries, regarding the bike, met with brick walls. Cargo flights were extremely limited, and the major companies couldn't even supply us with a quote. If we really wanted to get home, then we'd have to cast our net much wider.

Starting upon the mountain of antibiotics didn't exactly add to our cheer. One of them, Metronidazol, tasted disgustingly bitter, and no amount of brushing or mouthwash seemed to dispel it. We lost energy, both succumbing to 'Delhi belly' as the combined pills stripped away at our stomach linings and lowered our immunities. It was going to be a long ten days, not helped by the constant rain left in the wake of Eta's slow progress north. Barely had it departed before the news was warning of a second tropical storm forming out in the Caribbean. Within twenty-four hours, Iota had been reclassed as a hurricane and was again heading to Nicaragua. Two hurricanes in two weeks, and both making landfall on this relatively small country. It was unbelievable. Iota strengthened to category five and crushed the two days of sunshine we had tried to enjoy in between the storms.

In preparation, we made a sizable food shop and in the comfort of the apartment, hunkered down for its arrival. The power station cutting out and the generators firing up again forewarned us of the fast-approaching winds and rains. It was all pretty much a case of *déjà vu*, with the town flooding once again and the apartment springing its leaks. In the buffeting gales, our glass-shrouded balcony started coming apart and threatening to send thick glass panels crashing to the ground below. Mocha begrudgingly let workmen in to try and fix it, but I suspected they were happier outside in the rain than being growled at inside!

Along with the weather, the meds continued to pull us down, both physically and even emotionally. The fluctuating air pressure seemed to be giving us constant headaches and I had a growing complication to manage, one that couldn't be ignored. Years before, I'd suffered a deep vein thrombosis and a sizeable blood clot had lodged in one of my lungs. The Warfarin anticoagulant, that I still took daily, would be interacting with the antibiotics we were now taking, and needed to be closely monitored.

Every couple of days, I ventured out into the buffeting weather to a nearby laboratory and had an INR blood test carried out. The results kept coming back low; peculiar, as they should actually be getting pushed up higher by the antibiotics. Trying to get back 'in range', I'd been increasing the dosage between tests, up until a third identically low result set alarm bells ringing. This was near impossible; too implausible to have three identical results and they definitely shouldn't still be so low.

The next nearest lab was half an hour away, in the town where Roberto and Lucélia lived and despite the awful weather, we booked an appointment and immediately travelled over. Whilst waiting for the results, we called in on them and naturally the conversation tuned to the hurricane damage and how we were all coping. They showed us a bunch of photos from a nearby impoverished community and it was simply shocking. All 105 homes had been flooded to over a metre, twice, in just ten days. The families were very poor to start with and now they had lost most of what little they had. It just seemed so cruel, and the four of us discussed how it might be possible to help over 400 people.

My phone lit up, interrupting the conversations; the latest results were in. Oh dear, they were at the opposite end of the scale and dangerously high, so much so that the lab wanted me back first thing the following morning to repeat the tests and be sure. We finished up the coffees, said our goodbyes and decided to rent a car for early the next morning, repeat the tests and if necessary, drive straight to a hospital!

We were back at the lab by 8 am and sure enough the re-test came back way over the top once more. My head was spinning, three tests too low and now two results dangerously high, so high the doctor was worried I may have already suffered internal bleeding. We drove to a private hospital in the capital, explained the situation to the ER staff and let them see the string of results. Not trusting any of them, they repeated their own, my sixth in a week. I was supposed to have an INR of around 2.5 and the hospital's lab recorded it at over 11, requiring immediate admittance and intervention in the emergency ward.

The false results from the first lab had put me on a potentially lethal path. I was in danger of internal bleeds or even an aneurism. Fortunately, the treatment is straightforward enough; a good dose of vitamin K, given intravenously, would counteract the Warfarin. An ECG and a barrage of blood tests followed, to check for organ damage or signs of bleeding. Nothing came back ominous, but what a mess, though. The consultant confirmed I would have to stay in overnight for monitoring, maybe longer. Selly reluctantly said her good lucks and goodbyes, took a taxi with Mocha and arranged to stay with Blu and Roxana. Some Friday night this had turned into.

I was shown to a private room and once left alone in my comfy bed, my thoughts kept returning to the photos of the flooded villagers. Matteo's point, made months before, about all of us seemingly caring more for the dogs of Nicaragua than its people had struck a chord. Looking after and feeding Blacky, Canela and Mocha had become a preoccupation back at Paradiso, but now we had a chance to make a real difference. If we could raise enough money, maybe we could provide food, basic medicines and possibly even replace lost bedding, etc. With some of Roberto's photos forwarded, I drafted a fundraising appeal. Roberto's sister was doing the same over in Holland, and already forwarding donations.

My mind was made up, and with Selly in agreement we posted our own request for assistance. I had a typical hospital-sleepless night, as blood pressure and INR tests were taken every two hours, right up until the doctor did his morning rounds. He found me already dressed and sat in the visitor's chair, leaving him in no doubt I was eager to be discharged. As the latest results showed my INR to be back within a safe range, I was able to persuade him to let me pay up, leave and get myself reunited with Selly and Mocha. We had work to do!

As if it hadn't already been, things then started to get a little crazy. Within twenty-four hours, we had received over seven hundred pounds in donations. I phoned Roberto, to tell him I'd escaped the hospital and we had donations rolling in. The four of us hatched a plan to meet the next day, and as it was a Sunday, try and get the whole community together. On the basis of how much had jointly been raised so far, he would organise a local supermarket to make up 105 basic food parcels. One for each and every family. Discounted, of course!

After a much better sleep, I awoke the next day to find our own donations had nearly doubled overnight, to over thirteen hundred pounds. It was just amazing and we rode over to theirs with smiles on our faces and Mocha in the pannier. The four of us loaded up the hastily put-together parcels and headed out to the village. Despite Iota still battering the north-east, the sun actually came out for us, along with the whole community, and it couldn't have worked out any better.

We'd taken along a couple of large candy-filled *piñatas*, for the younger children to have a bash and play with as we organised the food parcels for the adults. After so much bad luck with the two hurricanes, a street-party atmosphere now prevailed and lightened everyone's mood. It took a couple of hours to ensure all the parcels were equally dished out, but the day had been a great success, a sea of grateful, heart-warming smiles. The day's work completed, the four of us retired to find a meal of our own and plot our next move. Twenty-six families had babies, or very young children, who desperately needed milk powder, soaps, nappies, etc. Several elders needed bedding and mattresses replacing, plus basic medications for all. We would continue to try to raise funds, shop and head out again the following Sunday.

The hurricane was beginning to ebb, but the weather was still constantly changing and continued to give us headaches. It had been a testing week; we needed to rest up a little and finish off our own medications. Fate had other ideas, though. The two-month lease was up on our apartment and although we had been given a verbal agreement to extend, we were now informed the place had been sold to a private buyer. We were about to become homeless and I could only wonder at how this had come about without us getting any heads-up. It was 3pm, two hours until the letting agencies in town closed, and we needed to be packed up and moved out by tomorrow lunchtime. Amongst all the apologies showered upon us, it turned out to be a classic case of the left hand not talking to the right, and neither hand talking to us!

We legged it down to the nearest agency, dog in tow and cash in pocket, to see what could be found. Thankfully, as it turned out, there was zero opportunity to be choosy. The agent had just one dog-friendly vacancy available, a comfy looking two-up two-down maisonette that we graciously accepted on the spot. The mild panic and rush soon became a blessing in disguise. Upon being given the address, we realised it was in the same complex as our stranded French friends. It looked like Didier and Nelly would now be just a couple of doors down from us!

The next morning, we didn't so much pack as call a taxi and throw everything into it. Mocha was utterly confused as to what was going on and laid down under the bike's back tyre, confident by now that where we went, the bike would surely follow. For half a day's pain, we had ended up in a cheaper but larger maisonette and with our Suzuki parked up alongside Didier and Nelly's matching BMWs.

Over BBQs and drinks, we quickly became firm friends, spending many of the evenings on each other's terraces, plotting ways of escaping the country. They had crossed into Nicaragua the same week we had and, likewise, had patiently waited over eight months for the situation to improve. Being by far the closest to us, Costa Rica was the favoured route for all of us and was scheduled to review its closed border policy on the 1st of December. This was less than a week away and we all had our hopes pinned on it opening up. It was a tantalising prospect; the four of us could take Mocha on walks along the coast and actually stand gazing at the Costa Rican countryside! If it did open up, then Selly and I could try trucking the bike down to Panama for shipping and jump on a flight out of San José. We might actually be home in time for Christmas, I dared to think.

Almost inevitably, the date came and passed without any change. In fact, it was worse than that; the next border review wasn't planned for at least another two to three months. Whilst still absorbing this predicament, another nugget of concerning and disheartening news reached us. From the 1st of January, the US government was introducing a ban on emotional support animals flying in the cabins. It was Wednesday the 2nd of December, England was celebrating emerging from its second national lockdown and in contrast, we just felt increasingly squeezed and trapped. Our travel insurance would now expire before the borders south opened up and by then, Mocha would be forced to travel in the hold. We just had to find a way to fly before the end of December.

As a distraction, we increasingly threw ourselves into the charity work. Donations continued to stream in, and we soon had over two thousand pounds to add to Rob and Lucélia's similar amount. Mid-week trips were made to Rivas, for coffee-laden planning sessions and further INR tests for me. On Sundays, we loaded up the latest goods and distributed them amongst the grateful community. Time was flying, though, time we didn't really have. Returning one evening, we found Didier waiting for us. He had both exciting news and a cunning plan to discuss with us. The land borders north had finally opened up to tourists and with negative Covid tests, we could theoretically head up through Honduras, El Salvador, Guatemala, and even as far as Mexico. The small catch was that all these countries had to be crossed within the seventy-two hours' validity of the Covid tests.

I jumped on the laptop and sure enough, though it would be a journey ten times further than nipping across the border to San José, there were flights we could take Mocha on from Guatemala City. It was the makings of a new, if not slightly audacious, plan. Although it was in the wrong direction for them, Didier and Nelly wanted to try getting to Guatemala. It was a country they felt sure they could sell their big bikes in, and then take flights down to Colombia, where they could buy much smaller machines for exploring South America.

They immediately stepped up to solve one of our first dilemmas. When we travelled around with Mocha, she occupied my pannier and I'd need to find a way of repacking the bike, not just for the contents of the pannier, but also the bag that would usually be strapped onto its lid. Without even asking, they offered to take two of our bags and strap one each onto their bikes. It was incredibly generous, and fortunate for us. I actually began to believe the three of us could make this trip happen.

There was no underestimating how tough it was going to be, though, a journey the length of John o' Groats to Land's End on broken roads, most likely full of broken trucks. Central and eastern Honduras had been pummelled by both hurricanes, with many routes still being cleared of landslides and rockfall. Hurricane Iota had weakened, but its aftermath and deluges still ravaged the country. Didier proposed staying as far west as possible, taking a shortcut up through El Salvador to then enter Guatemala; it made good sense.

The dry season was now overdue, and the temperatures were already mid-thirties daily. Could Mocha even endure sitting in a pannier for such a long journey? For sure, she and the bike would need some modifications, wind protection for her eyes and ears, and further protection if we encountered wet weather. My mind began to race and scramble. After months of relatively little activity, we were suddenly overwhelmed with thoughts, ideas and excitement.

The Covid tests would be a hundred and fifty dollars each, but without negative certificates, we'd be going nowhere. Before we took the tests and started the seventy-two hour race north, we needed all Mocha's paperwork in order, particularly her exit visa from the Ministry of Agriculture. As we worked through the details, it became a race against the clock, for Didier and Nelly were ready almost instantly! The vet was notified we needed Mocha's health, ownership and rabies certificates as soon as possible, plus the all-important psychiatrist's 'emotional support certificate' and official exit visa.

The timelines were heady; we'd need to cross three countries whilst our Covid tests remained valid, and Mocha's health certificates would need reviewing, or possibly renewing, at least twice before we reached the UK. Heathrow's Animal Reception Centre (the 'HARC') required an EU Health Certificate, completed within the ten days prior to flying in, and proof of tapeworm treatment having been carried out between one and five days prior to arrival. The flight we looked at getting Mocha on transited via Atlanta, and we decided it would be prudent to build in at least a two-night layover, to find a competent veterinary clinic there. Before we could board the London flight, the airline required a pre-approval letter from the HARC, which would only be emailed to us after we had supplied them with all the correct EU certificates stamped up. They required seventy-two hours' notice to oblige this; we probably wouldn't have more than twenty-four, at the very most!

We'd cross that bridge later; there was more to consider right now. Honduras required seventy-two hours' notice of our arrival, including the exact border crossing and copies of our (hopefully) negative Covid tests uploading with the online applications. That in itself was ridiculous; the tests were valid for seventy-two hours, but they requested seventy-two hours' notice of our arrival! Another bridge (or border) to be crossed later! Finally, we needed to remember to submit our 'UK Passenger Location' forms, within forty-eight hours prior to landing in England, or risk a hefty fine. There was already plenty of scope to get something wrong, and we hadn't even started looking for a shipping agent to handle the bike's return yet. I was already looking forward to the UK's ten days of self-isolation and enforced rest, if we managed to pull this off in time for Christmas!

Chapter Nineteen

Escaping Central America

On Tuesday, the 8th of December, I woke to a message from Didier and Nelly, inviting us to a farewell BBQ on their terrace, and could they borrow our gas BBQ for it! Wow, I knew they had itchy feet, but they were actually leaving us this week then. They planned to have Covid tests on the Thursday morning and head north that very same day. We couldn't be ready that quickly; our visas and bike paperwork would need renewing one last time and the vet needed a few days to get the paperwork cleared by the Ministry. Not wanting to be on the road too far behind them, we discussed heading into Managua, to make a start today. Fortunately, Didier scuppered the idea and saved us a wasted journey, informing us that everywhere would be closed until tomorrow. Today was a public holiday and the 'Feast of the Immaculate Conception'. Well, in that case then, we would pack the couple of bags they had offered to carry for us, relax and have that BBQ feast of our own!

That night was mostly sleepless as we pondered the ducks that needed lining up, before we ourselves could get back on the road again, and be in Didier and Nelly's wake. The following morning, grabbing Mocha and a hire car, we headed off into Managua, to plead one last time for extended visas. Mostly requiring the car was all the stuff we had accumulated over the last nine months of living in the country. A detour to Granada would allow us the chance to drop it all off for Blu and Roxana's new home, and check in on how the vet was coming along. The car soon filled up and it was a rude awakening as to how 'residential' and comfy we'd become over the months. There were pots and pans, food, storage containers, glasses and drink dispensers, exercise weights and mats. Even Mocha would be donating her bed, for their recently acquired and adorable puppy, Milo!

After about five hours of driving and another four of bureaucracy, we had convinced immigration to renew the visas this one last time, on the promise we would leave the country within days. Moving on to the border agency, we bought another month's insurance and submitted the final application to extend the bike's import certificate. Annoyingly, I would have to return to the capital in twenty-four hours to collect the stamped paperwork, but we had at least made a full day's progress. On the way out of the city, we called into a variety of hardware stores and large supermarkets, for anything useful in modifying the bike for Mocha. I wanted to fix some kind of transparent shield to the front of the pannier, something to block the wind and maybe allow a waterproof cover to be attached. It proved a time-wasting search that ended with us settling for a pair of workman's goggles, to be backed up by one of Selly's soft neck-tubes that could go over her ears.

With the capital behind us and the car now unloaded, we plonked ourselves down in Blu and Roxana's lounge, to briefly unwind and bring them up to speed. Running through the explanation for our sudden departure, I could see them looking over all the stuff we were leaving for them. For sure, it was gratefully received, but it reinforced we really were going to be leaving. It felt both sad and too rushed, definitely for us and also for them, it seemed. We would sorely miss each other's company and the easy banter between us all. Selly had a surprise gift for Blu, a pastel portrait that she'd painted for her birthday, a few weeks prior. With vibrant pastel colours, she'd captured Blu's 'blue' hair and blue eyes in fine detail. She was over the moon. They insisted we stay over at theirs the night before our Covid tests. At least the four of us could go out for a meal and a few drinks together one last time. We readily agreed; in any case, Granada was much closer to the capital for us and every hour would count.

The vet had pulled out all the stops; Mocha's exit paperwork would be stamped up by the Ministry in the morning and, along with the psychiatrist's 'emotional support certificate', could be collected tomorrow afternoon. Wow, there wasn't anything stopping us from packing up the apartment and leaving the coast tomorrow morning. Selly could then visit the vet and I could ride into Managua and collect the bike's paperwork. Friday morning, we could go for the Covid tests and we'd end up just one day behind Didier and Nelly.

So our farewell 'night on the town' with Blu and Roxana would actually be the very next night! Despite leaving Granada after dark and having an apartment to pack up, the day wasn't quite over. We desperately needed to see Roberto and Lucélia on the way home. Our last aid distribution together had been just a few days prior, on the Sunday, but donations were still trickling in, taking us to just shy of three thousand pounds. Aptly, and thankfully, we arranged with them to meet up at a pizzeria close to theirs. It may have been a long day already and running late, but it would be our first meal of the day! We retold our 'escape' story, but again it felt too rushed, too sudden, and we apologised for not being able to see the aid project through to the end. Everyone understood our reasons for leaving, but nobody wanted it to be so abrupt. There were too many people we should and needed to be saying goodbye to, but we were counting time in hours now, not days.

"What are you going to do with the bike when you reach Guatemala?" asked Roberto.

I honestly didn't know at this stage. I did know Roberto used to live there, still had a house and some business partners in the country.

"Let me make some calls, talk to some people over there and see who's shipping to Europe. Shouldn't be a problem," he confidently offered.

It was reassuring news to end the evening on and as we handed over the rest of the donations, another round of sad farewell hugs was exchanged. Driving home late that night, our heads and conversations were full of tomorrow's tasks; it would be another full day. To wave off Didier and Nelly, we would be up at five thirty. They planned to be on the road by 6am and in the capital early for their Covid tests. I would return the hire car and start loading up the bike as Selly got the apartment ready for handing back to the agency. After getting Mocha comfortable in the pannier, we would ride back over to Blu's, from where Selly could hound (excuse the pun!) the vet. With the bike unloaded at Blu's, I would push on into Managua, to hopefully collect the machine's import/export paperwork. If all this went well, then we'd enjoy a few well-earned drinks with the girls and, Friday morning, we would be chasing northwards, after Didier and Nelly's dust!

The alarm clock didn't have to work too hard; it had been another mostly sleepless night, pondering yet again over what we might have forgotten and what still needed to be done. I felt apprehensive about both loading up the bike and also riding it. Would Mocha cope with the distances and how would the bike handle with one side inevitably heavier than the other? I hadn't ridden it fully loaded for almost nine months, and now there were going to be three of us on it. Following the irresistible smell of freshly made coffee, I headed downstairs to be confronted by Mocha sat upright on the sofa, contentedly wearing goggles and a headscarf. Well, at least one of us appeared ready for this journey! I mentally ticked off another small worry: the princess wasn't rebelling against her new, if abhorrent, fashion look. Of course, she knew something was up; she'd witnessed and been part of several moves by now. I couldn't help feeling a little guilty, though; at least we had some idea of what lay ahead, but other than we seemed to be on the move again, she hadn't a clue. Her love and loyalty glued her to us. She trusted us completely and we couldn't, and wouldn't, push her too hard over the coming days. I took it for granted the journey would be memorable, but for me, it just needed to be completed safely and successfully, that's all. I say that's all, but my lofty definition of 'successful' meant the three of us being home and reunited with Giulia, before Christmas Day, without having had to crate Mocha up for the flights and no quarantining on arrival. What could possibly go wrong!

I could hear one of the BMWs being warmed up and we headed downstairs to wish them both luck. Mocha nervously swooned all over Nelly. The dog had often ventured down to theirs and just spent time with them. The five of us had taken long walks together and Mocha clearly enjoyed their company; she seemed to be saying goodbye also. We would try to stay in regular contact but could only guess when and where we would all be reunited again. As they finally rode off, just a little after six and with horns papping, we felt the weight of all the farewells we still owed. It felt like a tug-of-war. Silver lived just a few hundred metres from us, as did others we had come to know well, yet the race had now started. Last night. we hadn't got back until gone eleven and nobody we knew would be up at this hour of the morning. In any case, once Mocha was dressed and loaded into the pannier, I would only be making one brief stop, to drop the keys off at the letting agency.

To reach Granada we would be within a thirty-minute drive of Matteo and Iulia, down in the crater at Paradiso. Except it wouldn't be half an hour, it would be an hour return, plus maybe an hour or two explaining everything and saying goodbyes face to face! It felt awful not having the time to spare and call in, but it just wasn't possible if I wanted to reach Managua this afternoon and retrieve the bike's paperwork. Selly needed to be at the vet's, collecting and double-checking Mocha's paperwork. If anything was out of order then it wouldn't be worth going for our Covid tests early the following morning. The only clinic in the whole country carrying out the tests was at the capital's Ministry of Health, and it was closed over weekends! If we didn't get the tests sorted tomorrow, then another three days would be lost.

As inadequate as it felt to both of us, we would have to call Matteo instead. They had made 2020 not just bearable but incredibly fun and memorable, had given us our 'almost wedding' and allowed Mocha the opportunity to find us. A hasty phone call wouldn't cut it, though.

Matteo would find some way of guilting us into not only staying the weekend but cooking the Christmas turkey! We knew in our hearts that we'd all meet up again one day and our mission now was to reach Honduras by the weekend. The call would be made when we had some positive news, drinks in our hands and the time to relax.

Under a clear and windless sky, I looked over the loaded-up bike. The weight was distributed as best as could be, chain and tyre pressures adjusted and the tank was full. With her goggles and pink headscarf on, Mocha was gently lifted into her lined pannier, where she sat calmly and expectantly. Selly tucked in her only toy, a Teddy bear we'd picked up in a second-hand shop. It had been bought to try to teach and encourage her to play, something of an alien phenomenon, and progress was slow. For the last couple of years, she'd mostly fended for herself, driven by the need to find food, to survive. Become street-wise. Fun to her was hunting lizards, iguanas and chasing birds, not that we ever saw her hurt one. If she caught a lizard, she would hold it gently in her mouth, head and tail hanging out each side, and proudly walk around, before releasing it again. Through our playful perseverance, she had grown to like the Teddy bear, though, and it would be her pannier travel companion!

It wouldn't be long before the temperatures nudged over thirty degrees. She needed to be on the move; we all did. It was time to push aside any anxieties, any doubts, and get on the road. We swung past Silver's, on the off-chance she might be out on her balcony. With all the doors and blinds still closed and for no useful reason, I tooted my horn anyway. Every time I glanced into the mirror, Mocha appeared to be smiling, eyes no longer squinting behind her protective, if somewhat oversized, goggles. She took everything in as usual, sniffing the morning air and offering strangers those ritual, if unjustified, growls and barks. The bike felt incredibly heavy, but with each passing kilometre I relaxed a little more and decided to emulate Mocha. She sat almost serenely, thoroughly content with this new adventure and the world around her. With the luggage and backrest back on the bike, Selly was snug in her 'armchair' and kept a comforting hand around Mocha's shoulders. Life felt good, very good.

Reaching Lake Nicaragua revealed Ometepe's twin volcanoes, Concepción and Maderas, cloud-free and beautifully silhouetted against the blue horizon. Barely were they out of sight before Mombacho volcano came splendidly into view. It truly was a glorious day to be out for a ride. Plodding along sedately, I pondered on just how much of our time, out on the road, had been this easy to enjoy. The bike was riding great, the temperature was just perfect, the sky was as blue as the ocean we'd just left behind, the roads sumptuously smooth and near empty, and the scenery was to die for. It was frankly a rare combination and I hazarded a guess that it only accounted for about fifteen percent of our entire 26,000 kilometres! Not that it mattered much to my enjoyment; I just loved to be out riding bikes. All of the above was just a wonderfully added bonus, something to cherish and remember (when being rained on back in flat, flat Norfolk)!

It was never an issue getting Mocha into the pannier; she practically begged to hop in, but after ninety minutes she was also eager to have the goggles off and be let down again. Milo, the energetic bundle of puppy, was there to greet her and the pair legged it off together, for a pee and an explore. I briefly hugged Blu, before disappearing inside for a pee myself. Too many coffees whilst packing that morning! With the luggage safely inside, I wasted no time legging it into Managua, passing the fourth and arguably most impressive volcano of the day, Masaya. It wasn't at all tall, but it was constantly active and billowed clouds high into the sky.

Following the public holiday earlier in the week, the customs office was chaotically busy. I wasn't too surprised to learn that the documents I'd been promised just yesterday weren't ready. I dug in, basically stating I would wait as long as it took, but that I needed to have them today. Getting the Covid tests early tomorrow morning hinged on me having this paperwork today, and so they dug in! Having kept me there several anxious hours, I was again almost the last to leave the building. With no internet available, I'd sat in a vacuum of information, wondering how Selly was getting on with the vet and how Didier and Nelly had got on with their Covid tests. Walmart had free WiFi, though, and as I was still on the hunt for something to make a pannier shield out of, I diverted there on the way out of the capital.

The phone lit up as soon as I connected. Despite asking him not to, the vet had been trying to contact me instead of Selly. He had all the papers ready but had now left work and gone to the gym! In reverse, Selly had messaged me to say she hadn't heard anything and couldn't reach him at the clinic! Within a couple of calls, Selly was away in a taxi, relieved to know that I had the bike's paperwork and the vet was kindly heading back to his practice. Mooching around the store, I found an oversized and overpriced transparent storage box and bought that, along with a Stanley knife. The looks I got out in the car park as I hacked the brand-new box to pieces were priceless, but I ended up with a curved shield-shaped piece, which with a bit more finesse would surely suffice.

It was already dark, I was thirsty, hadn't eaten, but was avidly on the lookout for a repair shop, somewhere that would have some cutting tools. Just before reaching Granada, I spied a mechanic's roadside shed, where a tuk-tuk lay on its side and small motorbikes leant forlornly against the outside walls. An angle-grinder was put to work and within five minutes I had something resembling a half-decent shield. They even filed off all the burrs for the price of a couple of beers. Talking of which, Selly had thoughtfully diverted her taxi to pick up a chilled slab for my triumphant return.

As Roxana, Blu and I cracked into the beers and Selly poured herself a rum, we were nicely interrupted by a video call from Didier and Nelly. They'd had to wait several hours for their results but had both tested negative. Most of their riding day was lost, though, and they'd collapsed, tired but happy, into a hostel in Nicaragua's northern city of Leon.

"Get there early tomorrow, Mark. Friday will be busier, and try this hostel in Leon. You won't get any further than we have, I'm sure!" predicted Didier.

We hung up, with promises to keep each other updated, and I turned my attention to fitting Mocha's windshield before the beers got the better of me! It was easily bolted to the pannier, where the front lid clasp would normally be, and to her bemusement, Mocha was lifted in for a trial sizing. Simply put, she didn't like it, but it looked like it would do the job and spare her the ugly goggles. Pannier pantomimes over, we hit the town for what remained of the night. It all passed far too quickly, with much-needed food, several drinks and plenty of laughter, all followed by a surprisingly good sleep.

The morning's farewells were our last in Nicaragua; none of us enjoyed saying these goodbyes. Roxana needed to catch her bus to work and genuinely couldn't hang around. Blu had Milo snapping around at her feet and could sense we needed to get away. It was with heartfelt sadness mixed with anxious excitement that we pulled away and left Granada behind us. Every kilometre ridden north was in a one-way direction now. We found the street outside the Health Ministry buzzing with activity, and Mocha wasn't allowed in, of course. A young lad acting as a 'parking assistant' quickly sized us up and offered his services. Mocha lay down under the shade of the bike, water bowl at her side, and guarded our guard for the next hour!

The three of us kicked dust under the shade of a tree, awaiting the results. Four slow hours later, we found out we were both negative! Selly had found a kiosk, put some data on her phone and we sat an hour longer as we fiddled around online, completing applications for entry into Honduras. They wouldn't get their seventy-two hours' notice, but as it was now almost 4 pm, we wouldn't be trying to arrive at the border before tomorrow. It would have to suffice.

As predicted by our French comrades, we ended the day in Central America's hottest known city, Leon. It was surprisingly pretty, particularly as it was now thoroughly dark and the city had excelled in Christmas decorations. It had been thirty-two degrees riding up, and with a couple of 'watering' stops, not in any way too traumatic. Cars had randomly slowed beside us, for children to wave and for adults to photograph our unusual-looking party. I doubted it was particularly comfortable for her, but Mocha, nonetheless, appeared to take it all in her stride. All except the screen I'd laboured over! It just wasn't working; maybe it wasn't transparent enough for her, as she constantly strained to look either around or over the top of it. Back to the goggles then!

Pleasantly aching after the three-hour ride, I pulled up to the hostel Didier and Nelly had stayed at. We were welcomed, but unfortunately not Mocha. So back on the bike for another tour of Leon's decorations, until a cheap and less attractive hostel accepted three weary travellers! The day felt long, but stiff legs needed stretching and Mocha and I headed off to explore, settling in the main cathedral square for a bite to eat and a beer. I'd had several messages from Didier, a little disconcerting when taken together. They were now just over the border in El Salvador but had had to beg to be given a short forty-eight hour transit visa, and they weren't confident we'd be let in at all. They'd already been warned that upon reaching Guatemala, they'd only be given a maximum of five days and had already conjured up a backup plan. If they were only given the five days' entry, then they would continue on up to Mexico, stay a night and return to Guatemala, with a fresh three-month visa stamped in their passports.

Wow, our bags might be off to Mexico then. The bike had already started the adventure with a little holiday in Canada and it seemed everything else was getting further north than we could manage! I chewed over these developments with a second beer, absorbing the main square's Christmassy atmosphere of lights, stalls and festive decorations. Like arriving in the festive San Carlos de Bariloche the year before, I hadn't given much thought to Christmas, until it stared me in the face. Could we really get home in time for it, opening presents around our own tree in just two weeks' time? No flights were booked, no contact yet made with a shipping company, and still nearly 1,000 kilometres to travel. Mocha became fixated on a man blowing bubbles up into the light breeze. Admittedly huge shape-morphing glassy bubbles, which to Mocha were simply UFOs to be growled at and chased, along with the poor beggar, who ventured towards all the tables, except ours!

It was becoming normal to wake at five thirty. Even at a sedate pace we were on the road by seven and ready to tackle the border by ten. Finally, we were about to exit Nicaragua. We could hardly believe it. It was much busier than I'd expected and we were soon jumped upon by the usual gang of 'fixers', offering to smooth our path through the various channels. This help was usually brushed aside, but one young lad was speaking very good English and proving to be quite persuasive.

"I save you one hour, help clear dog, motorbike, two passports. Also, this friend watch everything. Just small tip, come on, five dollars only, everything much quicker," he successfully bargained.

It was a no-brainer really; every hour saved at the border was potentially an hour we didn't have to ride in the dark at the end of the day. We armed him with a myriad of papers and he duly dispatched his small workforce off in the direction of animal and vehicle customs, whilst ushering us pair into the passport queue. Another runner fetched photocopies, paid export taxes, returned with receipts and as advertised, we were all done in half an hour. These chaps often get a bad name for overly aggressive hassling (or changing money at scandalous rates!), but with hardly any tourists to look after they had treated us well. I happily parted with the dollars and our leftover *córdobas,* to be shared as tips.

Proceeding on a few hundred metres brought us to the much newer and posher-looking Honduran border. It was dead and empty, so much so that upon spying Mocha, a border official kindly took time out to walk us a couple of hundred metres over to the obscure and unsigned building that was the Ministry of Agriculture. With her paperwork stamped, we doubled back to sort ourselves and the bike out. Thankfully, the buildings were chilled by powerful air-con units and in each office Mocha laid herself flat out to cool down. The sun was blazing down and it was already hotter by mid-morning today than it was by mid-afternoon yesterday. Usually a bind, these border breaks were a godsend for her. We received our passport stamps with a firm warning.

"You are not allowed to go to El Salvador. They will not permit your entry," stated the official, with as much stern authority as he could muster.

Despite Didier's forewarning, it still put the cat amongst the pigeons. The logical and preferred route had us cutting straight up the west coast and keeping well away from the hurricane-damaged eastern side of the country. We wanted to stay in Nelly and Didier's shadows, riding on the smooth-ish PAH, all the way up through El Salvador and into Guatemala. As contradictory as it sounded, staying in Honduras looked like a convoluted detour that would take us virtually to the Caribbean coast. In the wake of the back-to-back hurricanes, our choices were limited; many routes were still being cleared and repaired. If we wanted to stay on passable main roads then we'd have to head over to the eastern city of San Pedro Sula, before doubling back south-westerly, to find a suitable Guatemalan border crossing. We were told to avoid the capital, Tegucigalpa, at all costs, and I was happy to oblige!

There was nothing for it then. We would forget El Salvador and head eastwards, for the city of Comayagua instead. The usual excitement of crossing a border was somewhat tempered by the feeling we were heading in totally the wrong direction, and getting further and further away from our bag-carrying French companions. We were starting to swelter in the riding gear; it was thirty-six degrees and the roads were deteriorating. Potholes and speed bumps were now the norm, along with the anticipated broken trucks on broken roads. I say broken, as we were routinely squeezing past half-cleared landslides, rockfalls and avoiding sections of road that had simply collapsed down mountainsides. The hurricanes had left their legacies and it began to feel like Peru all over again, except at least thirty degrees hotter!

Every hour, we made a short stop; we all needed it. Out on the road, Mocha was becoming even more of an attraction, but unfortunately many of the vehicles found it necessary to pap their ridiculously loud airhorns and it was beginning to spook her out. People meant well and wanted to fuss her, but when we tried to take her inside the air-conditioned rest stops, she was refused time after time. It was pretty heartbreaking, we all needed to cool down; but instead, we'd find some shade, buy some ice creams and chilled water and rest up for half an hour. If it was safe enough, we'd get her off the lead, and throwing her Teddy bear between us got all eight legs stretched off and Mocha thirsty enough to enjoy a good drink of water.

On these roads, we just couldn't progress like we were able to in Nicaragua. Yet again we arrived at our destination in the dark, and with no accommodation booked. At that moment, we'd take anything and pulled into the first hotel's car park we spied. A familiar scenario played out; we were welcome but Mocha wasn't. Comayagua is a sizeable city, but the receptionists couldn't even advise anywhere that might accept her. Having already helped Mocha down from the pannier and knowing all three of us were hungry, tired, dusty and sweaty, it was all a bit deflating. I got the feeling the hotel just wanted the 'nuisance' bikers out of their hair and it wasn't too difficult to prise the internet password out of them!

We did a little research and set the map to what looked like the main road through the town's centre, for sure it had several hostels and hotels marked along it. With no better plan, we again stopped at the first one we came to and bingo, they were dog-friendly and had a room available, even hot water! Poor Mocha, though, fireworks and bangers were being let off in earnest, somewhere behind the hotel, and she cowered, looking confused and scared as I tried to organise the room keys and secure parking. She'd had a day as taxing as ours, but at least we knew what was going on, what it was all for. I just felt sorry for her and proud of her all at once and gave her a long, reassuring hug.

We were that beat I literally threw the cover over the bike and locked it up. We didn't even dig out our toiletry bags. A nearby supermarket sold all we needed for a picnic in the room, including a bag of ice to turn the sink into the evening's fridge! Mocha was treated to a walk around the block, followed by roast chicken and diced pork, mixed into her biscuits. We were amazed by her, in awe of her. Including border stops we had been on the road thirteen hours today, more speed bumps than I could count, along with a good dosage of belching trucks and dusty roadworks. This was her third lengthy day on the bike and it looked like we needed at least two more similarly long days to reach Guatemala City.

We had more messages waiting from Didier; they were literally stuck in no-man's-land, between the El Salvadoran and Guatemalan borders. El Salvador had cleared them, but Guatemala wouldn't let them in for some reason. They were contemplating having to bed down on the roadside overnight and worse, if they were allowed in, they were pre-warned they'd definitely only be getting five-day visas. Our bags would be going to Mexico after all. This limitation had big implications for our plans. I doubted we could pull off finding a shipping company, sorting Mocha's vet visits and finding suitable flights, all within five days. Only three days in reality; we needed a day to reach Guatemala City, and a day to fly out of it!

If it wasn't for the alarm clock, I think we would all have slept until midday, a luxury that would have to wait. Hot showers and coffee got us into gear and a brisk walk did the same for Mocha. She watched us pulling on boots and gathering up the jackets and helmets, knowing too well it was destined to be another day in the pannier. In giving herself completely to us, the poor dog must have been thinking this was the life she'd signed up for. If it was as hot as yesterday, the stops would have to become more frequent, and longer.

It wasn't the same as yesterday; it was hotter. On the outskirts of Comayagua, we passed a pitiful 'tent city' sprawled under a large flyover. Every inch of the huge grassed roundabout, nestled in the shade of the flyover, was packed with a chaotic collection of tents and families. With no running water, electricity, or toilets, I couldn't comprehend their hopeless predicament. Children played at the road's edge and clothes hung everywhere, no doubt washed in the nearby dirty river. They'd been struggling here since the hurricanes had made them homeless, and I couldn't help thinking their plight made our little trip seem like a walk in the park.

Looking back on the communities we were helping in Nicaragua, I couldn't help feeling they actually had a lot to be thankful for. To be fair, we'd already witnessed scenes worse than this. Migrating Venezuelans, who'd escaped their country with nothing more than the clothes on their backs, begging for food, or lifts, or just someone to listen to them. However, 'Tent City' was still fresh in my mind when a sight even more troubling confronted us. To be honest, it was the smell that actually confronted us, and rounding a bend revealed the culprit to be a large, open but mostly flat, landfill. Barefoot children, just small kids really, ran and played amidst the filth and the stench of several stinking fires. A few scrawny adults and older kids scavenged for plastic and metal, as opportunistic vultures harangued them all. I didn't need the fires to burn this image into my brain; how hopeless I felt just seeing this. How hopeless their whole lives were destined to be.

We pressed on to find our first petrol stop and sure enough, despite the thirty-seven degrees, Mocha was again refused entry. With no words spoken, a pump attendant had witnessed our predicament and brought us a bucket, filled to the brim with cool water. We thanked him for his kindness and Mocha enjoyed a refreshing shower instead! As we pressed on, our hearts sank when the road turned to gravel, not just a short section, due to roadworks, or landslides, etc, but a lengthy dilapidated dirt and gravel road. Somewhat ridiculously, money was still found to keep up the love affair for speed bumps rather than saved up for asphalt. The road was so potholed that nothing could go fast if it wanted to! We crawled behind the traffic, breathing in the exhaust and dust clouds, and having to accept it just wasn't safe to overtake anything. Slowly, but surely, the three of us were being baked and choked, and this was supposed to be the good route!

To cap off the experience, my phone rattled out of its holder and dropped to the road below. Somehow I managed to pull over and retrieve it, before the next eighteen-wheeler crushed it into the gravel. It was to no avail, though, dying soon after and leaving me wondering how many important numbers were only in my phone and not stored in Selly's also. Like Didier and Nelly's for starters! The kilometres dragged painfully by as we searched for a fuel or rest stop until, at long last, out of the haze appeared a service station and we dismounted under some shade.

All three of us had the same dusty and somewhat bedraggled looks on our faces; we were thoroughly beat. The road had been, and still was, awful, the temperatures claustrophobic, the dirt clogged our lungs and eyes and once more, we weren't allowed inside with Mocha. Water and a run around weren't going to cut it this time and she sauntered off to find a better life, bless her. The protest didn't last too long, she'd made her point, but once seeing the helmets going back on and realising she risked being left behind, she walked back over to us, if somewhat resignedly. The message was clear enough, though. We were pushing her limits and the experience was stretching her endurance, taking its toll. We were all feeling the weight of the journey, but only Selly and I knew she had a loving home waiting for her, if she could only be patient a little longer.

We reached the Guatemalan border mid-afternoon on the Sunday and were greeted by a friendly young lady, dressed as a Honduran border official. With refreshing efficiency, we were informed both the Honduran and Guatemalan customs resided under one roof and that we'd only have to cross the road to process Mocha at the Ministry of Agriculture's small office. That was until she learned we hadn't applied, with seventy-two hours' notice, to leave the country! Explaining we believed that was only required for entering Honduras, Francia (we were on first-name terms by now!) took us down the road to a kiosk that, for a couple of dollars, would complete the online applications for us. Fortunately, as was the case on the way into Honduras, the seventy-two hours' notice seemed to be unimportant.

In the meantime, we would make a start with Mocha's exportation and importation. This was relatively simple and once a small fee was paid, inside the main customs building, she was free to go (preferably not without us, Mocha!). With our online applications still fresh on the kiosk owner's keypad, and Mocha already asleep in the cooling air-con, we joined a customs passport queue. The Honduran exit was simple enough, but all our fingers were crossed as we pleaded for thirty days' entry from the Guatemalan official. We had comfortably made the seventy-two-hour Covid deadline, but now we needed breathing space to organise the rest of the journey. He listened to our travel plans, read some helpful Nicaraguan notes scribbled into our passports and once he was satisfied we weren't trying to linger, issued us the full thirty days. We were overjoyed, for all of four minutes.

Sliding sideways to the 'vehicle' counter, I presented all the usual paperwork and permits. They were glanced at half-heartedly and 'presented' back to me.

"You need to pay the entry fee for Guatemalan importation first," the Honduran customs official instructed.

"Just over there, at the payment counter?" I gestured, pointing at the nearby window where I had previously paid Mocha's fee.

"No. At the bank, which opens eight thirty tomorrow morning," he replied, dismissively.

I couldn't quite take that in; was it a wind-up? We went out and found Francia, who confirmed that for no logical reason she knew of, the animal fees can be paid for inside, but the vehicle fees had to be paid at the bank. I couldn't get my head around why the vehicle counter was even manned on a Sunday then, if they couldn't process anything. A bigger concern was where we were going to sleep tonight. This was a border pretty much out in the sticks, with the nearest town several kilometres away and back in Honduras. My head was full of visions similar to poor Didier and Nelly's recent night spent sleeping on the pavement alongside their bikes and stuck between the borders in no-man's-land. As far as our passports were concerned, we were now in Guatemala, the bike was still in Honduras and poor Mocha, well, she was just in the dark, bless her!

It was the last thing we needed after a day like today, but Francia came to the rescue once more. She led Selly and Mocha on a walk through the Guatemalan barrier and down the road, to a house she understood would rent a room to people in our stranded predicament. In the meantime, I tried to find somewhere safe to park up the bike for the night, and came to the conclusion that outside the main doors of the customs building was as good as any! The girls came back trumps. For ten dollars we had a room for the night and Mocha was allowed to stay in with us. As it was a bit of a hike, Francia had again gone out of her way and solved another concern.

"I've spoken to the doctor here, and he says you can put all your bags and helmets in his office overnight, so you don't have to carry them down the road and back. It will be locked up and very secure," she offered with another smile.

We were so thankful. It was now dark, probably past the end of her shift, and yet she had stayed to make sure all three of us were sorted for the night. We hadn't experienced much of Honduras, but we'd certainly met one of its gems.

A few weeks previously, we'd hosted a BBQ and I'd been able to introduce Didier to Roberto. I had an idea they'd swapped numbers, and borrowing Selly's phone, I sent Lucélia a message, explaining my phone had died and could Rob please send us Didier's number, if indeed he had it. It turned out Rob had been trying to get hold of us also, to pass on the details of a shipping company he'd been liaising with. No prices, but he was fairly confident they could fly the bike to London for us. That was very welcome news and at the very least, a promising lead. An absolute gent, he forwarded these details along, plus Didier's number. I sent the pair of 'lost wanderers' an update from our end and collapsed on the bed, wondering where on earth they might be now!

It had been quite an exhausting day; we were all hungry, but only Mocha would be getting a meal this evening, unless we tried her biscuits! Despite the day's events, I don't ever recall being so thankful for such a sparse, dank room. It could easily have been put to shame by European prison cells. (It was just a 'borrowed' Christmas tree, and I'd only been locked up for one night... a long time ago!) The walls were still wet from recent floods, an ant nest had infested the bedding and mosquitoes droned around our ears. As I picked up my boots, to move them and their smell outside, a cockroach scuttled away, seemingly annoyed at our intrusion. It was hot, humid, smelled of mouldy dampness, but it wasn't a bleak pavement and with our clothes kept on, we slept just fine!

It was still early, but as we approached the covered motorbike, Francia was there to greet us with a cheery smile. We hung around for all the right officials to arrive, with Francia pointing out who I needed to see and in what order. Once armed with the correct paperwork, I nipped through the border to find the small bank as Selly and Francia retrieved our belongings from the doctor's office. The good news was that the bank had opened on time; the bad news was that there was already a huge queue, extending around a corner and down the road. With a mix of broken Spanish and broken English, the young chap next to me explained we had about a two-hour wait, and he was almost spot-on. I knew Selly would be reluctant to leave the bike and all our gear unattended, but she must have been worrying as my 'nip to the bank' approached the first hour.

Virtually everybody in the queue appeared to be traditionally dressed locals, evidently poor and looking desperately resigned to these long waits, but a sight far more heart-wrenching now greeted me. Sitting on the bank's steps was a pitiful girl of about twelve or thirteen, clutching a baby of around six to eight months. The way she was trying to care for it, I could only presume it was her own. She was vigorously shaking the bubbles out of a near-empty bottle of Pepsi and giving it to the grabbing infant. When the baby had finished drinking this, she produced a few fast-food sachets of tomato sauce and, ripping them open one by one, fed these to her little one. The 'meal' looked like it had been scrounged from some nearby bin, and the stains on the poor baby's clothes said this was all pretty run-of-the-mill.

The poor girl's plight seemed invisible to everybody except me. I couldn't stand the sight for more than a minute and felt I had to do something, anything. I had no food, no local currency yet, and a lengthy queue now extended out behind me, but I could see there was an ATM. I explained to my neighbour that I wanted to get some cash out and could he kindly save my place. I had no idea of the exchange rate but, after faffing with a couple of different cards, finally emerged with a handful of shiny Guatemalan *quetzals*. They were gone; in just the few minutes it had taken me to liberate the machine of some notes, the youngsters had been replaced by an anxious-looking Selly and the ever-helpful Francia.

"We were wondering what had happened to you," said Selly, as I took my place back in the world's slowest-moving queue!

Over the concluding hour, the young girl and her infant never did return. I wished I could have done something, but the opportunity was lost and so, with my bank receipts in hand, I returned to get the bike's entry stamps sorted. Mirroring our passports, I'd graciously been given thirty days for the motorcycle, a huge relief and something less to worry about. We loaded up the bags and an unenthusiastic-looking dog. Her scepticism for the day ahead was palpable and I sorely wished we could communicate this should be the final one. Turning to Francia, we couldn't even force a grateful tip upon her. She settled for goodbye hugs, selfies and promises we'd stay connected. It might have taken over twenty hours to cross the El Florido border, but it hadn't been all bad.

As we crawled past a long line of parked trucks and put the final border behind us, I was willing my passengers to hang in there. Selly had been gripped by chronic lower back pain, from sitting awkwardly on the bike. Mocha had a tendency to frequently stand up, which was understandable, but if she had her way she would climb all the way up onto Selly's lap. It came to a head one day when Mocha pushed her luck, lost her balance and half fell out of the pannier. We were riding slowly at the time, but I'd had to stop promptly and help settle her down again. We were all novices at this game and there were times I was actually amazed we'd made it as far as we had. Selly was constantly having to compensate, though, by leaning to one side and keeping a reassuring arm wrapped around her, at the expense of her own comfort. Almost on the hour, we found a modern service station that mercifully allowed all three of us inside. A different country, a different reception? We wanted – no, needed – something to look forward to, something to aim for, and plugging into the free WiFi, we made a search for dog-friendly accommodation. I'd had enough of turning up somewhere, in the dark usually, and being turned away! Selly found a suitable home-stay, great reviews, close to the airport and with a pretty garden for Mocha to chill in. We booked for three nights and would take it from there. At least we had an address to put into the map and we wouldn't be struggling to find something on the fly.

I think we were so excited to be nearing our destination that the similarly high temperatures didn't bother us so much that day. The roads were better and we hadn't been rained on in a thousand kilometres; there was plenty to be thankful for. Mocha continued to have her photograph taken, out on the road, and virtually everywhere we stopped. Our arrival in the capital was perfectly timed with rush hour, and still I didn't care. Even Mocha perked up to growl and bark at anybody not quite dressed up to her snobbish standards. The home-stay wasn't a straightforward find, but find it we did, and our helpful host made space for the bike, helped carry bags and showed us around the place. It really was lovely and Mocha was so impressed with all the green grass that she wasted no time thoroughly emptying herself!

I so wished I could have explained to her that she'd made it, no more goggles, scarves or pannier trips. She seemed content, though, had clearly decided the room's large armchair was hers alone and hopped up for a post-poo nap. We were chuffed to bits to have made it, to have the bike fully unloaded and the room turned into our homely mess! It called for a celebration and I popped out, returning with cold beers, Guatemalan rum and a selection of mixers. The host, Minore, caught me on the way back in, said I could use their fridge and handed me a bunch of menus for restaurants that would deliver. Easy-peasy, we wouldn't even have to venture out again tonight.

The room was more like a self-contained granny flat, nestled in the garden itself, but inside or outside, a new and wonderful noise punctured the solitude. We had seen two, maybe three, planes in the last nine months. Now they were regularly taking off and landing, almost on our doorstep. It certainly wasn't an annoying noise; if anything, it was all quite exciting. Fingers crossed, we would all be on one soon!

A little later, Selly's phone rang. Finally, it was a video call from a cheery Didier and Nelly, from inside Mexico! With stories briefly summarised and swapped, they informed us they'd hopefully be with us in just a couple of days. It was great news; we really looked forward to welcoming them both and catching up properly. Despite the noisy airport, Mocha could hardly be roused to eat. She looked how I felt, deadbeat. The journey from San Juan del Sur had been completed in five long bureaucratic days. We'd ridden just over 1,100 kilometres, a similar amount of potholes and speed bumps, and a similar amount of belching broken trucks! The heat and dust had been unrelenting and we'd lost count of the roadworks, landslides, rockfalls and diversions that randomly plagued the route. We weren't home yet, but it sure felt like the worst was behind us. There was one last pressing task, though, before allowing ourselves to get too relaxed. Borrowing Selly's phone and making use of Roberto's tip, I sent the shipping company an introductory email. Curled up in the armchair, Mocha looked thoroughly at home, but it took hot showers to semi-revive us and takeaways to fulfil us. An early night was enjoyed by all.

An encouraging reply awaited us in the morning. The shipping company confirmed they could send the bike, plus our gear; they just couldn't give us a price. Cargo costs, per kilo, were fluctuating daily and at this stage we could only provide an approximate weight. They had us over a barrel really. It had taken Mike and Charlie three months to get their bikes home from Costa Rica and they'd parted with roughly double the usual rate. I expected no less. It was still welcome news and on the back of it, we felt confident enough to go ahead and book the flights from Guatemala to Atlanta and then Atlanta to London. The first flight would be six days away and Minore happily extended our booking for us.

If all went to plan, the London flight was booked to get us in on the morning of the 23rd, and Selly wasted no time phoning Giulia, letting her know Mum should be home for Christmas! Feeling accomplished, I borrowed her phone, cracked a beer in the sun-filled garden and tried to get either Matteo or Iulia on the phone. They'd been on our minds the last few days and we were overdue a good chat. Unfortunately, neither picked up and we resorted to sending messages instead. Mocha lay stretched out on the grass, clearly not missing her goggles and looking totally at peace. It wouldn't last too long; we had a full day planned for her, involving a 'dry run' to the airport, followed by a trip to the vet's.

Although I'd submitted all the supporting documents to the airline's website, we physically wanted to see what would happen when we attempted to get through the airport and up to the check-in counters. It went surprisingly smoothly, other than finding out our adventurous dog was scared of riding inside lifts! We made it to the counters and explained we were flying out in a few days' time. The airline wasn't put off by Mocha's size, the paperwork seemed to be in order and they even arranged for the Ministry of Agriculture's official to come and have a chat with us. Again, all went well, and we left for the vet's feeling almost smug but definitely chuffed. The veterinary clinic I'd plucked from the internet turned out just to be a pet shop. Oh well, they had dog food on special offer; it wasn't a totally wasted visit. Now pointed in the right direction, we relocated and found an English-speaking vet that could produce all the certificates we would need for entering the USA, but not until the day before we were due to fly out. They were that busy.

We returned to the home-stay and set about emailing the HARC all the information and documents we currently had. They were prompt to reply, but it was all pretty disheartening. We'd allocated a two-day stopover in Atlanta and already had a vet's appointment, to organise the EU Health Certificate, but London still insisted they receive it with at least seventy-two hours' notice. If they didn't get the certificate, we wouldn't get the pre-approval letter and the airline might not let us on! Worse than this, though, I'd made a stupid blunder in Mocha's inoculation booklet. Noticing the microchip implantation date hadn't been completed, I inserted the date I thought it had been rather than properly checking when it actually had been!

From the booklet, it now looked like the rabies jabs and microchip dates were the wrong way around; a mistake, Heathrow pointed out, that would require Mocha to be quarantined for four months! I was gutted, and quickly sent over the Nicaraguan Ministry of Agriculture's certificate, which did have the correct dates, plus the vet's invoice, also with the correct dates. For some inexplicable reason, neither of these documents had Mocha's microchip numbers on them and weren't acceptable to the HARC. The room suddenly wasn't big enough to kick myself around in; we'd come so far and yet I'd managed to send us so far backwards.

There was some light at the end of the tunnel, though; every time I emailed Heathrow, I seemed to get a reply back from a different person. A follow-up email proposed I could have the vet add Mocha's microchip numbers to the relevant documents and if stamped, dated and countersigned, they would be acceptable. That wasn't so bad then, we just had to catch our Nicaraguan vet away from the gym and actually in his clinic, and we should be back in business. Then, as a backup, we'd ask the vet here to review all the documents, amend the inoculation booklet and add more stamps and signatures. Once all the grovelling emails were sent out, I felt a little better. Selly even stopped giving me 'the look'!

The following morning, Didier and Nelly messaged to confirm they would be with us late afternoon. With several hours to spare, I decided to take a ride across the city and meet face to face with the shipping company. Riding the bike, stripped of all luggage, was a dream. I effortlessly cut through the nose-to-bumper cars, or threaded my way to the front of traffic lights. Like most of the capitals we'd been in, the lights turning green resembled the start of a mad moped race, one I definitely had an advantage in at last. It was a quick and business-like visit to the company's modern warehouse and headquarters. The owner, a friend of Roberto's, introduced himself and, after a short chat, left me in the hands of one of his associates. She had photocopies of all my Guatemalan import documents made and we agreed to hand over the bike and the luggage at the end of the week. It would be the first motorcycle they had ever sent to Europe.

"Just one thing, Mark, as it's 'dangerous cargo', the bike needs to be thoroughly clean, empty of oil and gas, plus have the battery disconnected. Oh, and your luggage will need to go separately," she finished off with.

I was a little taken aback and explained that the bike had also flown to Buenos Aires as 'dangerous cargo'. The oil had stayed in, plus a little petrol, and the battery was left connected.

"That may be, but this is Guatemalan customs, not London, and we are signing the declaration. I will need a complete inventory of each bag and pannier," she stated, with slightly more professionalism than I'd hoped for!

The owner passed by within earshot and added his own pennies' worth.

"Mark, if you have three toothbrushes and only put two, we are going to have problems. It must be exact," he actually said. But we don't even brush Mocha's teeth, I worried. Should we?

I wasn't totally surprised to learn this was a German-based company. I now had total confidence the bike would be prepared and crated up as if made of gold, and I just hoped I didn't need to go out and find a large, shiny lump of it to pay for it all! The only bit of preparation I wholeheartedly agreed with was the thorough cleaning. The fuel tank was already virtually empty, but after the previous week's jaunts, the bike now flaunted a fully impregnated coat of dirt and brown dust.

I returned to find the pair of them sunbathing. Make the most of it, Mocha. Both Atlanta and Norfolk coincidentally happened to be just five degrees today! Selly had received more in-depth news from Didier. The Mexican detour had been a tiring addition to their journey and hadn't exactly been the visa run they'd expected it to be. For some inexplicable reason, they had been given three months in their passports, but just forty-eight hour transits for the two BMWs. They would come directly to ours and explain all, but just from the message, we really felt their frustration. All four of us had suffered at the hands of seemingly inept and illogical rules and processes. Nothing ever seemed to be straightforward and the Virgo in me would have loved to rip up most of the borders we'd crossed and start again, with some clear signage and huge arrows pointing us through the processes. The adventurer in me wouldn't change a thing, though, and hoped they didn't anytime soon!

We heard the BMWs arriving and chased after an excited Mocha, who also must have recognised their machines. Barely could they get off before she jumped all over them, tail-stump wagging crazily.

They looked haggard, tired, happy and bewildered, all at the same time. They also looked thirsty, like they needed a cold beer. Selly led them through to the garden terrace as I legged it to the corner shop, returning in minutes with snacks and a chilled six-pack. Their endurance story spilled out and made our trek north seem pretty run-of-the-mill. When they had passed through and exited Guatemala nine months previously, the customs officials hadn't closed down the bike's temporary import permits properly. On their system, the bikes had never left and they were refused a re-entry. It had taken a high-placed friend twenty-four hours to fix their predicament, but not before enduring a night on the pavement beside the bikes.

Coming back to Guatemala, from Mexico, they realised their seventy-two-hour Covid window had now lapsed. A backhander resolved that issue, but customs weren't quite finished with messing them around yet, issuing them three-month passport visas, but just forty-eight hours for the bikes. As lovely as the two machines were, they just wanted enough time in Guatemala to sell them and catch flights to Colombia. They'd lined up interested buyers, but tomorrow they would have to find the capital's customs HQ and go plead their case for extensions. It was a story and laughter-filled reunion, but with our bags returned we could understand they just needed to find their digs and recharge. It was so, so tempting to just sit in the sun and carry on drinking, but we all had a lot on our plates over the coming days and sadly, we didn't expect to see each other again before our flight out. With hugs and great memories banked, we bid each other farewell and much luck.

Over the next twenty-four hours, we excitedly told family and friends that flights were booked and we were truly on our way home. One friend stepped straight up and offered to collect the three of us from Heathrow, and drop us back home in Norfolk. It was my old buddy John who, armed with a stethoscope screwdriver, had embarrassingly found my loose spark plug cap sixteen months previously. Having both dogs and motorbikes of his own, he also had a neatly tricked-out van that could get us there in comfort. It was a great gesture, but best of all, we would have a friendly face meeting and greeting us.

"Am I making room for the bike as well? No problem, plenty of space," he'd asked.

"I wish, John. It's being left with a shipping company, who've never shipped a bike before!" I answered, visualising his frown.

"Good luck with that then," he unfortunately but accurately predicted in a tone of prophetic doom!

He was one of many who asked if we really had any idea of what we were coming back to. Other than knowing we were swapping our thirty-five degrees for five, we honestly couldn't get our heads around the juggling and confusing 'tier' systems in place back home. The Covid statistics, both in England and Italy, had become too mind-boggling, and the arguments over how the numbers were derived at were equally baffling. I had a sense that we'd be going back to a lot of pent-up resentment, even rage, as the news currently spoke of tumbling statues and mask-less protests.

The European figures were dwarfed by those in North America, though, and with their borders indefinitely shut, we knew that for us, returning home was still the right decision and the right time. In fact, boarding a plane and seeing Mocha trotting down the aisle was the most exciting thing we could think of right now! The following day, we popped out and bought suitcases each, the idea being to use the hold-luggage allowance to the limit and make our task of inventorying toothbrushes and tent pegs that much less time-consuming. It was still dark-o'clock before we finished that laborious task and as if I needed it pointing out, we still had too much stuff!

For four dollars, I was given a seat and a cup of coffee, as two lads set to with buckets, water and soap, attempting to remove several months' worth of muck. It was a roadside enterprise, comprising a couple of cones blocking off a single parking space. A tiny portable pressure washer sat on the pavement, with the well-worn and repaired power lead disappearing off into the café that had provided the seat and hot coffee. The top layer came off quite easily, but then they really did have to earn their fee, removing the accumulation of stubborn under-grime.

Today was the day we parted ways, until who knew when. I strapped on the luggage for the very last time, rode over to the shippers and stripped it back off, along with the screen, tent rack and the mirrors. As Gabriela scrutinised the inventory, I disconnected the battery but kept quiet about the oil and small amount of remaining petrol. With the keys handed over, I explained we flew out in a couple of days' time and could she think of anything else we needed to do?

"No, no, we are all good. Have a nice flight home and I will let you know when it is coming," she said with a smile as I glanced over at the bike and gear.

Leaving it all behind felt a bit like checking bags in at the airport, not my problem anymore! Even our room looked so much bigger and emptier when I got back. The last job before flying on Sunday was Mocha's vet's appointment in the morning, or at least so I thought. Sorting through all our remaining paperwork that evening, I was struck with a thought that sent alarm bells ringing. I messaged Gabriela to say I still had all the original import documents, and that she just had photocopies. Would that be a problem? Ten seconds after reading it, she was on the phone.

"Oh my God, we need those, Mark. I can't send the bike without them. They are very, very important," she stressed, adding that they were also now closed for the weekend!

I had kept a hold of them in case I was stopped whilst out riding the bike, but forgotten to ask if she now needed them. Their depot was in an enclosed business park and as it was likely that one or two of the businesses would be open until midday Saturday, I would need to get into the place and slide an envelope under the shipper's door! Typically, it was in a different direction to where the vet's appointment was, but it had to be done.

By 9am, we were knocking on the vet's door. I was beginning to feel like we were making down payments on new yachts for half of Central America's vets! Mocha's one hundred pound 'examination' literally consisted of me lifting her on and off the scales and the vet patting her on the head! Once we'd been handed a tapeworm and US health certificate, plus some autographs to correct my *faux pas* in the inoculation book, the bill had tripled to almost half the one we'd departed Nicaragua with the previous week. I didn't want to think about what size boat Atlanta's vet was saving for, and instead left Selly and Mocha to it whilst I disappeared off to deliver the 'very, very important' bike documents.

Back in the room, I emailed the latest documents to the HARC and they confirmed there'd be no 'airline pre-approval letter' prior to receiving the EU Health Certificate. Fair play, I guess. It was now Saturday evening and our last night in the country. Even if we'd wanted to, there was nothing more we could do. We collapsed with another lazy takeaway, a tipple of Guatemalan rum and thoughts gravitating excitedly towards North America.

Chapter Twenty

Taking Flight

Minore, helpful to the last, insisted upon driving us to the airport and seeing us safely off. At check-in, everything was going swimmingly, until the Ministry of Agriculture's official showed up. Of course, it had to be somebody different to the helpful lady we'd seen just a few days before.

"You don't have the dog's Guatemalan exit authority. It must be stamped at the headquarters," an officious and exasperated uniform told us, as the check-in lady tightened her grip on our boarding passes.

To no avail, Selly explained in her best Spanish that we'd had all the documents checked by one of his colleagues, and we'd even brought along the photocopies she'd said would be needed.

"I don't need any of these. What I need is the dog's Guatemalan exit authority," he repeated even more sternly. Things weren't looking good.

Attempting to match his exasperation, we thrust Mocha's thick file of paperwork into his hands, whilst declaring this had been sufficient to get us all the way from Nicaragua, without too many problems. I felt numb; it just seemed impossible to please everybody in a uniform, however hard we tried. The minutes ticked by as he sifted through the sizable wad of papers and tried to make sense of them.

"Oh, you are transiting? Then I just need to see the original Nicaraguan export certificate," he muttered, almost apologetically.

We had not only this but also several photocopies, which he declined to relieve us of. The check-in counter lady looked as relieved as we did, though I suspect this was because she'd pre-emptively sent our hold bags through fifteen minutes earlier! Avoiding escalators and carrying the normally brave Mocha in and out of lifts, we settled excitedly at the gate. The very last of our *quetzals* had been spent on stickers for the panniers, with which we sincerely hoped to be reunited soon! The cabin crew swooned over Mocha as she trotted happily down the plane's aisle and took her place at Selly's feet. There were hardly any passengers to board and we were soon accelerating down the runway and lifting off. Mocha woke up shortly after the seatbelt lights went out and climbed up onto Selly's lap. She was mesmerised, glued to the view, and every so often shot us a look, as if to say *Well, can't you at least open the window for me?*

Atlanta was two degrees that evening, and even sporting her new woolly dog-coat, we realised this was the coldest Mocha had ever experienced. Later, leaving the hotel room for her nightly walk, the grass twinkled and crunched under all our feet. The poor dog had gone from baking in a pannier to freezing her paws off; not that she seemed to care. Every smell was new to her and she turned into an excited bloodhound. Not wanting her to catch a cold, we kept the walks short and the room cosily warm. Tomorrow, she would be back at the vet's, for the final and most important certificate, the one that would negate a four-month quarantine.

It was quite exciting to be in the States. I'd taken a wander to a nearby gas station and gawped at the products inside. It was better stocked than most of the supermarkets we'd been inside over the whole of the last year. I couldn't stop myself filling a bag with treats and drinks, soon realising we'd need the two nights just to get through them!

We arrived promptly for Mocha's appointment and she was led inside, whilst we were asked to wait out in the parking lot. The brisk walk down had kept us warm, but now, stood waiting, it felt bitterly cold. Thankfully, her examination again appeared to consist of little more than a boxer's weigh-in, and for another chunk of cash, she was handed back to us with the relevant paperwork. Kind of.

"This EU certificate probably needs endorsing by the USDA by the way," said the vet, as dusk enveloped us.

My quizzical look begged for more information.

"The USDA, United States Department of Agriculture. They usually need to stamp these certificates, so I've uploaded it to their portal. Give them a call in the morning and see if it can be done sometime tomorrow is my advice," he elaborated, a little too matter-of-factly.

Thank goodness we'd booked an overnight flight and didn't need to be back at the airport until five thirty tomorrow evening. I must have read the UK government and HARC websites a dozen times by now, but not once had I come across the tip about getting the certificate endorsed by anything more than the vet's stamp and signatures.

"Here's their address and number to call. Make sure you tell them you're coming to collect it yourself, and good luck," was his parting shot.

I scanned and sent the certificate to Heathrow regardless, querying if the USDA endorsement was actually necessary. It was already nearly midnight in London, but with the reception centre open round the clock, I gave it a try. After a couple of hours without a reply, I backed it up with a phone call, explaining Mocha was 'in transit' through Atlanta and that she was exported originally from Nicaragua. I was desperately trying to get us the pre-approval email for tomorrow's check-in, without which, I feared, we could be denied boarding.

"Yes, as the EU certificate was issued in Atlanta, it would need to have the USDA endorsement carried out in Atlanta," confirmed the cockney accent.

Oh dear, so much for a last relaxing day, I thought, as I frowned at the phone's map. The USDA was nearly thirty miles away and a one-and-a-half-hour round trip. Let's hope they can sort this in the morning. (They didn't!)

The comfortable bed couldn't entice me into a decent night's sleep, supposedly and hopefully our last in the Americas. We were so close to getting back, but I kept dreaming up new loose ends, something missed that might block us getting on the flight. After breakfast, I somewhat nervously gave the USDA a call, reference number in hand.

"We already processed that application, refused it and returned it to your vet," and pre-empting my next question, followed up with, "your vet's payment didn't go through and the microchip number on page two was incorrect. What day do you fly?"

"Er, today, well, tonight actually," I responded, trying to sound calm, and hopelessly hopeful.

"You need to get back to your vet then. If you get it all corrected and submitted by noon, it might be ready to collect by five. Have a good day," he almost barked.

"But is there any way to get it sooner?" I rushed out, trying to catch him before the phone was hung up on us.

"No, there isn't. Our vet won't arrive before four thirty, to stamp up the day's paperwork. Five at the earliest, if it gets done today," he reaffirmed, and this time hung up before hearing my next potentially dumb question!

I'd had the phone on speaker, for Selly to hear first-hand, and we stared at each other nonplussed, heads full of questions. How could the vet get it so wrong? Turning to our copy of the health certificate, we could now see that on page two, a row of four zeros in the middle of Mocha's chip number was written with just three zeros.

"We need to get back to the vet's and collect a zero!" I tried to joke, lamely.

"We need to find out what they haven't paid," Selly replied.

We were supposed to be 'final' packing, checking out and chilling for the journey ahead. Instead, we charmed the receptionist into a freebie late check-out, pulled on jackets and hats and walked Mocha back to the clinic. They were suitably apologetic and we received a corrected certificate, an assurance their payment had now gone through and a new reference number for the USDA. That went OK, I thought as we walked back to the hotel, via the gas station to grab much-needed hot coffees. I should have known better than to let our hopes get up.

Sitting down, with our little travel laptop, I saw an email waiting from the HARC. It was a reply to my email of last night (one that I thought had now been negated by last night's phone chat). Somebody 'working from home' had reviewed the certificate we had sent (missed the microchip number being incorrect!) and wanted an extra bit of the form completing by the vet. A bit of the form that was auto-blocked off and only mirrored information already on the submitted rabies certificate. Were we being wound up? Our hands still hadn't warmed up from the last two-mile vet walk!

This particular email had only been sent in the last ten minutes, and before venturing back out into the cold, I replied, asking for confirmation this was really necessary. We had a speedy response, along the lines of 'Yes, sorry, if you could just get the vet to put something in there and countersign it, that would be great.' This was getting messy; it was already noon and we couldn't resubmit anything new to the USDA. If we made another trip to the vet's, we could possibly get our 'non-USDA' certificate amended, to present alongside the USDA-endorsed certificate, but would the HARC issue the pre-approval letter without the latest change being on the USDA certificate? That's if we even got that today and made it to the airport in time!

My head was spinning; both our heads were. Mocha slept at our feet, blissfully ignorant of the fuss around her and unaware she was supposed to be flying again this evening. Selly and I looked down at her, also unaware if we were flying this evening! Selly offered to go back out once more, to tackle the vet, and I stayed behind to check what our other flight options were, should we miss this one. I started with another call to the USDA, to confirm the vet's payment had gone through OK. I really didn't want to antagonise them, but we simply didn't have the hours left to keep correcting cock-ups. Without their endorsed paperwork, we wouldn't be getting on the plane. No way were we going to risk submitting Mocha to a UK winter in quarantine. Even if the paperwork was processed today, there was a good chance that we'd be arriving at the airport too late to make the flight. It's fair to say we weren't having a relaxing last day of our Pan-American dream adventure!

Our flight was due to take off just before seven thirty, and at 5pm we would be thirty miles across town, probably with rush-hour traffic to deal with. It was sporty to say the least. If we missed it, the next flight was overnight Christmas Eve. Not that that put John off, as he'd already messaged to say a Christmas Day pick-up was fine, despite coming all the way down from North Yorkshire. What a diamond!

By the time Selly returned, I was able to tell her I'd spoken once more to the USDA, thankfully to a different person, who'd confirmed the vet had made the necessary payment. Selly hadn't had a nice experience; she'd had to plead and insist that they please carry out Heathrow's latest request. I guess the hundreds they'd taken off us yesterday were banked and forgotten. With the changes begrudgingly made, they virtually slammed the door shut on her. What we had now would have to suffice.

We were getting emotionally ground down; even Mocha now looked despondent. Having moved out of the room and into the foyer, she correctly guessed we were on the move again and had nestled beside the cases. After a rushed late-afternoon lunch, we ordered a taxi. This was it; we were going for broke. Settling our bill, I couldn't push away the thought we might just be checking back in again later, though I sincerely hoped we wouldn't be.

We seemed to strike gold with our driver. She took an instant liking to Mocha and listened to our summarised plight. It was no problem for her to wait for us at the USDA and she would get us over to International Departures as quickly as she could. By ten minutes to five, I was in the USDA HQ and trying to find the correct floor and office. By five past five, I was excitedly back out and in the taxi, documents in hand. Selly was beaming, the driver was chuffed for us and Mocha jumped all over me as we sped back to the freeway.

It was a promising start. Shortly before six, we were at the check-in counter, having the cases taken off us and Mocha's paperwork glanced through. Behind my back, I had my fingers crossed.

We'd decided making the check-in on time was more important than faffing around trying to get the pre-approval letter out of the HARC. If at the counter they insisted upon it, well then, we'd have to cross that bridge with an insistent phone call. It wasn't asked for, or even mentioned! The boarding passes were handed over without anything more than a warm smile, directed at Mocha, of course. We were making the flight!

Once through security, we settled next to the gate and sent off the freshly endorsed paperwork to London. Glancing up at the screens, I could see we were due to board in just ten minutes. I backed the email up with a phone call. I didn't want any unforeseen hiccups upon landing. Silly me.

"Yes, I can see your email here, but have you paid the fee yet?" responded yet another different member of staff.

I hadn't, but made the payment there and then, waiting on the line for confirmation it had gone through OK. The first boarding announcement blared out and first-class passengers began to gather into a socially-distanced hubble.

"So that went through OK. Someone will meet you off the flight with a chip scanner and as long as it can be read OK, then we'll just need to check through her paperwork. Do you know if it is an ISO standard chip?" she casually asked.

"I've no idea, to be honest. It was implanted in Nicaragua, several months ago," I offered.

"Well, it should be OK, but if we can't read the chip then Mocha will have to be taken into quarantine, and the four-month process started off again, I'm afraid. Is that OK?" she asked.

Of course that wouldn't be OK! Wow, I hadn't enjoyed the tension of our last day and now the pleasure of drinking myself to sleep on an overnight trans-Atlantic flight had just been snatched away! This had come right down to the wire and my head began to swim with thoughts Mocha had some dodgy unreadable chip buried in her neck!

We were being called to the gate and my pause elicited a final offering from across the pond.

"Well, I'm sure everything will be fine and I'll get the pre-approval letter emailed to you within the next hour," she added cheerily, as if to end the call on a high note.

"Oh, not to worry, I'm about to board the plane as we speak," I said with empty satisfaction, though I definitely wouldn't be laughing if the scanner came back with the Chinese alphabet!

The last text, before losing the internet, was to John with a simple *We're on buddy, see you in the morning.* Dropping into our seats, Mocha must have sensed it was an overnight flight as she curled up, closed her eyes and ignored our spontaneous excitement. Microchips aside, we could hardly believe it was real, that the three of us were on the plane and it was finally happening.

"What would you like to drink?" enquired the smiling hostess.

All of it, I thought, but politely asked for a red wine. We couldn't stop smiling, toasting the recent journey, each other, Mocha and the whole adventure. It wasn't ending how we'd planned, but it had been a skip-load more adventurous than we ever could have dreamed of.

Stepping out into the air-bridge, Selly clutched Mocha's lead and I clutched the bulging file of Mocha's life history. The young lady flicked on the scanner and Mocha's chip number popped onto the scanner's display, before she'd even leant towards her. In that fraction of a second, I honestly felt a weight floating off me. Considering the too many hours spent with too many vets, just a cursory glance over the certificates was enough to have us dismissed and on our way.

A grinning John greeted Selly with a bottle of wine and myself with a bottle of beer. Mocha was just content to find he smelt of dogs and there was a comfy bed waiting for her in the van!

"So this is the travelling Mocha then. You do know most people are happy to come back with just a fridge magnet, don't you!" he teased.

Three hours later, we were pulling onto our driveway. We were home; a total flying-riding loop of 31,000 miles had been completed. Over the previous few months, and especially the last fortnight, every twist and turn had been a quest to bring Mocha to this front door without having to endure a four-month winter quarantine. We could hardly believe it had succeeded, could hardly take it in. There was even time to put up the Christmas tree and cook a turkey. We were simply over the moon!

Epilogue

Not Quite the End!

On the 8th of February, Mocha woke to find ten centimetres of snow had fallen overnight. It was the first she had ever seen and she sprinted around the garden, excitedly snatching snowflakes out of the icy air! Her adjustment to house-living had been seamless, despite us being either in self-isolation or confined by the third national lockdown since arriving home. Sofas and tables became her new indoor assault course and out on dog walks, she had found deer, rabbits and squirrels were a great 'hunting' substitute for Central America's iguanas, lizards and skunks. The hedgerows were of particular interest to her. Every plant and weed needed investigating, but none turned out to be her beloved snakeroot! Even without her 'fix', she was as relaxed as we'd ever seen her, if admittedly still prone to barking at scooters and strangers she didn't quite like the look of!

At the time of writing this, the motorcycle, panniers and the majority of our gear remains stranded in Guatemala. No amount of cajoling, by us or the shipping company, has so far overcome the red tape being regurgitated by the various officials. For unfathomable reasons, they persist in telling me I must return, and I'm convinced we will! In many ways, we are still living the adventure, or at least we are swept up in its aftermath, as we formulate plans to rescue the bike.

Blu and Roxana have added to their family, with a brand new motorcycle of their own! Didier and Nelly have criss-crossed the jungles of Colombia, having successfully sold the BMWs and bought a pair of much more nimble Hondas. Finding the borders south still frustratingly closed, they are now back in Central America, with a new plan to further explore Mexico. Matteo, Iulia and their two lovely children are still in Nicaragua, wowing visitors at the magical 'jungle hostel in a crater'. Roberto and Lucélia are continuing with the fundraising and uncovering ever new communities to assist. The twenty of us that were in lockdown together are spread around the world but connect regularly on the joint 'group chat'! We dearly miss everyone we met inside that volcano and outside, along the Pan-American Highway.

The joy of being back in our home, being a family again, has outweighed any withdrawal symptoms from not still being 'out on the road'. The experience still takes our breath away, lives within us and lifts us. The journey recalibrated what we thought we could endure and achieve together. Some of the testing days should have had us questioning what the hell we were doing this for, but with perseverance, they just turned out to be some of the most memorable parts of the journey.

I can't deny the PAH is a well-trodden path, if extremely remote at times, but each foray is uniquely adventurous and personal. The experience is a blend of so many changing aspects, from the people you meet along the way, the weather and road conditions you encounter, to those unfathomable strokes of both bad and good luck, shaping the journey. We all have different levels of experience and abilities to draw upon when making the many daily decisions, and a simple fork in the road can have trip-changing consequences. If a thousand PAH books were laid before you, they'd each tell a different tale, and we sincerely hope you've enjoyed ours!

In a post-pandemic world, we do plan on completing the second half of the mighty road that is the PAH. I doubt we could deny it, I'm sure it will be calling us, growing an 'itch' too irresistible to ignore. Just to shake it up a bit, maybe from north to south this time around, four wheels instead of two and eight legs instead of four?

First, though, we need to plan another wedding!